Software Engineering

SECOND EDITION

INTERNATIONAL COMPUTER SCIENCE SERIES

Consulting editors **A D McGettrick**
University of Strathclyde

J van Leeuwen
University of Utrecht

Software Engineering

SECOND EDITION

I. Sommerville

ADDISON-WESLEY PUBLISHING COMPANY

Wokingham, England · Reading, Massachusetts · Menlo Park, California
Don Mills, Ontario · Amsterdam · Sydney · Singapore · Tokyo
Mexico City · Bogota · Santiago · San Juan

The programs presented in this book have been included for their instructional
value. They have been tested with care but are not guaranteed for any particular
purpose. The publisher does not offer any warranties or representations, nor
does it accept any liabilities with respect to the programs.

Ada is a registered trademark of the U.S. Government – Ada Joint Program Office.
UNIX is a trademark of Bell Laboratories.

Cover design by Tektronix U.K. Ltd.
Typeset by Setrite of Hong Kong.
Printed in Finland by Werner Söderström Osakeyhtiö

British Library Cataloguing in Publication Data

Sommerville, Ian
    Software engineering.—2nd ed.
    1. Computer programs
    I. Title
    001.64′25   QA76.6

    ISBN 0-201-14229-5

Library of Congress Cataloging in Publication Data

Sommerville, Ian.
    Software engineering.

    Bibliography: p.
    Includes index.
    1. Electronic digital computers—Programming.   I. Title.
QA76.6.S645   1985   001.64′2   84-24504
ISBN 0-201-14229-5

 BCDEF 898765

PREFACE

The problems of constructing large software systems are immense. Some of these problems are akin to the problems which arise in any large engineering project — management and cost control, personnel management, tool selection, quality control and product design. Hence the term 'software engineering' was coined to describe the activity of large software system construction.

Software engineering has now emerged as a discipline in its own right. Although its principal base is in computer science, it also makes use of mathematics, psychology, ergonomics and management science. The software engineer must be able to assess and apply existing computing techniques in a cost-effective and usable way. He or she applies existing knowledge, derived from more fundamental subjects, in the same way as the electrical or mechanical engineer applies physics and mathematics.

Since 1968, when the problems of software system construction were brought to prominence, much progress has been made. High-level languages have ousted machine code for most applications; structured programming is widely used and can increase the readability and reliability of programs; some of the problems of software management have been tackled; formal software verification systems may become practicable in the near future and steps towards formal software specification have been taken.

However, many software systems are still being built which are unreliable, over-budget, poorly documented and not well suited to the user. The explosion of computer applications made possible by low-cost microprocessor systems and program development by people from a variety of disciplines has highlighted the need for effective software engineering education.

This is the second edition of a general textbook on software engineering. It has developed from courses in software engineering given to third and fourth year undergraduate students at the University of Strathclyde. It is assumed that readers are familiar with at least one high-level programming language such as Pascal, FORTRAN or Ada and that they have covered computer science fundamentals such as algorithms, machine organization and data structures. Although it is designed as a software engineering textbook, I hope the book will also be useful for practising software engineers in industry and commerce.

Broadly, the book is made up of two parts. The first part, which is modelled on the software life cycle, contains chapters covering requirements definition, software specification, software design, implementation and testing. The second part, linked to the first by a chapter on documentation, covers human aspects of software engineering. In this part of the book there are chapters which cover user interface considerations, management psychology and practical software management.

A book is like a software system in that it must continuously evolve to remain useful. It also invariably contains bugs and, perhaps most importantly, its requirements only become clear after the first version is complete. This is, thus, release 2. New features have been added, notably software specification, object-oriented design and algorithmic cost modelling; existing features have been improved (most chapters have been reorganized and partly rewritten) and known bugs have been eliminated. There are undoubtedly new bugs and I'd be pleased to receive bug reports from readers.

The changes to the chapters of the book may be summarized as follows. Chapter 1 has an extended discussion on the software life cycle. Chapter 2 has been reorganized and an Ada-based language for requirements definition has been introduced. Chapter 3 is a new chapter which introduces formal software specification. Chapter 4 covers software design and has a new section discussing object-oriented design. Again, an Ada-based notation is used in this chapter in preference to the design description language used in the first edition.

Chapters 5 and 6 correspond to Chapters 5 and 4 in the first edition, which covered programming languages and programming practice. They have been rewritten and reorganized. Chapter 7, which covers software testing, has been rewritten and reorganized as has Chapter 8 which discusses documentation and maintenance. Chapters 9 and 10 covering the user interface and management psychology respectively are only slightly changed versions of the corresponding chapters in the first edition. However, Chapter 11 which describes software management has new sections on algorithmic cost modelling and software quality assurance.

Throughout the book, there is an increased emphasis on Ada and Ada-based notations. The reason for this is that I believe that Ada will become the standard language for large systems development in the later years of this decade. However, detailed discussion of Ada has been avoided and Ada knowledge is certainly not a prerequisite to understanding this book.

Software engineering is an enormous subject and, in a general book, it is inevitable that some material is excluded. As before, the criterion for inclusion has been practical relevance, so research techniques which may be useful in future have not been discussed in detail here. However, this has still meant that some material has been left out, most notably parallel programming.

An appreciation of parallel programming requires an immense amount of background knowledge of both hardware and notations and I do not feel that readers of this book will necessarily have that knowledge. To include the necessary background, which is peripheral to software engineering, would mean that parallel programming would dominate the book. Thus, parallel programming has been excluded but it is covered in a forthcoming text covering large systems development using Ada.

I was very gratified that many teachers of software engineering found the first edition of this book useful. To increase the utility of this edition as a teaching text, I have made two important additions. Firstly, a section entitled 'Further reading' has been appended to each chapter. In this section, I list three or four references which are good starting points for further study of the material in that chapter.

Secondly, I have added an appendix to the book which covers software engineering education. In this appendix, I describe the approach adopted to the teaching of software engineering at Strathclyde University and I suggest projects and problems for students. I have deliberately collected these together in an appendix rather than included them with each chapter. This allows some common examples to be used and for cross-references between questions to be established.

I am grateful to a number of friends, colleagues and readers of the first edition for helpful comments and advice. Particular mention must be made of the editors Andrew McGettrick and Jan van Leeuwen, my colleagues Ray Welland and John Mariani and of Ron Morrison of St. Andrews University. In addition, Darrel Ince of the Open University commented on a draft of this edition and David Haas of the University of Wisconsin-Oshkosh, Wlad Turski of the Warsaw University and Alex Borgida of Rutgers University constructively criticized the first edition of this text. Thanks are also due to my colleagues Ray Welland and Richard Fryer for permission to include some of their examples in Appendix 1.

Finally, I must thank my wife Anne and daughters Alison and Jane for their tolerance whilst this book was being written. "Daddy's always writing" was Alison's remark after another sunny day was spent on this book. I hope the result is worthwhile.

CONTENTS

Chapter 1 INTRODUCTION

As the cost of computer hardware decreases because of new semiconductor technologies, computer systems are being incorporated in more and more products. Furthermore, some advanced computer applications, such as applications in artificial intelligence, have become economically viable. Hardware to support their heavy computation demands can now be built at moderate cost. The end result of this proliferation of computer systems into all aspects of life and business is that personal, corporate, national and international economies are becoming increasingly dependent on computers and their software systems.

Unfortunately, the costs of computer software have not fallen with hardware costs. In fact, these costs have shown a marked increase and for many types of system, software costs are 80%+ of the total system costs. The practice of software engineering is concerned with building large and complex software systems in a cost-effective way. Thus, it is probably not an exaggeration to suggest that the future prosperity of industrialized countries depends on effective software engineering.

The real costs of software development are immense. Although precise, up-to-date figures are very difficult to establish, it has been suggested (Lehman, 1980) that in 1977, software costs in the USA were in excess of $50 billion. This represented more than 3% of the American gross national product for that year. It can be estimated with confidence that these costs have now more than doubled and are comparable in other developed countries. Even small improvements in software productivity can therefore result in a significant reduction in absolute costs.

The problems encountered in building large software systems are not simply scaled up versions of the problems of writing small computer programs. An analogy may be drawn with a road bridge over an estuary and a footbridge over a stream. Although both are members of the class 'bridges' and hence have some common properties, a civil engineer would never consider designing an estuarial bridge simply by enlarging a footbridge design. The complexity of small programs (or bridges) is such that it can be easily understood by one person and all details of the design and construction held in that person's head. Specifications may be informal and the effect of changes immediately obvious. On the other hand, the complexity of large systems is such that it is impossible for any single individual to hold and maintain details of each aspect of the project in his or her mind. More formal techniques of specification and design are necessary; each stage of

1

the project must be properly documented, and careful management is essential.

The term 'software engineering' was first introduced in the late 1960s at a conference held to discuss the so-called 'software crisis'. This software crisis resulted directly from the introduction of third-generation computer hardware. These machines were orders of magnitude more powerful than second-generation machines and their power made hitherto unrealizable applications a feasible proposition. The implementation of these applications required large software systems to be built.

Initial experience in building large software systems showed that existing methodologies of software development were inadequate. Techniques applicable to small systems could not just be scaled up. A number of major projects were late (sometimes years late), cost much more than originally predicted, were unreliable, difficult to maintain and performed poorly. Software development was in a crisis situation. Hardware costs were tumbling whilst software costs were rising rapidly. There was an urgent need for new techniques and methodologies which allowed the complexity inherent in large software systems to be controlled.

There have been a number of proposed definitions of software engineering. Their common factors are that software engineering is concerned with building software systems which are larger than would normally be tackled by a single individual, uses engineering principles in the development of these systems and is made up of both technical and non-technical aspects. As well as a thorough knowledge of computing techniques, the software engineer, like any other engineer, must be able to communicate, both orally and in writing. He or she should appreciate the problems which system users have in interacting with software whose workings they may not understand. He or she should also understand the project management problems associated with software production.

Furthermore, the term 'software' does not simply encompass the computer programs associated with some application or product. As well as programs, software includes all documentation which is necessary to install, use, develop and maintain these programs. For large systems, the task of constructing such documentation is comparable in magnitude with the task of program development.

In the remainder of this introduction the notion of a software life cycle is introduced. This is followed by a description of life cycle models and software evolution which is the notion that large systems have a dynamic of their own. The importance of software reliability is then discussed and the final section defines some terms which are used in the remainder of the book.

1.1 The software life cycle

Like all other large-scale systems, large software systems take a considerable time to develop and are in use for an even longer time. A number of distinct stages in this period of development and usage can be identified. Together, they make up what is termed the software life cycle.

The initial model of the software life cycle was probably first proposed by Royce (1970) and, since then, there have been numerous refinements to and variations of the life cycle model. All of these can be encompassed in a 'macro' life cycle model as follows:

1. *Requirements analysis and definition.* The system's services, constraints and goals are established by consultation with system users. Once these have been agreed, they must be defined in a manner which is understandable by both users and development staff.

2. *System and software design.* Using the requirements definition as a base, the requirements are partitioned to either hardware or software systems. This process is termed systems design. Software design is the process of representing the functions of each software system in a manner which may be readily transformed to one or more computer programs.

3. *Implementation and unit testing.* During this stage, the software design is realized as a set of programs or program units which are written in some executable programming language. Unit testing involves verifying that each unit meets its specification.

4. *System testing.* The individual program units or programs are integrated and tested as a complete system to ensure that the software requirements have been met. After testing, the software system is delivered to the customer.

5. *Operation and maintenance.* Normally (although not necessarily) this is the longest life cycle phase. The system is installed and put into practical use. The activity of maintenance involves correcting errors which were not discovered in earlier stages of the life cycle, improving the implementation of system units and enhancing the system's services as new requirements are perceived.

It is not useful, at this stage, to identify sub-phases within each phase of the software life cycle. There is no general agreement on what these sub-phases are and individual projects are normally partitioned in different ways. For management purposes one, more detailed, view of the software life cycle is provided in Chapter 11.

It is useful for management purposes to consider the phases of the software life cycle to be distinct but, in practice, the development stages overlap and feed information to each other. This is illustrated in Fig. 1.1. The final life cycle phase has been deliberately left out of Fig. 1.1 as, during this phase, information is fed back to all previous life cycle phases. Therefore, to accommodate operation and maintenance, Fig. 1.1 must be modified as shown in Fig. 1.2. For simplicity, the information flows between development phases have been excluded from this diagram.

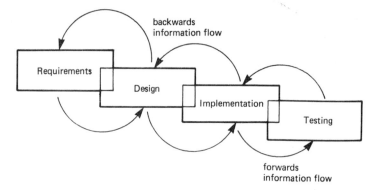

Figure 1.1   The software development cycle.

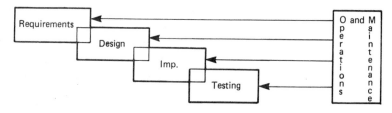

Figure 1.2   The software life cycle.

The reason why the operation and maintenance phase does not simply follow on from the system testing phase is that the maintenance activity may involve changes in requirements, design, and implementation or it may highlight the need for further system testing.

The testing phase of the software life cycle where the complete software system is integrated and exercised represents the ultimate validation stage in the development cycle. At this stage, the system developer must convince the system buyer that his requirements are met by the system. However, the activities of verification and validation pervade the earlier life cycle stages. It is during these activities that information which is to be fed back to earlier life cycle phases is normally identified.

Although verification and validation may appear to be synonymous, this is not in fact the case. Perhaps the most succinct expression of the difference between verification and validation is given by Boehm (1981):

Verification :   'Are we building the product right?'
Validation   :   'Are we building the right product?'

In short, verification checks if the product under construction meets the requirements definition, and validation checks if the product's functions are what the customer really wants.

Given this macro model of the software life cycle, it is instructive to examine the relative costs of each life cycle phase. These are obviously liable to vary quite dramatically from system to system. However, the figures given by Boehm (1975) for different types of software system (Table 1.1) are probably still approximately correct.

Table 1.1 Relative costs of software systems

System type	Phase costs(%)		
	Requirements/design	Implementation	Testing
Command/control systems	46	20	34
Spaceborne systems	34	20	46
Operating systems	33	17	50
Scientific systems	44	26	30
Business systems	44	28	28

More recently, Boehm (1981) has suggested somewhat different figures where the implementation costs are much higher and design costs much lower. These, however, appear to be based on a life cycle model whose emphasis is different from that used here. In this alternative model, detailed design is considered to be part of the implementation phase, whereas in the model proposed here detailed design is part of the overall software design process.

The inference which can be drawn from the above figures is that the software development costs are greatest at the beginning and at the end of the development cycle. This suggests that a reduction in overall software development costs is best accomplished by more effective software design and more effective life cycle verification and validation. This will lead to an ultimate reduction in testing costs.

What is not shown in the table is the costs of the final life cycle phase — operation and maintenance. Again there is immense variation in costs from system to system. However, for most large, long-lived software systems maintenance costs normally exceed development costs by factors which range from two to four. Indeed, Boehm (1975) quotes a pathological case where the development cost of an avionics system was $30 per instruction but the maintenance cost was $4000 per instruction.

The majority of software maintenance costs result not from system errors but from changing system requirements. Therefore, to reduce maintenance costs and hence total life cycle costs, a more accurate picture of the user's real requirements must be established. This has led to suggestions (McCracken and Jackson, 1982; Gladden, 1982) that the life cycle model discussed above should be scrapped and replaced by a more evolutionary model of software development.

This evolutionary mode of software development is based on the idea that the user ought to be presented with a prototype system for experimentation as quickly as possible. This prototype should be built in such a way that it may readily be re-implemented. As soon as a prototype is built, it is presented to the user who experiments with it and feedback information to the system builders. The prototype is then modified to reflect changed user requirements. This process of prototype e... continues until the user is satisfied with the delivered system.

Another life cycle view, put forward by Lehman (1984), also considers the software process as an incremental model. In his model, an application concept is successively transformed into a formal software specification. He calls this process abstraction. This involves reducing the amount of raw information in each transformation stage. Once the specification is established, information is added (this he calls reification) and the abstract system transformed through a set of formal notations to an operational program.

It is undoubtedly true that adopting an evolutionary approach to the development of some classes of system can result in systems which better meet the user's needs. This is particularly likely when the application being implemented is a completely new one with no non-automated analogue. In such cases, requirements formulation is very difficult indeed.

However, for systems which are based on existing manual systems which are reasonably well understood, the evolutionary approach is less likely to be cost-effective. Boehm (1984) suggests that, for large systems in particular, change control and integration may be more difficult using an evolutionary model. He also suggests that a mix of approaches may be the best overall solution with risk management analysis governing the approach adopted for particular sub-systems.

1.1.1 Software evolution

Large software systems are not static objects. They exist in an environment which is subject to constant change and which may not be completely understood by the implementors of the software. As the environment changes or becomes more fully understood, the software system must either adapt to these changes or become progressively less useful until, ultimately, it must be discarded. This process of change has been termed software evolution and is discussed in an important paper by Lehman (1980).

Software maintenance is the process of correcting errors in the system and modifying the system to reflect environmental changes. For large systems, this maintenance is accomplished in a series of system 'releases'. Each release is a new version of the system, with known errors corrected, and which incorporates new or updated system facilities.

If the system is implemented in a number of installations it is unlikely that all installations will include all changes in each system release. Furthermore, each installation may make local modifications, tuning the system to the particular environment in which it operates. As a result of these factors, it is inevitable that the versions of the system at each installation drift further and further apart and that general maintenance, applicable to all installations, becomes more difficult. Special software tools are necessary for management of this situation.

Lehman suggests that the evolution of a software system is subject to a number of 'laws'. He has derived these laws from experimental observations of a number of systems such as large operating systems (Lehman and

Belady, 1976). He suggests that there are five laws of program evolution:

1. *Continuing change*. A program that is used in a real-world environment — must change or become less and less useful in that environment.

2. *Increasing complexity*. As an evolving program changes, its structure becomes more complex unless active efforts are made to avoid this phenomenon.

3. *Program evolution*. Program evolution is a self-regulating process and measurement of system attributes such as size, time between releases, number of reported errors, etc., reveals statistically significant trends and invariances.

4. *Conservation of organizational stability*. Over the lifetime of a program, the rate of development of that program is approximately constant and independent of the resources devoted to system development.

5. *Conservation of familiarity*. Over the lifetime of a system, the incremental system change in each release is approximately constant.

Lehman's laws are not universally accepted in the same way as physical laws, but they do appear to have some validity for many types of software system. He has used them with some success in the management of new releases of a large operating system.

The reasoning which underlies the first of Lehman's laws is that when a software system (particularly a large software system) is built to model some environment and is then introduced into that environment, the original environment is modified by the presence of the software system. Therefore, users modify their behaviour as they become familiar with the software system and redefine what they expect of it. The system must then be modified and re-introduced into the environment after which the process starts anew.

The second law reflects the fact that the original program structure was set up to implement a set of initial requirements. As these requirements change incrementally, the original structure is corrupted. To reduce structural complexity thus requires the entire system to be wholly or partially restructured to reflect the requirements at a single point in time.

These observations have probably been made in every large software system which has ever been developed and the first two of Lehman's hypotheses are almost certainly valid.

The third, fourth and fifth laws are not based on software characteristics but are based on the inherent inertia of the human organizations involved in the software development process. Lehman suggests that organizations strive for stability and attempt to avoid sudden or drastic change. Thus, as more resources are added to a software project, the incremental effect of adding new resources becomes less and less until the addition of extra resources has no effect whatsoever. The project at this stage has reached resource saturation.

The latter three laws reflect the effect of individual and organizational behaviour on software systems. It is interesting to reflect that Lehman's work was carried out with the co-operation of a very large and successful organization which is in the happy position of being able to add resources to a project almost indefinitely. Furthermore, large organizations always have an internal bureaucracy which strives for stability.

Whilst the first two of Lehman's laws are almost certainly universally valid, it may be the case that in small, less formal, more responsive organizations Lehman's latter three laws are not valid. The organizational effects on the software may not be universal across organizations. This topic requires further research and investigation.

Given that Lehman's laws are valid, what are the implications for software life cycle management? Firstly, it is clear that software maintenance costs cannot ever be eliminated. The best that can be achieved is to adopt techniques which allow changes to be readily incorporated and which retard the deterioration of the system structure.

Secondly, management should not plan to make very large changes to software systems in a single increment. Rather, changes are best introduced in small increments which implies, perhaps, more frequent system releases. Furthermore, some releases should be dedicated to fault elimination with no attempt being made to introduce enhanced facilities in these systems. Finally, the laws imply that the most cost-effective way to develop software is to use as few people as possible in each project group, as the more people working on a project, the less productive is each individual project member.

1.2 Software reliability

As computer applications become more diverse and pervade almost every area of everyday life, it is becoming more and more apparent that the most important dynamic characteristic of most computer software is that it should be reliable.

The reliability of any system (not merely software systems) is dependent on the correctness of the system design, the correctness of the mapping of the system design to implementation and the reliability of the components making up the system. For example, the reliability of a motor car depends on the car design, on how well the car is put together, and on how long the components making up the car take to fail. In general, after initial teething troubles, the reliability of most systems is governed by how long it takes the system components to wear out. As the majority of systems have some moving parts, wear is inevitable and it is impossible for these systems to be 100% reliable.

Software systems are unique in this respect. They contain no moving parts and their reliability depends completely on design and implementation correctness. Hardware reliability can be achieved by duplication of com-

ponents with a new component automatically switching in if component failure is detected. This approach cannot be taken by software systems. If a procedure gives the wrong answer there is no point in trying to execute another identical copy of the same procedure. However, Randell (1975) suggests that greater software reliability might be attained by executing another functionally equivalent but non-identical copy of the procedure. Discussion of this topic is outside the scope of this book.

It is difficult to give a precise definition of what is meant by software reliability — some might say that software is reliable if it is correct. That is, if it meets its initial specifications and performs as specified. This is a possible definition but it does not take into account the possibility that the software specifications themselves are, almost certainly, both incomplete and incorrect.

It is often the case that for large useful programming systems it is impossible to produce a specification which is complete and invariant. The reason for this is that these systems are not stand-alone entities but operate in some environment which may not be wholly understood and which may be undergoing almost constant change. The notion of absolute correctness of such systems is therefore of limited utility. Rather as Lehman (1980) points out, it is the usability of the program in the real world and the relevance of its output in a constantly changing environment that is the main concern.

In fact, correct mathematically verified software is sometimes less reliable than tested but unverified software. Correctness proofs do not normally take into account the environment in which the software must operate and the proofs make the often unstated assumption that the environment is also correct. Whilst environmental effects are obviously a feature of program testing, program verification cannot detect environmental faults or inconsistencies.

A more realistic definition of program reliability is that a program should meet its specifications, should never produce 'incorrect' output irrespective of the input, should never allow itself to be corrupted, should take meaningful and useful actions in unexpected situations and should fail completely only when further progress is impossible.

In short, the reliability of a software system is a measure of how well it provides the services expected of it by its users. Of course, users do not consider all services to be of equal importance and a system might be viewed as unreliable if it ever failed to provide some critical service. For example, say a system was used to control braking on an aircraft but failed to work under a single set of very rare conditions. Should these conditions arise and the aircraft crash that software would be regarded as unreliable.

On the other hand, say the same software provided some visual indication of its actions to the pilot of the aircraft. Assume this failed once per month without the main system function being affected. It is unlikely, in spite of more frequent failure, that the software would be rated as unreliable.

To achieve high reliability inevitably involves a good deal of extra, often redundant, code built into the system to perform the necessary checking. This reduces the program execution speed and increases the amount of store required by the program. However, as computer users become more experienced, their principal criterion for system quality is reliability rather than efficiency. There are a number of reasons for this:

1. As equipment becomes cheaper and faster, there is less need to maximize equipment usage in preference to human convenience.

2. Unreliable software is liable to be avoided by users and, irrespective of how efficient it is, it will soon become worthless.

3. For some applications, such as a reactor control system or an aircraft navigation system, the cost of system failure is very much greater than the cost of the system itself.

4. An efficient system can be tuned with considerable success because most execution time is spent in fairly small sections of a program. An unreliable system is much more difficult to improve as unreliability tends to be distributed throughout the software system.

5. Inefficiency is predictable — programs take a long time to execute. Unreliability is much worse. Software which is unreliable can have hidden errors which can violate system and user data without warning and the results of an error might not be discovered till much later. For example, a fault in a design program used to design aircraft might not be discovered until a number of planes have crashed.

6. Unreliable systems can result in information being lost — hence much effort and money is expended in duplicating valuable data.

To achieve software reliability, the environment in which the software operates must be understood and a software specification prepared which, as far as possible, defines the role of the software system in that environment.

The software design should implement all parts of the specification and each part of the design should be correct. Although absolute correctness of the entire design is not necessarily meaningful because of constantly evolving specifications, each part of the design should be a well defined function and hence susceptible to demonstrations of correctness.

A reliable implementation of the software design means that all parts of the design should actually be implemented and that the implementation should be a correct mapping of the design notation into a programming language.

Finally, irrespective of the measurable system reliability, unless the system documentation is accurate that reliability will not be visible to users of the system. The documentation must describe system facilities correctly and should point out areas where contra-intuitive results might be obtained from using the system.

As well as being reliable at any one point in time, programming systems ought to be reliable over their lifetimes. Because the environments in which these systems operate do change, mechanisms must be built into the software so that it may evolve to reflect the changing environment. If the software cannot be readily maintained, its usability and relevance to users will decrease.

Throughout this book, reliability and maintainability are considered to be the most important attributes of a well engineered software system. Whilst hard and fast instructions on how to achieve this cannot be given, the text provides guidelines which should simplify the production of well engineered software.

1.3 Terminology

Software engineering is hindered by the fact that no consistent terminology exists to describe software systems. For example, the term 'module' is probably the most overloaded of any computing terms and covers a range of entities from hardware units to executable programs. Similarly, the terms 'task', 'job' and 'process' have different connotations for each individual, depending on that individual's background.

In such a young subject, this confusion of terms is inevitable and at this stage, standardization is probably undesirable. However, this text requires a consistent terminology and in this section a number of terms are defined. These terms are used in a consistent way throughout the remainder of the book.

A **programming system** is made up of a collection of autonomous **programs** possibly but not necessarily dedicated to a single application. Examples of programming systems are operating systems, command/control systems and office automation systems.

A **sub-system** is a programming system which is itself part of a larger programming system but which is always dedicated to a single application. For example, an office automation system might be made up of a number of sub-systems including a word processing sub-system, an electronic mail sub-system and a filing sub-system.

A **program** is a problem solution specification which may be executed by a computer.

A **process** is a program in execution. A number of processes may execute simultaneously on the same computer.

A **program object** is any entity which may be named in a program. This term therefore covers named program variables, constants, **modules, procedures,** and **functions**.

A **module** is a named collection of program objects. These objects are referenced by specifying both the module name and the object name and their visibility to objects outside the module may be explicitly controlled. If an object declared within a module is a data object, it may retain its value from one module reference to another. For readers familiar with Ada, the equivalent of a module is a package.

A **procedure** is an executable program object. If objects are declared within a procedure, they are deemed to come into existence when that procedure is activated and to go out of existence when execution of that procedure terminates.

A **function** is a procedure which always accepts at least one input value and returns a single output value. A function is an abstraction of an expression, so a function call is allowed anywhere that an expression may be used.

A **program unit** or **software component** is either a module, a procedure or a function.

The definitions given here do not necessarily correspond with the intuitive notions of these terms held by the reader. This does not necessarily mean that the reader's understanding of the terms is incorrect — for the purposes of this text it is necessary to adopt a consistent terminology and the aim of this section has simply been to establish that terminology.

Further reading

Software Engineering Economics, B.W. Boehm (1981) Englewood Cliffs, NJ: Prentice-Hall.
    In spite of the title, this book is a wide-ranging look at many aspects of software engineering by one of the best respected authorities in this field. Early chapters discuss the software life cycle and life cycle costs.

The Cost of Large Software Systems, ed. E. Horowitz (1975) Reading, Mass: Addison-Wesley.
    This is a relatively old collection of papers and it is surprising and somewhat depressing that so little has changed in ten years. Papers in this volume by Boehm, Schwartz and Wolverton are of particular interest.

'Programs, life cycles and the laws of software evolution', M.M. Lehman (1980) *Proc. IEEE*, **68 (9)**, 1060–76.
    This paper summarizes several years of work and thought on software evolution. It does take a bit of work to understand it properly but this is worthwhile as the author provides useful insights into software system characteristics.

'The operational versus the conventional approach to software development', P. Zave (1984) *Comm. ACM*, **27 (2)**.
    This is an interesting tutorial paper on an alternative system development model based on operational specifications rather than the conventional software life cycle. It provides a useful comparison of each approach but more detail of Zave's specification language and its applicability to large system construction would help make the writer's point.

Chapter 2 REQUIREMENTS DEFINITION

The problems which software engineers are called upon to solve are often immensely complex. Understanding the nature of the problem can be very difficult, particularly if the system is new and no non-automated system exists to serve as a model for the software to be developed. The process of establishing what services the system should provide and the constraints under which it must operate is called requirements analysis and definition. This is normally the first major phase of the software life cycle.

It is important to make a distinction between user needs and user requirements. An organization may decide that it needs a software system to support its accounting, but it is unrealistic to present this simple need to a software engineer and expect an acceptable and usable software system to be developed. Rather, information about the problem to be solved must be collected and analysed and a comprehensive problem definition produced. From this definition, the software solution can be designed and implemented.

It is also important to make a distinction between system goals and system requirements. In essence, a requirement is something that can be tested whereas a goal is a more general characteristic which the system should exhibit. For example, a goal might be that the system should be 'user friendly'. This is not testable, as 'friendliness' is a very subjective attribute. An associated requirement might be that all user command selection should take place using command menus.

The derivation of software requirements is not always considered the province of the software engineer. The systems analyst is sometimes considered responsible for this task, particularly where existing manual systems are to be automated. On the other hand, the definition of requirements for embedded systems and advanced systems is normally taken as a software engineering problem.

In fact, the roles of the systems analyst and the software engineer are complementary. The systems analyst should take responsibility for collecting data on the existing system and for performing a critical analysis of that data to factor out relevant information. He should consult with the software engineer so that each understands the required system and should formulate a set of software requirements. A discussion of techniques for requirements analysis or systems analysis is outside the area covered by this book. Indeed, it requires a book to itself and the interested reader is referred to texts such as those by Millington (1981) and Davis (1983) for further information on this topic.

This chapter actually concentrates on requirements definition and validation. The software requirements document described in the following section is the linking theme and the contents of the major sections of that document, namely the system model, functional requirements definition, database requirements and non-functional requirements definition, are each covered in a separate section. The final section in the chapter looks at requirements validation and introduces the idea of system prototyping as a requirements validation technique.

2.1 The software requirements document

The precise description of the requirements for a software system is called the software requirements document. This is defined by Yeh and Zave (1980) as:

> a set of precisely stated properties or constraints which a software system must satisfy.

The software requirements document is not a design document. It should set out what the system should do without specifying how it should be done. As Yeh states:

> A software requirements document establishes boundaries on the solution space of the problem of developing a useful software system.

A software requirements document allows a design to be validated — if the constraints and properties specified in the software requirements document are satisfied by the software design, then that design is an acceptable solution to the problem.

The task of developing a software requirements document should not be underestimated. Bell et al. (1977) report that the requirements document for a ballistic missile defence system contains over 8000 distinct requirements and support paragraphs and is made up of 2500 pages of text.

In principle, the requirements set out in such a document ought to be complete and consistent. Everything the system should do should be specified and no requirement should conflict with any other. In practice, this is extremely difficult to achieve, particularly if the requirements are stated as natural language text. Later in this chapter, more formal notations which allow some automatic consistency checking to be carried out will be discussed.

Heninger (1980) claims that there are six requirements which a software requirements document should satisfy:

1. It should specify only external system behaviour.
2. It should specify constraints on the implementation.
3. It should be easy to change.

4. It should serve as a reference tool for system maintainers.

5. It should record forethought about the life cycle of the system.

6. It should characterize acceptable responses to undesired events.

Heninger considers that the software requirements document should serve as a reference tool and should record forethought about the system life cycle because it will be used by maintenance programmers to find out what the system is supposed to do. In order to serve this purpose, information in the software requirements document must be precise and easily found. This implies that the software requirements document should have a detailed table of contents, one or more indexes, a glossary of terms used and a definition of the changes anticipated when the requirements were originally formulated. Bearing this in mind, a possible organization for a requirements definition is:

1. *Introduction.* This should describe the need for the system and should place the system in context, briefly describing its functions and presenting a rationale for the software system. It should also set out the structure of the remainder of the document and describe the notations used.

2. *Hardware.* If the system is to be implemented on special hardware, this hardware and its interfaces should be described. If off-the-shelf hardware is to be used, the minimal and optimal configurations on which the system may execute should be set out here.

3. *The conceptual model.* This section should describe the conceptual model on which the requirements are based. The conceptual system model is a very high-level system view showing the major services provided by the software and their relationship with each other. It is best expressed graphically in some notation such as data-flow diagrams, described by Constantine and Yourdon (1979).

4. *Functional requirements.* The functional requirements of the system, that is, the services provided for the user, should be described in this section. Depending on the nature of these requirements, the notation used might be natural language, a semi-formal language, a formal language or a mixture of all of these notations.

5. *Database requirements.* The logical organization of the data used by the system and its inter-relationships should be described here.

6. *Non-functional requirements.* The non-functional requirements of the system, that is, the constraints under which the software must operate, should be expressed and related to the functional requirements.

7. *Maintenance information.* This section of the software requirements document should describe the fundamental assumptions on which the system is based and describe anticipated changes due to hardware evolution, changing user needs, etc. Wherever possible, functions

and constraints which are particularly subject to change should be explicitly specified.

8. *Glossary.*   This should define the technical terms used in the document. This is principally intended to help non-technical users understand the software requirements document. However, it is also useful for development staff as it establishes a precise definition of terms used in the document. In formulating the glossary, no assumptions should be made about the experience or background of the reader.

9. *Index.*   It may be desirable to provide more than one kind of index to the document. As well as a normal alphabetic index, it may be useful to produce an index per chapter, an index of functions and so on. These indexes are best prepared with automatic aid so that, after changes to the software requirements document, it may be readily re-indexed.

Because requirements are liable to change, it is essential that the software requirements document should be organized in such a way that changes can be accommodated without extensive rewriting. If this is not done, changes in the requirements may be incorporated in the system without recording these changes in the definition. This causes the program and its documentation to become out of step — a situation which can result in immense problems for the maintenance programmer. Techniques for producing maintainable documentation are described in Chapter 8 of this book.

2.2 The system model

Once an initial analysis of the user's needs has been carried out, the next step, which is the first stage in requirements definition, is to produce a conceptual model of the software system. This conceptual model is a very high-level view of the system in which the major user services are identified and their relationships documented.

For trivial systems this model may exist only in the mind of the engineer responsible for establishing the requirements. He or she understands the systems and knows which functions must be provided as well as the constraints on the operation of these functions. For any non-trivial system, however, a mental model is likely to be inadequate. Because the system being modelled is inherently complex, mental models tend to be incomplete and contain ambiguities and conflicts. It is necessary to establish an explicit, precisely defined system model at an early stage and to use this model to understand the system.

Salter (1976) has used finite state machines for system modelling and considers a general system model to be a function of three elements — control, function and data. Intuitively, functions are the information transformers in the system, data are the inputs and outputs of functions, and control is the mechanism that activates functions in the desired sequence. The notion of states and state transformations also underlies the conceptual modelling systems described by Yeh and Zave (1980) and Heninger (1980).

Heninger describes the derivation of requirements for an embedded software system used on board a military aircraft. This system receives 70 separate input items and transmits 95 distinct output data items. The system was modelled by considering each separate output item and associating a function with that item. It was found to be impossible to express each output as a function of one or more inputs, so the requirements were expressed in terms of aircraft operating conditions. These conditions were then expressed in terms of input data items. As no direct functional relationship between input and output was defined, the system designer was not constrained by how particular operating conditions were detected.

The most effective notations for describing the conceptual model of a system are graphical notations. The reason for this is that pictures and diagrams are usually understandable by users who have no technical background in software engineering. For example, consider an office system providing electronic mail, spreadsheet, document preparation and information retrieval services. A high-level conceptual model of this system is shown in Fig. 2.1. From this model, the major user facilities (spreadsheet, electronic mail, document preparation and information retrieval) can be identified along with their support systems (communications and database).

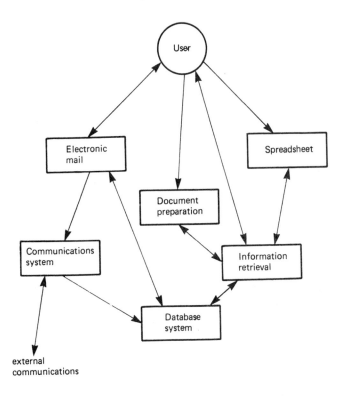

Figure 2.1 Conceptual model of an office system.

The next step in the conceptual modelling process is to take each major user service and establish a conceptual model for that service. This is illustrated in Fig. 2.2 which shows the conceptual model for the electronic mail service shown in Fig. 2.1. A similar model can be derived for the other major user services and these models may be refined to further levels of detail if necessary.

The reason for establishing a conceptual system model is to provide a framework on which a more detailed and complete requirements definition may be based. The creator of the model must take care not to imply a system design. However, it is inevitable, in many cases, that the high-level system design will have the same general form as the conceptual system model.

If a system is completely new, the conceptual system model may be incomplete because the system specifier does not know exactly what is required of the system. Software requirements derived from such a model are inevitably imprecise. The Stoneman document (DoD, 1980), describing the requirements for an Ada programming environment, is an example of such an imprecise definition. More precise requirements can be formulated only after design experiments have been carried out. The results of these experiments are fed back to allow a more complete conceptual model to be established.

The Stoneman requirements definition document is typical of the state of the art of requirements specification for software systems which are not a development of an existing automated or manual system. Examples from it are used in this chapter because it is publicly available and not because it is a particularly bad or particularly good example of a software requirements

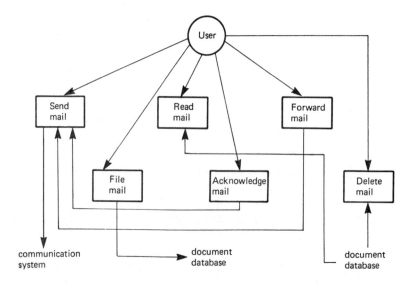

Figure 2.2   Conceptual model for an electronic mail system.

document. By contrast, most requirements definitions are proprietary documents and may not be freely quoted.

2.3 Functional requirements definition

Usually, most of the software requirements document is taken up with a definition of the functional system requirements. Systems analysts sometimes use the term 'functional specification' for this part of the requirements definition. However, this term is avoided here because it is used in a different way by many computer scientists.

The functional system requirements are those system services which are expected by the user of the system. In general, the user is uninterested in how these services are implemented, so the software engineer must avoid introducing implementation concepts in this section of the software requirements document.

In principle, the functional requirements of a system should be both complete and consistent. Completeness means that all services required by the user should be specified, and consistency means that no one requirements definition should contradict any other. In practice, for large, complex systems, it is practically impossible to achieve requirements consistency and completeness in the initial version of the software requirements document. As problems are discovered during reviews or in later life cycle phases, the software requirements document must be modified accordingly.

There are three ways of expressing the functional requirements of a system:

1. in natural language,
2. in a structured or formatted language which has some rules but no rigorous syntactic or semantic specification,
3. in a formal specification language with rigorously defined syntax and semantics.

Of these notations, the most commonly used is natural language simply because it is the most expressive and because it may be understood by both users and system developers. Some use has been made of structured languages. These have the advantage that, because of the rules governing their use, software tools for checking consistency and completeness can be constructed. The development of methods of formal specification is still a research problem and only very limited use of formal specification has been made in industrial software engineering.

As formal specification is the subject of the following chapter, this section concentrates on the use of natural language and structured languages for requirements definition. Rather than use an existing structured requirements definition language, however, a variant of the language Ada is used. This is likely to become an increasingly widespread method of requirements definition as Ada becomes known in the software engineering community and becomes widely used for systems development.

2.3.1 Natural language requirements definition

The most extensively used method of requirements definition is to set out the system requirements as numbered paragraphs of natural language text. For example, requirements 4.A.5 and 4.C.1 taken from the Stoneman document are as follows:

> 4.A.5   The database shall support the generation and control of configuration objects; that is, objects which are themselves groupings of other objects in the database. The configuration control facilities shall allow access to the objects in a version group by the use of an incomplete name.

> 4.C.1   A virtual interface which is independent of any host machine shall be provided for APSE communication.

Notice that these requirements are imprecise, descriptive and very high-level. For an innovative system such as the APSE it is neither possible nor desirable to use anything but natural language for requirements definition. The reason for this is that the exact services to be provided by the system can only be established in outline and a more definitive statement of requirements can only be established after experiment with prototype APSEs.

There are two major problems which sometimes arise when natural language is used for requirements definition.

1. Functional requirements, non-functional requirements and system goals are not clearly distinguished.
2. Each paragraph may encompass several individual requirements in a single statement. This makes consistency and completeness checking very difficult indeed.

These problems are illustrated with examples from the Stoneman document.

The APSE control requirements as expressed in this document consist of nine paragraphs of natural language text with supporting notes. Paragraph 4.C.1 which is set out above defines a high-level functional requirement. However, 4.C.2 states the following:

> The virtual interface shall be based on simple overall concepts which are straightforward to understand and use and which are few in number.

This is an admirable system goal, not a requirement, as it is very difficult to assess the simplicity, straightforwardness, usability and overallness of system concepts.

Requirement 4.C.8 states:

> It shall be possible for all necessary communication between the APSE and the user to be expressed in the standard Ada character set.

Rather than describe a function to be provided, this is a practical limitation on the design of an Ada programming support environment. That is, this is a non-functional requirement which is mixed with statements of functional requirements and system goals.

It is very difficult to avoid mixing functional and non-functional requirements and system goals when using natural language for requirements definition. The reason for this is that there is no notational distinction between them and the separation can be accomplished only with the assistance of careful requirements reviews.

The second problem outlined above can again be detected during requirements reviews. The original definer must make a conscious effort to avoid including multiple concepts in a single paragraph. However, this is also difficult to achieve as these concepts tend to be closely interlinked in the definer's mind.

Perhaps the best way of tackling this problem is to have the requirements definition analysed and rewritten by someone who is less closely involved in the process of requirements formulation. This is illustrated below where part of the Stoneman requirements defining the APSE database have been rewritten.

The original requirements and notes which have been revised are:

4.A.3   A separately identifiable collection of information in the database is known in this document as an 'object'. Every object stored in the database is accessed by the use of its distinct name. The database shall permit relationships to be maintained between objects.

4.B.1   OBJECTS: A separately identifiable collection of information in the database is known as an object in this document. An object has a name by which it may be uniquely identified in the database, it has attributes and it contains information. Typically, an object may contain a separately compilable Ada program unit, a fragment of Ada text, a separable definition, a file of test data, a project requirements specification, an aggregation of other project names (i.e. a configuration; see below), a documentation file, etc.

A revised version of these requirements where each requirement expresses a single notion is shown below. Notice that upper-case letters are used in the first reference to entities which are defined later in the requirements definition.

1. KAPSE DATABASE REQUIREMENTS

1.1 The KAPSE database (hereafter termed the KDB) shall be made up of named entities termed OBJECTS. [4.A.3]

1.2 The KDB shall permit relationships between objects to be recorded and maintained. [4.A.3]

1.3 The KDB must ensure that objects in the database are only accessed by the use of the distinct object NAME. [4.A.3]

1.4 KDB Objects

1.4.1 A KDB object is a separately identifiable collection of information. Examples of the information held in KDB objects include but are not restricted to a separately compilable Ada program unit, a fragment of Ada text, a separable definition, a collection of test data, a project requirements specification, an aggregation of other object names (a CONFIGURATION), a descriptive document, etc.

1.4.2 A KDB object is made up of two distinct components — INFORMATION CONTENT and ATTRIBUTES. [4.B.2]

1.4.3 Each KDB object shall have a NAME which uniquely identifies that object. [4.B.2]

This rewriting process can obviously be continued for the remainder of the requirements. Rewriting the requirements in this way is not a particularly difficult task but it makes the requirements definition much easier to read. The reason for this is that each statement in the requirements definition addresses a single concept and the reader need not work to separate the individual requirements in each paragraph.

From the foregoing, it may seem that natural language is an unhelpful notation for expressing software requirements. Indeed, in the following section of this chapter the limitations of natural language are discussed in more detail. However, it is necessary to use natural language when formulating high-level requirements, as the generality of these cannot be expressed in a more restricted notation.

In addition, a natural language statement of requirements may be used to supplement and document a more detailed requirements definition. Indeed, it is probably essential that some natural language definition is provided so that users with no experience of formal or structured notations may understand the requirements definition. Parnas (1979) also found that the expression of requirements in natural language was more understandable and, surprisingly, less misunderstood by software developers than more formal requirements definitions.

Therefore, it is unlikely that natural language will ever be supplanted completely by formal or semi-formal languages for requirements definition. Rather, a structured requirements definition will be produced with high-level requirements expressed in natural language and languages of increasing formality used as these requirements are expanded in more detail.

2.3.2 Structured languages for requirements definition
Whilst natural language is probably the only means of expressing high-level system requirements, a more detailed expression of requirements is best expressed using a more restricted and machine-processable notation.

The inadequacies of unstructured paragraphs of natural language for precise requirements definitions are:

1. They rely on the shared linguistic experience of those responsible for reading and writing the requirements definition. The writer of a definition assumes that the terms which are used in that specification mean the same to the reader as they do to him or her. This is a dangerous assumption because of the inherent ambiguity of natural language and because a standard computing terminology has not yet been established.

2. They are unable to express the functional architecture of the system in a clear and concise way. Schoman and Ross (1977) define the functional architecture of a system to be a description of the activities performed by the system and the interacting entities within the system. Essentially, it is a formalization of the conceptual model built by the system specifier. As this model is based on abstractions, the notation provided for specifying the model should be capable of expressing these abstractions in an unambiguous manner.

3. They are over-flexible as they allow related requirements to be expressed in completely different ways. This means that the reader of the definition is left with the task of identifying and partitioning related requirements with the consequent likelihood of error and misunderstanding.

4. They do not partition requirements effectively. As a result, the effect of changes can only be determined by examining every requirement rather than a group of related requirements.

To counteract some of these disadvantages of natural language definition there have been a number of notations developed specially for defining software requirements.

Notations which have been developed to define requirements all rely on natural language as an expressive base. Instead of using it in an unstructured way, however, they impose some structure on the definition, limit the natural language expressions which may be used and, in some of these languages, enhance the natural language definition by use of graphics.

Languages which have been designed to express software requirements include PSL/PSA (Teichrow and Hershey, 1977), SADT (Schoman and Ross, 1977) and RSL (Bell *et al.*, 1977). Although each language is intended as a general-purpose notation for specifying requirements, these languages were originally designed with different types of application in mind. RSL is designed for specifying time-critical real-time systems, PSL/PSA for information processing systems, and SADT for management information systems. RSL and PSL/PSA are designed to be used in conjunction with software tools which produce reports directly from formally stated requirements. By contrast, an SADT definition is intended to act as finished documentation so there is no need for an associated report generator.

SADT is the proprietary name of a notation developed by Ross (1977) based on a technique called Structured Analysis. Structured Analysis is not intended solely for specifying requirements but is designed as a technique for partitioning, structuring and expressing ideas, irrespective of the language in which these ideas are stated. Structured Analysis relies heavily on graphics to indicate structure and relationships, making use of about 40 distinct graphics symbols. Ross considers a description expressed in this way to bear the same relationship to the implemented system as a blueprint does to the engineering system which it describes.

Although Structured Analysis diagrams use special symbols, Ross maintains that they are easy to read and clear, even to the non-specialist. They are a tool for facilitating human communication, but it is difficult to collect the ideas expressed in these diagrams and to check their consistency and completeness with software tools. This is not the case with PSL/PSA and RSL which have been specifically designed for machine processing.

RSL was designed as part of a requirements engineering methodology described by Bell *et al.* (1977) and Alford (1977). Statements in RSL are machine processable and information derived from these statements is collected into a database called the Abstract System Semantic Model (ASSM). A set of automated tools processes the information in the ASSM to generate simulators, produce reports and check the consistency and completeness of the requirements.

The language is simple in concept and based on four distinct primitives. These are elements, relationships, attributes and structures. Elements correspond roughly to nouns in English, relationships to verbs, and attributes to adjectives. Structures model the flow of information through the functional steps which process that information. Fundamental elements, relationships and attributes are predefined in RSL and a facility exists for the user to add new elements, relationships or attributes if this is necessary to express new concepts.

The basic structure of PSL/PSA is similar to that of RSL. It allows objects to be identified and named and allows relationships between objects to be specified. It also collects the specified information into a centralized database where it can be processed by software tools.

An alternative to the use of a requirements statement language to structure and restrict natural language is to use standard forms to achieve the same purpose. A project which used this approach is described by Heninger (1980). Special-purpose forms were designed to describe the input, output and functions of an aircraft software system. The system requirements were specified by filling in these forms. Although the system described by Heninger is a manual one, standardization of the forms would allow machine processing of the requirements to be carried out.

Another method of requirements definition which is likely to become of increasing importance is to make use of a derivative of a powerful high-level language such as Ada. This approach has been described by Mander (1981) and Hill (1983). Pure Ada is probably too restrictive to be suitable on its own as a language for requirements definition. However, by relaxing some of the rules of the language and establishing new rules specifying what information must be provided, an Ada-based notation is suitable for requirements definition.

Mander compares requirements definition in Ada to definition in notations such as SADT and PSL/PSA. He concludes that Ada is as expressive as these languages as long as extensive use is made of comments to provide additional information to the reader. A similar approach is described by Kreig-Bruckner and Luckham (1980) who describe a formal specification language based on Ada. In this language, extra information is provided as formal comments. These are introduced by a special comment symbol so that they may be identified for machine processing.

The example below illustrates how a variant of Ada may be used to define the electronic mail system whose conceptual model is set out in Fig. 2.2. A brief explanation of the less-familiar Ada constructs is provided in comments. In this notation, some relaxation of Ada rules has been made:

1. Semi-colons need not be used as statement delimiters when an end-of-line character may perform the same function in an unambiguous way.

2. Ada **with** and **use** clauses may be included anywhere within a definition unit to indicate that declarations made in another definition unit may be used. The **use** clause on its own is taken to include an implicit **with** clause. This means that these clauses may be encapsulated within a definition unit.

3. The requirement for a **private** part in an Ada package, where private types are declared, is relaxed. This is obligatory in Ada programs for implementation reasons but, as it provides implementation information only, is unnecessary for requirements definition.

In addition, the following rules have been introduced to make the requirements definition more readable:

1. Individual user services should be defined as Ada procedures. A set of related services may be gathered together into an Ada package. An Ada package is a construct for controlling the visibility of the declarations made inside that package. It allows logically related objects to be grouped together and referenced as a single unit. In terms of the terminology introduced earlier, Ada packages allow modules to be defined.

2. If an error can occur during a user service, the definition of that user service must include an exception handler setting out the action to be taken in the event of an error. No other method of defining error actions may be used. Ada's exception handling constructs allow the user to define actions to be taken in the event of some unexpected event such as an error. The actions to be taken are grouped together at the end of a program unit into what is termed an exception handler.

3. All services must have at least three comment sections describing the input, the function and the output of that service. These are introduced by the special comment symbols −− input, −− Function and −− Output respectively and terminated by the comment lines −−* Input, −−* Function and −−* Output.

An Ada package definition may be used to define the highest level of the electronic mail system:

```
package ELECTRONIC_MAIL_SYSTEM is
     procedure SEND_MAIL
     procedure FILE_MAIL
     procedure ACKNOWLEDGE_MAIL
     procedure READ_MAIL
     procedure DELETE_MAIL
     procedure FORWARD_MAIL
end ELECTRONIC_MAIL_SYSTEM
```

The user view of the electronic mail system is of a set of related commands which can be activated to perform particular electronic mail functions. The Ada package construct allows all these functions to be gathered together and considered as a single entity — the ELECTRONIC_MAIL_SYSTEM.

The next step in the definition of requirements is to define those constants and types which may be shared by all of the mail system functions. Although this is the next part of the requirements definition, as set out in the software requirements document, these will probably be formulated after the user services have been defined. Again, these shared types and constants may be encapsulated in Ada packages.

```
package EM_CONSTANTS is
     NUMBER_OF_USERS : constant := 1000
     MAILBOX_CAPACITY : constant := 500
     TEXTSIZE : constant := 5000
end EM_CONSTANTS

package EM_TYPES is
     use EM_CONSTANTS
−− The use clause, simplistically, means that
−− the declarations in EM_constants should be included
−− here. Thus the constants declared in
−− EM_constants may be used in this package
     type USER_ID is range −1 . . NUMBER_OF_USERS
−− USER_ID is an integer value which uniquely identifies a
−− system user.
     type DATE is record
              MINS : 0. .60
              HOURS : 0. .24
              DAY : 1. .31
              MONTH : 1. .12
              YEAR : 84. .99
     end record
     type TEXT is ARRAY (1. .TEXTSIZE) OF CHARACTER
```

```
-- items of electronic mail have a structure defined
-- as follows:
    type MAIL_RECORD is record
            SENDER : USER-ID
            RECEIVER : USER-ID
            DISPATCH_DATE : DATE
            MESSAGE : TEXT
    end record
end EM_TYPES
```

One possible model for defining the actions of electronic mail services is to assume that each user has a personal mailbox for incoming mail and that this mailbox may be accessed using the user's system identifier. The mailbox can be defined in an Ada package definition without a decision having to be made on details of how the mailbox is to be implemented. Indeed, implementation of the mail system need not use mailboxes at all.

```
package MAIL is
    type BOX is limited private

-- defining BOX as a limited private type means that
-- its structure may not be accessed from outside MAIL
-- and that the operations on BOX are restricted to
-- those defined in the package MAIL

    use EM_TYPES
    procedure PUT (MAIL : MAIL_ITEM; NUMBER : USER_ID)
    procedure GET (MAIL : out MAIL_ITEM;
            NUMBER : USER_ID)

-- The allowed operations on mailboxes are put to
-- enter mail and get to retrieve mail

end MAIL
```

Assume that the user interacts with the electronic mail system using an interactive terminal. The operations on this terminal are the collection of mail and the display of mail. Again, these can be specified in an Ada package.

```
package TERMINAL is

-- Notice that the operations here have the same names
-- as the operations in MAIL. This is not ambiguous
-- as the operations must be accessed through their
-- own package whose name must be unique
    use EM_TYPES
    procedure GET (MAIL : out MAIL_ITEM)
    procedure PUT (MAIL : MAIL_ITEM)
end TERMINAL
```

Now, enough background has been included to define the individual user services. Space does not allow a complete definition here. Rather, the principles of requirements definition will be illustrated by defining the send mail service.

```
procedure SEND_MAIL
  -- Input
  -- interactive input from users terminal collected using the
  -- terminal handler operation get
  --* Input

  -- Function
  -- Collects mail to be delivered, identifies the receiver
  -- and delivers the mail to his or her mailbox.
  -- After delivery, an acknowledgement is sent to the sender
  -- indicating that the mail has been delivered
  --* Function

  -- Output
  -- The mailboxes of both the mail sender and receiver are
  -- affected by this operation. The input mail is appended
  -- to the receivers mailbox and an acknowledgement is
  -- appended to the senders mailbox
  --* Output

use EM_TYPES
INPUT_MAIL, ACKNOWLEDGEMENT : MAIL_ITEM
  -- Possible errors are defined as exceptions
UNKNOWN_SENDER, UNKNOWN_RECEIVER : exception
SENDERS_ID, RECEIVERS_ID : USER_ID
INVALID_USER : constant := -1
ANON : constant := 0

begin
    with TERMINAL, MAIL, CALENDAR
  -- the with clause is similar to the use clause except
  -- that the package name must precede the declaration
  -- CALENDAR is a standard Ada package
    TERMINAL.GET (INPUT_MAIL)
    SENDERS_ID := INPUT_MAIL.SENDER
    -- if an error is detected, the exception should
    -- be signalled
    -- in Ada, this is called raising the exception.
    if SENDERS_ID = INVALID_USER then
        raise UNKNOWN_SENDER
    end if
    RECEIVERS_ID := INPUT_MAIL.RECEIVER
    if RECEIVERS_ID = INVALID_USER then
        raise UNKNOWN_RECEIVER
    end if
    MAIL.PUT (INPUT_MAIL, RECEIVERS_ID)
    ACKNOWLEDGEMENT.SENDER := INPUT_MAIL.RECEIVER
    ACKNOWLEDGEMENT.RECEIVER := INPUT_MAIL.SENDER
    ACKNOWLEDGEMENT.DISPATCH_TIME := CALENDAR.CLOCK
    ACKNOWLEDGEMENT.MESSAGE := ''MAIL DELIVERED''
    MAIL.PUT (ACKNOWLEDGEMENT, SENDERS_ID)
end
  -- Note that raising an exception when some error is detected
  -- causes transfer to the exception handler here
  -- Although there are other error handling techniques
```

```
-- defining error handling with an exception handler means
-- that all error information is collected together in one
-- place
exception
    when UNKNOWN_SENDER =>
    -- send to receiver and also log on anonymous
    -- message log
        SENDERS_ID := ANON
        INPUT_MAIL.SENDER := ANON
        MAIL.PUT (INPUT_MAIL, RECEIVERS_ID)
        MAIL.PUT (INPUT_MAIL, SENDERS_ID)
    end
    when UNKNOWN_RECEIVER =>
    -- return to sender
        RECEIVERS_ID. := ANON
        MAIL.PUT (INPUT_MAIL, SENDERS_ID)
    end
end SEND_MAIL
```

The process of requirements definition in Ada can be continued for all of the other system functions.

It may be argued that the above notation is too low level and that it defines the software requirements by means of an implementation. Hence, the freedom of the software designer to decide how to implement the user services is constrained.

These statements are partially true. It is the author's opinion that all requirements definition languages imply an implementation because they are based on some underlying model which is essentially computational. In this respect, Ada is no different from RSL, etc. This does not mean, however, that the implications in the requirements definition need be taken up by the software designer. He or she should be at liberty to translate the requirements definition into any equivalent design.

2.4 Database requirements

Many large software systems require the existence of a large database of information. The system takes information from and adds information to this database as it executes. In some cases, this database exists independently of the software system; in others it is created for the system being developed. In either case, there is a need for a definition of the logical form of this database.

One technique which has been used to define the logical form of a database is to use a relational model of data as described by Codd (1970). Using the relational model, the logical data structure is specified as a set of tables, with some tables having common keys. This model allows the relationships between data items to be defined without considering the physical database organization.

As an example of a relational definition, consider a document database as might be used in the previous model of an office system. Within that database, the information held on each document might include the text of the document, the author of the document, the time it was entered into the database and a list of those permitted to access that document. Each document is identified by a unique internal identifier. A relation describing this organization is shown in Fig. 2.3. Notice that some of the fields in the relation such as the access_list field refer to some other relation. This might be set out as shown in Fig. 2.4. Indexes into the document list may also be defined as relations as shown in Fig. 2.5, which illustrates a possible structure for an author index. It is up to the system designer to study the data definition and determine how that specification is best realized as a physical data structure. If a relational database management system is available, it may even be possible to implement the logical definition directly.

Although a relational definition of the data does not compromise data independence, it does contain implications of how the data is to be physically structured. For example, it implies that document creation time and owner are stored in such a way that they are accessed via D# rather than in their own right. This may or may not be intended, but it is difficult for the designer to ignore such implications as the design is obviously influenced by the definitions.

An alternative technique of data definition, described by Chen (1976) uses a modified relational model where each relation is simply a binary relation. The document identifier D# is used as the key linking each binary relation. Using binary relations, a document may be described as follows:

D# 'is composed of' text
D# 'has author' author
D# 'was entered at' creation-time
D# 'has permissions' access-permissions

Using this type of definition, there is no implicit relationship between the document access permissions, say, and the document owner. Furthermore, each binary relation may have a converse:

owner 'owns' D#

This means that access to documents need not all go through the document identifier D#.

D#	Text file	Owner	Time-in	Access#
1234	F1	S. Simon	16452702	AL1
5678	F2	H. Dumpty	09171603	AL2
9012	F3	J. Horner	11321704	AL3
3456	F4	J. Sprat	13132204	AL4

Figure 2.3 A relation in a document database.

Access#	User
AL1	H. Dumpty
AL1	P. Flinders
AL2	B. Shafto
AL3	S. Simon
AL3	T. Tucker
AL4	W. Winkie

Figure 2.4   Access list relation.

Owner	D#
Dumpty	5678
Horner	9012
Simon	1234
Sprat	3456

Figure 2.5   Author index relation.

Binary relations are used in the requirements definition language RSL, discussed above, and a number of database systems have been implemented using this approach (Frost, 1981; McGregor and Malone, 1980; Sharman and Winterbottom, 1979). The problem with the binary relational definition of a database is that it is often less intuitive, more difficult to formulate and harder to read than a relational definition. It is up to management to decide whether the greater generality of this technique compensates for these difficulties.

2.5 Non-functional requirements definition

A non-functional system requirement is some restriction or constraint placed on the system service. Examples of non-functional requirements are constraints placed on system response times, limitations on the amount of store to be occupied by the software, and restrictions on the representation of system data.

Although both functional and non-functional requirements are liable to change, non-functional requirements are particularly affected by changes in hardware technology. As the development time for a large system may be several years, it is likely that the hardware available at the conclusion of the project will be more powerful than that available when the project was conceived. Furthermore, the hardware will evolve throughout the lifetime of the developed software and the non-functional requirements will be modified whilst the software is in use.

Hardware changes which may occur whilst the software is being developed can be anticipated. Hardware-dependent non-functional requirements can be specified which assume hardware capability will be available on project completion although that may not be the case when the project commences. No such anticipation can be made for changes during the project's lifetime and an important characteristic of hardware-dependent requirements is that they should be specified in such a way that they may be easily changed.

Non-functional requirements are such that they tend to conflict and interact with other system functional requirements. The conflict between execution speed requirements and storage requirements is the obvious example here. A non-functional requirements definition should set out these requirements in such a way that conflicts are made clear and should allow possible trade-offs to be discerned.

Boehm (1974) has described a notation called the requirements/properties matrix which is useful for determining the trade-offs to be made when considering requirements. He identifies program properties such as run speed, storage needs, reliability, maintainability, etc., and definite requirements such as size < 64K, user response time < 4 s, etc. These are then put together in a matrix displaying requirements and system properties. An example of part of such a matrix is shown in Fig. 2.6.

Prop. / Req.	Run speed	Maintainability	Reliability	Storage	...
< 64K	A	B	O	D42	
Standard character set	O	D32	O	O	
Response < 4 s	D17, D31	B	O	A	

Figure 2.6   Requirements/properties matrix.

The matrix is filled in with one of the following:

O — irrelevant
A — analysed
B — in the process of analysis
Di — covered by definition Di
Rj — overlaps requirement Rj

The use of such a matrix relates each requirement/property to an explicit definition. It reduces the probability that unrealistic requirements will be introduced by ensuring that a complete analysis of the implications of that requirement is made. Although the matrix does not show the results of analysis, it documents whether an analysis has been carried out or not. The implications of a particular requirement are unlikely to be overlooked.

It is normal practice to express non-functional requirements in natural language. This may be as part of a natural language requirements definition or may be in a special section of a requirements definition in a structured language. For example, a non-functional requirement taken from the Stoneman document is:

> 4.C.8   It shall be possible for all necessary communication between the APSE and the user to be expressed in the standard Ada character set.

This requirement restricts the freedom of an APSE designer in his or her choice of symbols which might be used to activate APSE services.

Because of the variety and the complexity of non-functional requirements, it is unlikely that natural language will ever be replaced by formal notations for non-functional requirements definition. However, some types of non-functional requirement which are concerned with the representation of information may be expressed in an Ada-like notation which includes extended facilities for representation specification. Ada already has a for-use clause which allows some representations to be defined. For example:

```
type STATE is (HALTED, WAITING, READY, RUNNING);
for STATE use (HALTED => 1, WAITING => 4, READY => 16
    RUNNING => 256);
```

This declares that HALTED is represented by 1, WAITING by 4, READY by 16, and RUNNING by 256. It is clear that a similar, extended notation might be used to specify the representation of the MAIL_ITEM type used in the electronic mail system defined above. For example:

```
type MAIL_ITEM is record
    SENDER : USER_ID;
    RECEIVER : USER_ID;
    DISPATCH_TIME : DATE;
    MESSAGE : TEXT;
end record;

for MAIL_ITEM use record
    SENDER at 0 size 2 bytes
    RECEIVER at 2 size 2 bytes
    DISPATCH_TIME at 4 size 10 bytes
    message at 14 range 1..5000 bytes
        terminator ASCII'EOT
end record
```

This defines the representation of MAIL_ITEM. The sender's and receiver's identifiers are represented by 2-byte units starting at position 0 and 2 respectively. The date is a 10-byte unit starting at offset 4 and message may vary in size from 1 to 5000 bytes. Message is always terminated by ASCII'EOT character.

2.6 Requirements validation

Once a set of system requirements has been established, these requirements should be validated. If no validation is carried out, errors in the requirements definition will be propagated to the system design and implementation and expensive system modifications may be required to correct these errors.

The cost of errors in stating requirements may be very high, particularly if these errors are not discovered until the system is implemented. Boehm (1974) reports that in some large systems up to 95% of the code had to be rewritten to satisfy changed user requirements and also that 12% of the errors discovered in a software system over a three-year period were due to errors in the original system requirements. The majority of so-called program maintenance is not actually correction of erroneous code but code modification to support changes to or errors in the original system requirements.

There are four separate steps involved in validating requirements. These are:

1. The requirements should be shown to be consistent. Any one requirement should not conflict with any other.

2. The requirements should be shown to be complete. The definition should include all functions and constraints intended by the system user.

3. The requirements should be shown to be realistic. There is no point in specifying requirements which are unrealizable using existing hardware and software technology. It may be acceptable to anticipate some hardware developments, but developments in software technology are much less predictable.

4. The needs of the user should be shown to be valid. A user may think that a system is needed to perform certain functions but further thought and analysis may identify additional or different functions which are required.

Requirements reviews are the most effective way to validate requirements. During a review, the requirements are studied and considered by both users and software developer. Anomalies and inconsistencies are sought. This process is simplified if the requirements definition is compilable and software tools for analysing the definition are available. Although tools for analysing requirements definitions are very valuable, they are most useful for staff formulating the requirements definition. The information produced by these tools is likely to be meaningless to the system user.

An example of a tool to assist requirements validation, described by

Boehm (1974), is a keyword analyser. Given particular keywords such as 'protection', 'store', 'access', etc., this system scans all requirements and extracts those requirements which include that keyword. These requirements can then be compared to ensure that they do not conflict. Other automated tools might ensure that duplicate terms for the same object are not introduced, or compare function inputs and outputs. If a function A provides input for function B, A's output definition should match B's input specification.

The realism of requirements can be demonstrated, in some cases, by constructing a system simulator. The technique of system simulation is particularly useful to demonstrate that non-functional requirements can be met. One of the tools used in conjunction with the requirements statement language RSL is a simulator generator. This tool analyses an RSL definition and automatically generates a system simulator in Pascal. Procedures which simulate each functional definition are provided by the specifier as part of the requirements definition.

Davis and Vick (1977) point out that, for complex systems, it can be as expensive and as time-consuming to develop the system simulator as it is to develop the system itself. Furthermore, it may be difficult to change the simulator, so that changes in the requirements may be impossible to assess by simulation. As a result, simulation has not been extensively used in validating the requirements of large systems, although Davis and Vick state that it can result in a significant reduction in requirements statement errors.

The other steps involved in requirements validation, checking the completeness of requirements and demonstrating that the system meets the actual needs of the user, can only be carried out with the co-operation of the system user. The user must examine and understand the requirements and check that they specify the kind of system which is really required. Unfortunately, many users do not clearly understand their own needs and cannot effectively compare a requirements statement with the application functions needed. Their needs can only be accurately identified if they have some kind of working software system to assess and criticize.

Regular requirements reviews involving both users and software engineers are essential while the requirements definition is being formulated. During these reviews, the development team should 'walk' the user through the system requirements explaining the implications of each requirement. Conflicts and contradictions should be pointed out. It is then up to the user to modify his requirements to resolve these problems and contradictions.

2.6.1 Prototyping

The fundamental problem which faces the user involved in defining a new software system is that it is very difficult to assess how the existence of that system will affect his work. For new systems, particularly if these are large and complex, it is probably impossible to derive a consistent, complete and valid requirements definition before the system is built and put into use.

This has led to suggestions, discussed in Chapter 1, that an evolutionary approach to systems development should be adopted. This implies presenting the user with a system knowing it to be incomplete and then modifying and augmenting that system as the user's real requirements become apparent. One way to achieve this is via prototyping where a system prototype is transformed in a series of steps to the final delivered system.

Alternatively, a deliberate decision might be made to build a 'throwaway' prototype. This is a widely used approach to hardware development where a prototype is built to identify initial problems and, after experimentation, an improved specification is formulated. The prototype is then discarded and a production-quality system built. This approach may also be applicable to software development.

The benefits of using a prototype system during the requirements analysis and definition phase of the software life cycle may be summarized as follows:

1. Misunderstandings between software developers and users may be identified as the system functions are demonstrated.
2. Missing user services may be detected.
3. Difficult-to-use or confusing user services may be identified and refined.
4. Software development staff may find incomplete and/or inconsistent requirements as the prototype is developed.
5. A working, albeit limited, system is available very quickly to demonstrate the feasibility and usefulness of the application to management.
6. The prototype may serve as a specification for the development of a production quality system.

Given that prototyping is used to assist in the validation of requirements, a decision must be made on whether the prototype should evolve into the final system or whether it ought to be scrapped and the system to be delivered written afresh.

For small systems, it may be appropriate to develop the prototype into the final system, although this may be precluded by the inefficiency inherent in the prototype implementation. For large systems where maintainability is most important, it is probably better to discard the prototype and rebuild the system. The reason for this is that rapid development should be the aim of prototype developers whereas maintainability should be the aim of production-quality systems development. Rapid development and maintainability are rarely compatible and it is likely that the structure of the prototype would degrade rapidly as maintenance progressed.

Prototyping has not been widely used in software evaluation. The principal argument against it is that the cost of prototype development represents an unacceptably large fraction of overall system costs. It is more economic to modify a finished system to meet unperceived needs than to provide an opportunity for the user to understand and refine his needs before the final system is built. By contrast, the cost of a prototype for a mechanical or electronic system which is to be mass produced represents a very small increment in the final unit cost of the system and the cost of system modification after release is very large indeed.

Software prototyping is expensive if the prototype is implemented using the same tools and to the same standards as the final system. However, if a prototype is intended to demonstrate the functional rather than the non-functional aspects of a system it can be developed at a cost which is significantly lower than that of the final system. Rapid prototype development can be accomplished by using very high-level languages for prototype implementation, by ignoring considerations of error action, by compromising on the suitability of the user interface and by reducing reliability and program quality standards.

Because error detection, error recovery and user interface implementation comprise such a large part of most systems, their elimination drastically reduces the size of the system to be prototyped. Hence the prototype development time is much less than the final system development time. This time can be further reduced by lowering standards of reliability and program quality. As the prototype is thrown away after the final requirements have been established, there is no need for production software standards to be adopted.

By reducing the system size and standards, prototype software can be constructed in any programming language but prototype development time can be reduced by using a very high-level programming language. Very high-level dynamic languages are not normally used for large system development because they need a large run-time support system. This run-time support increases the storage needs and reduces the execution speeds of programs written in the language. As performance requirements can sometimes be ignored in prototype development, however, this is not necessarily a disadvantage.

The language APL (Iverson, 1962) is eminently suited to prototype development. It offers powerful operations such as matrix arithmetic, is concise so that little time need be spent typing characters, and is implemented interactively. Using APL, the software engineer can often put together a prototype system in a fraction of the time required to implement the final software system. APL is unsuitable for large system programming because of its run-time overheads, and because its syntax does not permit readable, well structured programs to be written.

Gomaa (1983) has reported the successful use of APL as a prototyping language. He describes the advantages which accrued from developing a prototype for a process management and information system and he estimates that prototype development costs were less than 10% of the total system costs. In the development of the production system, no requirements definition problems were encountered, the project was completed on time and the system was well received by users.

Another useful prototyping tool is the shell programming language available under Unix (Ritchie and Thompson, 1978; Bourne, 1978). The Unix shell is a command language which includes looping and decision constructs. It provides facilities for combining commands which operate on files and strings. In the author's experience, a prototype for an information retrieval system was built, using the Unix shell, in a day. By contrast, the final system took several weeks to design and implement in Pascal.

The reason why the Unix shell is an effective prototyping tool is that it provides a means of connecting existing programs together into different useful configurations. This is a very sensible approach, but prototyping using the shell is limited because the granularity of the software components which may be connected together is relatively coarse. This means that the function of the individual components is often too general-purpose to combine effectively with other components. There appears to be scope for further development of prototyping using existing components with more precise functions than the programs available under Unix.

An alternative to using a very high-level language for prototype development or configuring existing components into a prototype is to use languages and environments which are specifically designed for prototype construction. Examples of such systems are RAPID (Wasserman and Shewmake, 1982) and Gist (Balzer *et al.*, 1982).

RAPID is built around a relational database, an implementation language called PLAIN which is designed for building interactive information systems, and a transition diagram interpreter for prototyping user dialogues. Gist is a non-deterministic language designed for operational specification (see Chapter 3). Early experience with both RAPID and Gist for rapid prototyping has been encouraging, but more work remains to be done before such tools can be generally used in industrial software development.

Further reading

The state of the art of requirements definition does not seem to have progressed a great deal over the last two or three years. It seems that the focus of activity in this area has switched to formal specifications. Hence, the papers on requirements definition recommended below are all a few years old.

'Specifying software requirements', R. T. Yeh and P. Zave (1980) *Proc. IEEE*, **68 (9)**, 1077−85.

> An interesting tutorial paper on how software requirements may be derived from a conceptual model. The authors illustrate their work with the derivation of a natural language requirements definition for a process control system.

'Specifying software requirements for complex systems: New techniques and their applications', K. L. Heninger (1980) *IEEE Trans. Software Engineering*, **SE-6 (1)**, 2–13.

A clearly written paper (unlike some papers on requirements definition!) which describes how a requirements definition was derived for an avionics system. Well worth reading as it is a fairly detailed look at a real rather than an example system.

'Towards an Ada-based specification and design language', A. Hill (1983) *ADA UK News*, **4 (4).**

A tutorial paper on the use of an Ada variant as a specification and design language. This variant has extensions to support the VDM formal specification technique but the paper uses mnemonic rather than symbolic notation.

ACM Software Engineering Notes, **7 (5),** 1982.

The proceedings of a conference on prototyping. Many papers of interest.

Chapter 3 SOFTWARE SPECIFICATION

The first stage of the software life cycle is to establish the requirements definition; that is, to set out the services provided for the user and the constraints under which the software must operate. Once this definition has been agreed, the next major stage in the life cycle is software design. During this stage, the requirements definition is analysed and software components to provide the user services are designed. This design is expressed in such a way that these components may be subsequently realized in some programming language. Software specification is part of this design process where the design is expressed in a high-level abstract way.

For small systems, it may be possible to go directly from the requirements definition to a detailed component design but, for large software systems, the design activity may be split into three stages:

1. Associate abstract software components with the services set out in the requirements definition and construct precise specifications for these components.

2. Construct a high-level design showing how these abstract software components are related to each other.

3. Formulate a detailed design for each abstract component. This detailed design is expressed in terms of simpler abstractions which may be readily translated to executable code.

Naturally, there is no clear division of these stages and the designer must iterate between them as the design is formulated. However, it is convenient to consider them separately in this book. In this chapter we are concerned with the first of these stages, namely the precise specification of software components. The other stages of software design are covered in Chapter 4.

It is sometimes argued that the software specification and the requirements definition are one and the same thing. Indeed, this confusion is exemplified by the fact that the terms 'functional specifications', 'requirements definition' and 'requirements specification' are often used interchangeably. In fact, there is a clear distinction between the software specification and the requirements definition.

The principal function of the requirements definition is to set out those services which the software must provide for the user. The requirements definition should be a user-oriented document and must be expressed in terms which are understandable to him. On the other hand, the software specification is intended for the software designer rather than the user. It is made up of abstract definitions of software components, not user services. As the user is normally unconcerned about how services are provided, he or she need not understand this document.

Of course, there are cases where there is a one-to-one relationship between software components and user services. In these cases, the software specification and the requirements definition may well be equivalent. In other cases, however, a user service may be provided by the interaction of several software components so the requirements definition and the specification of these components are quite distinct.

It is also sometimes argued that a software component specification is quite distinct from a software component design. It is suggested that the specification phase should precede the design phase and that a specification should set out what the software should do, whereas a design should define how the software function should be provided. There are some merits to this argument in that a completely abstract specification does not constrain the freedom of the software designer. On the other hand, it is extremely difficult to express some specifications in purely abstract terms, and forcing a separation of specification and design places unnecessary constraints on the software designer.

The view of this author is that the activities of software specification and design are so closely connected that it is impossible to separate them. Hence, specification is seen as part of the process of software design with a software specification being an abstract representation of a design.

The topic of software specification is currently the subject of a good deal of research with most of this work dedicated to the study of formal software specification. Formal software specification implies that the specification is expressed in a notation which is mathematically sound. This means that both the syntax and the semantics of the specification language should be formally defined so that the meaning of a specification can be determined by reference to the specification language definition.

Whilst it has been possible for some time to define in a formal way the syntax of a (restricted) language using a notation such as Backus-Naur form, the problem of defining the semantics or meaning of the language constructs is a much more difficult one. There are three distinct approaches to this problem:

1. *The operational approach.*   In this approach to semantic definition, an abstract machine is defined and the language semantics are expressed in terms of abstract machine operations. This technique has been used to define the semantics of the programming language PL/1 using a notation called VDL, described in Pagan (1981). Other descriptions of the operational approach are given by Berg *et al.* (1982).

   The problem which arises with this approach is that it relies on the operations of the underlying abstract machine being unambiguous and well understood. Using an operational model to define semantics simply pushes the problem down a level so that instead of language semantics the semantics of the abstract machine operations must be defined.

2. *The denotational approach.* The denotational approach to the definition of programming language semantics has its foundations in the lambda-calculus which is a calculus of mathematical logic. The fundamental work in applying the lambda-calculus to the definition of programming languages was carried out by Strachey and Scott and is described by Strachey and Milne (1976) and by Stoy (1977).

   While the operational approach maps programming language constructs onto abstract machine states, the denotational approach is based on functions which map constructs onto an abstract value space. The values in this space are mathematical objects such as integers, truthvalues and functions, so that mathematical techniques can be used to reason about their properties.

   The denotational approach is the basis for a specification method called the Vienna Development Method (VDM) which has an associated specification language called META-IV. It has been suggested that this may be useful in the specification of large software systems but, as the associated notation is fairly complex, space does not permit a description of this method here. Interested readers should refer to texts by Jones (1980) and Jones and Bjorner (1982).

3. *The axiomatic approach.* The axiomatic approach to the definition of programming language semantics was developed by Hoare (1969). It is unlike the denotational or operational approaches in that it is not based on some model underlying the programming language. Rather, it is founded on the idea that each programming language construct should have associated axioms which state what may be asserted after execution of that construct. These assertions are made in terms of what was true before execution.

   This approach is the foundation for a great deal of work on formal program verification. However, it does have the disadvantage that axioms for complex programming language constructs are difficult (if not impossible) to devise. The axiomatic approach has been used to define a subset of Pascal (Hoare and Wirth, 1973) but it is better suited to the definition of simpler languages than most of today's widely used programming languages.

A discussion of formal language semantics is outside the scope of this book and in the remainder of this chapter it is assumed that it is possible to construct a formal definition of the specification languages used in illustrative examples.

   There are a number of advantages which accrue from using formal specifications of software components:

1. Given a formal specification and a definition of programming language semantics, it may be possible to prove that a program meets its specification. Thus the absence of certain types of program errors can be established given, of course, that the proof is correct.

2. Formal software specifications can be studied mathematically so that questions concerning the equivalence of specifications, for example, can be answered.

3. Formal specifications are processable by computers and software tools may be constructed to assist designers in the development, understanding and debugging of software specifications.

The advantages of using formal software specifications are quite clear. However, there is one fundamental problem which, so far, has militated against their use in the development of large software systems. This problem is that software specifications are often very difficult to construct and to understand. This is particularly true for high-level abstractions representing complex activities such as document formatting, aircraft navigation, etc. For this reason, the examples used in this chapter are simple ones which are intended to give the reader some insights into formal specification techniques.

Some of the difficulties encountered in software specification are due to the fact that our notations for software specification are at a very early stage of development. Others are due to the inherent complexity of the abstractions which we use and intuitively understand. It may never be possible to construct comprehensible, formal specifications for some types of software component.

Yet other difficulties are due to the fact that an effective set of software tools has not yet evolved for specification processing. Tools which might be developed include formatting tools to lay out specifications in a readable way, checking tools to ensure that the syntax of the specification is correct, and execution tools which attempt to evaluate the specification, perhaps in a limited way.

The difficulties in constructing formal software specifications mean that their practical usefulness is currently limited. It is not economic to spend the time required to develop and debug formal specifications for even a small part of a large software system except, perhaps, in very critical applications where it is intended to verify the resulting program.

However, it is still useful for the software engineer to have some insight into formal specification techniques. This insight may allow him or her to create more precise, if not completely formal, software specifications and this is likely to lead to higher standards of software design. It is the author's opinion that thinking about how to construct formal specifications means that the designer must concentrate on the essential elements of his or her design. Even if it is impossible to write a formal specification, consideration of this task is an important part of the design process.

A proper and complete understanding of formal software specification requires considerable mathematical background and a full description of this topic requires at least one book to itself. Rather than attempt to be complete, therefore, this chapter is intended as a gentle introduction to software specification. Little mathematical background is necessary to understand the material here and a deliberate decision has been made that, where necessary, rigour should be sacrificed to clarity and conciseness.

One of the problems which faces the software engineer interested in formal software specifications is that there is no generally agreed notation for software specification. Indeed, a great deal of good work is concealed by notations which are difficult to penetrate and understand. Accordingly, complex symbolic notations have been avoided here and mnemonics rather than special symbols are used in the examples in this chapter.

There are four major sections in this chapter. The first of these introduces the idea of interface specifications where the software component is considered as a black box and its actions are defined in terms of its inputs and outputs. The second section looks at operational specifications where some abstract implementation of the component is provided. Thirdly, the specification of data abstractions is described. This is particularly important as the effective formal specification of data abstractions underpins all other specification techniques. In the final section, some guidelines on the practical development of software specifications are given.

3.1 Interface specifications

The most abstract view of a software component is to consider it as a black box. The only externally visible characteristics of a black box are its inputs and outputs, so interface specification involves specifying input and output constraints which define the function of the software component.

This type of specification is sometimes called input/output specification and sometimes pre/post condition specification after work in this area by Hoare (1969). Hoare's work was concerned with program verification and this led to a natural expression of the specification using mathematical concepts, such as sets, whose properties are well understood.

As a simple illustration of how interface specification may be used, consider the specification of a procedure MAX whose function is to determine the largest member of a set of integers:

> $MAX (X : set\ of\ integer) -> integer$
>   **input** $not\ empty\ (X)$
>   **output** $member\ (X, MAX)$ **and**
>   **forall** $E,\ member\ (X, E) : MAX >= E$

The first line of this specification sets out the function name, MAX, and its input formal parameter, X, whose type is $set\ of\ integer$, and indicates that the function returns an integer value. This is referenced using the function name MAX. The second line establishes the input constraint that X should not be the empty set and the third and fourth lines define the output constraints. The first of these is that *MAX* should be a member of set *X* and the second specifies that *MAX* should be greater than or equal to all other set members. It may be read as 'for all elements which satisfy the inclusion condition, the condition following the : must also hold'. Notice that this specification is completely abstract, giving no indication of how the largest set member is to be found.

In the specification of *MAX* the input was constrained to have at least one set member — the empty set was not accepted. However, no indication was provided of the action to be taken if this input constraint was not met. In practice, software components often have to handle incorrect input, so it is necessary to have some mechanism for specifying output corresponding to both correct and incorrect input.

This may be accomplished by considering the state of the component on termination. If a valid input is provided, the component is said to terminate in a normal state (**N-state**). On the other hand, if the input is invalid, the component terminates in an exception state (**E-state**). There should be one **E-state** for each class of invalid input.

This is illustrated in the example below, which is the specification of a procedure to order the elements of a set.

> *ORDER* (*X* : **in out** *set of integer*)
>   **N-state**
>   **input** *not empty* (*X*)
>   **output** *ordered* (*X'*) **and** *perm* (*X, X'*)
>   **E-state**
>   **input** *empty* (*X*)
>   **output** *empty* (*X'*)

As well as illustrating how normal and exceptional states may be specified, this example also introduces two other important specification techniques. The first of these is the representation of a component's output as a transformation of its input. From the specification heading we can see that the set *X* is both the input and the output parameter. The notation *X* is used to refer to the set of input values and *X'* to refer to the set of output values. This 'priming' of an input name indicates a transformation; thus T' is a transformation of T, Y' is a transformation of Y, etc.

The second technique introduced in this example is that of structured specifications. Two functions, 'ordered' and 'perm', have been introduced but not defined. In the same way as associating a mnemonic name with a collection of related operations in a program makes that program more readable, structuring specifications using named functions makes these specifications easier to understand.

The functions 'ordered' and 'perm' may be defined as follows:

> *ordered* (*T* : *set of integer*) $\rightarrow$ *boolean*
>   **forall** *i*, $1 <= i < size$ (*T*) :
> $T(i) < T(i + 1)$

perm (*X*, *Y* : *set of integer*) −> *boolean*
  size (*X*) = *size* (*Y*) **and**
forall *i*, *1* <= *i* <= *size* (*X*) :
  there_exists *j*, *1* <= *j* <= *size* (*Y*) :
    X (*i*) = *Y* (*j*)

The function *ordered* is true if its input set is in ascending order. The function *perm* is the permutation function which states that its inputs have the same number of members and that for all members of input set *X* there exists a member of input set *Y*. The condition following the colon in the **forall** clause may be read as 'there is an element which satisfies the following inclusion condition such that the condition following the : is also satisfied'. The ordering of *X* and *Y* may be different.

The meaning of the specification of *ORDER* (*X*) is now clear. In the normal termination state, the output of *ORDER* is a set whose members are arranged in ascending order and which has exactly the same members as the input set. In the exceptional state where the input consists of the empty set, the output should also be the empty set.

Using sets as a fundamental object in specifications is very convenient because their properties have been studied and set operations defined. Unfortunately, however, it is often unnatural to consider all information to be held in sets, so other specification types must be introduced.

For example, say a system has to handle a number of processes which may exist in one of three states. Each of these processes is associated with a sensor held at a fixed location numbered from 1 to *n*, where *n* is the number of processes. It is most convenient to represent this information as an array rather than a set because not all elements have distinct values and there is a sequential relationship between processes. Thus, the data for procedures in this system might be declared as follows:

  type *status* **is** (*stopped, ready, running*)
  type *P* **is** *array* (*1..n*) *of status*

Now consider the specification of a function *CHANGE_STATUS* which alters the status of a numbered process. Effectively, this is the assignment operation for this type of array.

  CHANGE_STATUS (*S* : **in out** *P*; *i* : *integer*; *t* : *status*)
    N-state
      input *in_range* (*S*, *i*)
      output *no_change* (*S*, *S'*, *first* (*S*), *i-1*) **and**
        no_change (*S*, *S'*, *i+1*, *last* (*S*)) **and**
        ·*S'* (*i*) = *t*
    E-state
      input *not in_range* (*S*, *i*)
      output ERROR **and**
        no_change (*S*, *S'*, *first* (*S*), *last* (*S*))

define
> in_range $(S : set\ of\ integer;\ i : integer)$ $\rightarrow$ $boolean$
> > $first\ (S) >= i >= last\ (S)$
>
> no_change $(S,\ T : array\ of\ integer;\ i,\ j : integer)$ $\rightarrow$ $boolean$
> > **forall** $k,\ i <= k <= j : S\ (k) = T\ (k)$

This example introduces the fundamental array operations **first** and **last** which return the index of the first and last members of the array respectively. It also illustrates the structuring of a specification with the keyword **define** used to introduce the definition of functions used in the specification.

The specification itself states that if the input index i is a valid index of S then the value t is assigned to the ith member of S and all other members are unchanged. If the index i is an invalid index, an error is signalled and the input array is unchanged.

This example can be developed further by defining an operation $SWITCH\_STATUS$ which makes all stopped processes ready, all ready processes active and all active processes stopped:

> $SWITCH\_STATUS$ $(S :$ **in out** $P)$
> > **output forall** $j,\ first\ (S) <= j <= last\ (S)$:
> > > $S\ (j) = stopped$ **and** $S'\ (j) = ready$ **or**
> > > $S\ (j) = ready$ **and** $S'\ (j) = active$ **or**
> > > $S\ (j) = active$ **and** $S'\ (j) = stopped$

This specification has no input constraints apart from those implied by the fact that its input is of type P. Its output constraint states that if an input array value was stopped, the corresponding output value must be ready, if ready it must be active, and if active it must be stopped.

One of the problems associated with interface specifications is that the expression of conceptually simple operations is often quite lengthy. In fact, the specification of an operation may be longer than the program required to implement that operation. This defeats one of the purposes of a specification, which is to provide a concise functional definition.

For example, say the sensor associated with each process in the process array in the above example is mapped onto another array whose values are either HI or LO. If a sensor associated with a process goes HI, the state of that process should be switched as illustrated in the $SWITCH\_STATUS$ example. Say the sensor array is defined as follows:

> **type** Sa **is** $array\ (1..n)\ of\ (HI,\ LO)$

The specification of an operation which scans the sensors and switches process states when a HI sensor is detected is:

> $SENSOR\_SWITCH$ $(\ S :$ **in out** $P;\ sensors : Sa)$
> > **output forall** $j,\ first\ (S) <= j <= last\ (S)$:
> > > $sensors\ (j) = HI$ **and** $stateswitched\ (S(j),S'(j)\ )$

or
$\qquad$ *sensors* $(j) = LO$ **and** *nochange* $(S(j), S'(j))$
define
$\qquad$ *stateswitched* $(a, b : status) \rightarrow boolean$
$\qquad\qquad a = stopped$ **and** $b = ready$ **or**
$\qquad\qquad a = ready$ **and** $b = active$ **or**
$\qquad\qquad a = active$ **and** $b = stopped$
$\qquad$ *nochange* $(a, b : status) \rightarrow boolean$
$\qquad\qquad a = stopped$ **and** $b = stopped$ **or**
$\qquad\qquad a = ready$ **and** $b = ready$ **or**
$\qquad\qquad a = active$ **and** $b = active$

This operation might be implemented by a Pascal procedure which is comparable in length with the specification:

```
procedure SensorSwitch (var sensors : Sa;
        var ProcessStatus : P; size : integer);
    var i : integer;
begin
    for i := 1 to size do
        if sensors (i) = HI then
            case ProcessStatus (i) of
                stopped : ProcessStatus (i) := ready;
                ready : ProcessStatus (i) := active;
                active : ProcessStatus (i) := stopped
            end
end; {SensorSwitch}
```

It is clear that, even for this very simple operation, the specification is about the same size as its equivalent program. For more complex operations the specifications may become larger than implementations. In the author's opinion, this makes interface specifications, on their own, impractical for specifying all but the simplest operations. A complementary specification method, operational specification, which allows shorter specifications to be constructed, is discussed in the following section.

Another disadvantage of interface specifications as far as the software designer is concerned is that it is not possible to provide guidance about the design in the specification. For example, the interface specification of a search routine might be:

```
SEARCH (T : array of E; key : E; i : out integer)
    N-state
        input match (T, key)
        output unchanged (T, T') and
        T' (i) = key
    E-state
        input not match (T, key)
        output unchanged (T, T') and
        i = -1
```

define
> *match* (*T* : *array of E*; *k* : *E*) —> *boolean*
>> **there exists** *j, first* (*T*) <= *j* <= *last* (*T*):
>>> T (*j*) = *k*
>
> *unchanged* (*T, U* : *array of E*) —> *boolean*
>> **forall** *i, first* (*T*) <= *i* <= *last* (*T*):
>>> *T* (*i*) = *U* (*i*)

This specification simply states that either the output value of *SEARCH* is equal to the index of the input key in the array or it is −1, indicating that there is no element of the array equal to the key value.

In the discussion so far, it has been assumed that operations on types such as arrays and sets are well defined. A method of defining these type operations is described later in this chapter.

This type of specification, which does not include implementation information, may be useful as part of a requirements definition as the user should not care how the search operation is implemented. However, if specification is seen as the first stage in the design process, the specifier may wish to define the searching technique. Operational specifications must be used for this purpose.

3.2 Operational specifications

When interface specifications are used, the computation which performs the transformation of the input to the output is not described. By contrast, an operational specification defines this input/output transformation explicitly, although it may be expressed in an abstract, high-level way.

Liskov and Berzins (1979) state that the difference between a language for operational specification and an implementation language is that the specification language should be designed for clarity of expression. No account should be taken of implementation considerations. However, this does not preclude the specification being executable — this has advantages for testing and prototyping (Balzer *et al.*, 1982).

In fact, if the specification language is executable, the specification is simply another program. This does not mean, of course, that executable specifications make programming languages obsolete. Executable specification languages make very heavy demands on a run-time system and might execute several hundred times slower than equivalent programs. The main role of operational specifications is still to define what the program should do rather than actually carry out the operations. However, it seems likely that today's specification languages will be tomorrow's programming languages if we can design and build hardware to support their requirements.

It is possible to construct program specifications using very simple languages indeed. In an early paper, McCarthy (1962) showed how operational specifications could be written in a language which had no assignment statement. The only control mechanisms were functions which could be called recursively, and expressions which could be conditional expressions.

The advantage of using this type of language (sometimes called an applicative language) for operational specifications is that such languages are closely related to the lambda-calculus, discussed above in the description of denotational semantics. Therefore, it may be possible to define formally the denotational semantics of an operational specification language. Furthermore, specifications written using an applicative language are often shorter and more readily understood than equivalent programs written in languages like Pascal. Indeed, it has been suggested (Backus, 1978) that we ought to build machines to support the direct execution of applicative languages and this is now the topic of research work in the US, Japan and Europe.

To illustrate how a specification may be constructed using only recursive functions and expressions, the specification for a merge of two ordered sequences is shown below. A sequence is an unbounded list of elements which is always accessed sequentially, from the front. It may be represented as a file in programming languages like Pascal. Note that the operation head (S) returns the first item in sequence S and tail (S) returns sequence S with the first item removed. The function empty (S) is true if the length of the sequence S is zero. The operator ',' is the catenation operator which is used to add elements to a sequence.

> MERGE $(S1, S2 : sequence of E)$ $->$ *sequence of E*
>   **if** *empty*$(S1)$ **then** *S2* **else**
>   **if** *empty*$(S2)$ **then** *S1* **else**
>   **if** *head* $(S1)$ $<$ *head* $(S2)$ **then**
>   *head*$(S1)$, *merge*(*tail*$(S1)$, *S2*) **else**
>   *head*$(S2)$, *merge*(*S1*, *tail*$(S2)$))
>   **end** *MERGE*

If either sequence is empty, the value returned by merge is the other sequence. Otherwise, the head of sequence *S1* is compared to the head of *S2*. If the head of *S1* is smaller, the output sequence is formed by catenating that value with the result of merging the remainder of *S1* with *S2*. Otherwise, if *head* $(S2)$ is less than or equal to *head* $(S1)$, the converse applies.

This specification of *MERGE* may be considered as a high-level description of how to implement that operation. It is the author's opinion that, given familiarity with the notation, such a description is more concise and more readily understandable than an interface specification of the same merge operation. It is left as an exercise for the reader to construct such a specification.

However, operational specifications are not always more concise than interface specifications. Recall the interface specification of the operation *MAX* which determined the largest value in a set of integers:

> MAX $(X : set of integer)$ $->$ *integer*
>   **input** *not empty* (X)
>   **output** *member* (X, MAX) **and**
>   **forall** *E*, *member* (X, E): $MAX >= E$

The corresponding specification of this operation expressed in an applicative language is:

MAX (*X* : *set of integer*) $\rightarrow$ *integer*

−− assume a non-empty input set and the existence of an
−− operation called a_member_of which returns an arbitrary
−− member of an input set

   let *m* = *a_member_of* (*X*)
   if *largest* (*X*, *m*) **then** *m* **else**
    MAX (*X* − {*m*})
define
   largest (*X* : *set of integer*; *m* : *integer*) $\rightarrow$ *boolean*
    let *y* = *a_member_of* (*X*)
    if *m* > *y* **then**
     if *X* − {*y*} = { } **then**
      true
     else
      largest (*X* − {*y*},*m*)
    else
     false
   end *largest*
end *MAX*

The operational specification of *MAX* is significantly larger than the interface specification. It often seems to be the case that interface specifications are the most concise way of describing simple abstractions, whereas operational specifications are best suited to the description of more complex abstract procedures.

As a further illustration of the power of applicative languages, consider the following specification. This describes a function which processes a stream of characters and identifies integers, words and punctuation symbols. Integers and punctuation symbols have their usual form while a word is defined as a sequence of characters whose first character is a letter and which is terminated by any character which is not a letter or a digit. Blanks in the input sequence are ignored. The function consumes an input sequence of characters and its result is also a character sequence. Such a function might be used in text or in language processing operations such as the first phase of a compiler, a text formatter, etc.

SCAN (*S* : *sequence of char*) $\rightarrow$ *sequence of char*
  −− if a digit then start of a number
  if *digit* (*head* (*S*)) **then**
   number (*S*)
  else
   −− if a letter then start of a word
   if *letter* (*head* (*S*)) **then**
    word (*S*)

```
        else
            -- if not a blank, simply a single character
            if head ( S ) <> " " then
                head (S)
            else
            -- must be a blank, ignore it
            scan ( tail (S) )
    define
        digit (x : char) -> boolean
            x >= "0" and x <= "9"
        end digit
        letter (x : char) -> boolean
            (x >= "a" and X <= "z") or
            (x >= "A" and X <= "Z")
        end letter
        number (S : sequence of char) -> sequence of char
            if digit (head (tail(S)) ) then
                head (S), number ( tail (S) )
            else
                head (S)
        end number
        word (S : sequence of char) -> sequence of char
            if letter (head (tail(S)) ) then
                head (S), word (tail (S) )
            else
                head (S)
        end word
    end SCAN
```

It is left as an exercise for the reader to attempt to formulate an interface specification for the above procedure. Be warned that this is not an easy task!

Although it is possible to express any operational specification using only functions and expressions, this does not mean that iterative constructs should be completely avoided. In fact, some operations may be expressed more clearly if recursion is not used.

For example, consider the specification of the MAX operation above. A shorter specification using a repeat loop rather than recursion is:

```
MAX (X : set of integer) -> integer

-- assumptions as before

    let m = a_member_of (X)
    repeat
        let y = a_member_of (X)
        X := X - {y}
        if y > m then
            m := y
```

```
    until empty (X)
    MAX := m
end MAX
```

Of course, the penalty paid for a more concise specification is that the semantics of the specification language are more complex and hence more difficult to define. However, if specification is seen as the first stage of the software design process, an informal definition of the specification language semantics may be adequate. It is only when it is intended to carry out mathematical or automatic manipulations of a specification that complete formality is essential.

As a further illustration of how operational specifications may be constructed, consider the specification of the *SENSOR_SWITCH* operation whose interface specification is given in Section 3.1. Recall that this procedure switched the status of a process when an associated sensor became *HI*. It made use of the following type definitions:

type *status* **is** (*stopped, ready, active*)
type *P* **is** *array* (*1..n*) *of status*
type *Sa* **is** *array* (*1..n*) *of* (*HI, LO*)

The operational specification of SENSOR_SWITCH is as follows:

```
SENSOR_SWITCH (S : in out P; sensors Sa)
    forall j, first(sensors) <= j <= last(sensors) do
    if sensors (j) = HI then
        process_status (j) :=
            if process_status (j) = active then
            stopped
        else
            succ (process_status (j) )
end SENSOR_SWITCH
```

Notice that, in this specification, the use of the sequential **for** loop has been avoided and a **forall** statement used. This statement specifies that the loop should be executed for all the values of the loop counter in the given range, but does not specify that this execution must be in sequence.

The reason why such a construct is used rather than the simpler **for** loop is that an iterative **for** loop states that the sensor array must be examined in order. In fact, one possible design for this operation is to associate a separate process with each sensor so that sensor checking and process state updating might be carried out in parallel for all sensors. If this is permitted but not required, the specification should be expressed so that the designer is not constrained to either parallel or sequential implementations.

One of the disadvantages of interface specification, expressed in Section 3.1, is that the specifier cannot give clues to the designer about how a specification should be implemented. In some circumstances this is a good thing as it is desirable that the specification and the design should be quite distinct. In others, however, it may be very useful to provide an algorithm specification which is to be realized as a design.

The operational specification of a procedure (*SEARCH*) and of an algorithm to implement that operation (*BINARY_SEARCH*) might be expressed as follows:

SEARCH (*T* : *array of E*; *key* : *E*; *i* : **out** *integer*)
   i := −*1*
  forall *j*, *first* (*T*) <= *j* <= *last* (*T*)
   if *T* (*j*) = *key* **then**
     i := *j*
end *SEARCH*

This is a general specification of the search operation whose interface specifications are given in Section 3.1. Notice that if there are multiple occurrences of the key in array *T*, the procedure may not return the same value each time it is activated. This is a consequence of the use of the nonsequential *forall* construct which does not guarantee any particular search order.

Say it was known in advance that the input array *T* was always ordered. A more efficient search procedure might be specified:

BINARY_SEARCH (*T* : *array of E*; *key* : *E*; *i* : **out** *integer*)
  if *SIZE* (*T*) = *0* **then**
   i := −*1*
  else
    mid : *integer* := (*first*(*T*) + *last* (*T*))/2
    if *T*(*mid*) = *key* **then**
     i := *mid*
    else
     if *T* (*mid*) > *key* **then**
      BINARY_SEARCH (*T*(*first*(*T*)..*mid*−*1*), *key*, *i*)
     else
      BINARY_SEARCH (*T*(*mid*+*1*..*last* (*T*)), *key*, *i*)
  end *BINARY_SEARCH*

In this example, a binary search has been specified. Notice how array slices have been specified in the recursive calls to *BINARY_SEARCH*. If an array name is followed by a range of indexes, this slice is taken out of the original array and considered separately. If the second slice index is smaller than the first, the array size is deemed to be zero. The size may be evaluated using the function *SIZE*.

A very important area of software development which seems to be ignored in most discussions of software specification is that of input and output. Real programs take in information from and output information to their environment. If part of a system is responsible for I/O it must also be specified.

The reason why input and output operations are avoided in most discussions of formal specification is that it is very difficult indeed to establish a clean, general-purpose underlying model of I/O processes. The reason for this difficulty is that I/O processes must interact with underlying hardware whose design is often neither elegant nor formally specified. However, even an informal model of I/O operations is useful when building design specifications.

The I/O process model used in the examples below is based on the notion of I/O streams. An I/O stream is a randomly accessible list of slots with each slot holding a single instance of a typed object. Therefore, each slot in an integer stream holds an integer, each slot in a boolean stream holds a truthvalue, etc. Each stream has a logical slot marker associated with it which indicates the current slot, and I/O operations always act on the object at this slot. This model is based on the algebraic description of sequential files given by Guttag *et al.* (1978).

There are five fundamental I/O operations:

1. IN (streamname) — fetches the item at the current slot. The stream marker is unaffected.

2. OUT (streamname) — puts an item into the current slot. The stream marker is unaffected.

3. SEEK (streamname, n) — moves the slot marker n places, where n may be a positive or a negative integer.

4. RESET (streamname) — sets the marker to the first slot in the I/O stream.

5. FINISH (streamname) — true if the marker is positioned after the last slot in the I/O stream, false otherwise.

Streams are logical entities, not physical I/O channels. In practice, several streams may be mapped onto a physical file or I/O device. Streams are also inherently random access so, obviously, some restrictions must be placed on their use when they are mapped onto sequential I/O devices.

This model for I/O specifications is illustrated in the following examples. The first of these is an in-place update procedure which inputs records from an update stream and, if the record exists in some master-record stream, it is replaced by the record which has been input. If it does not exist in the master-record stream, it is placed on a new-record stream. This may be specified as follows:

```
type prec is record
    key : integer;
    value : integer;
end record

update, master, new : stream of prec

UPDATE
    x : prec
    RESET (update); RESET (new)
```

```
      repeat
        x := IN (update)
        SEEK (update, 1)
        find (master, x)
        if not FINISH (master) then
          OUT (master, x)
        else
          OUT (new, x)
          SEEK (new, 1)
      until FINISH (update)
  define
    find (S : stream of prec; x : prec)
      T : prec;
      found : boolean := false
      RESET (S)
      repeat
        T := IN (S)
        if T.key = x.key then
          found := true
        else
          SEEK (S, 1)
      until found or FINISH (S)
    end find
  end UPDATE
```

This example is almost exclusively concerned with input and output operations with very little computation involved. Another example, which illustrates the specification of a computational process which includes input and output is the specification of a procedure which reads a stream of numbers and, for each number, determines if it is prime and prints a message accordingly.

```
  numbers, primes : stream of integer;
  textout : stream of string

  PRINTPRIMES
    x : integer
    repeat
      x := IN (numbers)
      SEEK (numbers, 1)
      if prime (x) then
        OUT (textout, "prime ")
        SEEK (textout, 1)
        OUT (primes, x)
        SEEK (primes, 1)
        OUT (textout, "\n")      -- new line
        SEEK (textout, 1)
    until FINISH (numbers)
```

define
   prime (x : integer) —> boolean
     forall *j, 3 <= j <= SQRT (x) :*
      x mod j <> 0
end *PRINTPRIMES*

Notice that this model of input and output explicitly requires the movement of the stream marker, whereas in most programming languages I/O pointer movement is a side-effect of the input or output operation. It is an important general principle of software specification that side effects should be disallowed. All object modifications should be made explicit in the specification.

3.3 The specification of data abstractions

In all the specification examples in previous sections, the existence of particular data types such as arrays and sets, along with their associated operations, has been taken for granted. However, for specifications to be complete, it is important to define the meaning of the data type by specifying the behaviour of the type operations.

When a data type is represented as a set of operations and values, it is called an abstract data type. This is one of the most important notions which has emerged in computer science. The use of abstract data types allows structured specifications to be constructed and it also seems to lead to an implementation methodology which results in readily maintainable software. This latter point will be discussed in later chapters. In this section, we shall concentrate on the specification of abstract data types.

There are two approaches which may be adopted to the specification of abstract data types. These are described and compared by Liskov and Berzins (1979). The first approach involves specifying the behaviour of the type operations using an abstract model, the second is an algebraic approach developed by Zilles (1974), Guttag (1977) and, more formally, by Goguen *et al.* (1977).

The algebraic approach is by far the best developed of these specification techniques so we shall concentrate on this method of specifying data abstractions. Essentially, an algebraic specification has two parts. These are an interface part which names the allowed operations and specifies the types of their parameters, and an axioms part which defines the behaviour of these operations.

This is illustrated in the simple example below which is the specification of the abstract data type 'array'. In this example, it is assumed that there is a create operation which brings an array of a particular size into existence but does not assign values to its elements. An alternative view of arrays is given by Hoare (Dahl *et al.*, 1972) where all array elements have defined values. However, the approach adopted here is closer to that provided in most programming languages.

array of E
  Interface
    create (*a, b* : *integer*) $\rightarrow$ *array of E*
    first (*x* : *array of E*) $\rightarrow$ *integer*
    last (*x* : *array of E*) $\rightarrow$ *integer*
    eval (*x* : *array of E*; *i* : *integer*) $\rightarrow$ *E*
    put (*x* : *array of E*; *i* : *integer*; *v* : *E*) $\rightarrow$ *array of E*
  Axioms
    1. create (*a, b*) = **if** *b* < *a* **then** *ERROR*
    2. put (*x, i, v*) = **if** *first* (*x*) > *i* > *last* (*x*) **then**
                   ERROR
    3. first (*create* (*a, b*)) = *a*
    4. first (*put* (*x, i, v*)) = *first* (*x*)
    5. last (*create* (*a, b*)) = *b*
    6. last (*put* (*x, i, v*)) = *last* (*x*)
    7. eval (*create* (*a, b*), *i*) =
          if *a* <= *i* <= *b* **then** *UNDEFINED* **else** *ERROR*
    8. eval (*put* (*x, a, v*), *b*) =
          if *a* = *b* **then** *v* **else** *eval* (*x, b*)

To make references simpler, the axioms have been numbered, but these numbers are not part of the specification. Axiom 1 above refers to the *create* operation and specifies that the lower bound of an array must be less than the upper bound otherwise an error should be reported. Axiom 2 specifies that operations which assign values to array elements must take place within the bounds of the array. Axioms 3 and 4 define the *first* operation, stating that the result of *first* is a value equal to the lower bound of the array and that the *put* operation does not modify that bound.

Axioms 5 and 6 are the corresponding axioms for the *last* operation. Axiom 7 states that an attempt to evaluate an element whose index is outside the array bounds results in an error and that an evaluation of an element in a newly created array results in an undefined value. Finally, axiom 8 defines the effect of *eval* when operating on an array whose elements may be defined or undefined.

As well as arrays, sets were also used in previous examples in this chapter. The algebraic definition of this abstract data type is as follows:

set of E
  Interface
    create $\rightarrow$ *set of E*
    a_member_of (*set of E*) $\rightarrow$ *E*
    sub (*set of E, E*) $\rightarrow$ *set of E*
    add (*set of E, E*) $\rightarrow$ *set of E*
    empty (*set of E*) $\rightarrow$ *boolean*
    is_in (*set of E, E*) $\rightarrow$ *boolean*
  Axioms
    1. empty (*create*) = *true*

2. *empty (add (s,i)) = false*
3. *a_member_of (create) = ERROR*
4. *a_member_of (add (create, i)) = i*
5. *a_member_of (s) = j* **where**
   $\qquad$ *add (sub (s, j), j) = s*
6. *is_in (create, i) = false*
7. *is_in (add (s, j), i) =*
   $\qquad$ **if** *i = j* **then** *true* **else** *is_in (s, i)*
8. *sub (create, i) = create*
9. *sub (add (s, j), i) =*
   $\qquad$ **if** *i = j* **then** *sub (s, i)* **else** *add (sub (s, i), j)*

The first two axioms are fairly evident and define the empty operation. Axioms 3 to 5 define the *a_member_of* operation, where axiom 3 states that attempting that operation on an empty set should result in an error, axiom 4 states that *a_member_of* applied to a set with one member returns that member, and axiom 5 defines the more general case where the set has an indefinite number of members.

Axioms 6 and 7 define the *is_in* operation stating that *is_in* applied to an empty set is always false and that if *is_in* is applied to an *add* operation, it is true if its parameter value is the same as the value added. If not, the action is as if no *add* had taken place.

This may seem an inadequate and circuitous definition but an example illustrates its validity. Say *S* is a set of integers {7, 14, 21, 28} and the operation *is_in (S, 5)* is applied to that set. According to the axiom, this may be represented as:

$\qquad$ *is_in (add({7, 14, 21}, 28), 5) =*
$\qquad\quad$ *is_in (add({7, 14}, 21), 5) =*
$\qquad\qquad$ *is_in (add({7}, 14), 5) =*
$\qquad\qquad\quad$ *is_in (add ({ }, 7), 5) =*
$\qquad\qquad\qquad$ *is_in ({ }, 5) = false*

It is left as an exercise for the reader to attempt an expansion of *is_in* when the parameter is a member of the set.

Axioms 8 and 9 define the *sub* operation which removes an element from a set. Axiom 8 states that attempting to remove an element from an empty set has no effect, and axiom 9 states that only those elements which have been added to a set may be removed from it. Again this may be illustrated by example.

Say set *S* is {1, 2, 3} and it is intended to subtract 2 from this, leaving *S′* as {1, 3}. From the axioms above for the set operations, we get:

$\qquad$ *sub ({1, 2, 3}, 2) =*
$\qquad\quad$ *sub (add({1, 2}, 3), 2) =*
$\qquad\qquad$ *add (sub({1, 2}, 2), 3) =*
$\qquad\qquad\quad$ *add(sub(add({1}, 2), 2), 3) =*

$$add(sub(\{1\}, 2), 3) =$$
$$add(sub(add(\{\ \}, 1), 2), 3) =$$
$$add(add(sub(\{\}, 2), 1), 3) =$$
$$add(add(\{\}, 1), 3) =$$
$$add(\{1\}, 3) = \{1, 3\}$$

Arrays and sets are fairly primitive abstract data types, but higher-level abstract data types may also be specified using the algebraic approach. This is illustrated by a specification of an abstract data type *queue*, based on that given in Guttag (1977). The characteristic of a queue is, of course, that elements are placed on the queue at one end and removed from the other end. This is reflected in the specification below:

queue of E
  Interface
    create −> *queue of E*
    put (queue of E, E) −> *queue of E*
    get (queue of E) −> *E*
    is_empty (queue of E) −> *boolean*
    remove (queue of E) −> *queue of E*
  Axioms
    1. *is_empty (create) = true*
    2. *is_empty (put (q, v)) = false*
    3. *get (create) = ERROR*
    4. *get (put (q, x)) =* **if** *is_empty (q)* **then**
              x **else** *get (q)*
    5. *remove (create) = ERROR*
    6. *remove (put (q, x)) =* **if** *is_empty (q)* **then**
              create **else** *put (remove (q), x)*

Axioms 1 and 2 define the *is_empty* operation with axiom 1 stating that a newly created queue is always empty and axiom 2 specifying that a queue created by a *put* operation is not empty. Axioms 3 and 4 state that it is an error to attempt to *get* an item from an empty queue and that *get* fetches an item from the opposite end of the queue from *put*. Again, this may not be intuitively obvious but it can be demonstrated by example. Say a queue has the elements [2, 4, 6, 8] with 8 the last element put onto the queue.

$$get ([2, 4, 6, 8]) =$$
$$get (put([2, 4, 6], 8)) =$$
$$get (put([2, 4], 6)) =$$
$$get (put([2], 4)) =$$
$$\textbf{get } (put[], 2) = 2$$

Axioms 5 and 6 define the *remove* operation whose result is the original queue with the '*first*' item removed. Axiom 5 states that removal from an empty queue is meaningless and axiom 6 states again that items are removed from the opposite end to that which they are entered. It is left as an exercise for the reader to verify this by constructing an example.

The advantage of using algebraic specifications for abstract data types is that these specifications are often much shorter than corresponding operational specifications. However, constructing algebraic specifications is not always an easy task and it may be that operational specifications are intuitively simpler to construct by those with programming experience. Some guidelines on creating specifications are provided in the following section.

3.4 Practical software specification

So far, three approaches to software specification — namely, interface specification, operational specification and the algebraic specification of abstract data types — have been presented. These have all been illustrated by examples which, it is hoped, give the reader insights into these specification techniques.

However, the steps involved in creating system specifications have not been made explicit. The reason for this is that this is an intuitive rather than a definitive process. Thus, a recipe for developing specifications cannot be provided. However, some hints on specification creation may be given and this is the topic of this section.

Given that specification is seen as part of the activity of design rather than the first stage in a formal verification process, there is no reason why the specifier need restrict himself or herself to a single specification technique. In fact, there is much to be gained by using the most appropriate technique for different levels in the system in order to minimize the overall size of the specification. Thus, system specification might be seen as a three-stage process:

1. Construct operational specifications for the higher-level system abstractions, expressing these in terms of simpler abstractions and abstract data types.

2. Construct specifications for the system's abstract data types.

3. Construct interface specifications for the simpler system abstractions which may be readily specified in this way.

Expressed like this, this process seems straightforward. In practice, it is not so. Like software development, specification development is an iterative process and as the specifications for lower-level system abstractions are developed, errors in higher-level specifications may be highlighted and must be corrected.

First of all, let us look at how to build an operational specification using only recursion and conditional expressions. Take, for example, a spelling checker program. The design of such a program is discussed in Chapter 4. The initial stage in developing a specification is to write down an informal strategy of how the problem should be approached. This might be:

A dictionary exists which contains a list of correctly spelled words. Given an input document, the spelling checker takes each word in that document and checks if it appears in the dictionary. If it does, the spelling of the word is correct. If it does not appear in the dictionary, the spelling checker informs the user that the word may be mis-spelt. Note that non-appearance does not necessarily mean mis-spelling — the word may be a proper name or an acronym, or the dictionary may not be complete.

From this strategy, the general approach involving the looking up of all document words in the dictionary and the display of potential mis-spellings may be identified. This may be expressed in a very succinct way as follows:

display (lookup (dictionary, words_in (document)))

where *words_in* is a function which returns a list of words in the document, *lookup* checks this list against the dictionary and returns a list of those words which are not in the dictionary. The function *display* prints this list. The *display* function may be defined as follows:

> *display (W : wordlist)*
> **if** *empty (W)* **then** *"all done"* **else**
> **if** *head (W)* = *''''* **then** *display (tail (W))*
> **else**
> *head (W), display (tail (W))*
> **end** *display*

Here, an empty input list terminates the recursive calls of *display*. It is a common error when writing specifications as recursive functions to leave out the termination condition. This does not necessarily make the specification incorrect, it is simply incomplete and the termination condition must be decided in the next elaboration of the design. However, if termination is left out, this should be commented in the specification.

The *lookup* function takes a *wordlist* and the dictionary and generates a *wordlist* for display.

> *lookup (D : dict; W : wordlist)* −> *wordlist*
> −− *if list has a single item check it*
> **if** *empty (tail (W))* **then**
> *if is_in (D, head (W))* **then** *''''* **else** *head (W)*
> **else**
> −− *more than 1 item check the first then recursive lookup*
> **if** *is_in (D, head (W))* **then** *''''* **else** *head (W),*
> *lookup (D, tail (W))*
> **end** *lookup*

Notice here the common recursion termination condition which is a test if the input list is a single-member list. The operation *is_in* checks if a single word is in the dictionary *D* but a definition of this is postponed until later.

The remaining function in the high-level operational specification is *words_in*, defined as follows:

```
words_in (doc : charlist) –> wordlist
    – – input parameter is empty wordlist
    get_unique_words (doc, NULL_LIST)
define
    get_unique_words (doc : charlist; wl : wordlist) –> wordlist
        let x = SCAN (doc)
        let newdoc = strip (doc, x)
        if x = end_doc then
            wl
        else
            if is_in (wl, x) then
                get_unique_words (newdoc, wl)
            else
                get_unique_words (newdoc, add(wl, x))
    end get_unique words
```

The operation of this function is, perhaps, less intuitively obvious than the others. It is desired to return a list of words given a list of characters (*doc*). As recursion is the only method which is available to repeat operations, it is necessary to define a recursive function *get_unique_words* within *words_in* to build up this *wordlist*.

The function *get_unique_words* uses a modification of *SCAN* described in Section 3.2. As used here, *SCAN* is modified to return an end-of-document indicator when all of the input document has been scanned and a function *strip* is called to remove the scanned item from the input sequence. Again, *is_in* is used to determine if a word is already in a *wordlist*. In this case, if it is, it is not added to *wl*.

Although it is certainly possible to construct an operational specification for *is_in*, the interface specification for that function is probably more concise and easier to understand. It is therefore sensible to use this rather than a deeply recursive operational specification.

```
is_in (L : wordlist; w : word) –> boolean
    output
        there_exists t, member_of (L) :
            w = t
```

The function is true if there is a member of the input list *L* which matches the input word *w*.

This specification says nothing about the representations of the wordlist *L* but, presumably, a representation which allows efficient searching would be chosen by the designer. One such representation is the binary tree and, if this is used, an algebraic specification of this abstract data type might be constructed. A good description of such a specification for a binary tree is given in Guttag *et al.* (1978).

The first stage in the definition of an abstract data type is to identify the allowed operations on that type. In almost all abstract data types, the following operations are necessary:

1. create — Bring an instance of a data object into existence.
2. test_if_empty — Check if any data has been entered.
3. enter — Place an item of data in the data structure.
4. remove — Remove an item of data from the data structure.

Naturally, there will normally be additional operations which are data type dependent. In the case of a binary tree, these might be:

1. left — Return the left subtree.
2. right — Return the right subtree.
3. is_in — Check if a data value is held in the tree.

Thus, a complete set of operations along with parameter types may be defined for the abstract data type bintree as follows:

bintree of W
> *create −> bintree of W*
> *is_empty (bintree of W) −> boolean*
> *left (bintree of W) −> bintree of W*
> *data (bintree of W) −> W or UNDEFINED*
> *right (bintree of W) −> bintree of W*
> *is_in (bintree of W, W) −> boolean*
> *build (bintree of W, W, bintree of W) −> bintree of W*

The definition of axioms setting out the behaviour of abstract data type operations should start by identifying so-called 'constructor operations'. Constructor operations are those operations which are used to build instances of the data type and, in almost all cases, these constructor operations are the create operation and the operation which adds items to the data structure. Therefore, in the example of the binary tree, the constructor operations are *create* and *build*.

Using each constructor operation, an axiom is defined for all of the other data type operations. Therefore, for the create operation, the following binary tree axioms may be identified:

> *is_empty (create) = true*
> *left (create) = create*
> *data (create) = UNDEFINED*
> *right (create) = create*
> *is_in (create, w) = false*

It is usually the case that the definition of axioms for the create operations is simpler than axiom definition for the other constructor operation. However, in the case of the binary tree the axioms are straightforward:

is_empty (*build* (*l*, *w*, *r*)) = *false*
left (*build* (*l*, *w*, *r*)) = *l*
data (*build* (*l*, *w*, *r*)) = *w*
right (*build* (*l*, *w*, *r*)) = *r*
is_in (*build* (*l*, *w*, *r*), *W*) =
   if *w* = *W* **then** *true* **else** *is_in* (*l*, *W*) *or is_in* (*r*, *W*)

Thus, a complete specification of a binary tree may be put together as follows:

bintree of W
  Interface
    create –> *bintree of W*
    is_empty (*bintree of W*) –> *boolean*
    left (*bintree of W*) –> *bintree of W*
    data (*bintree of W*) –> *W or UNDEFINED*
    right (*bintree of W*) –> *bintree of W*
    is_in (*bintree of W, W*) –> *boolean*
    build (*bintree of W, W, bintree of W*) –> *bintree of W*
  Axioms
    is_empty (*create*) = *true*
    left (*create*) = *create*
    data (*create*) = *UNDEFINED*
    right (*create*) = *create*
    is_in (*create, w*) = *false*
    is_empty (*build* (*l*, *w*, *r*)) = *false*
    left (*build* (*l*, *w*, *r*)) = *l*
    data (*build* (*l*, *w*, *r*)) = *w*
    right (*build* (*l*, *w*, *r*)) = *r*
    is_in (*build* (*l*, *w*, *r*), *W*) =
      if *w* = *W* **then** *true* **else** *is_in* (*l*, *W*) *or is_in* (*r*, *W*)

It is facile to suggest, as some have done, that formal software specification will solve the software crisis and result in a dramatic reduction in the costs of software systems. However, it seems likely that more precise specifications of software components will lead to an improvement in component design and to some reduction in component design, implementation and validation costs.

For this reason, an understanding of the specification techniques described here is important to the software engineer. Even if completely formal (in the mathematical sense) specifications are too expensive to create, greater precision in specifications results from an understanding of formal methods. As notations and tools for supporting software specification techniques are improved, software specification will emerge from the research laboratory and become widely used in practical software production.

Further reading

There are few references which are good introductions to software specification. The papers recommended below are all several years old, as recent work has been more concerned with notations and techniques, rather than fundamental concepts.

'An appraisal of program specifications', B. H. Liskov and V. Berzins. In *Research Directions in Software Technology*, ed. P. Wegner (1979), Cambridge, Mass: MIT Press.

A very readable paper which is perhaps the best starting point for those wishing to explore this area in more detail. It is backed up by an informative discussion elsewhere in the same volume.

'The design of data type specifications', J. V. Guttag, E. Horowitz and D. R. Musser. In *Current Trends in Programming Methodology, Vol. 4*, ed. R. T. Yeh (1978), Englewood Cliffs, NJ: Prentice Hall.

An excellent introduction to the building of algebraic specifications for abstract data types. The book which includes this paper also contains other papers of interest.

'Specifications: Formal and Informal — A Case Study', N. Gehani (1982) *Software — Practice and Experience*, **12.**

This paper discusses the use of formal specifications in the development of a real rather than an example system. Gehani compares formal and informal specifications and concludes that both are probably necessary for the effective description of non-trivial software systems.

Chapter 4 SOFTWARE DESIGN

Software design is a creative process. It requires a certain amount of flair on the part of the designer and the final design is normally an iteration from a number of preliminary designs. Design cannot be learned from a book — it must be practiced and learnt by experience and study of existing systems. Good design is the key to effective software engineering. A well designed software system is straightforward to implement and maintain, easily understood and reliable. Badly designed systems, although they may work, are likely to be expensive to maintain, difficult to test and unreliable. The design stage is therefore the most critical part of the software development process.

Until fairly recently, software design was largely an *ad hoc* process. Given a set of requirements, usually in natural language, an informal design was prepared, often in the form of a flowchart. Coding then commenced and the design was modified as the system was implemented. When the implementation stage was complete, the design had usually changed so much from its initial specification that the original design document was a totally inadequate description of the system.

This approach to software design was responsible for many dramatic and very expensive project failures. Now it is realized that completely informal notations such as flowcharts, which are close to the programming language, are inadequate vehicles for formulating and expressing system design. It is recognized that precise (although not necessarily formal) specification is an essential part of the design process and that software design is an iterative, multi-stage activity which cannot be represented in any single notation. Accordingly, a number of design notations such as data flow diagrams, HIPO charts, structure diagrams and design description languages have been developed which are superior to flowcharts for expressing software designs.

Given a requirements definition, the software engineer must use this to derive the design of a programming system which satisfies these requirements. This derivation is accomplished in a number of stages:

1. The sub-systems making up the programming system must be established.

2. Each sub-system must be decomposed into separate components and the sub-system specification established by defining the operation of these components.

3. Each program may then be designed in terms of interacting sub-components.

4. Each component must then be refined. This normally entails specifying each component as a hierarchy of sub-components.

5. At some stage of this refinement process, the algorithms used in each component must be specified in detail.

As well as these various stages of programming system design, the software engineer may also be required to design communication mechanisms allowing processes in the system to communicate. He or she may have to design file structures, and will almost certainly have to design the data structures used in his programs. He or she will have to design test cases to validate his programs.

There is no definitive way of establishing what is meant by a 'good' design. Depending on the application and the particular project requirements, a good design might be a design which allows very efficient code to be produced, it might be a minimal design where the implementation is as compact as possible, or it might be the most maintainable design. This latter criterion is the criterion of 'goodness' adopted here. A maintainable design implies that the cost of system changes is minimized and this means that the design should be understandable and that changes should be local in effect. Both of these are achieved if the software design is highly cohesive and loosely coupled.

A program unit is said to exhibit a high degree of cohesion if the elements in that unit exhibit a high degree of functional relatedness. This means that each element in the program unit should be essential for that unit to achieve its purpose, for example sort a file, lookup a dictionary, etc. Elements which are grouped together in a program unit for some other reason, such as to perform actions which take place at the same time or which implement a number of distinct functions, have a low degree of cohesion.

Coupling is related to cohesion — it is an indication of the strength of interconnections between program units. Highly coupled systems have strong interconnections, with program units dependent on each other, whereas loosely coupled systems are made up of units which are independent or almost independent.

The obvious advantages of highly cohesive, loosely coupled systems is that any program unit can be replaced by an equivalent unit with little or no change to other units in the system. This is important when designs are refined. Loosely coupled units mean that a designer has the option of changing his mind about the design of a unit without adverse effects on the rest of the system.

Effective software design is best accomplished by using a consistent design methodology. There have been a vast number of design methodologies developed and used in different applications. Some of these are described by Peters (1980) and by Blank and Krijger (1983). In essence, most of these methodologies can be classified into one of three areas:

1. *Top-down functional design.* The system is designed from a functional viewpoint, starting with a high-level view and progressively refining this into a more detailed design. This methodology is exemplified by Structured Design (Constantine and Yourdon, 1979) and step-wise refinement (Wirth, 1971; 1976).

2. *Object-oriented design.* The system is viewed as a collection of objects rather than as functions with messages passed from object to object. Each object has its own set of associated operations. Object-oriented design is based on the idea of information hiding which was first put forward by Parnas (1972) and which has been described more recently by Robson (1981) and Booch (1983).

3. *Data-driven design.* This methodology, suggested by Jackson (1975) and Warnier (1977) suggests that the structure of a software system should reflect the structure of the data processed by that system. Therefore, the software design is derived from an analysis of the input and output system data.

Top-down functional decomposition has been widely used for both small-scale and large-scale projects in diverse application areas. Data-driven design has been mostly used in relatively small-scale data processing system projects although recent work by Jackson (1982) demonstrates that this approach to design is not confined to these systems. Object-oriented design is a relatively recent development which has not been widely tried but which shows considerable promise. Large software systems are such complex entities that all of these might be used at some stage in the design of different parts of the system. There is no 'best' design methodology for large projects.

Space does not permit a proper description of all these methodologies here. As a result, a decision has been made to concentrate on top-down functional decomposition because this is the most widely used technique. However, because of the potential importance of object-oriented design, it is also described here (in slightly less detail) and contrasted with top-down functional decomposition.

To illustrate the difference between functional and object-oriented approaches to software design, consider the structure of a compiler. It may be viewed as a set of functional transformations with information being passed from one function to another. This is shown in Fig. 4.1.

An alternative, object-oriented view of the same system is shown in Fig. 4.2. Here, the objects manipulated by the compiler are central with transformation functions associated with object communications.

It has been suggested that this object-oriented approach to software design results in better, more readily maintained software systems than those

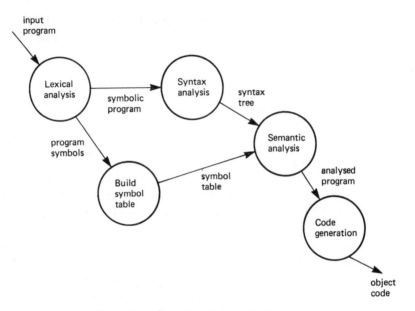

Figure 4.1   Functional view of a compiler.

developed using top-down functional decomposition. However, this has not yet been demonstrated in practice for large software systems. It is rather dangerous to discard the well-tried top-down design methodology completely in favour of this approach. Rather, a combination of these methodologies is probably the most appropriate. The high-level view of a system might be a set of functions reflecting those in the requirements definition with these functions built on top of a collection of interacting objects.

The major sections in this chapter reflect this view. Both top-down design and object-oriented design are illustrated by example and, in ad-

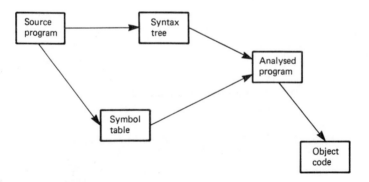

Figure 4.2   Object-oriented view of a compiler.

dition, sections are included discussing design description notations and design validation.

4.1 Design notations

Consistent and complete notations are immensely valuable in the creation of abstract objects such as software systems. Without such notations, designs cannot be evaluated, compared, tested or communicated. Although the computer program itself is the absolute design specification, the level of detail presented in the program is such that it is unsuitable for conveying the design to human readers. This is particularly true of the higher levels of design where a large system is decomposed into functional units such as sub-systems or programs. It is very difficult to express this clearly using a programming language.

There is no single notation which is ideally suited to the expression of a software design. Indeed, there have probably been hundreds of different notations invented, each of which may be useful for describing different levels of the design or for describing designs of systems in a particular application area. It would be quite impossible in a book of this nature to describe all of these, so three complementary notations have been chosen which may be used together to describe a software design.

The notations which are described are:

1. *Data-flow diagrams.* These are diagrams used to describe high-level system design. They show how data is transformed as it moves from one system component to another.

2. *Structure charts.* These are hierarchy diagrams which show the structural relationship of components in a software design. Again, this notation is most useful for describing high-level system design.

3. *A design description language.* This is a notation with some pro-gramming language attributes which is suitable for describing control and detailed design operations. It may be used at any level in the system design.

It must be emphasized that these notations are complementary and that there is no single notation which is suitable for describing all levels in a design. Thus it is normal, particularly for large systems, to use all of these in the documentation of the system design. Graphical notations, in particular, are very important as they are very useful for illustrating the complex structure inherent in large software systems.

4.1.1 Data flow diagrams

The notation of data flow diagrams described here derives from the work of Constantine and Yourdon (1979), Yourdon (1975) and Myers (1975). These diagrams document how data input is transformed to output, with each stage in the diagram representing a distinct transformation.

Data flow diagrams are made up of three components:

1. annotated arrows,
2. annotated bubbles,
3. the operators * and ⊕.

The annotated bubbles represent transformation centres with the annotation specifying the transformation. The arrows represent data flow in and out of the transformation centres with the annotations naming the data flow. Data flow diagrams describe how an input is transformed to an output. They do not, and should not, include control information or sequencing information. Each bubble can be considered as a stand-alone black box which transforms its inputs to its outputs. The operators * and ⊕ are used to link arrows — * means AND and ⊕ means EXCLUSIVE OR.

Figure 4.3 shows input data D1 and D2 being transformed to either D3.1 or D3.2. By convention, inputs enter from the left and outputs leave to the right. In this example, D1 is transformed by T1 to D1.1 which is transformed by T2 to D1.2. D1.2 is combined with D2 at transformation centre T3 to produce D3. D3 is transformed by T4 producing either D3.1 or D3.2.

Using a practical example, consider a spelling checker program which looks up each word used in a document in a dictionary. If a word appears in the dictionary it is deemed to be correctly spelled, otherwise it is displayed on the user's terminal. The user may then decide if the word is mis-spelled or if it is correctly spelled. If mis-spelled, the word is held in a file of mis-spelled words; if correctly spelled, it is added to the dictionary. A specification of this spelling checker was given in the previous chapter.

There are a number of possible ways of implementing this system. The data flow diagram for one of these possibilities is shown in Fig. 4.4.

One of the principal advantages of data flow diagrams is that they show transformations without making any assumptions about how these transformations are implemented. In Fig. 4.4, the user at a terminal is represented as a transformation and the other transformations might be implemented in a variety of ways. For example, the system could be

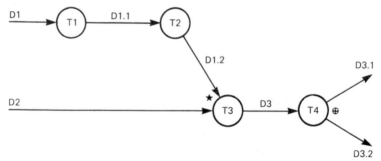

Figure 4.3   A data flow diagram.

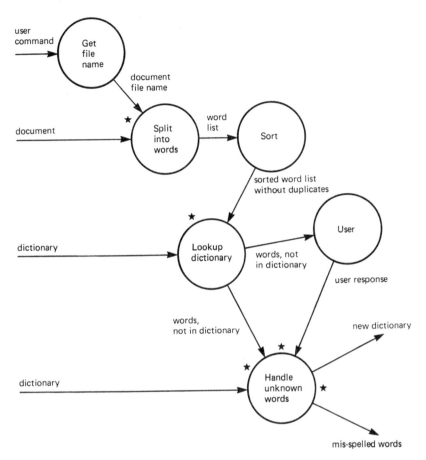

Figure 4.4   Data flow diagram for spelling checker.

implemented as a single program using program units to implement each transformation. Alternatively, it might be implemented as a number of separate interacting programs, using files to communicate with each other or, perhaps, the implementation might be an amalgam of these methods.

The preparation of data flow diagrams is best approached by considering system inputs and working towards system outputs. Each bubble must represent a distinct transformation — its output should, in some way, be different from its input. There are no rules for determining the overall structure of the diagram and constructing a data flow diagram is one of the creative aspects of system design. Like all design, it is an iterative process with early attempts refined in stages to produce the final diagram.

4.1.2 Structure charts
Structure charts describe the programming system as a hierarchy of parts and display this graphically, as a tree. They document how elements of a

data flow diagram can be implemented as a hierarchy of program units. The form of structure chart described here follows closely that of Constantine, Yourdon and Myers but without the control conventions used in their notation. The reason why a simplified structure chart notation is used here is that it is the opinion of this author that control is best described using a design description language rather than by extending the structure chart notation.

A structure chart shows relationships between program units without including any information about the order of activation of these units. It is drawn using three symbols:

1. a rectangle annotated with the name of the unit,
2. an arrow connecting these rectangles,
3. a circled arrow $\circ\!\!\longrightarrow$, annotated with the name of data passed to and from elements in the structure chart. Normally, the circled arrow is drawn parallel to the arrow connecting the rectangles in the chart.

An example of a structure chart is shown in Fig. 4.5

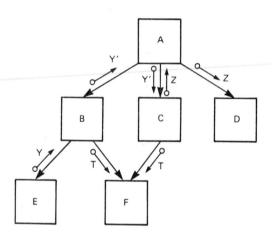

Figure 4.5   A structure chart.

Unit A calls on units B, C and D. Unit B calls on units E and F, and unit C calls on unit F. Notice that nodes at level n in the tree may be shared by two or more nodes at level $n-1$ but that nodes at level n may not utilize other nodes at the same level. The left-to-right ordering of B, C and D does not imply that the units are called in that sequence.

In the above chart, data Y originates in unit E, is transformed by B to Y' and passed to A. Unit B also passes data T to unit F. Unit A passes Y' to C and C passes T to F. C returns Z to A which passes Z on to D. Data arrows which originate at a lower node are taken to be input.

Nodes which do not return data to a higher level node are assumed to output that data.

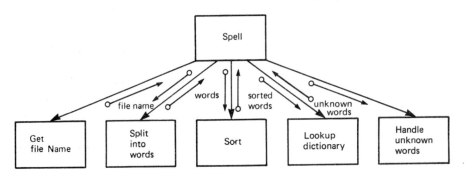

Figure 4.6   Spell structure 1.

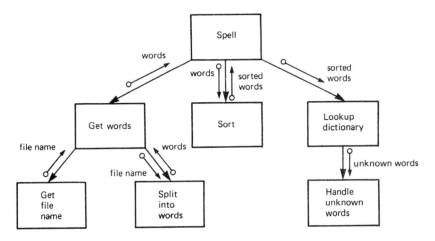

Figure 4.7   Spell structure 2.

From any non-trivial data flow diagram, it is possible to derive a number of different structure charts. For example, Figs. 4.6, 4.7 and 4.8 show three structure charts representing different ways of organizing a spelling checker program.

A major problem facing the software engineer is how to derive the most appropriate structure chart from a data flow diagram. This will be discussed later in the chapter.

4.1.3 Design description languages

The lowest level of a software design is best described using some formal language. It has been argued that the most appropriate notation for this is a high-level programming language such as Ada or Pascal. Whilst this has the obvious advantage that the design is executable if a suitable language compiler is available, there are disadvantages to this approach. These are:

1. High-level programming languages — because they must be compilable — are not readily extended to include new concepts.

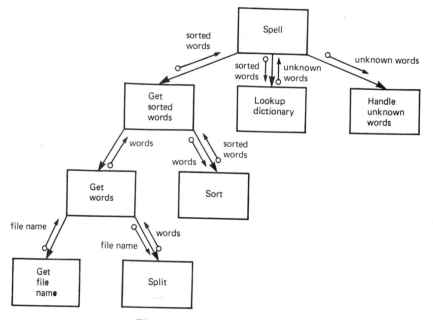

Figure 4.8 Spell structure 3.

2. The data types, structures and operations available as primitives in programming languages are often relatively low-level. This means that the representation of some intuitively simple high-level constructs such as an unbounded sequence of data items sometimes becomes detailed and confused.

3. As thinking is constrained by language, the lower the level of constructs available to the designer, the more his thinking is liable to be influenced by language constructs.

4. If an initial implementation of a design, specified in a programming language, must subsequently be re-implemented, it is difficult to carry out this re-implementation in a higher-level language than the design specification language.

Rather than using an existing programming language as a vehicle for design expression, a better alternative is to use a design description language specifically intended for documenting and communicating software designs. A number of such languages have been invented, such as those described by Chu (1978), Van Leer (1976) and Linger *et al.* (1979).

In essence, design description languages make use of the familiar control constructs of high-level programming languages to specify flow of control but allow the designer considerable flexibility in the description of operations. In this chapter, a variant of Ada (Ada/PDL) is used as a design description language. This notation has been chosen partly because Ada is likely to become the most common software engineering language and because Ada is one of the few programming languages which are rich enough in constructs to serve as an adequate base for a program description language.

Like the Ada-based notation used for requirements definition, an Ada/PDL need not conform to the strict rules of Ada. In the notation which is used here, English descriptions of operations are used, Ada punctuation conventions are not adhered to and additional constructs (such as forall) are added if this improves the clarity of the design description. However, wherever appropriate, we use Ada control constructs and operators in the description. We have avoided the use of Ada constructs which are likely to be unfamiliar to readers who have no knowledge of this language.

Generally, a design in an Ada/PDL is refined through a number of levels of abstraction from a high-level statement of the operation to a detailed design whose representation is close to the programming language. For example, consider the design of a program intended to detect misspelled words in a document:

```
procedure SPELLCHECK is
begin
      split document into single words
      look up words in dictionary
      display words which are not in dictionary
      create a new dictionary
end SPELLCHECK
```

This very high-level design description may be refined in more detail as shown below. On occasions, it may be useful to import a high-level design description into a refinement in the form of comments. Thus the comment symbol $--^*$ means that the associated comment represents a higher level operational description. A next level of refinement of spellcheck might be:

```
procedure SPELLCHECK is
begin
      --* split document into words
      loop
            get next word
            add word to word list in sort order
            exit when all words processed
      end loop
      --* look up words in dictionary
      loop
            get word from word list
            if word not in dictionary then
                  --* display words not in dictionary
                  display word, prompt on user terminal
                  if user response says word OK then
                        add word to good word list
            else
                        add word to bad word list
                  end if
            end if
            exit when all words processed
```

end loop
−−* create a new dictionary
DICTIONARY := merge dictionary and good word list
end SPELLCHECK

In this example, some PDL control constructs have been used to describe the decisions made in the program but all actual operations have been described in natural language. Readers familiar with a high-level programming language should have no difficulty understanding the above fragment as it uses only familiar programming language constructs.

One of the advantages of using a design description language is that new abstract data types may be introduced and used without previous definition. Naturally they must eventually be defined. This is illustrated in the next example, where an abstract data type called a sequence is used. A sequence is an unbounded list which may only be accessed in order, from the front.

An operational model of a sequence is an ordered pair of lists, the first list (the past list) being those members already accessed and the second list (the future list) those members to be accessed. The operation **current** returns the last member of the past list, the operation **next** returns the first member of the future list. **Reset** defines a new sequence whose past list is the empty list and whose future list is a catenation of the two lists of the old sequence. Informally, it sets an implicit list pointer to the beginning of the list. The application of next to a sequence has the effect of increasing the length of I.past by 1 and reducing the length of I.future by 1. Informally, it moves the pointer along the sequence. The **length** function returns the number of items in the sequence and the catenation operator ++ puts sequences together to make a new sequence.

Thus, if a sequence p is $(a,b,c), (x,y,z)$, current refers to c, the last member of the first list and next refers to x, the first member of the second list. The operation reset(p) creates a new sequence $p = (a,b,c,x,y,z)$. The length operator applied to this sequence returns a value of 6. It is possible to refer to each of these lists separately as p.past and p.future. Therefore p is always equal to p.past ++ p.future.

Sequences are used in the example below which describes the final part of the spelling checker, namely the merging of the dictionary and the properly spelled words from the document which do not appear in the dictionary.

```
type WORDSEQ is SEQUENCE of WORD
DICTIONARY, GOODWORDS, NEWDICT : WORDSEQ

procedure MERGE (A, B : WORDSEQ; C : out WORDSEQ) is

    X, Y : WORD
begin
    if LENGTH (A) = 0 then
        C := B
    elsif LENGTH (B) = 0 then
        C := A
```

```
    else
        X := NEXT (A); Y := NEXT (B)
        -- execute till one sequence exhausted
        while LENGTH (A) > 0 and LENGTH (B) > 0 loop
            if X < Y then --select from 1st sequence
                C := C ++ X; X := NEXT (A)
            else -- select from 2nd sequence
                C := C ++ Y; Y := NEXT (B)
            end if
        end loop
        -- assign remainder of non exhausted sequence
        if LENGTH (A) = 0 then
            C := C ++ B.FUTURE
        else
            C := C ++ A.FUTURE
        end if
    end if
end MERGE
```

It is hoped that the reader familiar with a high-level programming language such as Pascal will appreciate the general notion of program description languages from these examples. Space does not permit a more complete definition of this Ada/PDL, but additional concepts will be introduced as required in subsequent examples.

4.2 Top-down design

The design of software is a creative process which cannot be formulated as a set of rules. Nevertheless, the use of a systematic design methodology simplifies the design process and results in software which is understandable, verifiable and reliable. One such methodology is called top-down design or stepwise refinement. Top-down design is based on the notion that the structure of the problem should determine the structure of the software solution. It makes use of the most fundamental human problem solving facility — abstraction.

According to the *Concise Oxford Dictionary*, abstraction is the 'process of stripping an idea of its concrete accompaniments'. The idea is considered as an abstract entity without details of how that entity is actually realized. The previous example of the spelling checker illustrated the process — checking spelling involved splitting the document into words, sorting these words, then looking them up in a dictionary. These were identified as fundamental operations and, initially, how they actually worked was ignored. As the design progresses, each component is refined into its own fundamental operations with the process continuing until a low-level design is formulated.

The formulation and description of a software design involves a number of different stages:

1. Study and understand the problem. Without this understanding, effective software design is impossible.

2. Identify gross features of at least one possible solution. At this stage it is often useful to identify a number of solutions and evaluate each of these. The simplest possible solution should be chosen. It is particularly important not to allow low-level implementation details, of which the designer may be aware, to interfere with the choice of solution.

3. Construct a data flow diagram showing gross data transformations in the system. If this seems impossible, it is likely that the problem is not properly understood.

4. Using the data flow diagram, construct a structure chart showing the program units involved in the solution.

5. Describe each abstraction used in the solution in a description language such as Ada/PDL. It is likely that at the first stages of the design this will consist, almost exclusively, of natural language description.

After the initial, highest-level, solution has been formulated and described, the problem solving process should be repeated for each abstraction used. This process of refinement continues until a low-level specification of each abstraction has been prepared. Although the list above implies that there are clear and distinct stages of design, the boundaries between stages are fluid. For some systems, the best approach might be to follow that above; for others, the designer might leave out the structure chart stage initially and go back and fill it in after describing the design in a program description language.

It is very important that the representation of each stage of the design is clear and concise. A useful rule-of-thumb which may be adopted is to express the design in such a way that each part of the specification can normally be described on a single, standard-sized sheet of paper.

4.2.1 Deriving structure charts

An important stage in the design process is the transformation of a data flow diagram to a structure chart. This stage converts abstract transformations into a hierarchy of program units, thus representing an important step in the transition from an abstract problem solution to a concrete realization of that solution.

Recall that in the previous example of a spelling checker program, three different structure diagrams were derived from the system data flow diagram. No comment was made at that stage as to which of these represented the 'best' solution. Although this notion of a best solution is to some extent subjective, our aim should be to derive a design where program units exhibit a high degree of cohesion and a low degree of coupling.

The identification of loosely coupled, highly cohesive units is simplified if units are considered to be principally responsible for dealing with one of four types of data flow.

1. Input — the program unit is responsible for accepting data from a unit at a lower level in the structure chart and passing that data on to a higher-level unit in some modified form. Yourdon and Constantine use the term 'afferent' to describe such units.

2. Output — the program unit is responsible for accepting data from a higher-level unit and passing it to a lower-level unit. This is termed 'efferent' by Yourdon and Constantine.

3. Transform flow — a program unit accepts data from a higher-level unit, transforms that data and passes it back to that unit.

4. Co-ordinate flow — a unit is responsible for controlling and managing other units.

Typical representations for each type of unit in a structure chart are shown in Fig. 4.9.

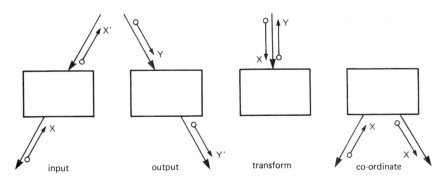

Figure 4.9 Structure chart representation.

The first step in converting a data flow diagram to a structure chart is to identify the highest-level input and output units. These units are those still concerned with passing data up and down the hierarchy but furthest removed from physical input and output. This step, generally, does not include all bubbles and the remaining transforms are termed central transforms.

Identifying the highest-level input and output bubbles depends on the skill and experience of the system designer. One possible way to approach this task is to trace the inputs until a bubble is found whose output is such that its input cannot be deduced from output examination. The previous bubble then represents the highest-level input unit. A similar criterion is used to establish the highest-level output bubble. The first level of the structure chart is produced by representing the input unit as a single box and each central transform as a single box. The box at the root of the structure chart is designated as a control unit. This factoring process may then be repeated for the first-level units in the structure chart until all bubbles in the data flow diagram are represented. Consider again the data flow diagram for the spelling checker program shown in Fig. 4.10.

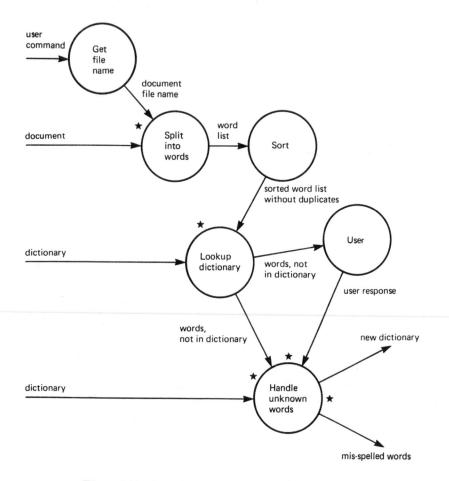

Figure 4.10 Data flow diagram for spelling checker.

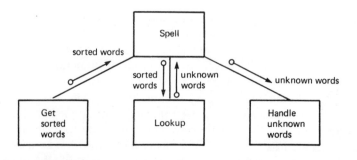

Figure 4.11 First-level structure for spelling checker.

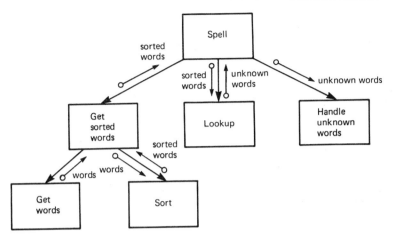

Figure 4.12 Second-level structure for spelling checker.

Applying the above criteria to the data flow diagram of the spelling checker suggests that the bubble 'lookup' represents a central transform whereas 'sort' represents the highest-level input unit, and 'handle unknown words' the highest-level output unit. Up to the lookup bubble, the transformations are fundamentally rearrangements of the system input, after the lookup bubble they are cosmetic transformations of the system output. The lookup operation, on the other hand, is a transformation where input disappears and output emerges and thus can be identified as the central transform.

This results in the following first-level structure being derived as in Fig. 4.11. Applying the same process to the sort unit to derive the second-level structure, we get Fig. 4.12. Notice that sort has now taken on the role of a central transform. The derivation process is applied a third time to derive the final structure chart as Fig. 4.13.

It is generally (although not necessarily) true that each node in the structure chart of a well structured design will have between two and seven subordinates. If a node has only a single subordinate, this implies that the unit represented by that node may have a low degree of cohesion — the unit encompasses more than a single function and the existence of a single subordinate means that one of the functions may have been factored out. If a node has many subordinates, this implies that the design has been developed to too low a level at that stage.

4.2.2 An example of top-down design

As with other creative processes, the concepts of top-down design are best illustrated by example and, in this section, an information retrieval system intended for use in an office is described. As a full system description is lengthy, only an overview of the system is presented. Aspects of the system will be expounded in more detail as required.

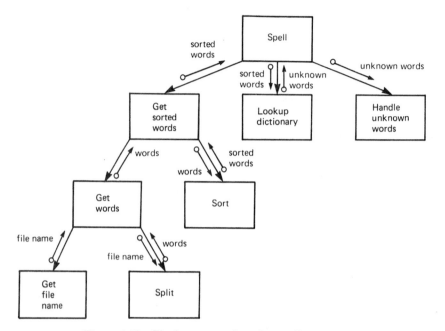

Figure 4.13   Final structure chart for spelling checker.

The Office Information Retrieval System (OIRS) is an automatic file clerk which can file documents under some name in one or more indexes, retrieve documents, display and maintain document indexes, archive documents and destroy documents. The system is activated by a request from the user's terminal and always returns a message to the user indicating the success or failure of his request.

When a document is filed, the location of the document, a document name and the indexes under which it should be filed must be specified. Retrieval requests involve the specification of one or more indexes along with the document name. Index examination involves specifying an index name and a qualifier. This qualifier is a condition determining which parts of the index are required for examination.

It is neither possible nor useful to provide a full description of the office information retrieval system here. Rather, some of its functions will be illustrated by example. Typical commands which might be issued by an OIRS system user are:

1. **file as** *smithletter* **under** *letters, smith*
2. **lookup** *letters s-v*
3. **get** *books on-loan*
4. **edit**
5. **file as** *on-loan*
6. **get** *proposal*

The numbers are not part of the command — they have simply been included for easy reference. A general principle of operation of this system is that each user has an anonymous personal workspace and, if no name is specified in a command, the command operates on that workspace. This is illustrated in commands 4 and 5 above. Command 4 specifies a workspace edit and command 5 specifies that the contents of the workspace should be filed under the name on-loan. All commands which return information copy that information into the user's workspace.

Commands also execute in a context defined by an earlier command. Therefore, if command parameters are left out they are deduced by the OIRS system. Thus, command 3 above establishes a context 'books' (this is the name of the index) and retrieves the document called *on-loan* from that index. Command 4 causes it to be edited and command 5 files it as *on-loan*. There is no need to specify the index name as it is established by command 3.

Command 1 above files the user's buffer under the name *smithletter* and makes entries in indexes called *letters* and *smith*. Command 2 is used to examine the index letters and it lists those documents whose filenames start with a letter between s and v.

4.2.3 Designing an office information system

The initial stage of the design of OIRS can be tackled by considering the system as a black box and examining the inputs and outputs of the system. This can be represented as a data flow diagram as shown as Fig. 4.14.

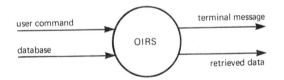

Figure 4.14   Inputs and outputs of OIRS.

A possible development of this is to assume that a data flow bubble exists to handle each input and each output. Connecting these bubbles might be a transform converting input to output as shown in Fig. 4.15

Examination of the problem description shows that there are a number of different user commands, each of which may have parameters. There is, therefore, a need to check command syntax and to 'understand' the command parameters before passing it on for transformation. This leads to a development of the input command bubble as shown in Fig. 4.16. After the user command has been analysed, it is transformed to a request for information retrieval.

Attention must now be paid to the other input bubble — that responsible for accessing the OIRS database. This database consists of many distinct files and, clearly, the function of this input bubble is fairly complex. A possible way of tackling this problem is to postulate the existence of a database management system (DBMS) responsible for all information

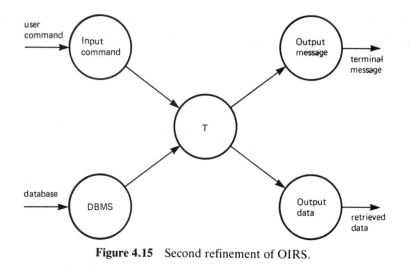

Figure 4.15   Second refinement of OIRS.

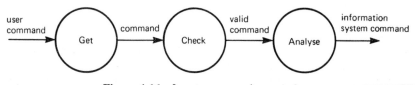

Figure 4.16   Input command processing.

transfers to and from the OIRS database. This DBMS represents an abstraction and allows the database to be considered as a single entity rather than as a number of files. The data flow diagram for input is shown Fig. 4.17.

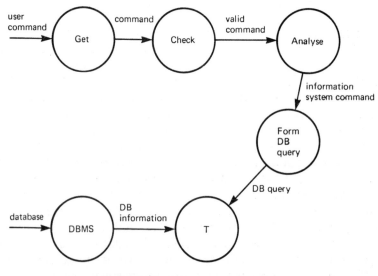

Figure 4.17   Input transformations.

The DBMS returns the information retrieved to bubble T and this must be transformed to appropriate user output. The output part of the system might be represented as shown in Fig. 4.18.

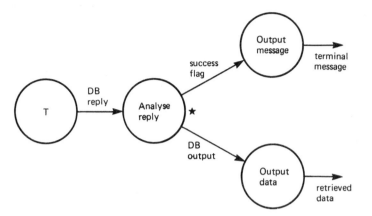

Figure 4.18   Output data flow diagram.

In each of these diagrams, the bubble T has been shown as the sink for input and as the source of output. However, examination shows that T is actually redundant and that the central transform is that carried out by the DBMS. The highest-level data flow diagram for OIRS therefore is illustrated as Fig. 4.19.

The next stage in the design is to derive a structure chart. The highest-level 'input' bubble is 'form DB query', the highest-level output bubble is 'analyse reply' and the only central transform bubble is 'DBMS'. This identifies the first level in the structure chart and the process is continued until all levels are identified. The structure chart shown in Fig. 4.20 is thus derived.

The next stage in the design process is to consider the data flow diagram and specifications and work out which bubbles should be expanded in more detail.

Consider the bubble 'form DB query'. This accepts a 'compiled' user command and translates it to one or more database management system commands. Examination of the specifications shows that, on occasion, the compiled user command is incomplete — it may require additional information derived from previous commands. This may be obtained from a history file which stores all previous user commands. The expanded data flow diagram for this bubble is illustrated as Fig. 4.21.

A similar expansion can be carried out for other bubbles in the data flow diagram and second-order structure charts prepared for each of these.

Having prepared data flow diagrams and structure charts, the next design activity is to derive and document the design using a description language. Before doing so, however, the data flow diagrams should be re-examined to see where error reports should be generated.

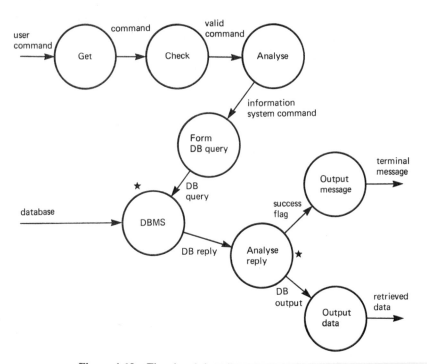

Figure 4.19   First-level data flow diagram for OIRS.

In the preparation of data flow diagrams, it is sensible to ignore data flows resulting from error conditions as these tend to clutter the diagram. However, as the design is documented in more detail, it is important to take errors into account. A modified data flow diagram for the system which includes error information is shown in Fig. 4.22.

For clarity, error data flow is not shown flowing to a bubble — it is clearly indicated by specifying ERROR in upper-case letters.

The refinement of the design and specification in a description language is illustrated below by describing the design of 'ANALYSE_COMMAND' which generates a compiled OIRS request. Such a request has the form:

```
type IR_REQ is record
    OK : BOOLEAN; -- true if valid request
    COMMAND : range 1..MAXIMUM_NUMBER_OF_COMMANDS;
    LOCATION : FILENAME; -- where its held
    NAME : STRING; -- user-supplied name
    INDEXES : INDEX_LIST; -- filed in these indexes
end record

REQUEST : IR_REQ;
```

The program unit ANALYSE_COMMAND is called with a structure of this form as a parameter. A description of ANALYSE_COMMAND is:

```
procedure ANALYSE_COMMAND(REQ : in out IR_REQ) is
    COMMAND_STRING : STRING;
```

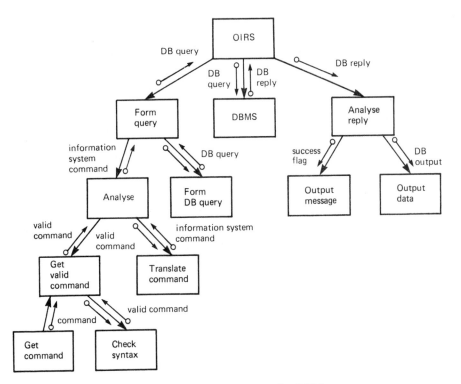

Figure 4.20   Structure chart for OIRS.

```
        ERROR_INDICATOR : BOOLEAN;
begin
        GET_VALID_COMMAND(ERROR_INDICATOR,COMMAND_STRING);
        if ERROR_INDICATOR then
             REQ.OK := FALSE;
        else
             COMPILE_COMMAND(COMMAND_STRING,REQ);
        end if;
end ANALYSE_COMMAND;
```

Now the design of each unit which is referenced in ANALYSE_COMMAND can be refined. This is illustrated by describing the design of 'COMPILE_COMMAND'. The string returned by 'GET_VALID_COMMAND' is terminated by a colon and holds the command name, the location, the user supplied name and the list of indexes. All of these are separated by commas:

<COMMAND_STRING> ::= <C_NAME>,<LOC>,<U_NAME>,<INDEXES>:

This command is generated by another program unit so its syntax can be assumed to be correct. Therefore, COMPILE_COMMAND does not need syntax checking statements.

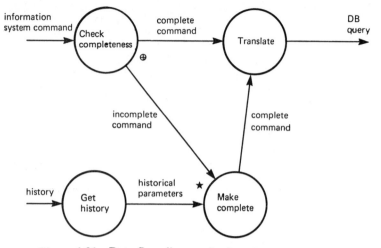

Figure 4.21   Data flow diagram for form DB command.

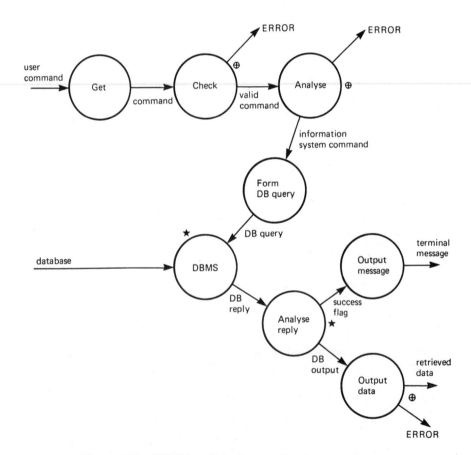

Figure 4.22   OIRS data flow diagram showing error flows.

```
procedure COMPILE_COMMAND(COMMAND_STRING : STRING;
                          REQ : IR_REQ) is
    SP : INTEGER := START OF STRING; -- pointer to command string
begin
    COMMAND := GET_TO_COMMA(SP,COMMAND_STRING);
    LOCATION := GET_TO_COMMA(SP,COMMAND_STRING);
    NAME := GET_TO_COMMA(SP,COMMAND_STRING);
    INDEXES := MAKE_INDEX_LIST(SP, COMMAND_STRING);
    case COMMAND of
    when FILE => -- file command
        if NAME = '' THEN
            REQ.OK := FALSE;
            ERROR_MESSAGE('FILE COMMAND NEEDS A NAME');
        else
            REQ := (TRUE,FILE,LOCATION,NAME,INDEXES);
        end if;
    when LOOKUP => -- lookup command
        if NAME /= '' OR LOCATION /= '' THEN
            ERROR_MESSAGE ('ONLY INDEXES NEEDED IN LOOKUP');
        end if;
        REQ := (TRUE,LOOKUP,'','',INDEXES);
    when GET =>
        .......
        -- code for remaining commands
        .......
    end case;
end COMPILE_COMMAND;
```

The final refinement step is to describe the program units GET_TO_COMMA and MAKE_INDEX_LIST but as the details of these are straightforward, they will not be shown here.

The design specification is continued for all other program units in a similar way. Notice that no account is taken of implementation details such as the efficiency of data representations or programming language control constructs. The intention of the designer is to develop a language-independent design which may be understood and validated. Taking implementation considerations such as efficiency and representation into account serves to confuse the design.

4.3 Object-oriented design

Rather than develop a software system design using top-down functional decomposition, it has been suggested that a better design methodology is object-oriented design. In object-oriented design, the software components are seen as objects rather than functions. Each object has an associated set of permitted operations and objects communicate by message passing where the message usually includes an instruction to activate a particular function.

Object-oriented design was founded on the idea of using information hiding as the principal criterion for decomposition (Parnas, 1972) and on the notion of abstract data types. This methodology has been enthusiastically adopted by some software developers and educators with Abbot (1983) going as far as to say 'well written Ada programs are usually object-oriented'. This implies that, unless the program is object-oriented, it is not well written. Such unsubstantiated generalizations are not helpful and it is unlikely that any one design methodology is superior in all circumstances. To place such comments in perspective, many large systems have been built using top-down design. Few large systems have been built using an object-oriented approach.

As an illustration of the object-oriented approach to system design, consider the spelling checker program discussed in Section 4.2.1. Using a functional approach, the following operations were identified:

1. split document into words,
2. check if words are in dictionary,
3. form lists of words which are not in dictionary,
4. merge good words with dictionary giving new dictionary.

An object-oriented view of this system might have as generalized objects (abstract data types) documents, dictionaries and word lists. The system can be represented as a set of interacting objects as shown in Fig. 4.23. Notice that sequencing is shown by numbering the messages passed between objects.

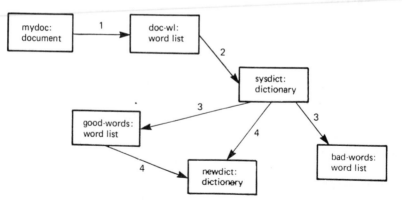

Figure 4.23 An object-oriented spelling checker.

It is straightforward to identify the objects in this simple system. In general, however, there is a need for a strategy to be used in the derivation of an object-oriented design. One such strategy is suggested by Abbot (1983) and is also described in Booch (1983).

This strategy relies on writing an informal natural language description of how to tackle the design problem. Given such a description, common nouns such as dates, messages, documents, dictionaries, etc., are picked out and considered as abstract data types. So-called mass nouns such as units of measure, the names of qualities, activities, etc., also fall into this category.

Proper nouns and direct references to common nouns such as system delivery date, my birthday, the project proposal, etc., are considered to be instances of abstract data types. Verbs and adverbs are used to identify operators (insert, create, etc.) and attributes of an object (is it empty, how many are there, etc.). These are associated with the corresponding abstract data type.

This strategy is best illustrated by example. Consider the example of a 'head-up' display available to the pilot of an aircraft. This is described by Booch (1983). An informal description of this system is:

> The pilot sees a display consisting of flight parameters, a target box with an aiming point, the actual target with state vector and armament status. During the target engagement, these elements will change at arbitrary times forcing an immediate update of the display. The pilot may terminate the head-up display processing upon command.

Using the approach outlined above, Booch identifies the following objects:

1. actual target including state vector,
2. armament status,
3. flight parameters,
4. head-up display,
5. target box including aim,
6. user command.

The operations associated with each object are also identified:

1. Actual target
   get_status
2. Armament status
   get_changes
3. Flight parameters
   get_changes
4. Head-up display
   update
5. Target box
   get_changes
6. User command
   is_terminate

After identifying objects and their associated operations, Booch goes on to establish which objects must communicate and then to define each object using Ada packages. Object definition using Ada/PDL will be discussed later in this section.

This approach to object-oriented design which relies on a natural language problem description appears to be useful in some circumstances. However, it is not clear how it may be applied to the design of large, complex systems. When a system is complex with many interacting functions, it is very difficult indeed to produce a concise and complete natural language system description. It is thus likely that errors, omissions and inconsistencies will be present in the informal description of the problem.

Whilst the resolution of such errors is always a design problem, the lack of structure and inherent ambiguity of natural language makes the derivation of a complete problem description difficult. This suggests that a combination of strategies is probably necessary to derive object-oriented designs where the designer uses his or her experience and intuition to derive a design from a natural language description, a high-level system design, a top-down functional model, etc.

It has been suggested that an object-centred view of software systems should entirely replace the functional view. It is this author's opinion that this would be a mistake. Rather, top-down functional decomposition and object-oriented design complement each other and each is applicable at different stages in the system design.

To illustrate this, consider the software systems which might be part of a modern civil airliner. Some of these might be:

1. the navigation system,
2. the radar system,
3. the external communications system,
4. the instrument display system,
5. the engine control system.

These systems and their interactions are illustrated in Fig. 4.24.

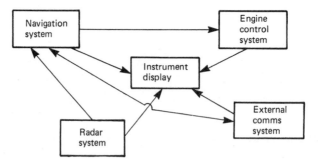

Figure 4.24   Interacting aircraft sub-systems.

Our natural high-level view of the overall software system is as a set of objects (sub-systems) rather than as a set of functions. Thus at very abstract design levels, an object-oriented viewpoint seems to be appropriate.

However, once the system is examined in more detail, its natural description is as a set of interacting functions rather than objects. For example, some of these functions might be:

1. Display_Track (radar sub-system),
2. Compensate_for_Wind_Speed (navigation sub-system),
3. Reduce_Power (engine control sub-system),
4. Indicate_Emergency (instrument sub-system),
5. Lock_onto_Frequency (communications sub-system).

This functional view is that taken by the requirements definition. Whilst it may be possible to convert this to an object-oriented view, this may be difficult to validate because there is not a simple correspondence between design functions and requirements definitions. A single logical function in the requirements definition may be implemented as a complex sequence of object interactions.

As the system design is further decomposed, an object-oriented view may again become the natural way to view the system. At the detailed design stage, the objects manipulated might be THE_ENGINE_STATUS, THE_AIRCRAFT_POSITION, THE_ALTIMETER, THE_CLOSEST_TRACK, etc. Thus an object-oriented approach to the lower levels of the system design is likely to be effective.

In summary, an object-oriented approach to software design seems to be the most natural at the highest and lowest levels of system design. At these levels, it may lead to higher component coherence and lower component coupling and it is these characteristics which lead to a maintainable design. In between these levels, however, the functional view seems more apt. This confirms the notion that large software systems are such complex objects that it is unwise to adopt any single, dogmatic approach to the building of these systems.

4.3.1 An example of object-oriented design

To illustrate how an object-oriented design may be derived, this section presents an example of the technique. To contrast the design with that produced using functional decomposition, the office information system described above is redesigned using an object-oriented approach.

A useful starting point is to use Abbot's natural language-based strategy to make a preliminary identification of objects. Recall that the system was described as follows:

The Office Information Retrieval System (OIRS) is an automatic file clerk which can file documents under some name in one or more indexes, retrieve documents, display and maintain document indexes, archive documents and destroy documents. The system is activated by a request from the user's terminal and always returns a message to the user indicating the success or failure of his request.

From this informal description, it is possible to identify some objects, namely:

documents
indexes
user_requests

It is also possible to identify some operations:

file documents
retrieve documents
archive documents
destroy documents
display indexes
maintain indexes
get user_request

In itself, the information provided in the single paragraph description of the system is not adequate. More information is available in the succeeding paragraph:

When a document is filed, the location of the document, a document name and the indexes under which it should be filed must be specified. Retrieval requests involve the specification of one or more indexes along with the document name. Index examination involves specifying an index name and a qualifier. This qualifier is a condition determining which parts of the index are required for examination.

From this paragraph, we see that the file operation involves specifying indexes and there is the implicit assumption that when a document is filed, its name is entered in an index. We also get the information that index examination requires the specification of the index name and qualifier. There is also the implicit statement that all of this is specified as part of the user command.

In fact, the description of the system stated above was not intended as a starting point for object-oriented design, so was not written with this end in view. Nevertheless, it illustrates the general problem with this approach. The production of a complete description of a system is neither straightforward nor concise. We actually need much more detailed information about operations, system parameters, restrictions, etc., than can normally be provided in a one or two paragraph description.

As this stage, therefore, it is usually worth producing a very high-level description of the system.

```
procedure OIRS is
begin
    COMMAND := GET_USER_COMMAND;
    case COMMAND.ACTION of
        when FILE =>
```

```
            FILE_DOCUMENT (COMMAND.PARAMETERS);
         when RETRIEVE =>
            RETRIEVE_DOCUMENT (COMMAND_PARAMETERS);
         when LOOKUP =>
            LOOKUP_INDEX (COMMAND_PARAMETERS);
         when DESTROY =>
            DESTROY_DOCUMENT (COMMAND PARAMETERS);
         when ARCHIVE =>
            ARCHIVE_DOCUMENT (COMMAND_PARAMETERS);
      end case;
   if COMMAND IS SUCCESSFUL then
         OUTPUT SUCCESS MESSAGE
      else
         OUTPUT FAILURE MESSAGE
      end if
   end OIRS
```

Using a combination of the natural language description, the high-level system description above, and the information about the system which has already been derived from the data-flow analysis above, the following objects and associated operations may be identified:

document
   file
   retrieve
   destroy
   archive

index
   display
   delete_entry
   add_entry

user_request
   get_request
   get_action
   get_index
   get_index_list
   get_qualifier
   get_location
   get_name

The next stage in the derivation of an object-oriented design is to specify these objects and associated operations in more detail. This is accomplished in Ada/PDL by using the package construct, which is a means of gathering together type declarations, associated operations, etc. This construct has already been introduced in Chapter 2 and is discussed in more detail in Chapters 5 and 6.

An Ada package is a means by which the visibility of names may be controlled. It is made up of two parts — a specification which makes known the names which may be used externally, and a package body which defines the implementation of operations made known in the package specification. Here, we are not interested in the implementation of objects, so only package specifications are given.

The DOCUMENT object and associated operations may be specified as follows:

```
package DOCUMENT is
    -- Access is required to some types declared in the
    -- index object. Specify that this object is
    -- required using Ada's with/use constructs.
    with INDEX; use INDEX;
    type A_DOC_NAME is private;
    type A_DOC_LOCATION is private;
    procedure FILE (D : A_DOC_NAME;
                    L : A _DOC_LOCATION
                    I : AN_INDEX_LIST);
    procedure RETRIEVE (D : A_DOC_NAME;
                    I : AN_INDEX_LIST);
    procedure DESTROY (D : A_DOC_NAME;
                    I : AN_INDEX_LIST);
    procedure ARCHIVE (D : A_DOC_NAME;
                    I : AN_INDEX_LIST);
private
    -- at this stage, the structure of private types
    -- is not of interest so their design is deferred
end DOCUMENT;
```

Notice how the types declared in this package are private types. This means that their structure may not be accessed from outside the package document. Thus, they may only be manipulated directly by operations in the document package and are protected from external interference.

The INDEX object is specified in the same way:

```
package INDEX is
    with DOCUMENT; use DOCUMENT;
    type AN_INDEX is private;
    -- Now assume that it is possible to declare a
    -- composite link list type. This might be
    -- accomplished using Ada generics but these
    -- are not of interest here
    type AN_INDEX_LIST is list of AN_INDEX
    type A_QUALIFIER is private;
    procedure ADD_AN_ITEM (I : AN_INDEX;
                    N : A_DOC_NAME;
                    L : A_DOC_LOCATION);
    procedure DELETE_AN_ITEM (I : AN_INDEX;
                    N : A_DOC_NAME);
    procedure LOOKUP (I : AN_INDEX;
                    Q : A_QUALIFIER);
private
    -- design deferred
end INDEX;
```

Finally, the object representing a USER_REQUEST may be specified:

```
package USER_REQUEST is
    type A_LINE is private;
    type A_COMMAND is (FILE, RETRIEVE, ARCHIVE,
                        DESTROY, LOOKUP);
    with INDEX, DOCUMENT;
    use INDEX, DOCUMENT;
    procedure GET_REQUEST (L : out A_LINE);
    function GET_ACTION (L : A_LINE) return A_COMMAND;
    function GET_INDEX (L : A_LINE) return AN_INDEX;
    function GET_QUALIFIER (L : A_LINE) return A_QUALIFIER;
    function GET_LOCATION (L : A_LINE) return A_DOC_LOCATION;
    function GET_INDEX_LIST (L : A_LINE) return AN_INDEX_LIST;
    function GET_NAME (L : A_LINE) return A_DOC_NAME;
private
    -- design deferred
end USER_REQUEST;
```

Using these object descriptions, it is now possible to derive a more detailed description of the information retrieval system:

```
procedure OIRS is
    with USER_REQUEST; use USER_REQUEST;
    C : A_COMMAND;
    L : A_LINE;
begin
    GET_REQUEST (L);
    C := GET_ACTION (L);
    if C = LOOKUP then
    declare
        with INDEX; use INDEX;
        I : AN_INDEX;
        Q : A_QUALIFIER;
    begin
        I := GET_INDEX (L);
        Q := GET_QUALIFIER (L);
        LOOKUP (I, Q);
    end;
    else
    declare
        with DOCUMENT; use DOCUMENT;
        I : INDEX_LIST;
        D : A_DOC_NAME;
    begin
        if C = FILE then
        declare
            LOC : A_DOC_LOCATION;
        begin
            LOC := GET_LOCATION (L);
            D := GET_NAME (L);
            I := GET_INDEX_LIST (L);
            FILE (LOC, D, I);
        end;
        else
```

```
            I := GET_INDEX_LIST (L);
            D := GET_NAME (L);
            case C of
            when RETRIEVE =>
                RETRIEVE (D, I);
            when DESTROY =>
                DESTROY (D, I);
            when ARCHIVE =>
                ARCHIVE (D, I);
            end case;
        end if;
    end;
    end if;
    if COMMAND SUCCESSFUL then
        OUTPUT SUCCESS MESSAGE
    else
        OUTPUT FAILURE MESSAGE
    end if;
  end OIRS;
```

Object-oriented design is a design methodology, not an implementation methodology. Whilst the availability of a language like Ada makes the implementation of object-oriented designs much easier, it is not essential. It is quite possible to simulate, in an imperfect way, Ada packages in languages like Pascal. This is described in Chapter 5.

It is not possible to be definitive about whether the object-oriented OIRS is superior or inferior to the system design developed using functional decomposition. Certainly the object-oriented approach gives the designer more flexibility in decisions on representation of objects, as access to these objects is confined to a single package.

Object-oriented design is a natural precursor to a programming methodology based on information hiding. This methodology seems to lead to more maintainable (and thus cheaper) systems. However, as Jamsa (1984) points out, object-oriented design does not yet have a well developed graphical notation to back it up, nor is it easy to describe unless an Ada-like PDL is used. As more experience is gained with this methodology and as notations are improved, it will undoubtedly become of increasing importance in large systems development.

4.4 Design validation

Validation of a software design is extremely important. Undetected errors and omissions which are carried forward to the implementation phase of the project and not detected until system testing can be extremely expensive to correct. They may require a complete redesign and re-implementation of parts of the system.

The validation of a software design is intended to achieve two objects:

1. To show that the software design is 'correct'; that is, the design should correctly implement the intentions of the designer. This

process is sometimes called verification to distinguish it from the more general process of validation discussed below.

2. To show that the software is valid. That is, it should be demonstrated that the design meets the requirements in full. For each requirement a design fragment should exist to meet that requirement.

The first of the objects above, the verification of design correctness, is best achieved by providing a mathematical proof that each software fragment is correct. However, proving correctness is time consuming and intellectually demanding, with the consequence that the formal verification of a design is expensive. Because of this cost, formal verification is not yet generally used for demonstrating design correctness. It is the author's opinion that formal methods ought to be more widely used to verify critical parts of systems.

It is arguable whether a correctness proof should be applied to a detailed design or to an implementation. Clearly, it depends, to some extent, on the programming language used for the implementation. If it is a language like Ada, proving the implementation is usually the best approach, but if an implementation language such as FORTRAN or C is used, the proof process is best applied to the detailed software design.

The second design validation objective, to check that all requirements have been met by the design, is accomplished by the use of design reviews. At a design review, a set of requirements and the design to meet these requirements are studied and compared. This task is considerably simplified if the requirements are stated in a formal way. If requirements are stated informally, ambiguities in the requirements may result in uncertainties in the design which are difficult to resolve.

4.4.1 Design verification

The most secure way of verifying a software design is to verify mathematically the correctness of a detailed design description. However, this is usually a difficult and expensive process and it is not currently a cost-effective method of design validation. The process is illustrated in Chapter 7, where it is discussed in the context of program rather than design verification.

Correctness can also be demonstrated in a non-formal way by presenting an argument explaining why a program is correct. Although less rigorous, this technique is much easier, quicker and cheaper than more formal verification methods. An example of a non-formal demonstration of correctness is shown below. The algorithm specified takes two strings A and B as input. If B is a substring of A, it returns the index of the first character of B in A; otherwise it returns -1.

```
procedure MATCH (A, B : STRING; OFFSET : INTEGER) is
    I : INTEGER;
    DIFF : constant := LENGTH (A) - LENGTH (B);
begin
    if DIFF < 0 then
```

```
            OFFSET := -1;
        elsif DIFF = 0 then
            if A = B then
                OFFSET := 0;
            else
                OFFSET := -1;
            end if;
        else
            I := 0; OFFSET := -1;
            loop
                if B = A(I..(I + LENGTH (B))) then
                    OFFSET := I;
                    exit;
                else
                    I := I + 1;
                    exit when I > DIFF;
                end if;
            end loop;
        end if;
    end MATCH;
```

A correctness argument for this routine involves showing that the routine terminates — that is, does not contain an endless loop — and explaining why the routine does what it is supposed to do. This latter step involves looking at each of the statements in the routine and explaining its function.

Termination
There is only a single loop in the program which is made up of an **if-then-else** statement. Each arm of that statement has an **exit**. The **then** branch has an unconditional **exit** so, if this is chosen, termination is assured. The **else** branch terminates when I becomes greater than DIFF. As I is always increased in this branch, it must eventually exceed the value of DIFF and termination is thus assured.

Correctness argument
1. The length of B is greater then the length of A so B cannot be a substring of A. OFFSET is set to −1.
2. If the lengths of A and B are equal, B is contained in A if A = B, so OFFSET = 0 if equal, otherwise −1.
3. If LENGTH(A) > LENGTH(B) the algorithm moves a pointer character by character along A. B is compared with the selected substring of A each time the pointer is moved. If B is equal to the substring of A, offset is set to I, the first character of the matching substring.
4. The comparison continues until the last substring checked is the last LENGTH(B) characters in A. The > test is OK because the characters in A index from 0 thus the last possible match is at position LENGTH (B) — LENGTH (A).

Because of the importance of design correctness, the software engineer should provide some form of verification — informal or formal — with each program design specification. The testing of a design after implementation is so expensive that the cost of producing this verification is justified.

4.4.2 Design reviews

At the time of writing, the most practical, widely used and cost-effective design validation technique is the design review. During a design review, the designer's work is scrutinized by a team of reviewers with the intention of finding out the current state of the software design. Reviews take many forms — their common factor is that they are not personnel reviews. Rather, their aim is to validate the software design and not to evaluate an individual's activities.

There are at least three types of design review that may be used in the development of a large software system. These are:

1. *Informal design reviews.* The design work of an individual is reviewed by fellow members of the design team.

2. *Formal technical reviews.* The design work of an individual or of a team is reviewed by a panel made up of project members and technical management. As well as design validation, formal technical reviews are also concerned with whether the design is on schedule, the state of the development of different parts of the design, the correspondence between the specifications and the design, etc.

3. *Management product reviews.* This type of review is intended to provide information for management about the progress of the software design. It is not intended for detailed design validation. Although the design should be 'walked through', the main concerns of this type of review are design costs, plans and schedules. This review is an important project checkpoint where major decisions about the readiness of the project for implementation or even product viability are made. This type of review is a management activity and is not principally intended for design validation. Thus, it is not discussed further here.

Informal design reviews should be carried out at regular intervals by a design team. Their objective is to detect as many errors as possible in the software design. The design specifications and software requirements should be distributed before the review for study by the members of the review team. The designer should lead the rest of the team through his design step by step, explaining the function and need for each statement. The intention is that the review team will detect errors and inconsistencies in the design and point them out to the designer. If errors are detected, they should be noted for subsequent correction. The review team should not waste time attempting to correct these errors.

It is not yet common practice to verify software designs in a formal way or even in the informal way discussed above. However, if some form of verification has been carried out by a designer, this should be distributed with the software for review. The verification can act as a framework for the review with the design discussed in that context.

The principal task of an informal design review is to check the correspondence between the software specification and the software design. It is probably inevitable, at this stage, that the review will also detect errors in the specification and, perhaps, errors in the requirements definition. These should not be corrected by the design team but should be passed on to the next level of review (formal technical review) for clarification.

A formal technical review usually involves a less detailed study of individual design components. It is more concerned with the validation of component interactions and with determining whether the design meets the user's requirements. This kind of review is conducted in essentially the same way as an informal review. The software designer describes his design to the review team, errors are noted, and actions to be taken by various individuals are recorded. In addition, the technical review team is also concerned with the design schedule and how slippage in one part of the design might affect other component designs.

An important task of the formal technical review is to decide how to handle errors in the software specifications and requirements definition which have been detected by design teams. In some cases, where these errors are in the description of user services, they must be reported to the software contractor. In other cases, the impact of changing the requirements or the specification must be evaluated. If the cost of a change is high (that is, if it means that many associated components must be changed) it may be necessary to live with the error and instruct the design team to design around it rather than correct that error.

An essential component of both formal and informal reviews is the review report. Whilst it is possible to conduct informal reviews with only informal notes, this is not advisable. Rather, a more formal account of the review along with reported errors and specified actions should be produced and distributed to all participants. This should then form the first item of discussion at the following review.

Further reading

There are an immense number of books and papers available which describe the activity of software design. Almost any of them may be used as a starting point for further reading but, inevitably, most put forward the author's opinions on how to design software. As yet, there is no way to compare design methodologies in a quantitative way.

Structured Design, L. L. Constantine and E. Yourdon (1979), Englewood Cliffs, NJ: Prentice-Hall.

> This is the definitive text on structured design and the methods are explained in great detail and in a very clear way. Unfortunately, all the examples chosen are from data processing systems, although the method is applicable to other types of software system.

Principles of Program Design, M. A. Jackson (1975), London: Academic Press.

Describes the methodology of data-driven design which is not covered in this chapter. Well written but a little old-fashioned.

'Object-oriented software systems', D. Robson (1981), Byte, **6 (8).**

A well written introduction to the concepts underlying object-oriented design. Robson worked for the SMALLTALK research group which first brought the notion of object-oriented design to light.

Software Engineering with Ada, G. Booch (1983), Reading, Mass: Benjamin Cummings.

Presents a description of object-oriented design in the context of Ada. Booch uses Abbot's method of deriving designs from a natural language description and whilst his examples are interesting and well written, they are somewhat simplified (I suspect) to make the design derivations work.

Chapter 5 PROGRAMMING PRACTICE

Programming is a craft, dependent on individual skill, attention to detail, and knowledge of how to use available tools in the best way. Just as a craftsman such as a potter must know his materials, understand the principles of glazing and firing and learn by experience, the programmer must understand the computer system, some theory of programming, and must practise programming. Programming is a practical activity which can only be learned by experience. Nevertheless, the experience of others can be distilled and provide guidelines for the programmer to help him or her avoid some pitfalls.

Good programming — the production of reliable and maintainable programs — is a language-independent process. Whilst high-level languages such as Ada or Pascal simplify the process of converting a design into an implementation, there is no reason why good programs may not be constructed in any language whatsoever. Even assembly code can be written in an understandable and reliable way.

The material in this chapter covers some of the language-independent aspects of the programming process. These include programming methodology, programming style, the use of software tools to assist programming and how programs may be written so that portability problems are reduced.

Section 5.1 briefly describes alternative methodologies of programming — top-down and bottom-up programming. Top-down programming has much in common with top-down design and is the general programming methodology preferred here. Bottom-up programming is the reverse process. As it has many disadvantages, it is not described in detail in this book. The notion of top-down development carried out in conjunction with information hiding is also discussed.

Section 5.2 discusses programming style. The style of programming used by an individual programmer is possibly the most important factor affecting the readability and understandability of programs. A well written program is neatly laid out, makes use of meaningful names, is sensibly commented, and uses language constructs so that program security and readability are maximized. The creation of such a program requires care, discipline and pride in workmanship on the part of the programmer.

Section 5.3 describes software tools which can assist the programmer in producing a well written program. Software tools improve programmer productivity by taking over mundane clerical tasks previously carried out by the programmer himself. The information gathered by software tools about static and dynamic program attributes can be used by the software engineer to refine his or her work, improving the quality of the developed programs.

This leads on to Section 5.4, which covers programming environments. Rather than use a collection of unrelated tools, recent research suggests that an integrated toolkit — a programming environment — could improve programmer productivity. This section describes what this toolkit might contain and introduces the notion of a software engineering environment which supports every stage in the software life cycle.

Section 5.5 addresses program portability. As software costs increase, it is clearly desirable to write programs in such a way that they do not depend on the underlying computer hardware. In practice, complete independence is impossible but the way in which a program is written significantly influences its portability. The material in this section describes how operating system and hardware dependencies can be minimized.

5.1 Programming methodology

The process of developing a program from a software design may be tackled in two ways. These are top-down development and bottom-up development. If the program is viewed as a hierarchy of components, top-down development involves starting at the top of the hierarchy and working downwards, whereas bottom-up development implies starting at the bottom and working upwards. This is illustrated in Fig. 5.1.

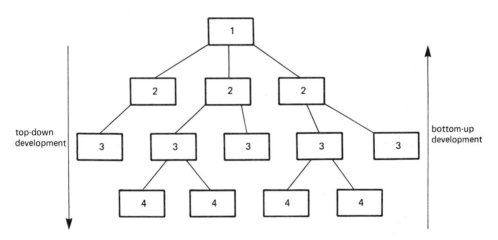

Figure 5.1   Top-down and bottom-up development.

Top-down development parallels the top-down process which should be used in system design, with the program structure being hierarchical. The programmer implements the higher levels of the design and represents the lower levels by stubs which simulate their function in a simplified way. As the implementation of a level is completed, the programmer moves on to the next lower level and implements that in terms of its sub-levels. Ultimately, the lowest level of the system is implemented using basic programming language facilities.

Bottom-up development is the converse of this process. Implementation starts with the lower levels of the system and the system is built up until, finally, the highest design level is implemented. Effectively, the programmer creates basic building blocks and uses these to build more complex blocks which are themselves used as building blocks for higher levels of the system.

Authors such as Wirth (1971), Dijkstra (1968a) and Naur (1972) argue that top-down development is a superior methodology because it results in the creation of programs which are more readable and more reliable than those implemented using bottom-up techniques. Bottom-up development, it is argued, tends to result in local optimizations at the expense of system quality because the programmer is never given the opportunity to view the system as an entity. Rather it always appears as a collection of parts.

At this point it is appropriate to introduce the term 'structured programming', which is widely and rather loosely used in discussions of programming. There appears to be no generally accepted definition of the term — in some cases it means programming without the use of **gotos**, in other cases it means adopting a top-down design methodology, and in yet others it means confining programming control constructs to **while** loops and **if** statements. It is not the intention here to present an exact definition of the term structured programming. As it is used, it embraces a philosophy rather than a methodology. The philosophy embraces the design and programming guidelines covered in this book and if these are followed the reader can claim to program in a structured manner.

For small programs which are hierarchical, it is almost certainly true that a top-down approach to development results in the most elegant, modifiable and reliable programs. However, large software systems are usually built of interconnected sub-systems so that it is impractical to build them as a strict component hierarchy. Their structure is that of a graph rather than a tree. This is shown in Fig. 5.2.

Given this structure, it is less clear what top-down and bottom-up development really means. The situation is further complicated by the fact that there may already exist some components which may be re-used and that it may be virtually impossible to implement other components in stub form.

In practice, then, neither a strict top-down nor a bottom-up approach is appropriate for large system construction. A strict top-down approach is likely to lead to an unacceptable amount of component duplication, whereas a bottom-up approach has the disadvantages discussed above. It is most appropriate to factor those components which provide services to other components out of the system, leaving a structure which is approximately hierarchical. This may then be implemented in a top-down way with the service components implemented in advance or in parallel with other development work.

In this discussion of software development, it has been assumed that the

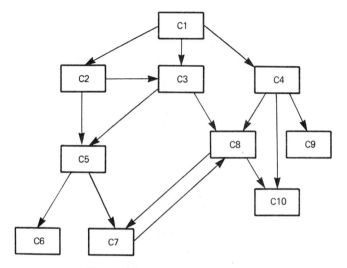

Figure 5.2 Large system structure.

majority of software components do not exist and have to be built by the programmer. If we compare this situation with hardware development, a quite different situation pertains. In hardware development, much more use is made of existing components with the minority of system components being specially built. In future, it seems likely that software development will involve much more component re-use than is currently practised. This implies that the main emphasis in programming will be on component interconnections rather than on program development. We will thus need to develop new notations and methodologies to support this process, perhaps along the lines of that suggested by DeRemer and Kron (1976). In their paper, they propose a notation which shows what services are provided by components and how components interact. Since the original publication there seems to have been little further work in this area.

5.1.1 Information hiding

A security principle adopted by military organizations is the 'need to know' principle. Only those individuals who need to know a particular piece of information to carry out their duties are given that information. Information which is not directly relevant to their work is withheld. When programming, an analogous principle should be adopted to control access to system data by program units.

In principle, each program unit should be allowed access only to program objects which are required to implement that unit's function. Access to other objects, not needed by the unit, should be denied by using the scope rules of the programming language to conceal the existence of these objects. This is called 'information hiding'. We have already seen examples of this in the formal specification of abstract data types and in object-oriented design.

The advantage of hiding unnecessary information is that there is no way in which the hidden information may be corrupted by a program unit which is not supposed to use that information. This means that programs are more secure and, in some circumstances, may provide data independence. The data representation may be changed without changing the program units which make use of that data. Furthermore, if objects are declared close to where they are used, this improves the readability of the program. The reader need not search through pages of listing to find the definition of an object.

As we have seen, the package construct in Ada is intended to support information hiding. The definition of an object and its associated operations may be separated from the code implementing that object. Take, for example, the following Ada package header which defines a queue of integers:

```
package QUEUE is
    type Q is limited private;
    procedure ADD (IQ : in out Q; X : in INTEGER);
    procedure REMOVE (IQ : in out Q; X : out INTEGER);
    function IS_EMPTY (IQ : in Q) return BOOLEAN;
private
    Q_SIZE : constant := 100;
    type INTVEC is
        array (INTEGER range <>) of INTEGER;
    type Q is record
            Q_VEC : INTVEC (1 . . Q_SIZE);
            FRONT : INTEGER range 0 . . Q_SIZE := 0;
            BACK : INTEGER range 0 . . Q_SIZE := 0;
    end record;              ;
end QUEUE;
```

The package header makes a type Q available for use outside the package but, as it is declared as a **limited private** type, operations on it are restricted. Declaring the type as a **private** type means that its structure may not be accessed from outside the package. The **limited** keyword specifies that the only permitted operations on that type are ADD, REMOVE and IS_EMPTY. The rules of Ada require that the structure of some types be declared in the package header but this may not be accessed by users of the package.

This package definition defines a type Q and associated operations ADD, REMOVE, and IS_EMPTY but gives no information on how integer queues are implemented. In fact, several possible implementations are possible — one possibility is shown below:

```
package body QUEUE is

    procedure ADD (IQ : in out Q; X : INTEGER);
    begin
        IQ.FRONT := IQ.FRONT + 1;
        IQ.Q_VEC (IQ.FRONT) := X;
    end;
```

```
procedure REMOVE (IQ : in out Q; X : out INTEGER);
begin
    IQ.BACK := IQ.BACK + 1;
    X := IQ.Q_VEC (IQ.BACK);
end;

function IS_EMPTY (IQ : Q) return BOOLEAN;
begin
    if IQ.FRONT = IQ.BACK then
        return TRUE;
    else
        return FALSE;
    end if;
end;
end QUEUE;
```

For brevity, the procedures which operate on the queue have been simplified. In practice, code to check for queue overflow and underflow must be included in the queue operations.

Programming languages such as FORTRAN and Pascal do not have constructs which allow access to information on a 'need to know' basis. FORTRAN's single-level locality of declarations in subroutines and Pascal's simple block structure mean that, in most programs, unnecessary information is available to some or all program units.

In languages without information hiding constructs, a very disciplined approach to programming is necessary if such constructs are to be simulated. The approach which must be adopted is to define special-purpose procedures to access particular types. Access to objects of these types in any other way should be avoided.

For example, an integer queue type may be defined in Pascal as follows:

```
type IntQueue = record
    Qvec : array [1..100] of INTEGER;
    front : 0..100;
    back : 0..100;
end;
```

Associated procedures *AddtoQueue*, *RemovefromQueue*, and *IsQueueEmpty* may be defined. Although direct access to *IntQueue* is not forbidden by the language, disciplined use of these access procedures simulates the Ada information hiding mechanism. These procedures are not given here as they are identical apart from syntactic details to the Ada procedures above.

A type like Q in the Ada package above which is defined in conjunction with its associated operations is called an abstract data type. This notion was first proposed by Liskov and Zilles (1974) and has been described in detail by Guttag (1977) and many others. Using the above Ada package queues, instances of that type are declared as follows:

```
with QUEUE; use QUEUE;
declare
    JOBS_RUNNING, JOBS_WAITING : Q;
```

The fact that type Q is declared to be a **limited private** type means that its structure is not available to other software components which use that package and that the only permitted operations on Q are those defined in the package header.

The importance of abstract data types for software specification has already been discussed, but they are an equally important practical programming technique. Even if no language construct which directly supports the creation of abstract data types is available, thinking in such terms and hiding as much information as possible is likely to result in more readily maintained programs.

For example, say an abstract data type representing a hash table is defined as follows:

```
package HASH is
    type TABLE is limited private;
    procedure ENTER (T : in out TABLE; S : KEY; V : VAL);
    procedure RETRIEVE (T : TABLE; S : KEY; V : out VAL);
private
    type TABLE_ENTRY is record
        PRIMARY_KEY : KEY;
        OBJECT_VALUE : VAL;
    end record;
    type TABLE is ARRAY (1 . . 100) of TABLE_ENTRY;
end;
```

The procedures ENTER and RETRIEVE are defined in the package body. In an initial implementation of these procedures, linear rehashing may be used to handle hash table collisions but, after the system has gone into use, it is decided to handle collisions using chaining. Naturally, the procedures ENTER and RETRIEVE must be modified to reflect this. In addition, the **private** part of the package header must be changed so that a link field is included in each table entry. However, as HASH.TABLE is defined as a **limited private** type, no code which uses hash tables is affected by the representation change.

5.2 Programming style

The requirements for the programming language Ada made the cogent observation that a program is read more often than it is written and that it is the responsibility of programming language designers to design languages which allow readable programs to be constructed. However, program readability does not just depend on language facilities. The style in which a program is written determines its readability or otherwise — a well written program in a language such as FORTRAN might be more readable than a badly written program in Pascal.

The creation of a readable and reliable program is a creative process and it is impossible to lay down rigid rules governing programming style. However, a number of guidelines can be established which, if followed, improve program readability. In addition, recognition and avoidance of error-prone language constructs and the utilization of language facilities which allow compile-time and run-time checks to be carried out increases the overall reliability of a program.

In this section aspects of programming style relating to the naming of program objects, structuring programs and paragraphing program listings are discussed. By following the guidelines set out here, it is possible to produce readable and understandable programs in any programming language.

5.2.1 Program names

The objects in a program such as constants, variables, procedures, functions, and types model real-world entities. The function of some entity in the real world is mirrored by the function of the object representing that entity in a program. Accordingly, the names of objects in a program should be closely related to or, if practical, identical to the names of the real-world entities which are modelled.

For example, if a program is computing satellite orbits, it is concerned with entities such as the mass of the satellite, the mass of the earth, the velocity of the satellite, and the acceleration of the satellite. These should be represented in the program by objects which might be named satellite_mass, earth_mass, satellite_velocity, and satellite_acceleration. It is not enough to use names such as mass, velocity and acceleration to refer to the satellite mass, velocity and acceleration, because it is not immediately obvious to the program reader that these names refer to the satellite rather than to some other entity such as the earth.

Even worse, is to choose names which are unrelated to the entities being modelled, such as the names of footballers, cryptic abbreviations or single-letter identifiers. Poor programmers frequently choose names which are short and therefore easy to type. This procedure often results in programs which are almost incomprehensible.

Consider the following example, programmed using short names, and compare it with the next example which is the same program coded using meaningful names. As well as illustrating the use of names, the example below also illustrates that the use of a reasonable programming language such as Pascal does not guarantee that the function of programs in that language is necessarily immediately obvious.

```
program CT(input, output);
  var t,f : real;
  begin
    read(t);
    f := t*9/5+32;
    write(f)
  end.

program ConvertCentigradeToFahrenheit(input, output);
  var Fahrenheit, Centigrade : real;
  begin
```

```
    read(Centigrade);
    Fahrenheit := Centigrade * 9/5 + 32;
    write(Fahrenheit)
end.
```

In the first instance, if the reader did not know the formula for converting centigrade temperature to fahrenheit temperature, it is unlikely that he or she would ever deduce what the program was doing. In the second example, not only does the program name explain the function of the program, but the conversion formula is also made explicit. The use of meaningful identifiers makes it immediately obvious that the program reads in an input value representing a temperature in degrees centigrade and outputs a number representing that value in degrees fahrenheit.

Unfortunately, one of the most commonly used programming languages, FORTRAN, places an arbitrary restriction on the length of program names. Early versions of FORTRAN introduced this restriction to simplify the task of the compiler writer, and revisions of the language have not removed the restriction. It is not clear why this is so. Our compiler technology is now such that names of any length can easily be handled and longer names do not invalidate any existing programs.

The FORTRAN programmer has no alternative but to choose abbreviations for program names. There are a number of ways of going about this:

1. If the meaningful name is made up of several words such as 'ConvertCentigradeToFahrenheit', the programmer may choose a name made up of the initial letters of each word — CCTF.

2. He may choose to abstract important information from the name and abbreviate that. The name 'ConvertCentigradeToFahrenheit' may become CENFAH.

3. If a meaningful name consists of a single word such as 'velocity', the best abbreviation convention is to drop vowels from the right in the name so that 'velocity' becomes VELCTY.

Whatever abbreviation technique is chosen, it is important that it is applied consistently. For example, if a program abbreviates 'satellite_velocity' to SATVEL, rocket_velocity should be abbreviated to ROCVEL rather than RCTVEL or ROCKV.

In addition, the abbreviation convention should be described in a program comment, and an index relating abbreviations to names and their function should be included. Essentially, this index should provide that type and range information which may be explicitly specified in Pascal or Ada.

For example:

```
C   SATVEL    satellite velocity, real > 0
C   SATMSS    satellite mass, constant = 250 kg
C   SATACC    satellite acceleration, real
    ........
```

A mechanism which is sometimes used to provide meaningful names in a FORTRAN program is to make use of a preprocessor which takes as input a version of the program in 'extended FORTRAN' which has no practical limit on name lengths. The preprocessor's output is a standard FORTRAN program ready for input to a FORTRAN compiler. This preprocessor may be either a general-purpose macro processing system or one of the many preprocessors implementing structured versions of FORTRAN such as RATFOR (Kernighan and Plauger, 1976).

5.2.2 Program control constructs

Control constructs in a program should be used so that flow of control is strictly top-down. As loops can be considered as single compound statements, execution should commence with the first program statement, each statement should be executed in turn, and execution should terminate with the last statement. Program units, loops and decision statements should have a single point of entry and a single exit.

Strictly, this precludes the use of conditional and unconditional **goto** statements in languages like Pascal which offer adequate decision and loop constructs. The use of gotos in FORTRAN and machine code should be restricted to simulating the action of higher-level constructs such as **if** statements, **case** statements and **while** statements.

However, as long as the rule stating that each compound construct should have a single entry and exit point is observed, **goto** statements may be used to escape from within a compound construct in the event of some exceptional condition occurring. If a **goto** is used in this way, the programmer must ensure that it transfers control to the statement immediately after the compound construct and never elsewhere. If this discipline is observed, the readability of a program is not compromised and it may even be improved by the use of a **goto** statement. Knuth (1974) presents a number of examples where the use of a **goto** is justified.

A circumstance where the use of a **goto** may be justified is to exit from a procedure in the event of some exception. If the exception is such that it is pointless to continue execution, an immediate return can be made by jumping out of the procedure. **Goto** statements should only ever be used for the handling of exceptional situations which arise during program execution. They should be used to skip over code and never to repeat code sections. This means that gotos should only transfer control forward in a program. If higher level constructs are available, there are no circumstances when backward transfers of control using gotos are justified.

Another control construct whose misuse can lead to programs which are difficult to understand is the **if-then-else** two-armed conditional statement. If such statements are deeply nested, it can become very difficult to follow the flow of control and to determine which 'else' is associated with which 'if'. Unfortunately, the nature of the **case** statement in most languages is such that it cannot be used to code situations where one of a number of conditions may occur and when these conditions involve objects of different

types. To encode this situation involves the use of multiple conditional
statements:

```
if C1 then
    S1
else
    if C2 then
        S2
    else
        if C3 then
            S3
        else
            if C4 then
                S4
            else
                . . . . . . . .
```

The nesting of conditionals can become so deep that, even with disciplined
paragraphing, it is difficult to determine under what circumstances a statement is executed. Some languages, such as Ada, have introduced explicit **if**-
statement delimiters which help to improve readability. However, if a
language like Pascal must be used, use of the alternatives below can make
programs easier to read.

One way of avoiding deeply nested **if-then-else** statements is to use
multiple conditions:

```
if C1 then S1
if C2 then S2
if C3 then S3
if C4 then S4
```

Although this introduces inefficiency because conditions are tested even
when they must be false, the program is shorter and more readable. A more
serious drawback, however, to this form of implementation is that the
conditions must be mutually exclusive, otherwise more than one condition
might be true. For example, the following conditions could not be directly
implemented in this way:

```
if C1 and C2 then
    S1
else
    if C2 or C3 then
        S2
    else
        . . . . . . . .
```

In this example, if both C1 and C2 are true, S1 is executed and the
remainder of the statement skipped. However, if this was implemented

using single-armed conditionals as shown above, both *S1* and *S2* would be executed — clearly not what was intended by the programmer.

This situation is one where a **goto** statement can be used to improve program readability. Using single-armed conditionals and **goto** statements, a guarded conditional statement like that described in the following chapter can be simulated:

> **if** *C1* **and** *C2* **then** { *S1*; **goto** *out* }
> **if** *C2* **or** *C3* **then** { *S2*; **goto** *out* }
> **if** *C4* **then** { *S3*; **goto** *out* }
>
>   . . . .
> *out* :

Any loop construct in a program can be simulated using a while or repeat loop but where a loop is to be executed a known number of times, a **for** loop should be used. **for** loops should be used only in situations where no program exceptions should occur — escape should never be made from inside a **for** loop.

If this convention is observed, the reader of the program can identify the exact circumstances under which a loop will terminate, simply by reading the first statement in that loop. Of course, termination can be compromised in languages such as ALGOL60 or FORTRAN if the user alters the loop parameters. It is very poor programming practice to make assignments to the **for** loop variable, the increment or the final terminating value within the loop.

If a language without high-level control constructs is used, the program should be designed as if these constructs were available. It is relatively straightforward to simulate the action of any control constructs using **if** statements and **goto** statements. The FORTRAN programmer should translate the higher-level control constructs in his design to this form. For example, consider the following **while** loop:

> **while** $x < y$ **do**
> **begin**
>   *someprocess* (x);
> $x := x + 1$
> **end**;

Although FORTRAN has no equivalent looping construct, the **while** construct may be simulated using I F and GOTO statements.

```
10 IF X.GE.Y GOTO 20
   CALL SPRCSS.(X)
   X = X + 1
   GOTO 10
20 ....
```

So-called 'facilities' of FORTRAN such as arithmetic I F statements, assigned GOTOs, alternative subroutine entry and return points are inherently dangerous constructs and should be avoided.

5.2.3 Program layout

The majority of programming languages are free format languages where the meaning of a program is not affected by how it is laid out on a page. Exceptions to this are FORTRAN and some assembly languages where the position of a field in an input record can affect its meaning. This is a hangover from the days when punched cards were almost universally used for preparing programs.

Layout affects the readability of a program. The liberal use of blank lines, reserved word highlighting and consistent paragraphing makes the program appear more elegant and easier to read. They act as separators which distinguish one part of the program from another. The example procedure below illustrates how the readability of identical procedures is affected by the way the text is laid out.

```
procedure CountElementOccurrences(var inarray : intarray;
arraysize : integer);
{Given a sorted array of integers, this procedure prints each
distinct integer and the number of occurrences of that integer}
var i,count : integer; begin
count := 1; for i := 1 to arraysize−1 do
begin if inarray[i] = inarray[i+1] then count := count+1 else
begin write(inarray[i], count); count := 1;
end; write(inarray[arraysize],count);
end;
```

The same procedure laid out using consistent indentation and blank lines is much more readable.

```
procedure CountElementOccurrences(var inarray : intarray;
                              arraysize : integer);
{ Given a sorted array of integers, this procedure prints each distinct
integer and the number of occurrences of that integer }

    var i,count : integer;

begin
    count := 1;
    for i := 1 to arraysize−1 do
        if inarray[i] = inarray[i+1] then
            count := count + 1
        else
        begin
            write(inarray[i],count);
            count := 1
        end;
    write (inarray[arraysize],count)
end;
```

Distinct parts of the program such as the header comment, variable declarations and the procedure body can be clearly identified by separating them from each other with blank lines. Statements executed in the same loop and in each arm of a conditional statement are picked out by consistent indentation.

It is very difficult to establish hard and fast rules for program layout which cope successfully with each and every program. There are inevitably circumstances such as very long or very short statements where layout rules break down and elegant layout relies on the judgement of the programmer. For this reason, prettyprinters, programs which automatically layout listings, are sometimes unsuccessful.

However, some general guidelines can be established which are adequate for laying out the majority of Pascal programs. There is no single set of guidelines which are accepted as the 'best'. The conventions used by the author are set out below but it must be emphasized that any consistent set of layout conventions which separates distinct parts of the program will improve readability.

In the guidelines below, T stands for some standard tab indent and n the block level of a procedure. In experiments to measure the effectiveness of indentation as an aid to program understanding, Miara *et al.* (1983) discovered that the value of T should be between 2 and 4 to be most effective. Smaller and larger values were found to be detrimental to the understandability of the program.

1. Label, constant, type, and variable declarations made at the outermost block level (level 0) should start in column 1 of a line. Declarations made at subsequent block levels should start at column $T*n$.

2. In procedure declarations, the procedure header should start at column $T*n$ and the procedure body, that is, those statements between 'begin' and 'end' should start at column $T*(n+1)$. The 'begin' and 'end' bracketing the procedure body should, however, be indented at column $T*n$.

3. Local declarations should be separated from the procedure header by at least one blank line.

4. If the procedure has a header comment, it should appear before the local declarations and be separated from both the procedure header and the local declarations by at least one blank line.

5. The statement within a loop whose initial statement (**for, while, repeat**) is indented by N blanks should be indented by $N+T$ blanks. If this statement is a compound statement, however, the 'begin' and 'end' brackets of that statement should be on a line by themselves and should be indented by N spaces. Statements within these brackets should be indented by $N+T$ spaces.

6. Where a conditional statement is indented by N spaces, the statement in each arm of the conditional should be indented by $N+T$

spaces. If the statement is a compound statement, the rule for compound statements given above should be applied. If the conditional statement is a two-armed conditional, the reserved word 'else' should be indented by N spaces and should be on a line by itself.

7. When records are declared, the reserved words 'record' and 'end' should occur on lines by themselves as should the declaration of each field of the record. The indentation of the field name declarations should be consistent and such that the field declaration with the greatest number of characters can fit on a single line.

8. Wherever possible, each assignment or input/output statement should appear on a line by itself.

These rules do not describe how each and every Pascal construct is to be laid out. Constructs which are not covered are those for which it is difficult to establish strict rules and the layout of these depends on the actual program text. The important principle which must be adhered to in program layout is consistency — once a set of conventions has been established, the same conventions should be used throughout the same program.

5.3 Software tools

Historically, the most significant productivity increases in a manufacturing or building process have come about when human skills are augmented by automated tools. For example, one man and a bulldozer can probably shift more earth in a day than 50 men working with hand tools. The practice of programming is certainly akin to manufacturing and by supporting programmers with automated tools dramatic improvements in programmer productivity can be achieved.

Before the widespread introduction of timesharing computer systems, the majority of program development was carried out off-line. Programs were prepared and debugged without the aid of the computer system. Preparing a program involved punching it onto cardboard cards, submitting the cards to a batch processing system and then retrieving the cards along with a listing of the results of executing or compiling the program. Program modifications were made by repunching those cards in the deck which contained the program statements to be modified.

Even in this situation, some programming tools were available. Apart from compilers, assemblers and other language processors, most systems provided a link editor which allowed parts of the program to be independently compiled then linked together to form an executable program. The link editing process also allowed the creation and maintenance of subroutine libraries.

Subroutine libraries are probably the earliest instance of organized program sharing. If a generally useful subroutine is prepared by one individual, that routine can be entered in a public library of subroutines and any other user may refer to that subroutine in his or her program. It is the task of the link editor to search the appropriate subroutine libraries, abstract the code of the called routine and link that routine with the calling program.

As well as these tools, a variety of other software to assist the process of program development has now been developed. The use of timesharing systems allows interactive editors and debugging tools to be used and large amounts of backing store means that library programs to keep track of code and documentation can be developed.

For convenience, an arbitrary distinction has been made between software tools to support the programming process and software tools to support testing and debugging. Although some of these tools are described in this chapter and some in Chapter 7, in practice the tools are used in tandem to support both program development and debugging. In this section, the emphasis is on development tools and tools to assist program preparation, translation, analysis and configuration management are discussed.

5.3.1 Program preparation tools

An important software tool in an on-line programming environment is the editor. The function of the editor is to enable the user to create and modify files kept on-line in the system. A variety of different types of editor have been implemented and these can be broadly classified as follows:

1. *Line editors.* These allow the user to replace one line of his program by some other line. They rely on the user determining the number of the line to be changed. Editors in a BASIC programming environment, as provided on many microcomputers, are inevitably line editors, although they may have some context editing features.

2. *Screen editors.* The text to be modified is displayed on the screen of the user's terminal and those parts to be changed are modified by overtyping. Facilities also exist to delete and insert characters.

3. *Context editors.* The editor obeys a sequence of commands which relate to the text to be modified. These commands allow parts of the text to be related by their context and often provide facilities for the repetition of commands.

Many editors include features of all the above types and each type of editor is useful in particular environments. For program development the most generally useful editor is a screen editor, such as vi available under Unix, which includes line editing and context editing features.

A context editor should include commands which allow the user to locate text by its position in the file, by its position relative to the text on which the user is currently working, and by its context. It should be possible to add, delete and replace complete lines and change text within a line. There should also be a mechanism for the repetitive execution of command sequences so that the same modification may be made at a number of places in the file.

Although some editors such as Unix's vi have some facilities which are designed to support program preparation, most editors are general-purpose text preparation systems. This naturally means that it is possible for the user to prepare syntactically incorrect programs with these editors.

To circumvent this problem, some work has been done in developing language-oriented editors designed to prepare and modify programs in a specific programming language. An example of such a system is the Cornell Program Synthesiser, described by Teitelbaum and Reps (1981) which is intended to help beginners prepare programs written in a subset of PL/1 called PL/C. Such a system must include a PL/C syntax analyser as well as editing features. Rather than manipulate unstructured text, the system actually manipulates a tree structure representing the program. In fact, the Cornell system is more than just a syntax-directed editor but is a complete language-oriented environment with integrated editing, translation and program execution facilities.

Such systems are very valuable for beginners wrestling with the idiosyncrasies of our current programming languages. At the moment, however, they do have limitations — handling context-sensitive language constructs is very difficult, particularly in large programs where the whole program is not visible on the screen. More fundamentally, perhaps, these systems do not recognize the fact that many experienced programmers work by laying out an (incorrect) program skeleton then filling in that skeleton. They force a sequential mode of working on the user. It thus remains to be seen if such syntax-directed systems are of value for large-scale software development.

5.3.2 Program translation tools

The most important tool available to the programmer is the language processing system used to convert his or her program to machine code. The provision of a helpful compilation system can reduce the costs of program development by making program errors easier to find and by producing program listings which include information about program structure as seen by the compiler. Obviously, the error diagnostic facilities of a compiler are partially dependent on the language being compiled. A Pascal compiler, for example, can detect many more errors than a FORTRAN compiler. Not only are the rules which govern the validity of a program more strict for Pascal than for FORTRAN, the Pascal programmer must also supply more information to the compiler about the objects to be manipulated by the program. This information allows the compiler to detect forbidden operations on these objects.

As well as providing information to the programmer, a compilation system must also generate efficient machine code. This latter task involves a good deal of program analysis and can be very time consuming. This has the consequence that it is generally uneconomic to carry out this operation for anything apart from completely developed programs. A programming environment, therefore, might contain two compatible compilers for each language — a development compiler and an optimizing compiler.

Development compilers should be written to compile code as quickly as possible and to provide the maximum amount of diagnostic information to the programmer. Optimizing compilers, on the other hand, should be tailored to generate efficient machine code without considering compilation speed and diagnostic facilities. Programs are developed using the development system and, when complete, the optimizing system is used to produce the final version of the program for production use.

Within the confines of the language being processed, development compilers should provide as much information as possible about the program being compiled. For instance:

1. The compiler listing of the program should associate a line number with each program line.

2. When a program syntax or semantic error is discovered, the compiler should indicate where it found the error and what the error appears to be. It may also be appropriate to indicate the possible cause of the error.

    The design of meaningful error messages is not a simple task as the meaningfullness or otherwise of an error message depends on the knowledge and experience of the reader of that message. In environments where the users of the system are professional programmers, it may be acceptable to couch error messages in programming language jargon. In other environments, such as engineering laboratories, where the programmers are those involved in the application itself, the compiler should produce error messages in plain language which can easily be understood, As the users of a system can rarely be classified exactly, it is a good general rule that error messages should be couched in plain language and should include a reference to a more precise error specification. This is discussed further in Chapter 9.

3. The compiler should include directives which allow the programmer some control over the program listing generated by the compiler. These directives should allow the suppression of parts of the listing, control over the pagination of the listing, and the enhancement of program keywords by bold printing or underlining.

4. When a program in a block-structured language is compiled, the compiler should indicate the lexical level at the beginning and the end of each block. This facility allows misplaced 'begin'/'end' brackets to be easily identified.

5. The compiler should separate source text provided by the user from information provided by the compiler. This can be accomplished by delimiting the input source using special characters such as | and prefacing compiler messages by some string of punctuation characters such as ****.

6. The compiler should identify where each procedure in a program

starts and finishes. When a program listing is searched for a particular procedure, the location of that procedure is often not immediately obvious because the name of the procedure is not distinguished from the remainder of the source text. When compiling a procedure heading, the procedure name should be abstracted and, as well as listing the procedure heading normally, the procedure name should be reprinted so that it stands out from the rest of the program text. This can be accomplished in a number of ways such as that used by the XPL compiler (McKeeman *et al.*, 1970). In XPL, the procedure name is abstracted and reprinted on the right-hand margin of the listing for each statement in that procedure.

If an environment supports both development and optimizing compilers, there is no need for the optimizing compiler to provide comprehensive diagnostic facilities for the user. Rather, given that code optimization is a time-consuming business, it may allow him or her to specify the degree of optimization to be carried out by the compiler or whether time or space considerations are most important. The Ada language has a specific construct called a pragma which, amongst other things, provides facilities for the user to control compiler optimization.

5.3.3 Program analysis tools

An important tool which may be incorporated with the compiling system is a program cross-referencer. Such a system indicates the names used in the program, the types of the named objects, the line in the program where each name is declared, and the line numbers where a reference is made to that object. More sophisticated cross-referencers can also provide, for each procedure in the program, a list of the procedure parameters and their types, the procedure local variables and the global variables referenced in the procedure.

This latter facility is particularly useful to the programmer who must modify the value of some global variable. By examining the cross-reference listing, either manually or with an automatic tool, those procedures which reference that variable can be identified and checked to ensure that global variable modification will not adversely affect their actions.

In addition to cross-reference systems, other source code analysis tools include layout programs (prettyprinters) which set out programs in some standard way, and structured listing systems which allow the user to list parts of his program by referring to the code itself rather than source line numbers. For example, to list a procedure in a Pascal program, the user might issue the command:

plist someproc

The effect of this would be to list the procedure *someproc* on the user's terminal, and he need have no knowledge where it is actually located within the program.

Like cross-referencing systems, these tools are language-oriented and must include a language syntax analyser. This has led to suggestions that the process of analysis normally carried out by the compiler should be factored out. Program analysis would be distinct from compiling and the analyser output would be processable by translation tools, editors, analysis tools, etc.

5.3.4 Configuration management tools

A large software project may involve many programmers, hundreds of distinct modules and thousands of lines of code. This code may be distributed over many files and libraries and exist as both source code and object code. A number of distinct versions of a system, tailored to different environments, may be produced at different times. Major problems which exist with any large software system are keeping track of the development and maintenance of program modules, determining the interdependence of modules, and ensuring that the common code in different versions of a system is consistent.

This is part of the task of configuration management. Configuration management is sometimes seen as a management activity and it encompasses all those practices and standards required to create and maintain multiple versions of software systems. However, the tools described here are used by programmers rather than managers and it thus seems most apt to describe them in this chapter. Configuration management is discussed further in Chapter 11.

If programs are developed under a batch processing system, the problems of version control may be handled by a program librarian. The notion of program librarians was first publicized by IBM in a description of a project management technique known as Chief Programmer Teams (Baker, 1972). The librarian removes much of the administrative burden from programmers, allowing them to get on with constructing the system.

The job of a program librarian is to maintain the information pertaining to a project, and all programmers working on a project must funnel their work through the program librarian. The program librarian has no programming responsibilities although he may be involved in file editing. Because all work must be submitted through the librarian, he can ensure that system updates are carried out in such a way that consistency is maintained. Furthermore, the librarian can keep detailed records of which files relate to which system modules and how different system versions can be generated. The program librarian may use specially developed library maintenance programs for this task.

The use of a program librarian is beneficial in a batch environment because it ensures that there is only a single person interface between the programming team and the computer. This is perfectly acceptable when program development is an off-line process but, if an interactive system is used, the notion of funnelling work through a single individual is not tenable. In such circumstances, there is a need for an automated system to carry out system housekeeping — maintaining information about files, system modules, updates and different versions of the system.

A number of systems have been developed to automate and extend the task of the program librarian. These include MAKE (Feldman, 1979), SCCS (Rochkind, 1975) and CADES (McGuffin *et al.*, 1979). These systems may be either stand-alone systems such as CADES or may operate in conjunction — MAKE and SCCS are both available under the Unix operating system. Many other configuration management systems exist but these have not been documented in widely available publications.

To illustrate code control systems, MAKE and SCCS will be used as examples of software tools for controlling code modifications and maintenance. These code control systems are complementary — SCCS keeps track of system modifications and different system versions, whereas MAKE ensures the consistency of source code and its corresponding object code.

SCCS (Source Code Control System) was originally developed for IBM 370 hardware but is now provided as part of the Unix system. The aim of SCCS is to allow different versions of the system to be maintained without unnecessary code duplication. It controls system updates by ensuring that no part of the system can be updated by more than one programmer at any one time. It also records when updates were made, what source lines were changed and who was responsible for the change.

SCCS is principally a system for storing and recording changes to a system module. Each time a module is changed, that change is recorded and stored in what is termed a delta. Subsequent changes are also recorded as deltas. To produce the latest version of a system, SCCS applies the deltas in turn to the original module until all deltas have been processed. Conceptually, a chain of deltas is involved as shown in Fig. 5.3.

The user of SCCS can specify that the system should be generated up to any point in this chain, allowing systems at different stages of development to be produced.

An extension of this feature is the ability to freeze a system at any point in the chain. When a module is added to SCCS originally, it is deemed to be release 1.0. Subsequent deltas create 1.1, 1.2, 1.3, etc. At some stage, the programmer may wish to freeze his system, for testing say, although further system development — the addition of more deltas — may be continuing in parallel. Freezing a system simply involves specifying that new deltas constitute a new release of the system (Fig. 5.4.).

In order to obtain release 1 of the system, the SCCS user requests that release and only those deltas pertaining to release 1 are applied. Furthermore, release 1 can be modified after development of release 2 is in progress by adding new level 1 deltas. In the above example, D1.4 could be inserted between D1.3 and D2.1.

As deltas are date stamped and owner stamped, the user of SCCS can specify that a system version at any particular date should be created and can also generate management reports on system development.

MAKE is a complementary code control system which maintains the correspondence between source code and object code versions of a system.

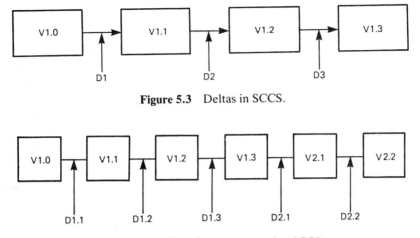

Figure 5.3 Deltas in SCCS.

Figure 5.4 Freezing a system using SCCS.

Typically, a system is made up of code abstracted from a number of files. In some cases, dependencies exist between those files; that is, changing one file also necessitates changing some other file or group of files. MAKE provides a mechanism for specifying those dependencies. Using built-in information and user-specified commands, MAKE can cause the object code of a system to be recreated when a change is made to part of the system source code.

Using MAKE, the programmer must initially state file dependencies. For example, if the object code file x.o depends on the source code files x.c and d.c, this can be stated. If d.c is changed, this change can be detected by MAKE and x.o recreated by recompiling x.c and d.c. There is no need for the user to recompile files after an editing session — MAKE works out necessary recompilations and initiates them automatically.

As an example of how MAKE can be used, consider a situation where a program called comp is created out of object modules scan.o, syn.o, sem.o, and cgen.o. For each object module, there exists a source code module called scan.c, syn.c, sem.c, and cgen.c. A file of declarations called defs.c is shared by scan.c, syn.c, and sem.c. Modifications can be made to any of scan.c, syn.c and sem.c without requiring any other files to be recompiled but a modification to defs.c requires that scan.c, syn.c, and sem.c be recompiled. This is illustrated in Fig. 5.5, where an arrow implies a dependency.

A file stating these dependencies which can be processed by MAKE might be created as follows:

```
comp : scan.o syn.o sem.o cgen.o
      cc scan.o syn.o sem.o cgen.o -o comp
scan.o syn.o sem.o : defs
```

This states that comp is dependent (: means dependence) on scan.o, syn.o, sem.o and cgen.o. The modules scan.o, syn.o and sem.o are stated to be dependent on defs.

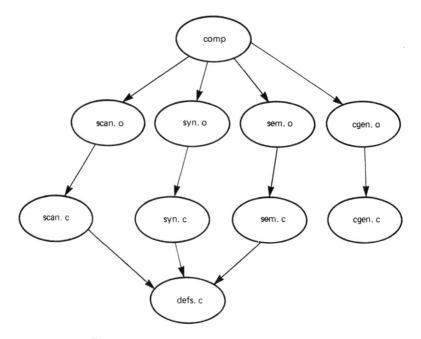

Figure 5.5   Component dependency graph.

Associated with the dependency of comp is a command sequence stating how comp may be created. Consider a situation where the files defs.c and cgen.c are modified. When MAKE is applied to the dependency information, it examines defs.c and notes that its modification time is later than the time scan.o, syn.o and sem.o were created. It therefore causes the files scan.c, syn.c and sem.c to be recompiled to create new versions of the object files.

The file comp is now examined and its creation date is seen to precede the creation dates of the object files on which it depends. Therefore, MAKE recreates comp. In this case, there is no need to recompile scan.c, syn.c or sem.c since that compilation step has just been carried out. However, MAKE notes that the file cgen.c has been modified so that it causes that file to be recompiled and the entire system relinked.

Because of its built-in assumptions regarding name conventions, such as the assumption that all files ending in .o have .c equivalents, MAKE is strictly Unix-specific. However, it illustrates a general class of software tool designed for code control.

Another problem which might be handled by configuration management systems is change control. This is discussed in Chapter 11 but, in essence, if a software component is shared, it is unacceptable for that component to be changed without the consent of all users. A configuration management system may provide some automated support for change control maintaining records of who uses a component, whose permissions must be granted before the component may be changed, who is the original component owner, etc.

5.4 Programming environments

So far, software tools have been discussed in isolation and it has been suggested that these tools can aid the practice of programming. An environment designed for program development should provide the tools already discussed and should be specifically geared for the production of programs.

There are a number of different classes of programming environment such as language-oriented environments intended to support programming in one particular programming language and teaching environments which are intended to help beginners learn to program. A survey by Howden (1982) describes these in broad terms. The type of environment which is of most interest to us here is one intended to support the development of large software systems. Such environments are sometimes called 'software engineering environments'.

Most existing programming environments support the later stages of the software development process and do not provide tools to support requirements specification and software design. However, a number of research projects are underway (Willis, 1981; Standish, 1981; Stucki and Walker, 1981) which aim to develop a software engineering environment. This would provide a consistent environment and a set of tools to support all stages of the software life cycle from requirements definition to maintenance and software management.

Although a programming environment may be provided as a sub-system of some general-purpose system, the requirements of a system whose main task is the execution of programs need not coincide with the requirements of a system whose function is to support program development. For example, a mainframe may support a transaction processing system which requires a guaranteed amount of dedicated processor time. Developing programs on such a system can be very frustrating, as the programming process must give precedence to the transaction processing system.

In some cases, it may even be impossible to develop software for a computer using the facilities of that computer. This is often the case when software is developed for microprocessor systems which have relatively small memories and little support software. For these reasons, it is often better to support a programming environment on a special development machine which is distinct from the target machine on which the program will eventually execute.

As well as the software tools to support programming discussed above, a programming environment might provide the following facilities:

1. Communications software linking the development computer to the computer on which the software is to execute (the target machine).

2. Target machine simulators — these are particularly valuable when microprocessor software is being developed.

3. Testing and debugging tools — these might include test drivers, dynamic and static program analysers and test output analysis programs. These tools are discussed in Chapter 7.

4. Text processing tools — these programs allow documentation to be developed on the same machine as the program. This simplified the task of producing and updating documentation as the program is developed. Documentation tools are discussed in Chapter 8.

5. Requirements specification and analysis tools as discussed in Chapter 2.

6. A computer aided design system to support some of the more clerical aspects of software design, such as the draughting of design diagrams. Such a tool is included in the AIDES (Willis, 1981) system.

7. Project management tools — these software tools allow estimates of the time required for a project and the cost of that project to be made. Furthermore, they may provide facilities for generating management reports on the status of a project at any time.

The best known programming environment is probably the Unix Programmers Workbench (Unix/PWB) System (Ivie, 1977; Dolotta *et al.*, 1978). This system is designed to support the development of software for IBM, UNIVAC, XDS and DIGITAL computers. The system developers point out that, as well as providing an environment conducive to program development, the use of the Unix/PWB system means that the same system interface is presented to the programmer irrespective of which machine is actually being used for program execution. The programmer need not learn the details of several different systems. He is also preserved from disruptions caused by changes in the target hardware.

The Unix/PWB system is a file-oriented programming environment where the user may interconnect different tools, either explicitly via shared files or by using Unix pipes. This file-oriented approach has the disadvantage that the user must be aware of the specific I/O conventions of co-operating tools and, if these do not happen to match, it is not easy to use these tools in tandem.

To obviate this problem, current thinking now suggests that programming environments should be built around a database system. All tools should output information to and collect information from this database, which thus provides a standard tool interface. Furthermore, the use of a database system also opens up the possibility of building powerful information retrieval tools which can collate and present component information generated at different stages in the life cycle.

The Stoneman proposals for an Ada programming environment (APSE) envisage that the APSE should be portable and available on a variety of different machines. To achieve this degree of portability, three levels of program support are required — a kernel environment (KAPSE), a minimal environment (MAPSE) and the full Ada program support environment (APSE). The proposed organization of the APSE is shown in Fig. 5.6.

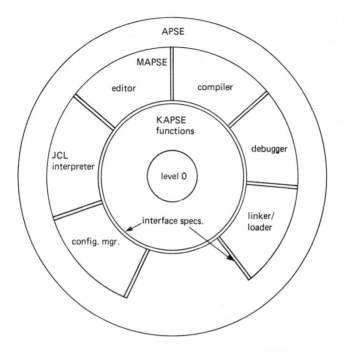

Figure 5.6 The organization of the APSE.

The innermost level of the APSE is the Kernel-APSE, which provides the interface between Ada programs and the underlying operating system. Thus the KAPSE must include an Ada run-time support system, database primitives and the interface to peripheral devices such as terminals. In principle, the KAPSE should insulate the remainder of the APSE from the underlying machine. Therefore, to transfer the APSE from machine to machine should simply require a re-implementation of the KAPSE system.

The next level in the APSE is the so-called Minimal-APSE. This is built on top of the KAPSE and should provide facilities for the development of Ada programs. Obviously the MAPSE must include an Ada compiler, an editor and a loader but other tools such as static and dynamic program analysers, command interpreters and configuration management systems are also to be provided at this level.

The top-level APSE is, at the time of writing, fairly nebulously defined and no examples of an APSE have been developed. As described in the requirements document, the APSE might provide tools to support all phases of the software life cycle and tools to support particular development methodologies. The form which these tools should take is currently an important software engineering research problem. As well as providing a comprehensive toolkit to support the development of Ada programs, an APSE must also provide database facilities for tools to communicate and to allow relationships between objects to be recorded and maintained. The information in the database may be used to produce management reports detailing the current state of a project, project development cost, etc. A more detailed description of the APSE is provided in McDermid and Ripkin (1984).

Because of the advantages offered by the use of a comprehensive programming environment, it is inevitable that more and more software engineering projects will use such a system. Just as there is no ideal programming language, there is no ideal programming environment, and different projects will make use of different environments. The identification, development and integration of software tools for use in such environments is still a major research problem.

5.5 Program portability

The rate of change of computer hardware technology is such that computing machinery becomes obsolete long before the programs which execute on these machines. It is therefore very important that programs should be written in such a manner that they may be implemented under more than one computer/operating system configuration. This is doubly important if a programming system is widely marketed as a product — the more machines on which a system is implemented, the greater the potential market for it.

Techniques for achieving program portability have been widely documented (Brown, 1977; Tanenbaum et al., 1978; Wallis, 1982). They include emulating one machine on another using microcode, compiling a program into some abstract machine language then implementing that abstract machine on a variety of computers, and using preprocessors to translate from one dialect of a programming language to another.

A full discussion of program portability requires a book to itself. Therefore, it is not the intention here to cover general techniques of moving programs from one machine to another. Rather, programming practices which reduce and isolate the amount of machine and operating system dependent code in a program are described below.

An important aspect of portability which is covered in Chapter 8 is the portability of documentation. A programming system without documentation is of little use and it is important that documentation is ported along with the program.

A characteristic of a portable program is that it is self-contained. The program should not rely on the existence of external agencies to supply required functions. In practice, complete self-containment is almost impossible to achieve and the programmer intending to produce a portable program must compromise by isolating necessary references to the external environment. When that external environment is changed, those dependent parts of the program can be identified and modified.

Throughout this section, it will be assumed that a high-level language is used for programming and that a compiler for that language is available for each machine on which the program is to be implemented. It is also assumed that some standard version of the high-level language is used rather than a dialect unique to a particular installation. The work involved in implementing a program on more than a single system is significantly increased if non-standard language 'extensions' are used in the initial coding of the program. Inevitably, compiler writers have different ideas concerning which extensions should be made to a language, and different compilers rarely include exactly the same additions.

Even when a standard, widely implemented, high-level language is used for programming, it is virtually impossible to construct a program of any size without some machine dependencies. These dependencies arise because features of the machine and its operating system are reflected directly in the language implementation. For example, the precision of numbers is dependent on the machine word size, and the access to backing store files is dependent on the primitives provided by the operating system. Even the character set available on different machines may not be identical, with the result that programs written using one character set must be edited to reflect the alternative character set.

Portability problems which arise when a standard high-level language is used can be classified under two distinct headings — those problems caused by language features influenced by the machine architecture and those caused by operating system dependencies.

5.5.1 Machine architecture dependencies

The principal machine architecture dependencies which arise in programs are due to the fact that, whatever high-level language is used, the language must rely on the conventions of information representation adopted by the host machine. Different machines have different word lengths, different character sets and different techniques for representing integer and real numbers.

The length of a computer word directly affects the range of integers available on that machine, the precision of real numbers and the number of characters which may be packed into a single word. It is extremely difficult to program in such a way that implicit dependencies on machine word lengths are avoided.

For example, say a program is intended to count instances of some occurrence where the maximum number of instances which might arise is 500000. Assume instance counts are to be compared. If this program is implemented on a machine with a 32-bit word size, instance counts can be represented as integers and comparisons made directly. However, if the program is subsequently moved to a 16-bit machine, it will fail because the maximum possible positive integer which can be held in a 16-bit word is 32 767.

Such a situation poses a difficult problem for the programmer. If instance counts are not represented as integers but as real numbers or as character strings, this will inevitably introduce unnecessary overhead in counting and comparisons on the 32-bit machine. The cost of this overhead must be traded off against the cost of the inevitable reprogramming which is necessary if the system is subsequently implemented on a 16-bit machine.

If portability considerations are paramount in such a situation and if a programming language which permits the use of user-defined types is available, an alternative solution to this problem is possible. The user must define a type, say *CountType*, whose range encompasses the possible values of the instance counter. In Pascal on a 32-bit machine this might be defined:

```
type CountType = 0..500000;
```

If the system is subsequently ported to a 16-bit machine, then *CountType* may be redefined:

```
type CountType = array [1..6] of char;
```

Instead of using an integer to hold the counter value, it may be held as an array of digits. Associated with this type, must be the operations permitted on instance counters. These can be programmed in Pascal as functions. On 32-bit machines, these functions simply consist of the appropriate integer operations. On 16-bit machines, on the other hand, the functions would be more complex, and must simulate integer operations on digit strings. For example, consider a Pascal function to compare counters for equality. On a 32-bit machine, this might be written:

```
function Cequals(c1,c2 : CountType) : boolean;
  begin
    Cequals := c1=c2
  end;
```

On a 16-bit machine, where large integers are represented as strings of digits, the function could be written:

```
function Cequals(c1,c2 : CountType) : boolean;
  var i : integer;
      comp : boolean;
  begin
    comp := true; i := 1;
    while comp and (i <= 6) do
    begin
      comp := c1[i] = c2[i];
      i := i + 1
    end;
    Cequals := comp
  end;
```

Irrespective of how the type *CountType* is represented, the user always has exactly the same operations available and transporting the program simply involves changing the type definition and rewriting the functions which operate on that type.

Ideally, the type definition and its related operations should be grouped together into a self-contained unit like an Ada package. This is shown below:

```
package COUNTER is
    type C is private;
    procedure INC (CNT : in out C);
    procedure DEC (CNT : in out C);
private
    C : INTEGER 0..500_000 := 0;
end;
```

Only the type name and related operations need be visible outside the package with all representation details confined to the package. If the program is ported to another system which uses a different counter representation, only the counter package need be changed. None of the uses of counter are affected. In languages such as Pascal, where no module facility is available, the operations on each type should be grouped together and clearly delimited by comments.

Different machine word lengths also mean that the precision of real numbers varies from machine to machine. For example, if a real number is represented using 32-bits, 8-digit precision may be possible, whereas 64-bit representation allows 17 or 18-digit precision. On a 32-bit machine, no distinction could be made between the numbers 10001.3214 and 10001.3210, whereas they would be considered different numbers on a higher-precision machine.

The problem of differing precision has been recognized in Ada and, in defining a numeric type, the user may explicitly state the precision to which values of that type are held. For example, 6-digit precision is specified:

```
type SHORT is digits 6 range 0..SOMEMAX;
```

This specifies that numbers of type short lie in the range 0 to SOMEMAX and should be held to 6-digit precision.

This facility eliminates some of the problems involved in porting software which uses real numbers and, theoretically, implementations of Ada should support the specification of any precision whatsoever. In practice, the specification of precisions which cannot be accommodated in one or two machine words is difficult to implement and will probably involve heavy run-time overhead.

A portability problem related to but distinct from the problems caused by machines having different word lengths is caused by the fact that different machines may represent exactly the same information in different ways. For example, a 16-bit machine which uses two's complement notation to represent negative numbers would represent −1 as 1111111111111111, whereas a machine which uses one's complement notation would represent the same number as 1111111111111110.

In some machines, the most significant bit of a number is the leftmost bit and on others it is the rightmost bit. On 16-bit machines where it is the leftmost bit, the number 2 would be represented as 0000000000000010, whereas if the rightmost bit is significant, 2 is represented 0100000000000000, assuming two's complement representation is used.

These representation considerations do not normally cause problems for the high-level language programmer because the objects which he uses have values which are consistent from one representation to another. If, however, the programmer wishes to generate specific bit patterns and the programming language does not allow the programmer to operate directly on binary objects, the user might simulate these binary objects using integers. The representation of integers on a particular machine must be known if appropriate bit patterns are to be generated.

If the program is moved to another machine which uses a different representation for integers, the bitstrings generated from integers will be incorrect. As a general rule, when bitstrings are generated by using integers, absolute integer values should never be used in the program. Rather, the integers representing the bitstrings should be given names appropriate to their function, with these names defined as constants. For example, if it is required to define a mask which will select the rightmost bit of a number, this might be declared:

const *RIGHTMOST = 1*;

If the program containing this declaration is subsequently moved to a machine where the most significant bit is the rightmost bit, this constant might be redefined:

const *RIGHTMOST = −(MAXINT+1)*;

Again, if packages are available, these declarations can be grouped in a package and their representation concealed from the remainder of the program. Otherwise, declarations of such machine-dependent constants must be grouped together and clearly identified by comments in the program text.

Unfortunately there is no single worldwide standardization of the character sets used in computers. The majority of systems use a character set named ASCII (American Standard Code for Information Interchange) but other representations are also used, principally EBCDIC (Extended Binary Coded Decimal) which is used on IBM and IBM-compatible systems.

Not only do different character sets use different values to represent each character, they also differ in the punctuation characters provided. As a result, programs written using character set A, say, cannot be directly translated to another character set B. The programs in character set A must first be edited to replace characters available in A but not in B by some equivalent. For example, in the original definition of Pascal, it was specified that text enclosed in braces { } is treated as a comment. Many implementations of Pascal execute on machines which do not provide braces so, in these implementations, comments are enclosed within the compound symbols (* and *).

The editing procedure required to resolve character set differences is tedious but does not cause serious portability problems. The transformation is clearly defined and easy to implement if a reasonable context editor is available. Portability problems are caused by character representations when the system depends on a character having a particular value. For example, in ASCII, the digits 0−9 have values 60−69 and, to obtain the integer value of a digit, 60 is subtracted from the character value. In Pascal:

$digitvalue := ord(digit) - 60$;

If this code were transported to machine using the EBCDIC character set, it would be legal but would deliver an incorrect result. In EBCDIC, digits are represented by the values 240−249, so the above statement would consider the character '2' to have an integer value of 182.

Assumptions about the values used to represent characters should never be built into a program. If the above statement were written:

$digitvalue := ord(digit) - ord('0')$;

no portability problems arise. Not only is the statement character set independent, it is also a clearer description of the operation being implemented.

A further difficulty which arises because of different character sets results from the fact that different machines use different collating sequences for the letters of the alphabet. In ASCII, the letters A to Z are assigned ascending values in consecutive sequence whereas in EBCDIC, A to Z do not have consecutive values. A program statement may test a value to see if it represents a letter of the alphabet by checking that it lies between the value representing A and the value representing Z. For example:

if$(someval >= ord('A'))$ **and** $(someval <= ord('Z'))$ **then** ...

On EBCDIC machines, this is not guaranteed to work because the sequence of values between A and Z includes other characters. If the programmer is faced with such a situation and knows that his program may be implemented on machines with differing character sets, the only solution is to isolate such machine dependencies in clearly identified procedures. The above statement might be written:

if *letter(someval)* **then**...

The procedure letter must be rewritten when the program is transferred to a machine with an incompatible character set.

5.5.2 Operating system dependencies

One of the reasons for using high-level programming languages is that the languages conceal low-level machine details from the programmer. Inevitably, this involves the use of machine operating system facilities. As there is no general consensus on what operating facilities are necessary, there is little or no operating system standardization. Each implementation of a particular language reflects the facilities of the operating system under which that language executes.

In this section, those features of a high-level language program which are dependent on operating system facilities are discussed. The major problem areas are libraries, files, input-output and job control.

A well known and widely used operating system facility is the provision of subroutines which are available to all users for inclusion in their programs.

Subroutine libraries fall into 2 classes:

1. Standardized libraries of routines associated with a particular application. An example of such routines are the NAG library routines for numerical applications. These routines have a standard interface and exactly the same routines are available to all installations which subscribe to the library.

2. Installation libraries which consist of routines submitted by users at a particular installation. These routines rarely have a standard interface, nor are they written in such a way that they may easily be ported from one installation to another.

The re-use of existing software should be encouraged whenever possible as it reduces the amount of code which must be written, tested and documented. However, the use of subroutine libraries reduces the self-containedness of a program and hence may increase the difficulty of transferring that program from one installation to another.

If use is made of standard subroutine libraries such as the NAG library, this will not cause any portability problems if the program is moved to another installation where the library is available. On the other hand, if the library is not available, transportation of the program is likely to be almost impossible.

If use is made of local installation libraries, transporting the program either involves transporting the library with the program or supplementing the target-system library to make it compatible with the host library. The user must trade off the productivity advantages of using libraries against the dependence on the external environment which this entails.

One of the principal functions of an operating system is to provide a file system — primitive operations which allow the user to name, create, access, delete, protect and share files. There are no standards governing how these operations should be provided, with the consequence that each operating system provides them in different ways.

As high-level language systems must provide file facilities, they interface with the file system. Normally, the file system operations provided in the high-level language are synonymous with the operating system primitives. Therefore, the least portable parts of a program are often those operations which involve access to files.

There are a number of different problems which can arise because of file system incompatibilities:

1. The convention for naming files may differ from system to system. Some systems restrict the number of characters in a file name, other systems impose restrictions on exactly which characters can make up a file name, and yet others impose no restrictions whatsoever.

2. The file system structure may differ from system to system. Some file systems are hierarchically structured; the user may create his own directories and sub-directories. Other systems are restricted to a two-level structure where all files belonging to a particular user must reside in the same directory.

3. Different systems utilize different schemes for protecting files. Some systems involve passwords, other systems use explicit lists of who may access what, and yet others grant permissions according to the attributes of the user.

4. Some systems attempt to classify files as data files, program files, binary files, etc. Other systems consider all files to be files of characters.

5. Most systems restrict the user to a maximum number of files which may be in use at any one time. If this number is different on the host machine from that on the target machine, there are problems in porting programs which have many files open at the same time.

6. There are a number of different file structuring mechanisms enforced by different systems. Systems such as Unix support only character files, whereas other systems consider files to be made up of logical records with many logical records packed into each physical block.

7. Related to the structure of the file are the random access primitives supported by the system. Some systems may not support random access, others allow random access to individual characters and yet others only permit random access at the block level.

There is little the programmer can do to make file access over different systems compatible. He is stuck with a set of file system primitives and those parts of the system must be modified if the program is moved to another installation. To reduce the amount of work required, file access primitives should be isolated, whenever possible, in user-defined procedures. For example, in Unix, the mechanism to create a file involves calling a system function called 'create' passing the file name and access permissions as parameters:

```
create ("myfile",0755)
```
This creates a file called myfile with universal read and execute access and owner write access. In order to isolate this call, a synonymous user function which calls create can be included:

```
access_permissions = "rwxr_xr_x"
create_file ("myfile",access_permissions)
```

In Unix, create_file would simply consist of a single call to the system routine create. On other systems, create_file could be rewritten to reflect the conventions of the system. The parameters to create_file could be translated into the appropriate form for that system.

It might be imagined that the input/output facilities in a programming language would conceal the details of the operating system input/output routines. Input/output should therefore cause few problems when porting a system from one installation to another.

This is true to some extent. In some programming languages, such as FORTRAN, input/output facilities are defined and each implementation of the language provides these facilities. In other languages, such as Pascal, the input/output facilities are poorly defined or inadequate. As a result, the implementors of a compiler 'extend' the I/O facilities to reflect the facilities provided by the operating system and this leads to portability problems because of incompatible extensions. Particular problems arise in many widely used programming languages with interactive terminal input/output. These problems arise because the programming languages were designed before interactive terminals came into widespread use and interactive input/output was not considered by the language designers.

Different systems consider interactive terminals in different ways. In Unix, a terminal is considered as a special file and file access primitives are used to access it. In other systems, terminals are considered to be devices distinct from files and special terminal access primitives are provided.

There are advantages and disadvantages in considering a terminal as a file. The advantage is that input and output to and from a program can come from either a terminal or a file on backing store. The disadvantage is that the characteristics of a terminal are not exactly those of a file. In fact, a terminal is really like two distinct files, an input file and an output file. If this is not taken into account, portability problems are likely to arise.

Further problems with terminal I/O arise because terminal characteristics differ. Different terminals have different screen sizes, some terminals offer cursor addressability, others do not, some terminals support tab characters, and so on. So-called 'intelligent' terminals make use of control characters. These usually differ from terminal to terminal. Again, the only advice which can be given to the programmer wishing to write portable interactive programs is to isolate hardware-specific code in clearly defined procedures. These procedures must be rewritten when the system is moved to another installation.

Alternatively, the user may chose to construct a special table-driven terminal driver which can handle all kinds of terminal likely to be used with the system. The terminal table contains details of terminal characteristics and the user must explicitly inform the driver what type of terminal is being used. This approach to isolating terminal dependencies is quite an expensive one but is probably worthwhile where a system (like Unix) is to be used with a wide variety of terminal types.

Many systems are made up of a number of separate programs with job control language statements used to co-ordinate the activities of these programs. There is absolutely no standardization of job control in different systems, with the consequence that all job control must be rewritten when transferring a system from one installation to another. There is nothing the programmer can do to reduce the work involved.

This sad note concludes this section on program portability. Apart from the problems described here which can arise when transferring high-level language programs from one installation to another, other portability problems not directly connected with programming also occur. Different installations may have incompatible peripheral devices so that physical media written on the host system cannot be read on the target system. This is a common and extremely frustrating problem.

Further reading

Software Tools in Pascal, B. W. Kernighan and P. J. Plauger (1981), Reading, Mass: Addison-Wesley.

This is not just a book about software tools; it is also a book about programming style, and the authors illustrate how a coherent set of tools can be developed. The book is illustrated with many examples of how to program well.

Software Engineering Environments, ed. H. Hunke (1981), Amsterdam: North-Holland.

A collection of papers from a conference on environments for software engineering. As is always the case with such collections, it contains good, bad and indifferent papers, but in general it is well worth consulting if you are interested in this area.

'Contemporary software development environments', W. E. Howden (1982), *Comm. ACM*, **25 (5)**.

A survey of the basic principles underlying software development environments. A good starting point for reading in this area.

'Guidelines for software portability', A. S. Tanenbaum, P. Klint and W. Bohm (1978), *Software — Practice and Experience*, **8.**

A well written exposition of the problems of achieving portable software.

Chapter 6 PROGRAMMING LANGUAGES

This chapter concentrates on a discussion about the programming languages which may be used to implement a software system. Although apparently an academic preoccupation, language design is of vital importance to the software engineer. Programming languages are his most basic tools and he must feed back information on the reliability and usability of programming languages to the language designer. The software engineer should have some knowledge of programming languages so that he can make reasoned decisions about which programming language is best suited for particular applications.

In this chapter, different classes of programming language are described and this is followed by a discussion of programming language features which affect the readability and reliability of programs. These include declarations, types, modules, control constructs and exception handling. Section 6.3 discusses the factors which should be taken into account in choosing a programming language for a major project, and Section 6.5 discusses the need for languages to be designed to allow separate compilation of different parts of a system.

6.1 Programming language classification

Since 1960, literally thousands of different programming languages have been designed and implemented. The majority of these languages have been implemented as part of research projects and only a relatively small number of them have been widely used. The language most widely used for professional applications is COBOL, which is used for most data processing activities. For scientific programming, FORTRAN is the most common language, with Pascal and C used for systems programming. In future, however, the US DoD-sponsored language Ada is likely to supplant both FORTRAN and Pascal for many applications, and much COBOL programming will be replaced by program generation. In addition, languages such as LISP and PROLOG will be used for artificial intelligence applications as hardware to support them becomes available at relatively low cost.

In general, programming languages fall into one of five categories:

1. *Assembly languages.* These are machine languages with a one-to-one correspondence between programming language statements and machine operations. Programming in assembly code involves the

programmer translating his program design into sequences of machine actions. Because these two notations are quite dissimilar, assembly code programming tends to be difficult and error-prone. Each assembly language is specific to the computer family on which it is implemented.

2. *Systems implementation languages.* This class of programming language evolved from assembly languages when the difficulty of assembly code programming was recognized. Systems implementation languages provide some facilities such as control statements and variable type checking, but they also allow the programmer direct access to machine operations and addresses. In theory, therefore, anything which may be programmed in assembly language may also be programmed in a systems implementation language. Well known systems implementation languages which are available on a number of computers are BCPL and C.

3. *Static high-level languages.* These are languages which provide the programmer with some control statements and variable declarations and which have no facilities for the programmer to control the machine operations generated by the compiler. They are characterized by static storage allocation. The storage space required for program variables can be computed by the language compiler and reserved in advance of program execution. Whilst this has some implementation advantages for the compiler writer, it imposes constraints on the programmer. High-level languages in this class were amongst the first high-level languages and have consequently become very widely used. The best known examples of this type of language are COBOL and FORTRAN.

4. *Block-structured high-level languages.* These languages are developments from static languages, and provide the programmer with a selection of control constructs, and the ability to classify program objects as being of a particular type. They are distinguished by their provision of a limited form of dynamic storage allocation called block structure. The language compiler cannot make all decisions on the amount of store required by program variables, and program execution is supported by a store management system which can allocate and de-allocate store on entry to and exit from a program block.

A program block is a clearly delimited area of a program and execution of the program is interrupted on entry to a block in order to allocate store. The programmer must know on entry to a block exactly how much store is required. Until fairly recently, languages in this class were not widely used commercially, but this situation is changing as the advantages of block-structured languages over COBOL and FORTRAN are recognized. Examples of this class of language are ALGOL and Pascal.

Languages such as Ada and Modula also fall into this category, although their scope rules are not strictly those of block-structured languages. Rather, Ada and Modula provide extended facilities for data abstraction, allowing information hiding to be enforced by the language compiler. However, their storage allocation strategies are the same as block-structured languages, with storage being allocated and de-allocated at the beginning and the end of a program block.

5. *Dynamic high-level languages.* This class of programming languages is distinguished by a requirement that all storage management is carried out dynamically. That is, the execution of individual language statements can cause store to be allocated and de-allocated. In general, the structure of these languages tends to be quite different from the structure of static or block-structured high-level language. Indeed, languages in this class rarely even resemble each other. Dynamic languages tend to be tailored for a particular application and are not general-purpose programming languages. Examples of this class of language are APL, PROLOG and LISP.

These languages are not yet widely used commercially but are sometimes useful in research and prototyping applications. However, as hardware to support the heavy run-time demands of these languages becomes available at moderate cost, their use will become much more widespread. By the 1990s, a significant number of applications will make use of this type of language.

In general, there is a one-to-many correspondence between high-level programming languages and machine code. This means that a number of machine instructions are generated for each high-level language instruction. As well as this, high-level languages allow the user to associate meaningful names with program variables and subroutines where the object name relates to the entity represented by that object. Consequently, high-level language programs are easier to read, easier to write, easier to debug, and easier to maintain than assembly code programs.

The availability of certain programming language constructs simplifies the construction of reliable and maintainable programs. Some constructs, such as Ada packages, allow a system to be partitioned into independent units and hence enhance program maintainability. Other constructs, or the lack of certain features, have inherent disadvantages and cause what are termed 'characteristic errors'. Examples of characteristic errors are un-initialized variables caused by the lack of an explicit initialization construct and object mistyping caused by default type allocation based on the initial letter of an identifier.

It is important that the software engineer understands the ramifications of different programming language constructs. Without this understanding, it is not possible to make reasoned technical decisions about which programming language should be chosen for a project. Therefore, in the following sections, a number of different constructs are discussed along with their advantages and disadvantages. In essence, high-level language constructs provide support for control abstraction and for data abstraction. Data abstraction facilities allow the programmer to divorce himself or herself from how data is represented in the computer, whereas control abstraction facilities provide a convenient way of expressing flow of control in a program.

6.2 Control abstractions

The importance of control abstractions in creating readable, maintainable and checkable programs was first brought to prominence by Dijkstra (1968b) in his classic letter entitled 'Goto Statement Considered Harmful'. Dijkstra's comments, however, were based on sound theoretical work by Bohm and Jacopini (1966), who demonstrated that the flow of control in any program could be expressed using **if** statements and **while** loops.

The whole structured programming debate which raged in the late 1960s and early 1970s revolved around the **goto** statement and whether it should be used in programs. Much of this debate was fairly sterile and it is now generally accepted that expressive control constructs such as **while** statements, **case** statements, etc., should normally be used to express flow of control in a program. However, there are situations where using **goto** statements improves program readability and the wholesale banning of **goto**s is unnecessary.

In this section, the design of various control abstractions in different programming languages is described. In particular, loop control constructs, decision constructs and exception handling are covered here.

6.2.1 Loop control constructs

Loop control constructs are those language control constructs which specify that a statement or a group of statements in a program should be executed a number of times. That number may be specified explicitly or it may depend on some condition becoming true. The most common loop constructs are **for** statements, **while-do** statements and **repeat-until** statements.

The numeric **for** statement is used when it is intended to execute a loop a given number of times. It has the general form:

for <*counter*> := <*initial value*> **step** <*increment*> **to** <*final value*>

Different languages differ slightly in the exact nature of their **for** statement.

Normally, the **for** statement is a very safe construct as, in most languages, loop termination is guaranteed. However, ALGOL60 allows the statement parameters (initial value, step, final value) to be modified by statements within the loop so that it is possible to construct **for** loops which never terminate.

This problem is circumvented in languages such as Pascal by considering the loop counter, starting value and terminating value to be **for** loop parameters. The parameters are evaluated by value rather than by name as in ALGOL60, which means that changes made to these parameters are purely local to the loop. Pascal does have the disadvantage that the loop counter variable must be declared as any other program variable at the head of a block. However, its value on completion of the loop is, according to the Pascal report, undefined — the user may not assume that it has any particular value on loop termination.

A more satisfactory **for** statement design causes the loop counter to be implicitly re-declared as a constant after each execution of the loop as described by Cole and Morrison (1982) in a variant of ALGOL. The value of this constant is one greater than the constant value after the previous loop execution. Not only does this form of implementation ensure that the loop counter cannot possibly be modified within the loop, it also means that the counter name need not be declared in advance by the programmer and that the name disappears on loop termination. There is no possibility of accidental usage. Similarly, the final value and the increment, if any, should also be constant and not subject to modification. This design and its implementation is illustrated below:

> **for** $i := 1$ **to** N **do**
>   *somestatement*(i)

In low-level notation, this is equivalent to:

> **begin**
>   **integer** *counter* $:= 0$
>   **constant** *finalvalue* $= N$
>   *1* : **begin**
>   **constant** $i = counter + 1$
>   **if** $i >$ *finalvalue* **goto** 2
>   *somestatement* (i)
>   *counter* $:= counter + 1$
>   **goto** *1*
>   *2* $:=$ **end**

Notice that the loop counter value and the value passed as a parameter are distinct so that the constant can be properly re-declared.

repeat and **while** statements allow the user to specify that the loop should be executed until some condition is true or while some condition is true.

> **while** $<condition>$ **do** $<statement>$
> **repeat** $<statement>$ **until** $<condition>$

These types of loop do not suffer from the same problems as some **for** statement designs because the loop control variable is under the direct control of the programmer, rather than the language system. The **while** statement allows the programmer to place the test for loop termination at the beginning of the loop and the **repeat** statement allows the test to be placed at the end of the loop. Neither construct allows the test for termination to be placed in the middle of the loop.

There are many practical programming situations where it is necessary to place the termination test within the loop. For example, consider the situation where a program reads some input, then processes that input in some way. If the number of input items is unknown but it is known that the last item is −1, an intuitive implementation of this might be:

```
repeat
    read.item;
    process.item
until item = −1
```

Unfortunately, this is incorrect because this loop will cause the terminating item −1 to be processed. This can be avoided by the introduction of a boolean variable which is set when the terminator is input:

```
finished := false;
repeat
    read.item;
    if item = −1 then
        finished := true
    else
        process.item
until finished
```

The implementation of termination from within a loop by the use of **if** statements and boolean variables is clumsy and increases the length of the program. A number of different control constructs have been proposed which provide for the placing of the loop termination test anywhere in the loop. These have been described by Zahn (1974) and Bochmann (1973).

The variety of proposed constructs will not be described here. Rather, the solution adopted in Ada is described. This provides a facility which allows programmer control over the placing of the loop termination test.

In Ada, the loop statement has the form:

```
[<iteration specification>]<basic loop>
```

where the iteration specification is optional. When included, it has the form:

```
for <loop parameter> in [reverse]<discrete range>
while <condition>
```

The iteration specifier allows the specification of **for** or **while** loops. Unlike Pascal, the loop parameter is implicitly declared by its use in the **for** specifier.

The basic loop in Ada has the form:

```
loop <sequence of statements> end loop;
```

Examples of Ada loops are:

```
for I in 1..10 loop
    PROCESS(I);
end loop;
```

```
while I < 10 loop
    PROCESS(I);
    I:=I+1;
end loop;

for C in COLOURS loop
    PROCESSCOLOUR (C);
end loop;
```

It is possible to escape from within a loop by using an **exit** statement. This has the form:

exit [<identifier>][**when** <condition>]

The **exit** statement causes control to be transferred to the statement following the loop unless it is followed by an identifier. In this case, control is transferred to the statement following the loop labelled with that identifier. The **exit-when** construct can be used to place the loop terminating condition within the loop. The previous example might be coded:

```
loop
    READ (ITEM);
    exit when ITEM = −1;
    PROCESS (ITEM);
end loop;
```

In fact, it is possible to use the **exit** statement to exit from an inner loop to the end of some enclosing loop. This is accomplished by preceding the outer loop with an identifier which looks like (but which is not) a label. The identifier is referenced explicitly in the **exit** statement as shown in the example below:

```
LOOP1:
    loop
        . . .
        . . .
        loop
            . . .
            exit LOOP1 when SOMECONDITION;
            . . .
        end loop;
    end loop; −− LOOP1
```

This exit to an enclosing loop does not actually violate the requirement that loops should only have a single exit point. It merely saves the programmer multiple **exit** statements which test the same condition after each inner loop.

6.2.2 Decision constructs

Decision constructs in a high-level language are control constructs which allow a statement or group of statements to be selected for execution on the basis of some condition being true. These constructs encompass the one-armed conditional (**if-then**), the two-armed conditional (**if-then-else**) and the multi-armed conditional construct (**case**).

The form of the one-armed and two-armed conditional statements is familiar:

> **if** <*condition*> **then** <*statement*>
> **if** <*condition*> **then** <*statement*> **else** <*statement*>

There are no practical problems in using these statements.

There are a number of different forms of case statement in use but, unlike one- and two-armed conditionals, each form has some disadvantages and may be responsible for certain types of program error.

In ALGOLW and ALGOL68, the case statement takes an integer expression as the case selector and the case statement includes a number of separate executable statements. If the case selector has the value M, the Mth statement is chosen for execution.

> **case** <*integer expression*> **of**
> <*S1*>
> <*S2*>
> <*S3*>
> . . .
> . . .
> <*Sn*>

After the selected expression has been executed, execution continues with the statement after the **case** statement.

This form of the **case** construct suffers from two problems:

1. The action taken if the value of the case expression is less than zero or greater than N is not specified.

2. The correct ordering of the statements to be selected by the case expression is crucial. If an error should be made in this ordering, it is undetectable at compile-time or run-time. The statement actually executed will not be that statement intended by the programmer. This situation is most likely to arise where the range of the case selector expression is not continuous and dummy statements are inserted into the statement list to ensure that the appropriate statement is selected.

Pascal offers an alternative **case** statement design which eliminates the dependence on correct programmer ordering of the executable statements. In Pascal, the case selector expression may evaluate to any scalar type except real. Each executable statement in the case construct is labelled with one or more special constant labels called case labels. Execution of the **case** statement involves evaluating the case selector expression, matching that value against the case labels and selecting for execution that statement whose label matches the case selector value. For example:

```
case inputcharacter of
begin
    ',' : setcomma;
    ':' : setcolon;
    ';' : setsemicolon;
    '0','1','2','3','4','5','6','8','9' : setdigit;
    ' ','.','@' : setotherchar
end;
```

The Pascal **case** statement makes no attempt to provide a solution to the first problem identified above — what action is taken if the case selector fails to match any of the case labels.

The **case** statement in Ada has been designed so that the problem associated with the Pascal **case** statement has been eliminated. In Ada, if the **case** expression is of type T, **case**s for all possible values of T must be included. If explicit mention is not made of all values, a default statement must be included. For example, consider a type DAY, defined:

type DAY **is** (MON,TUE,WED,THUR,FRI,SAT,SUN);

and a variable TODAY of this type. An Ada **case** statement using TODAY might be:

```
case TODAY of
    when MON => FIRST_WORKING_DAY;
    when TUE..THUR => MIDDLE_DAYS;
    when FRI => LAST_WORKING_DAY;
    when OTHERS => WEEKEND;
end case;
```

The default is stated as '**when** others'.

Although the Ada **case** statement is safe, inasmuch as user error can always be detected by the compiler and no undefined situations can arise, it is the author's opinion that a guarded command mechanism as suggested by Dijkstra (1975) is superior to existing forms of case statement. This construct is essentially an abstraction over a condition and allows all conditional statements to be expressed in the same way. The user need not learn several different ways of expressing program conditions.

This guarded command construct is a generalization of the two-armed conditional so that each statement is preceded by a boolean expression 'guarding' that statement. This may be expressed:

```
if
    <condition1> : <statement1>
    <condition2> : <statement2>
    . . . .
    . . . .
    <conditionN> : <statementN>
else
```

```
  <statement>
end if
```

An appropriate shorthand notation might be invented if the left-hand side of each condition was identical. Evaluation of the multi-armed conditional involves evaluating the conditions until some true condition is found and then executing the statement following that condition.

6.2.3 Exception handling

When an error of some kind or an unexpected event occurs during the execution of a program, this event is termed an exception. Exceptions may be caused by hardware or software errors which may or may not have been anticipated by the programmer. In general, where an exception has not been anticipated explicitly by the programmer, control is transferred to a system exception-handling mechanism which handles the exception. If the exception is serious the executing program is terminated. If an exception has been anticipated by the programmer, he must include code to detect that exception and to take appropriate action when that exception occurs. In general, if a program is running under an operating system, the programmer will not be able to detect or handle hardware exceptions in his program. It is the responsibility of the operating system to handle such cases.

Programming languages such as FORTRAN or Pascal offer the programmer little help in detecting and handling exceptions. The programmer must use the normal decision constructs of the language to detect the exception and the control constructs to transfer control to the exception handler.

Whilst this is possible in a monolithic program, in programs where a sequence of procedure calls is nested, there is no convenient and safe mechanism for transmitting the exception from one procedure to another.

Consider the following example:

```
procedure A;
  ....
  B;
  ....
end; {A}

procedure B;
  ....
  C;
  ....
end; {B}

procedure C;
  ....
  ....
end; {C}
```

Procedure A calls procedure B which calls procedure C. If an exception occurs during the execution of C this may be so serious that it is pointless to continue execution of B after the call of C. Similarly, it may be necessary to transmit the fact that an exception has occurred from B to A.

The only mechanism which the programmer has for this in Pascal, say, is a global boolean variable which is set to indicate that an exception has occurred. This must either be passed as a parameter to every procedure or be set globally. The programmer must test the value of this variable after each procedure call so that, in a sequence of nested procedure calls, the same test is carried out a number of times. The existing mechanism forces the programmer to test for the exception each and every time that exception might occur. Unanticipated exceptions cause transfer to a system exception handler and, normally, program termination.

Whilst such a situation is acceptable in situations such as a student learning environment, it is not acceptable in situations where reliability considerations are paramount. In those situations, usually where the computer is acting as a controller or providing an essential time-critical service, the system must not fail. Furthermore, program size is often critical in such situations so that it is unacceptable to include a number of largely redundant statements to test for exceptions.

Ideally, an exception-handling facility should be available which does not force the programmer to increase the length of his program inordinately and which makes possible the transmission of exceptions from one program unit to another. Such exception handling facilities are not easy to design or implement. When designing exception handling constructs, a number of factors must be taken into account:

1. How should exceptions be declared?
2. Where should exception handlers be placed in a program?
3. Should exception handlers be a distinct program structure or should exceptions be handled using existing structures such as procedures?
4. How should exceptions be signalled and transmitted from one program unit to another?
5. Should exceptions and exception handlers be subject to the normal scope and extent rules of the language? If so, which exception handler should be selected if a number of handlers of the same name are provided at different levels?
6. Should exception handlers cause control to be returned to the point where the exception occurred after it has been dealt with?

The majority of widely used programming languages offer no specific exception-handling constructs. An exception to this is PL/1 which recognizes the importance of exception handling and provides special constructs for this purpose.

In PL/1, the ON statement is used to specify what action should be taken when an exception occurs. As well as built-in exceptions, such as end-of-

`file, integer-overflow, divide-by-zero,` etc., the programmer can define his own exception names and can indicate that an exception of that name has occurred. Exception names and actions to be taken are defined using an `ON` statement:

```
ON end-of-file call closefile
ON condition(HEAPFULL) call garbage_collect
```

The first `ON` statement above specifies an action to be taken in the event of the standard exception 'end-of-file' occurring. The second example introduces an exception name `HEAPFULL` and specifies an action associated with that exception.

PL/1 `ON` statements essentially set up an exception action and this action is triggered either when a built-in system exception occurs or when a `SIGNAL` statement is used by the programmer to indicate that an exception has occurred. The `SIGNAL` statement has the form:

```
SIGNAL condition(HEAPFULL)
```

When the `SIGNAL` statement is executed, this causes control to be transferred to the language statement specified in the `ON` statement. This action may be a code sequence, a procedure call or a goto statement. Unless the `ON` action branches to a location elsewhere in the program, control returns to the statement following the `SIGNAL` statement after the `ON` action has been executed.

The programming language Ada was designed for constructing embedded computer systems, and a general characteristic of such systems is that they should be highly reliable. Therefore, care has been taken in the design of Ada exception handling facilities and the language provides powerful and adaptable constructs for indicating and handling exceptions.

In Ada, exception names are declared like any other names; that is, as a name associated with some type. Exception names are always declared to be of the special built-in type exception. Drawing attention to an exception is termed 'raising an exception' in Ada and executing a sequence of actions in response to an exception being raised is called 'handling the exception'.

Any program unit in Ada may have an associated exception handler which must appear at the end of the unit. An exception handler is distinguished by the reserved word exception and resembles an Ada case statement inasmuch as it states exception names and appropriate actions for each exception. However, not every exception raised in a program unit need necessarily be handled by that unit — the exception may be propagated to some other unit at a higher level.

Exceptions in Ada may be used as an error-handling mechanism to deal with unanticipated events such as hardware failure, or may be used as a form of control construct where it is expected that the exception will arise. This is particularly useful when the situation causing the exception is to be propagated to some calling procedure. Without explicit exception handling facilities, the propagation would be the responsibility of the programmer.

He or she would be forced to include explicit parameters to signal that an exception had occurred.

The example below illustrates the use of Ada exceptions. It is assumed in this example that the files INPUT_FILE and OUTPUT_FILE have been opened as textfiles and that the file USER_CONSOLE is associated with the user's terminal. Naturally, this presupposes that the package TEXT_IO is used and has been included in the user's compilation unit.

```
-- This program copies characters from an input
-- file to an output file. Termination occurs
-- either when all characters are copied or
-- when a NULL character is input
NULLCHAR,EOF : exception;
    CHAR : CHARACTER;

loop
    GET(INPUT_FILE,CHAR);
    if END_OF_FILE(INPUT_FILE) then
        raise (EOF);
    elsif CHAR = ASCII'NUL then
        raise (NULLCHAR);
    else
        PUT (OUTPUT_FILE,CHAR);
    end if;
end loop;
exception
    when EOF => WRITE(USER_CONSOLE,'NO NULL CHARACTERS');
    when NULLCHAR => WRITE(USER_CONSOLE,'NULL TERMINATOR');
end;
```

In this example, exceptions are handled in the same program unit in which they are declared. To illustrate how exceptions may be propagated to a higher-level unit, consider a modification of the above example. Assume that copying of characters ceases whenever any character apart from a letter or a digit is detected:

```
EOF,NOT_LETTER_OR_DIGIT : exception;
function CHAR_IS_LETTER_OR_DIGIT (CHAR : in CHARACTER)
                        return BOOLEAN is
begin
    if CHAR in '0'..'9' or CHAR in 'A'..'Z' or
    CHAR in 'A'..'Z' then
        return TRUE;
    else
        raise NOT_LETTER_OR_DIGIT;
    end if;
end;

loop
    GET(INPUT_FILE,CHAR);
    if CHAR_IS_LETTER_OR_DIGIT(CHAR) then
        PUT (OUTPUT_FILE,CHAR);
    end if;
```

```
    if END_OF_FILE(INPUT_FILE) then
        raise EOF;
    end if;
  end loop;
  exception
        when EOF => PUT (USER_CONSOLE,"FILE COPIED");
        when NOT_LETTER_OR_DIGIT =>PUT (USER_CONSOLE,"ERROR");
  end;
```

The exception NOT_LETTER_OR_DIGIT which is raised in the function CHAR_IS_LETTER_OR_DIGIT is propagated to the calling program because no handler for it exists in the function. In general, exceptions are propagated outwards until a handler is found or until the Ada system exception handler is activated.

The exception handling mechanism of Ada, unlike that of PL/1, does not provide for the exception handler recovering from the event which caused the exception and resuming program execution at the point where the exception occurred. Instead, an exception occurring within a program unit always results in the execution of that unit being terminated. However, the exception propagation mechanism can be used to effect recovery if an exception occurs in a program unit X. That exception can be propagated to a higher-level unit Y, the conditions causing the exception corrected or modified and the program unit X explicitly reactivated.

6.2.4 The goto statement

Although not strictly a control abstraction, as it is a direct reflection of a machine code operation, the use and abuse of goto statements has engendered such controversy as to be worthy of some comment here. We have already seen situations where the use of gotos can improve program readability. In this short section, the arguments for and against the inclusion of a goto statement in a programming language are summarized.

It has been demonstrated by Bohm and Jacopini (1966) that any program can be expressed without goto statements as long as language facilities include a while statement, an if-then-else statement and boolean variables. Furthermore, they showed that any program written using goto statements can be transformed into a program without gotos, although this usually involves increasing the program size.

Programs which make extensive use of goto statements to modify the flow of control are more difficult to read and more prone to error than gotoless programs. Undisciplined use of goto statements to share small code sections and to make a program 'more efficient' result in the flow of control in a program being extremely circuitous. In extreme cases, 'spaghetti' programs can result from the uncontrolled use of gotos where the flow of control is as tangled as a bowl of spaghetti.

For these reasons, it has been advocated that the goto statement is so dangerous and powerful that it has no place in high-level programming languages. This is true for languages used in applications such as the teaching of programming. Inexperienced programmers cannot be expected to understand the rare circumstances where it may be sensible to use a goto statement and, by removing temptation, the possibility of misusing the goto statement is avoided.

However, experienced programmers who program in a disciplined manner can use the goto statement responsibly and there are certain programming circumstances where it is the most apt construct to apply. Specialized forms of the goto statement, such as a statement allowing exit from within a loop or a statement allowing immediate return from a procedure, are easier to read and understand than the extensive use of boolean variables and two-armed conditionals which can accomplish the same function. Handling exceptional situations where an error may occur anywhere in a sequence of procedure activations is another circumstance where the goto statement may be useful.

6.3 Data abstraction

As well as simple control abstractions such as DO-loops, the first widely used high-level language, FORTRAN, had some data abstraction facilities. These were the provision of real and integer numbers which concealed the representation of numbers in the underlying machine from the programmer. The ideas introduced in FORTRAN were extended and refined in ALGOL60 and its associated derivatives such as ALGOLW. With the emergence of Pascal, the importance of data abstractions became widely known. It is now accepted that data abstraction facilities are at least as important an issue in programming language design as control abstraction constructs. Recently designed languages, such as Ada, thus incorporate powerful mechanisms for data abstraction.

In this section, a slight liberty in the use of the term 'data abstraction' has been taken, as notions such as the importance of initialization facilities are also covered here. The topics discussed are the need for variable declarations and initialization facilities, simple types, composite types, constants and, finally, modules allowing the definition of abstract data types.

6.3.1 Declarations

The declaration of names for objects used in a program has a triple function; it provides information to the compiler about the storage requirements of that object and it informs the system exactly which names may be used in the program. In addition, they document the programmer's intention and give hints to the program reader about the meaning of the program. A type may be associated with a declaration and this allows the compiler to check that objects of a particular type are used only in operations which are defined for that type. For example, if an object is declared to be type real, the compiler should signal an error if that object is used as an operand in a logical 'and' operation where only boolean-type operands should be used.

Not all programming languages force the user to declare names for all the objects used in his program. In languages such as FORTRAN or BASIC, the first use of a name is deemed to be its declaration. In FORTRAN, declarations are optional and they may associate one of a limited number of types with a name. If a name is introduced without declaration, the initial letter of that name determines its type — if the name starts with any letter from I to N, it is presumed to represent an integer, otherwise it is taken as a real number.

Optional declarations are dangerous because they allow programmer errors which result in legal but incorrect FORTRAN programs. For example, consider the legal FORTRAN statement:

```
IPOINT = IPOINT + 1
```

The effect of this statement is to set IPOINT to 1. A new integer object called IPOINT is created and initialized to zero and that value plus 1 is assigned to IPOINT. On many printers, the letter O and the character zero (0) are almost indistinguishable and should O be accidentally substituted for zero or vice versa, a new object is created by the use of the mis-spelt name.

In programming languages which enforce declarations, the above error is easily detected by the compiler because only IPOINT (say) would have been declared. The use of the name IPOINT would be illegal.

6.3.2 Simple types

Closely associated with name declarations are type declarations, which allow the user to associate a type name with a declared object. This type name serves to classify the object and operations on the object are restricted to operations defined on that class of objects. If the programmer uses an object of a particular type in an invalid manner, this error can be detected and signalled by the compiler.

The notion of type checking was introduced in ALGOL60 and the concept has been considerably refined since then. Programming languages such as Pascal allow the user to define his or her own types, relevant to a particular application, and to declare objects of that type. For example, if a traffic light system is being modelled in Pascal, the following declarations might be made:

type *TrafficLightColour* = *(red,redamber,amber,green)*;
var *ColourShowing* : *TrafficLightColour*;

The object *ColourShowing*, which is modelling the colour displayed by the traffic light, may be assigned only the values *red, redamber, amber* and *green*.

Contrast this with the modelling of such a situation in FORTRAN. Here, integers must be used to represent the entities associated with the traffic light:

```
INTEGER RED,REDAMB,AMBER,GREEN,COLSHW
DATA RED/1/,REDAMB/2/,AMBER/3/,GREEN/4/
```

Integers are associated with each possible colour, and assignments such as

```
COLSHW = RED
```

can be made.

Disciplined programming in FORTRAN, which means associating a relevant name with each constant used to represent an entity, improves program readability. However, there is no mechanism to restrict statements which directly assign integers or real numbers to COLSHW. If names are not associated with constants, assignments such as:

```
COLSHW = 3
```

must be made, forcing the program to consult documentation or program comments to find out which colour is actually represented by 3.

If a statement such as

```
COLSHW = 13
```

is made, there is no way that the error can be detected either by the compiler or the run-time system. Detection of such an error depends on explicit checking code being included by the programmer.

Another important class of Pascal type declarations are sub-range type declarations. These allow the programmer to declare a type whose values make up a subset of the values of some other type. For example:

> **type** *PositiveInteger* = *1..maxint*;
> *LowerCaseLetters* = '*a*'..'*z*';

These declarations introduce a type called *PositiveInteger* whose range covers positive integers and the type *LowerCaseLetters* which encompasses characters between '*a*' and '*z*'. Objects which are declared as one of these types are restricted to values within the specified range. The Pascal compiler automatically generates code to check, at run-time, that assignments to these objects do not cause violation of the range constraint. In languages without the facility of sub-range types, they can only be modelled by the inclusion of explicit checking code by the programmer.

6.3.3 Composite types

Most programming languages allow the user to declare arrays. Arrays are sequential collections of elements, all of the same type, where each individual element can be identified by its position in the collection. As well as one-dimensional arrays, it is usually possible to define multi-dimensional arrays to represent objects such as matrices which are inherently two-dimensional.

A decision which has to be made by the language designer is whether arrays should be static or dynamic. Static arrays are arrays whose bounds are fixed at compile time, whereas dynamic arrays have their bounds determined at run-time. Static arrays, where the array bounds are built into the user-defined array type, simplify type checking but are somewhat unreal as they imply that an array of six integers (say) has little in common with an array of five integers. The designers of Pascal have been widely criticized for including only static arrays in that language. This criticism is certainly valid if Pascal is considered as a systems programming language. However, the original intention of the designers was to design a language for teaching programming and, for this purpose, dynamic arrays are probably unnecessary.

The mechanism used in Ada to provide dynamic arrays without compromising type checking is the notion of a subtype. It is possible to define a generalized array type where the array bounds are unspecified then create specific instances of that type (subtypes) which set up the array bounds. For example:

type INT_VECTOR **is array** (INTEGER **range** <>) OF INTEGER;

This introduces a type INT_VECTOR which is a one-dimensional array of integers whose index is also an integer. By specifying the range of the index as <>, the type declaration states that array bounds are not fixed.

To create specific instances of this type, subtypes are declared as follows:

subtype SMALL_VEC **is** INT_VECTOR (1..5);
subtype LARGE_VEC **is** INT_VECTOR (0..10_000);

The first of these subtype declarations defines a type SMALL_VEC whose index must lie in the range 1 to 5, whereas the second declaration declares LARGE_VEC whose index is in the range 0 to 10000.

An object whose type is a subtype of some parent type may be used anywhere that objects of the parent type are allowed. Therefore, unlike Pascal, individual functions need not be created to manipulate array objects with different bounds. For example:

function COUNT (V : **in** INT_VECTOR) **return** INTEGER;

This function can be called with objects whose type is either SMALL_VEC, LARGE_VEC or any other subtype of INT_VECTOR. For example:

```
declare
    SV : SMALL_VEC;
    LV : LARGE_VEC;
begin
    COUNT (SV); COUNT (LV);
end;
```

Arrays are an important data type, but they are not particularly suitable for representing objects which model entities made up of a collection of elements of different types. For example, consider a personnel record in an organization. This might be made up of a number of fields with each field modelling an individual attribute:

Name : string of letters and blanks
Address : string of letters, numbers, and blanks

Age : integer between 16 and 65
Department : the name of one of a number of known departments
Salary : integer between 3000 and 15000

In Pascal a facility exists for declaring structured types made up of collections of elements, not all of which need be of the same type. A name is associated with each element and reference to the element is made via that name. The fields of the record type have the same names as the entities which they are modelling. If a variable, say employee, is declared to be of type *PersonnelRecord*, *employee.name* references the name field, *employee.dept* references the dept field and so on.

The above personnel record could be represented in Pascal as follows:

```
type PersonnelRecord =
  record
    name : array [1..NAMESIZE] of char;
    address : array [1..ADDRESSSIZE] of char;
    age : 16..65;
    dept : (sales,personnel,production,DP,admin);
    salary : 3000..15000
  end;
```

In languages which do not provide such structured data types, arrays must be used to represent entities such as the personnel record. Each field of the record is held at a known offset from the start of the array. For example, in a FORTRAN77 character array, the first 20 characters might be the name, the next 30 characters the address, the next 2 characters the age, the next characters a code representing the department, and the final 5 characters the salary. This might be declared:

```
CHARACTER PERSRC(40)
```

A disciplined FORTRAN programmer declares names for each field in the record and initializes these names to refer to the appropriate locations in PERSRC. Therefore reference could be made to PERSRC(SALARY), PERSRC(NAME), etc. Because all elements in the array must be of the same type, numbers in the record are represented as character strings and these strings must be converted to numbers before they can be used in arithmetic operations.

Furthermore, it is impossible for the compiler to carry out any checking to ensure that appropriate values are assigned to fields. For example, the following assignment is permitted:

```
PERSRC(SALARY:SALARY+4) = '25500'
```

The FORTRAN77 feature of substring assignment is used to assign the string '25500' to the salary field of PERSRC. As the maximum salary is 15000, this is an invalid value.

Type declarations in a programming language are not just a safety feature. As well as providing information which allows the compiler to carry out some program checking, they are also an important abstraction mechanism. The definition of type names allows reference to be made to entities such as personnel records, traffic light colours, etc., without considering the representation of these entities. The importance of abstraction has already been discussed and the sensible use of typing is a powerful abstraction technique for the system designer.

6.3.4 Initialization

One of the most common programming errors is the failure to initialize declared variables before these variables are used. Some languages, such as FORTRAN and Ada, provide facilities for variable initialization but they do not force the programmer to use them — if a variable is not initialized, it is assigned some standard, system-dependent value.

Other languages, such as Pascal, have no explicit initialization features and the programmer must use assignment statements to perform initializations. The separation of variable declarations and program statements in Pascal means that it is impossible to write the initialization assignment immediately after the variable declaration. This is an aspect of Pascal which is likely to cause programming errors.

The lack of initialization facilities and purely voluntary initialization is unsatisfactory. To reduce the error proneness of a programming language, the programmer should be forced to provide an initial value of the appropriate type for all variables declared in his program. This removes all possibility of a programmer forgetting to initialize some variable and also makes it impossible for a programmer to rely on the system initializing variables to some default value. Relying on system initialization is particularly dangerous. Should the program be transferred to some other system with different initialization conventions, an incorrect initialization will be given to his variables and, consequently, the result of executing the program will be unpredictable.

An alternative to enforced programmer initialization of variables is for the system to assign a special 'not yet initialized' value to a variable when it is declared and to signal an error if an attempt is made to read that variable before an assignment has been made to it. This solves the problem of 'forgotten' initialization but would have to be enforced on every system if the program were run on different machines. In terms of existing hardware, such a system would be expensive to implement but the design of hardware to support such a system is not difficult (Scowen, 1979).

6.3.5 Constants

Many of the entities modelled in a program are not variable but constant. These may be mathematical entities such as pi, physical constants such as the speed of light, or defined constants such as the current standard rate of income tax. During the execution of a program, the values of the objects representing these entities do not change.

There is another class of constant which is commonly used in programming. This is a constant which is a program parameter, used for deriving a particular instance of a program. For example, if a program object represents a name, it may have an associated constant NAMESIZE, indicating the maximum number of characters in a name. Although constant for any one instance of a program, it may be convenient for NAMESIZE to have different values in different instances of the program.

Of course it is possible to represent constants by using program variables, initializing these variables to the constant value and making no further assignments to that variable. This has the disadvantages that the reader cannot distinguish constants and variables by examining the program and that the compiler cannot enforce constancy — it cannot prevent assignments to a supposedly constant variable.

In Pascal, constants are declared explicitly using a **const** declaration. Constant declarations in Pascal must precede the declaration of types and this imposes the limitation that the type of Pascal constants is restricted to one of the predefined language types — integer, real, char or boolean. This limitation means that the advantages of Pascal typing only apply to program variables. Declarations such as the following are not permitted:

type *TrafficLightColour* = (*red,redamber,amber,green*);
const *GoColour* = *TrafficLightColour*(*green*);

This lack of typed constants is a serious inconsistency in the design of Pascal.

This has been remedied in Ada, which not only allows typed constants but also permits the dynamic assignment of values to constants. This is in contrast to Pascal where only manifest constants — constants whose values are fixed at compile time — are allowed. The dynamic initialization of constants means that the important safety aspects of constants — the ability to guarantee that a name is always associated with the same value — is maintained without forcing the programmer to determine that value at compile time.

Examples of Ada constant declarations are:

```
GO_COLOUR : constant COLOUR := GREEN;
LIMIT : constant SMALL_INTEGER := M*N;
PI : constant := 3.14159_26536;
MAX : constant := 1000;
```

Notice that when the value of a constant is a number it is not necessary to include the constant type in the declaration as this can be determined by the Ada compiler.

6.3.6 Modules

Block-structured languages such as Pascal provide some control over the visibility of object names because names that are declared in an inner block are not accessible from an outer block. However, the programmer has no control over the accessibility of outer block objects. They cannot be protected from access from within an inner block except by re-using the object name. Furthermore, because of the dynamic storage allocation philosophy of block-structured languages, it is not possible to preserve the value of an object from one activation of a block to another.

Consequently, objects which may only be used by one or two routines in a program, but whose values must be maintained from one activation of the routine to another, must be declared globally and must, therefore, be potentially accessible by any routine in the program. Again, this can cause program maintenance problems as code modifying these objects may be accidentally introduced into the program.

An example where global objects must be used is shown below in Pascal:

```
var sp : 0..STACKSIZE + 1;
   stack : array [1..STACKSIZE] of integer;

procedure push (v:integer);
begin
  if sp > STACKSIZE then
    error (stackoverflow)
  else
  begin
    sp := sp + 1;
    stack [sp] := v
  end
end; {push}

function pop : integer;
begin
  if sp = 0 then
    error (stackunderflow)
  else
  begin
    pop := stack [sp];
    sp := sp - 1
  end
end; {pop}

function testempty : boolean;
begin
  testempty := sp = 0
end; {testempty}
```

Assume that STACKSIZE, stackoverflow and stackunderflow are declared elsewhere.

In this example, the variables sp and stack must be implemented as global program variables because they are shared by the routines push, pop and testempty. They must maintain their values from one access to another and therefore cannot be declared in an inner block.

Block structure on its own is an inadequate mechanism for controlling the visibility of names. There is a need for some additional mechanism which allows the user much closer control over what local names may be accessed from outside the program unit in which these names are declared. It should also be possible to specify that a local variable should maintain its value from one activation of a program unit to another.

A construct providing these facilities has been introduced in several programming languages under a number of different names — a class in SIMULA, a module in MODULA, and a package in Ada. In describing this construct, terminology and syntax derived from Ada is used.

The provision of modules such as Ada packages offers a number of advantages to the programmer:

1. Abstract data types, as proposed by Liskov and Zilles (1974) may be constructed. These are data types whose representation is concealed from the user. The stack example above is an instance of an abstract data type. The user may manipulate the stack but its actual representation is concealed. Conceivably, the stack representation might be modified, to a linked list, say, without affecting the user's view of the stack and without any changes in the programs which make use of the stack package.

2. Related operations may be grouped together and may share variables in a controlled way. An example of this type of module might be an I/O package. Within the package, necessary I/O buffers would be declared and shared by the I/O procedures declared in the package.

3. A module is a convenient unit for independent compilation. A module may be constructed as a self-contained unit, making no reference to its outside environment except via other module activations. This means that it can be compiled without the presence of a global environment and stored in a library.

Because of these advantages, the availability of modules in a programming language makes that language particularly suitable for major software projects.

An Ada package allows the programmer to declare a named program unit which may contain declarations of local objects. These objects may be strictly local, that is, their names may only be used within the package body, or the programmer may choose to 'export' the names of some objects. This means that the names may be used outside that package body and will refer to the objects declared in the package. If those objects are variables, they maintain their value from one activation of the package to another. We have already come across Ada packages in earlier chapters in discussions of abstract data types, object-oriented design and programming methodology. This illustrates the importance of this construct.

The declaration of an Ada package is made up of two parts — a package header which specifies the local package names accessible outside the package, and a package body which defines the objects making up the package. A package is simply a lexical mechanism providing control over the visibility of names. Consequently, a package body consists entirely of declarations — type declarations, variable declarations and procedure declarations.

The example below is a recoding in Ada of the previous Pascal example of stack implementation:

```
package STACK is
    procedure PUSH (V : in INTEGER);
    procedure POP return INTEGER;
    procedure TESTEMPTY return BOOLEAN;
end STACK;
```

This is the package header which declares the local package names 'exported' from the package. In this case, the user may refer only to the procedure names PUSH, POP and TESTEMPTY. A package body declaration specifies the objects associated with these names together with local package objects.

```
package body STACK is

    -- declare stack pointer and array to represent the stack
    -- these are local variables but they retain their value from
    -- one activation of STACK to another

    SP : INTEGER range 0..STACKSIZE+1 := 0;
    STACK : ARRAY (1..STACKSIZE) OF INTEGER;

    type ERRORTYPE is (OVERFLOW,UNDERFLOW);

    procedure PUSH (V : in INTEGER);
    begin
        if SP > STACKSIZE then
            ERROR (OVERFLOW);
        else
            SP := SP + 1;
            STACK (SP) := V;
        end if;
    end push;

    procedure POP return INTEGER;
    begin
        if SP = 0 then
            ERROR (UNDERFLOW);
        else
            SP := SP - 1;
            return STACK (SP + 1);
        end if;
    end pop;

    procedure TESTEMPTY return BOOLEAN;
    begin
        return SP = 0;
    end testempty;
```

```
procedure ERROR (T : in ERRORTYPE);
begin
    - - A standard I/O package called TEXT_IO is required
    - - this is included using a with statement
    with TEXT_IO;
    case T is
        when UNDERFLOW => TEXT_IO.PUT ("STACK UNDERFLOW");
        when OVERFLOW => TEXT_IO.PUT ("STACK OVERFLOW");
        when OTHERS => TEXT_IO.PUT ("SYSTEM ERROR");
    end case;
    - - communicate error to calling procedure
    raise STACKERROR;
end ERROR;

end STACK;
```

The package body defines the accessible procedures PUSH, POP and TESTEMPTY and local objects STACK, SP, STACKSIZE, ERRORTYPE and ERROR. In order that the package might be self-contained, the error-handling procedure is included in the package.

The error procedure illustrates how package names are referenced. This procedure calls the procedure PUT, declared in a package called TEXT_IO. A procedure name, exported from a package, is preceded by the package name. Therefore:

```
TEXT_IO.PUT ("SOME MESSAGE")
```

calls the procedure put in the package TEXT_IO.

```
X := STACK.POP
```

calls the procedure POP in the package STACK and

```
if STACK.TESTEMPTY then ...
```

calls the procedure TESTEMPTY declared in STACK.

In the above stack example, the stack structure itself is completely concealed from users of the package. However, the user may wish to have a number of stacks in his or her program, in which case the type stack should be declared as a **limited private** type in the package header. This means that the type name may also be exported from the package but that operations on it are limited and its structure is concealed. This creation of an abstract data type was illustrated for queues in Chapter 5 and examples illustrating abstract data types will not be repeated here.

This mechanism for referencing names exported from a package means that different packages may export the same names and that these names may refer to different objects without ambiguity. For example, a package concerned exclusively with character input/output, say CHARIO, may export a name 'PUT'. This would be referred to as CHARIO.PUT. Because the package name precedes the procedure name there is no confusion with the procedure TEXT_IO.PUT.

6.4 Choosing a programming language

One of the most important decisions which must be made when designing and building a large software system is which programming language to use in the implementation of the system. As most of the costs in a software system are incurred during the testing and maintenance phases of the system life cycle, an inappropriate notation used to represent the system can introduce difficulties at later stages of the life cycle. Choosing an appropriate programming language minimizes the difficulties in coding a design, reduces the amount of program testing required, and makes for a more readable and hence more easily maintained program.

There is rarely any justification for choosing assembly code as the programming language for a major project. Wichmann (1978) has asserted that there appear to be only three application areas where it may be necessary to use assembly code:

1. some aerospace applications where very tight time and space constraints are placed on the program;
2. engineering test programs where arbitrary, perhaps illegal, sequences of instructions must be generated;
3. some microprocessor systems with unusual or special-purpose architectures so that it is impossible or uneconomic to construct an efficient high-level language compiler for these machines.

As well as these applications, it might be added that the coding of small time-critical parts of large systems may be justified. The identification of which parts are to be coded in a low-level language cannot be carried out before the system is implemented. Only after implementation and evaluation can those parts be discovered and recoded if necessary.

To reduce total life cycle costs, the implementation of the system should be readily maintainable. This implies that the system should be encoded in a high-level language which provides facilities to build the system as a number of autonomous, co-operating modules. The language should have control and data structuring facilities which allow a 'readable' program to be produced.

It should be possible to use meaningful names; structuring facilities such as procedures and functions should be available and the language should have adequate control constructs so that the use of goto statements may be avoided. As it is obviously desirable that the system should detect as many errors as possible, the language should be typed so that user errors due to object mistyping may be detected by the compiler. These are ideal criteria for selecting a programming language for a major project but pragmatic considerations often mean that the most suitable language, in theory, cannot be used.

Some of these important pragmatic criteria are:

1. *The requirements of the system contractor.* The contractor of a software system may specify that a particular programming language is to be used and, in general, this requirement must be adhered to. Alternatively, the contractor may provide a list of approved languages and one of these must be chosen for the project implementation. It is up to the system designers and implementors to decide which is the most appropriate language for each particular project.

    Contractor specification of programming language is the normal practice where the contractor takes over system maintenance from the implementors after an agreed period, as is common in systems contracted for defence purposes. As the contractor's staff are involved in program maintenance, the project must be implemented in a language which they can understand.

2. *The availability of language compilers.* If a project is to be implemented using a particular hardware/operating system configuration, there must be an acceptably efficient translator for the implementation language available.

3. *The availability of software tools to support program development.* Software tools such as context editors, cross-referencers, code control systems and execution flow analysers have an important role to play in supporting the programming process. The availability of such tools for a particular language is likely to make a system easier to implement and validate.

4. *The size of the project.* If the project is very large, it may be appropriate to design and implement a programming language specifically for that project. This is especially true where no reasonable implementations of existing languages are available. An example of a well known system where this approach was adopted was in the development of the Unix operating system and its associated programming language C.

5. *The knowledge of existing programming staff.* Although it is not particularly difficult for experienced programmers to learn a new programming language, they require some practice in a language before they become fully competent. If other factors do not militate against it, it is desirable to choose a language with which programming staff are already familiar.

6. *The programming language used in previous projects.* This is related to the above consideration inasmuch as programmers who have worked on previous projects are already familiar with some programming language. Another important consideration is that program maintenance is made more difficult if many languages are in current use. If programmers are expected to maintain a number of systems, coded in different languages, there will inevitably be mistakes made because of confusion of language features.

7. *The need for software portability.* If the software is intended for only a single hardware configuration, and has a limited lifetime, software portability considerations are not important. On the other hand, if the system is intended to operate on a number of different machines, it is important to select a programming language which allows portable programs to be constructed.

8. *The application being programmed.* Although so-called general-purpose programming languages can be used for any application, some languages are more suitable than others for particular applications. For example, a language such as FORTRAN is best suited to scientific/mathematical applications and is quite unsuitable for compiler writing or operating system construction. COBOL, on the other hand, was designed for business applications and Ada for programming embedded computer systems. However, the general-purpose nature of Ada means that it may eventually supplant both COBOL and FORTRAN in their respective application areas.

One area of increasing importance which cannot be readily programmed using languages such as Pascal or Ada is artificial intelligence applications. In this area, it is virtually essential to use a language such as LISP or PROLOG which supports dynamic storage allocation and allows the creation of complex linked structures.

The choice of a programming language is a very important one and all the above factors should be taken into consideration when making that choice. At present, there are no programming languages which are really suitable for all applications and rigid standardization on any one language is not recommended. A better approach is to have a list of approved programming languages, each tailored towards a particular application. The language on the list which is best suited to the application should be chosen.

6.5 Independent compilation

Independent compilation of program units means that units may be compiled separately and subsequently integrated to form a complete program. The integration process is carried out by another program, known as a linker or link editor. Without the facility of independent compilation, a language cannot be considered as a viable language for software engineering.

Typically, a large program is made up of a number of distinct program units — procedures, functions or modules. In total, it may consist of several thousand lines of source code and it may take hours to compile the complete program. If every program unit needed to be recompiled each time any one of the units is changed, this would impose significant overhead and increase the costs of program development, debugging and maintenance. If independent compilation is available, compiling the whole system is unnecessary

— only the modified unit need be recompiled and the system relinked.

To compile a program unit on its own, that unit must be self-contained. All objects referenced in a unit should either be defined explicitly in that unit or their properties — type, name, parameters of a procedure — should be specified in a special declaration commonly known as an external declaration. As long as the properties of all objects are explicitly specified, compiler checking is not compromised by independent compilation.

An independent compilation facility is vital for the development of large systems and this is one of the principal reasons why FORTRAN, in spite of its shortcomings, has been so widely used in software engineering projects. The design of FORTRAN subroutines is such that independent compilation is straightforward and large libraries of precompiled FORTRAN routines can be developed. As well as this, routines specific to some application such as mathematical routines are available at almost all large FORTRAN installations and this increases the real power of the language enormously.

In FORTRAN, the basic program unit which is independently compiled is the subroutine. Because FORTRAN is not a block-structured language, there is no concept of global names — all names used in a subroutine are either parameters, locally declared or explicitly stated in a COMMON block. A COMMON statement specifies those program variables which are defined outside the subroutine. If reference is made to other subroutines, the FORTRAN compiler assumes them to be externally declared and creates a list of external references to be resolved by the link editor. Because the user need not specify external references made in a subroutine, the compiler assumes that all external references, whether to subroutines or COMMON variables, are correct. It cannot check, for example, if a subroutine call has the correct number of parameters and consequently there is no way to detect programmer error.

The design of block-structured languages is such that independent compilation must be implemented as a special feature and restrictions must be imposed on language usage if independent compilation is permitted. The scope rules of block-structured languages mean that all names accessed in a block need not be declared in that block — access to names declared in outer blocks are permitted. Consequently, according to the rules of the language, a procedure may refer to global variables and the compiler must obtain the specifications of these variables by compiling their declarations. Clearly, procedures which refer to global variables cannot be independently compiled. Non-standard implementations of block-structured languages like Pascal which offer an independent compilation facility generally forbid the use of global names in independently compiled procedures. In order that independently compiled procedures may make reference to other procedures, the language is usually extended by the provision of an external procedure specification facility.

An external procedure specification allows the programmer to introduce the name of an external procedure and to specify the types of its parameters. There may be a restriction on the parameter types permitted in an external procedure or, alternatively, the system may not guarantee compiler checking of external procedure references. Each external procedure which is referenced must be specified, and after compilation a special purpose linker is used to create the final program.

Because of the rules governing visibility of names, block-structured languages are not particularly suitable for independent compilation. Procedures which share variables cannot be written and compiler checking is either compromised or the programmer is severely restricted in his use of the language.

In Ada, the need for independent compilation of programs has been explicitly recognized by the language designers. An Ada program may be submitted to the compiler as a single unit or as a number of separate compilation units. A compilation unit may take several forms but, simplistically, it is either a subprogram or a package.

An integral part of the Ada compilation system is one or more libraries containing those compilation units which have already been processed. When a compilation unit requires the services of a library unit, this is indicated by a **with** statement. For example:

with QUEUES, STACKS, LISTS;

This statement tells the Ada compiler that library units called 'QUEUES', 'STACKS' and 'LISTS' are required.

An additional independent compilation facility is also provided in Ada. This is the ability to define the body of a compilation unit as separate and to compile the unit specification (package header, etc.) before the unit body. This allows the parallel development of dependent units to take place. Once the specification of a unit is available in a library it may be used by any other unit, although obviously execution is impossible until the unit body is available.

Separate compilation of the bodies of compilation units is indicated by means of the keyword **separate**:

package body LISTS **is separate**;
procedure COUNT (X : **in** SOMEARRAY) **is separate**;

The independent compilation facilities of Ada make the separate development of Ada programs a straightforward task. However, the disadvantage with Ada's approach to independent compilation is that the order of compilation of units is critical — a unit must be compiled before it is referenced. This is most liable to cause problems when units in the library are being changed at the same time as some other units are relying on their services. To reduce clashes between unit versions, the management of Ada libraries must be automated using a configuration management system.

Further reading

In spite of the enormous number of publications in this area, it is difficult to find some general work which is both up-to-date and not overconcerned with the translation of programming languages. There is a need for a study of programming languages which takes data abstraction, Ada, etc., into account.

An Introduction to the Study of Programming Languages, D. W. Barron (1977), Cambridge: Cambridge University Press.

A well written little book but its usefulness is limited because it does not cover either Pascal or Ada.

Programming in Ada, J. G. P. Barnes (1984), London: Addison-Wesley.

Every software engineer ought to know something about Ada and there are literally dozens of introductory texts on that language. This seems to be one of the best, although this is largely personal preference.

'Programming languages for reliable computing systems', J. J. Horning. In *Program Construction*, LNCS 69, Berlin: Springer-Verlag.

A first-class summary of how programming language features affect the reliability of systems. Highly recommended.

Real-time Languages, Design and Development, S. J. Young (1982), Chichester: Wiley/Ellis Horwood.

This is a general survey of the facilities required in real-time languages. The author compares Ada, MODULA and RTL/2.

Chapter 7 TESTING AND DEBUGGING

The validation of a software system is a continuing process through each stage of the software life cycle. In earlier chapters, validation of particular stages of the software life cycle has been discussed. However, program testing is still by far the most widely used system validation technique, so this chapter is devoted to that topic and its associated process of debugging.

Program testing is that part of the validation process which is normally carried out during implementation and also, in a different form, when implementation is complete. Testing involves exercising the program using data similar to the real data the program is designed to execute, observing the program outputs and inferrring the existence of program errors or inadequacies from anomalies in that output.

It is sometimes thought that program testing and debugging are one and the same thing. Although closely related, they are, in fact, quite distinct processes. Testing is the process of establishing the existence of program errors. Debugging is the process of locating where these errors occurred in the program and correcting the code which is incorrect.

It is very important to realize that testing can never show that a program is correct. It is always possible that undetected errors exist even after the most comprehensive testing. Program testing can only demonstrate the presence of errors in a program, it cannot demonstrate their absence. Following Myers (1979), therefore, a successful test is considered to be one which establishes the presence of one or more errors in the software being tested. Notice that this differs from the normal definition of a successful test, which is a test displaying no output anomalies.

Program testing is a destructive process. It is intended to cause a program to behave in a manner which was not intended by its designer or implementor. As it is a natural human trait for an individual to feel some affinity with objects which he has constructed, the programmer responsible for system implementation is not the best person to test a program. Psychologically, the system programmer will not want to 'destroy' his creation with the result that, consciously or subconsciously, program tests will be selected which fail. These tests will not be adequate for demonstrating the presence of system errors.

On the other hand, detailed knowledge of the structure of a program or programming system can be extremely useful in identifying appropriate test cases, and the system implementor plays an important part in this. The key to successful program testing is to establish a working environment where system implementors and outsiders involved in program testing can play a complementary role. This must involve the management premise that program 'errors' are inevitable because of the complexity of the systems involved and that errors are not blameworthy. The testing process must not be seen as threatening those individuals involved in implementation, otherwise they are liable to be uncooperative with outsiders responsible for testing.

Although only a part of the overall validation process, program testing is the only technique used to validate a program in most programming organizations. Program verification and inspection (described below) are not widely used validation techniques. Unfortunately, testing, on its own, cannot completely validate a program, with the result that unreliable systems are very common indeed.

As well as covering program testing techniques, this chapter also discusses the role of verification and formalized inspections in the software validation process. Test-case design is illustrated by example, and software tools which may be used in the testing process are described. The final sections in the chapter discuss debugging. They describe how programs can be written to facilitate debugging and discuss a number of automated debugging aids.

7.1 The testing process

Except for very small computer programs, it is unrealistic to attempt to test systems as a single unit. Large systems are built out of sub-systems which are built out of modules which may themselves be built out of procedures. If an attempt is made to test the system as a single entity, it is unlikely that more than a small percentage of the system 'errors' will be identified. The testing process, like the programming process, must proceed in stages with each stage being a logical continuation of the previous stage.

It is possible to identify five distinct stages in the testing process. These are:

1. *Function testing.* Function testing or unit testing is the basic level of testing where the functions making up a module are tested to ensure that they operate correctly. In a properly designed system, each function should have a single, clearly defined specification. It should be relatively straightforward to design test cases to ensure that the function meets its specification. Functions should not depend on other functions at the same level, so it should be possible to test each function as a stand-alone entity, without the presence of other functions.

2. *Module testing.* A module is made up of a number of functions which may co-operate with each other. After each individual function has been tested, it is necessary to test the co-operation of these

functions when they are put together as a module. It should be possible to test a module as a stand-alone entity, without the presence of other system modules.

3. *Sub-system testing.* Sub-system testing is the next step up in the testing process where modules are put together to form sub-systems. As modules co-operate and communicate, sub-system testing should concentrate on testing module interfaces under the assumption that the modules themselves are correct.

4. *System testing.* System testing (sometimes called integration testing) is carried out when the sub-systems are integrated to make up the entire system. At this stage, the testing process is concerned with finding errors in design and coding. It is also concerned with validating that the overall system provides the functions specified in the requirements and that the dynamic characteristics of the system match those specified in the requirements definition.

5. *Acceptance testing.* Until this stage, all testing is carried out using data generated by the organization responsible for constructing the system. Acceptance testing is the process of testing the system with real data — the information which the system is intended to manipulate. The process of acceptance testing often demonstrates errors in the system requirements definition. The requirements may not reflect the actual facilities and performance required by the user, and acceptance testing may demonstrate that the system does not exhibit the anticipated performance and functionality.

Normally, function testing and module testing are carried out by the implementor of the function or the programming team without a formal test specification. The programmer makes up his own test data and may incrementally test his code as it is being developed.

The other stages of testing involve integrating work from a number of programmers and must be planned in advance. They are usually undertaken by an independent team of testers. The testing procedure should be formally specified and set out in the project plan. It is desirable to start test planning at a relatively early stage in the software development process. Module and sub-system testing should be planned as the design of the sub-system is formulated with system test and acceptance test specifications prepared either at the system design stage or while system implementation is in progress.

This description of the stages involved in the testing process is the classical one which is widely adopted in the testing of large systems. However, if strict top-down testing, as described below, is used, the order of the stages of testing may be changed. Sub-system testing may precede module testing with function testing as the final stage in the testing process.

System testing is not part of this top-down testing process but is carried out after sub-systems have been completely developed. Rather than simultaneously combining all sub-systems into a single unit, they should be incrementally integrated so that errors may be more easily detected and localized.

One approach to testing is to test each system module individually. Once satisfied that modules are fully tested, all modules are put together to make up the final system. That system is then tested as an integrated whole. This approach leads almost inevitably to a non-working system with no clear indicators of exactly which aspects of the system are causing the problems. A much better approach which should be adopted irrespective of whether a top-down or bottom-up strategy is being used, is to introduce modules incrementally, one at a time.

The system should start off as a single module and thus should be tested using appropriate test cases. Once the testing of this module is satisfactory, a second module can be introduced and further testing carried out. The process continues until all modules have eventually been integrated into a complete system. If a module is introduced at some stage in this process and tests, which previously did not detect system errors, now detect system errors, it is likely that these errors are due to the introduction of the new module. The source of the error is thus localized, simplifying the task of locating and correcting the error.

7.1.1 Top-down and bottom-up testing

There are two different testing philosophies which have been used in sub-system, module and function testing. These are called top-down testing and bottom-up testing as they are based on the corresponding top-down and bottom-up software development methods. An illustration of how these approaches differ is shown in Fig. 7.1.

Top-down testing involves starting at the sub-system level with modules represented by stubs — objects which have the same interface as the module

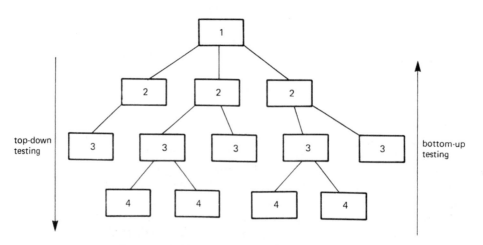

Figure 7.1 Top-down and bottom-up testing.

but which are very much simpler. After sub-system testing is complete, each module is tested in the same way — the functions are represented by stubs. Finally, the functions are replaced by the actual code and this is tested.

Bottom-up testing reverses the process. Firstly, the functions making up a module are tested individually. Then they are integrated to form a module and this is tested. After each module has been tested, the modules are integrated and, finally, the sub-system is tested.

Top-down testing is not an activity which should be carried out in isolation. Rather it is used in conjunction with top-down program development so that a module is tested as soon as it is coded. In principle, therefore, coding and testing are a single function with no clearly defined function or module testing phase.

If top-down testing is used, it is likely that unnoticed design errors will be detected at an early stage in the testing process. These errors are usually built into the top levels of the system and, if they are detected early, a good deal of time can be saved. Early error detection before much of the system has been implemented means that extensive redesign and re-implementation may be avoided.

As well as this, top-down testing has the advantage that a working, albeit limited, system is available at an early stage in the development process. Not only does this provide an important psychological boost to those involved in the system development, it also demonstrates the feasibility of the system to management.

Unfortunately, strict top-down testing can be extremely difficult because of the requirement that program stubs, simulating lower levels of the system, must be produced. The mechanism for implementing these program stubs involves either producing a very simplified version of the function required, returning some random value of the correct type, or interacting with the tester who inputs an appropriate value, simulating the action of the function.

If the function is a complex one, it may be virtually impossible to produce a program stub which simulates that function accurately. For example, consider a function which converts an array of objects into a linked list. The result of that function involves internal program objects — the pointers linking elements in the list. It is unrealistic to generate some random list and return that object. The list components must correspond to the array elements. It is equally impossible for the programmer to input the created list as he has no knowledge of the internal representation of pointers. Therefore, the routine to perform the conversion from array to list must exist before top-down testing is possible.

A further disadvantage of top-down testing is that test output may be difficult to observe. In many systems, the higher levels of that system do not directly generate output but, in order to test these levels, they must be forced to do so. The tester must create an artificial situation, in order to generate test results.

Bottom-up testing, on the other hand, involves testing the modules at the lower levels in the hierarchy, and then working up the hierarchy of modules until the final module is tested. The advantages of top-down testing are the disadvantages of bottom-up testing and vice versa.

If bottom-up testing is used, drivers must be constructed for the lower-level modules which present these modules with appropriate inputs. Using a bottom-up approach to testing usually means that it is easier to create test cases and observe test input. Bottom-up testing has the disadvantage that no demonstrably working program is available until the very last module has been tested. Furthermore, if design errors exist in high-level modules these are not detected until a late stage in the system test. Correction of these errors might involve the rewriting and consequent retesting of lower-level modules in the system.

In view of the advantages and disadvantages of each method of testing, there can be no definitive statement made about the best method of testing a program. The techniques adopted must depend on the programming organization, the application being programmed and the individual programmers working on a project. In practice, some combination of top-down and bottom-up testing is usually used to test a system. It is normal to test at least some of the lower-level components illustrated in Fig. 7.1 in parallel with the components nearer the top of the tree.

If limited system facilities are provided it is better that a few facilities are provided completely rather than many facilities in a primitive state. For example, say an operating system is being developed in language D. This operating system is designed to offer language processing, text processing, editing and other facilities to many users. A strict top-down approach would make limited versions of all these facilities available as early as possible.

However, all facilities are not equally important and, as the system is being programmed in language D, it is obviously advantageous to make a full compiler for D available as early as possible. A practical testing strategy therefore involves a controlled top-down approach, carried out in conjunction with program development. The system facilities can then be ranked, developing them in order of importance and ignoring any formal top-down/bottom-up testing techniques.

7.1.2 The design of test cases

Planning the testing of a programming system involves formulating a set of test cases which are akin to the real data that the system is intended to manipulate. Test cases should fully exercise the system. Test cases consist of an input specification, a description of the system functions exercised by that input and a statement of the expected output. Thorough testing involves producing cases to ensure that the program responds as expected to both valid and invalid inputs, that the program performs to specification and that it does not corrupt other programs or data in the system.

It is important to distinguish between test cases and test data. Test data is simply the input which has been formulated to test the system, whereas test cases are composed of input and output specifications plus a statement of the function under test. It is sometimes possible to generate test data automatically, but impossible to generate test cases as the generator would have to have the same functions as the program being tested.

It is impossible to present an example of the test cases for a large system as they would normally occupy a volume much thicker than this book. Rather, a very simple example is presented — the testing of a routine to search a table of integers to determine if some given integer is present in that table.

Assume that this routine is called as follows:

$S := SEARCH (AnArray, ArraySize, InValue)$;

If *AnArray* has an element equal to *InValue*, the index of that element is returned by *SEARCH*, otherwise -1 is returned. The size of *AnArray* is passed to *SEARCH* as *ArraySize* and it may be assumed that the lower bound of the array is 1. If *SEARCH* is written in a programming language which permits type checking, such as Pascal, the compiler detects parameters of incorrect type. There is no need to test *SEARCH* with parameters of the wrong type or with incorrect numbers of parameters.

According to our list above, *SEARCH* must be tested for its reaction to valid and invalid input, system corruption and performance. As invalid input is trapped by the compiler and performance is not specified, there is no need to design specific test cases for them. The requirement that a call of *SEARCH* should not modify any program variables apart from that assigned the value returned by *SEARCH* cannot be tested using specific test cases.

To detect if *SEARCH* actually corrupts global values, a dump of the program global variables is taken. This is taken each time *SEARCH* is called and repeated immediately after the call of the procedure. These dumps may then be compared automatically, to ensure that only the variable assigned a value by *SEARCH* has been changed. It is not realistic to require this process to be explicitly programmed into the system as the extra work involved is considerable. Rather a software tool designed to assist with program testing is used.

Now let us consider the minimum set of test cases which are required simply to establish a reasonable level of confidence in *SEARCH*:

1. Array is a single value equal to required value.
   Input : $AnArray = 17$; $ArraySize = 1$; $InValue = 17$
   Output : function returns 1

2. Array is a single value not equal to required value.
   Input : $AnArray = 17$; $ArraySize = 1$; $InValue = 0$
   Output : function returns -1

3. Array is empty.
   Input : $AnArray = -$; $ArraySize = 0$; $InValue = 1$
   Output : function returns -1

4. The array size is even and the first value is the required value.

Input : *AnArray* = 17,23; *ArraySize* = 2; *InValue* = 17
Output : function returns 1

5. The array size is even and the last value is the required value.
Input : *AnArray* = 17,23; *ArraySize* = 2; *InValue* = 23
Output : function returns 2

6. The array size is even and no value matches the required value.
Input : *AnArray* = 17,23; *ArraySize* = 2; *InValue* = 3
Output : function returns −1

7. The array size is odd and the first value is the required value.
Input : *AnArray* = 17,23,29; *ArraySize* = 3; *InValue* = 17
Output : function returns 1

8. The array size is odd and the last value is the required value.
Input : *AnArray* = 17,23,29; *ArraySize* = 3; *InValue* = 29
Output : function returns 3

9. The array size is odd and no value matches the required value.
Input : *AnArray* = 17,23,29; *ArraySize* = 3; *InValue* = 4
Output : function returns −1

10. Array has multiple values, one of which is the required value.
Input : *AnArray* = 17,23,29,35,41; *ArraySize* = 5; *InValue* = 23
Output : function returns 2

This set of input values is in no way exhaustive — *SEARCH* may fail if the input array happens to be 1, 2, 3, 4 but there are no grounds for supposing this. Test cases have been designed to check *SEARCH* for a number of classes of input and it is reasonable to surmize that if it works successfully for one member of a class, it will do so for all members of that class. For example, a test case has been designed to check that *SEARCH* works with arrays which have an odd (3) number of values. It may be that *SEARCH* would fail if an array whose size is a different odd number is used, but there is no reason to suspect that this will be the case.

By identifying these classes and selecting a test case from each class, errors in *SEARCH*, if they exist, should be detected. The classes which have been identified for possible input values in this example are:

1. Array size of 1, element in array.
2. Array size of 1, element not in array.
3. Empty array.
4. Even array size, element 1st element in array.
5. Even array size, element last element in array.
6. Even array size, element not in array.
7. Odd array size, element 1st element in array.
8. Odd array size, element last element in array.
9. Odd array size, element not in array.
10. Multiple-valued array, element in array, not first or last.

This form of input classification for determining test inputs is called equivalence partitioning. Equivalence partitioning is a technique for determining which classes of input data have common properties so that, if the program does not display an erroneous output for one member of a class, it should not do so for any member of that class.

The equivalence classes must be identified by using the program specification or user documentation and by the tester using his or her experience in guessing which classes of input value are likely to detect errors. For example, if an input specification states that the range of some input values must be a 5-digit integer — that is, between 10 000 and 99 999 — equivalence classes might be those values less than 10 000, values between 10 000 and 99 999 and values greater than 99 999. Similarly, if 4 to 8 values are to be input, equivalence classes are less than 4, between 4 and 8, and more than 8.

In some cases, program specifications may not be precisely detailed, so the tester must use his experience to determine equivalence classes. For example, if a program accepts an integer as input, it should be tested using integers less than zero. If a program manipulates tables it should be tested using tables with no entries, a single entry and many entries.

When equivalence classes have been determined, the next step is to choose values from each class which are most likely to lead to a successful test. The values chosen should cause the program to display an erroneous output. Testing experience has shown that the most useful values to select for test input are those at the boundaries of each equivalence class.

Not only input equivalence classes should be considered. Output equivalence classes should also be taken into account and the input values which generate outputs at the boundary of each output class should be chosen as test input. For example, say a program is designed to produce between three and six outputs, with each output lying in the range 1000–2500. Test input should be selected which produces 3 values at 1000, 3 values at 2500, 6 values at 1000 and 6 values at 2500. Furthermore, input should be selected so that erroneous output values would result if that input was processed as correct input. This input should attempt to force the program to produce less than 3 values, more than 6 values, values less than 1000 and values greater than 2500.

To illustrate this technique of choosing test input, consider a procedure designed to convert a string of digits to an integer. Assume that the procedure is implemented in Pascal in an environment where 16-bit two's complement notation is used to represent integers.

This conversion procedure header and associated type declaration are as follows:

type *shortstring = array [1..6] of char*;
function *StringToInteger (digits : shortstring) : integer*;

The string of digits to be converted to an integer is right-justified in digits and may be positive or negative. If less than 6 characters long, digits is padded with blanks on the left and, if the input is negative, a minus sign occupies the character position immediately to the left of the most significant digit. Because of built-in compiler checking, there is no need to test this function using arrays of more or less than 6 characters or to test it with any other invalid type of parameter.

Inspection of the function specification results in the identification of the following input equivalence classes:

1. inputs with 1–5 non-blank characters (C1),
2. inputs with 6 non-blank characters (C2),
3. empty inputs (C3),
4. inputs consisting of a minus sign on its own (C4),
5. inputs with a minus sign as the most significant character (C5),
6. inputs with a digit as the most significant character (C6),
7. inputs which are left-padded by some character apart from a blank or zero (C7),
8. inputs which are left-padded with zeros (C8),
9. inputs whose most significant character is a digit but which contain non-digits mixed with digits (C9),
10. inputs where the minus sign is not immediately to the left of the most significant digit (C10).

Output equivalence classes can also be identified:

1. negative integers between the minimum integer which it is possible to represent and zero (C11),
2. zero (C12),
3. positive integers between zero and the maximum possible integer which may be represented (C13).

Using two's complement 16-bit representation for integers means that the minimum integer which may be represented is $-32\,768$ and the maximum positive integer is $32\,767$.

By selecting test input values at the boundaries of each of these equivalence classes and eliminating possible duplicate values derived from consideration of input and output classes, the following test cases can be constructed:

INPUT	EXPECTED OUTPUT	CLASSES TESTED
" 1"	1	C1, C6, C13
" 32767"	32767	C1, C6, C13
" 32768"	Error, invalid input	C1, C13
"−32768"	−32768	C2, C5, C11
" 032767"	32767	C2, C13
" 123456"	Error, invalid input	C2

" −32769"	Error, invalid input	C2, C5, C11
" "	Error, invalid input	C3
" −"	Error, invalid input	C4
" −1"	−1	C5, C11
" 0"	0	C6, C12
" xxxxx1"	Error, invalid input	C7
"xxxx−1"	Error, invalid input	C7
" 000001"	1	C8, C6, C2
"−00001"	−1	C8, C5, C2
" 2x1"	Error, invalid input	C9
" 2−1"	Error, invalid input	C9
" −1"	Error, invalid input	C10
" 000000"	0	C2, C12

Thirteen input and output equivalence classes can be identified, and from these nineteen distinct test inputs identified. Notice that tests derived from input and output equivalent classes can overlap. For example, testing the function with the input −32 768 tests the function's reaction to an input containing six significant characters, and also if it converts strings representing the maximum negative integer correctly.

The technique of equivalence partitioning is a useful one for selecting instances of each possible input for test. However, even when a program operates successfully for individual test inputs, combinations of these inputs may detect program error. Equivalence partitioning provides no help in selecting these combinations. Generally, the number of possible input combinations for even a relatively small program will be immense. It is quite impossible, usually, to carry out tests of all possible combinations, and the experience and intuition of the tester must be used to select combinations likely to cause program failure.

The most productive way of choosing input combinations is to combine the process of testing with code examination. For example, code examination may reveal that two separate program routines use and modify shared variables. This is potentially error prone as incorrect or unthinking modification of these variables by one routine could cause the other routine to fail. A useful test case would cause both routines to be exercised during the same program execution.

Code inspection may also reveal the pointlessness of testing other input combinations. If routines are entirely self-contained, it is impossible for the execution of one routine to affect the execution of other routines and thus there is no need to test them together. Dependencies, also, may be revealed by code inspection. For example, an arithmetic function may accept character strings as input and depend on conversion functions, such as the StringToInteger function above, to translate its input into numeric quantities. Not only the conversion function must be tested but also routines which call that function for their reaction when the conversion function is presented with invalid input.

7.1.3 Testing real-time programs

Real-time systems are those systems which interact with their environment in 'real time'. That is, the processes in the system must respond to events under time constraints. If the system response is not timely, information may be lost. Examples of real-time systems are operating systems, message switching systems, and process control systems. The effective testing of such systems poses particular problems for the tester.

Real-time systems are usually made up of a number of distinct co-operating processes and are often interrupt driven. This means that an external event such as an input from a sensor causes control to be trans-ferred from the currently executing process to the process which handles that event.

The peculiar problems of testing real-time systems are caused by the subtle interactions which may arise between the various processes in the system. System errors may be time dependent, only arising when the system processes are in a particular state. The exact state of the system processes when the error occurred may be impossible to reproduce.

The testing of real-time systems is often further complicated because the reliability requirements of these systems are usually greater than the requirements for systems which are not time critical. The reason for this lies in the applications for which real-time systems are used — controlling complex machinery, air traffic control, military communications, etc. The consequences of system failure are potentially disastrous. This has the consequence that system testing must be both exhaustive and stringent.

Consider the real-time system made up of five processes shown in Fig. 7.2. These processes interact with each other and some of them collect inputs from their environment and generate outputs to that environment. These inputs may be from sensors, keyboards or some other computer system. Similarly, outputs may be to control lines, other computers or user terminals.

Because real-time systems are composed of a number of processes, the first step in testing such systems is to test each process individually. In the above system model, therefore, P1, P2, P3, P4 and P5 would first be tested in isolation and debugged until each process meets its specification.

Following this, it may be appropriate to test threads; that is, test the system's reaction to a single event. This will normally involve control passing from process to process — actions 'thread' their way through the system. In the above model, threads might be I1(P1) -> P1 -> P3 -> P4 -> O1(P4), I(P2) -> P2 -> P1 -> P3 -> P4 -> O1(P4) and so on.

After a single thread has been tested, that thread can then be exercised by introducing multiple events of the same class but without introducing events of any other class. For example, a multi-user system might first be tested using a single terminal then multiple-terminal testing gradually introduced. In the above model, this type of testing might involve processing all inputs in multiple-input processes. For example, I1(P1), I2(P1), I3(P1)

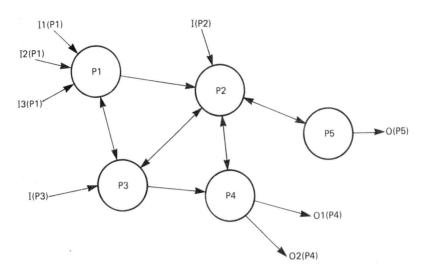

Figure 7.2   A real-time system.

-> P1 -> P3 -> P4 -> O1(P4) might be a possible test, as might I123(P1) -> P2 -> P5 -> O(P5).

After the system's reaction to each class of event has been tested, it can then be tested for its reactions to more than one class of event occurring simultaneously. At this stage, new event tests should be introduced gradually so that system errors can be localized. In the above model, this might be tested as shown in Fig. 7.3.

Finally, the system must be tested in an operational environment, again gradually increasing the number of operations which the system must perform.

An important software tool which has been developed to assist the

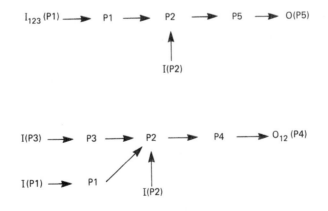

Figure 7.3   Thread testing.

construction of real-time programs is the MASCOT system (Jackson, 1977). This system provides a framework for constructing real-time systems and is particularly useful for testing such systems, as it allows processes to be introduced and removed without halting other processes in the system. Furthermore, it strictly controls process communications so that the possibility of one process corrupting another is reduced.

7.2 Program verification

The notion of program verification is an attractive one. Rather than validate a program by testing, verification involves demonstrating the correspondence between a program (or a design) and its specifications using mathematical methods. Essentially, the program is proved to be correct.

It has been suggested that the development of effective methods of program verification will make the need for a system-testing phase redundant. This is a false premise. Whilst part of the testing activity involves checking that a program meets its specifications, system testing also checks that these specifications are correct and that non-functional constraints are satisfied by the system. While program verification can reduce testing costs, it cannot completely replace testing as a means of system validation.

It is arguable whether it is best to carry out verification on the program itself or on the detailed design. If the design is verified, it is possible to introduce errors during the implementation which would be detected if the verification process was carried out on the finished program. However, there are a number of disadvantages to verifying a program rather than a design. These are:

1. The program may be written in such a way that verification is very difficult. Implementation-dependent constructs whose semantics are not clear may have been used in order to satisfy efficiency requirements.

2. The programming language used may be so low level that verification is impossible — there is no way a FORTRAN or machine code program can be proven to be correct.

3. If verification follows implementation and design errors are discovered, this may involve considerable work in redesign and re-implementation of the program. It is far better to detect these errors at the design stage and accept the possibility of implementation errors which are usually relatively cheap to correct.

4. As an implementation is usually larger than a design, program verification is longer, more complex and more expensive than design verification.

5. It may be possible to transform the design automatically into several different programs, depending on the system required. Thus, by verifying the design, only a single verification is necessary for all of these generated programs.

Much depends, of course, on the implementation language. If this is close to or the same as the language used for specifying the detailed design it is obviously sensible to verify the program. If it is a lower-level language, it makes more sense to verify the detailed design. Ideally both the design and the implementation should be verified, but because of the cost of the verification process this is quite unrealistic.

At the moment, program verification is only likely to be cost-effective for highly critical parts of large systems. It is unlikely that formal verification of complete systems will be practiced in the near future because of the associated costs and difficulties.

The verification of programs by providing a mathematical proof of their correctness was built on the work of McCarthy (1962) and a number of other authors such as Floyd (1967), Hoare (1969), Dijkstra (1976) and Manna (1969). There are a variety of different techniques for proving program correctness, but the general principle underlying these techniques is straightforward.

Assume that there are a number of points in a program where the designer can provide assertions concerning the program variables and their relationships. At each of these points, the assertions should be invariably true. Say the points in the program are P(1), P(2),...,P(n). The associated assertions are a(1), a(2),...,a(n). Assertion a(1) must be an assertion about the input of the program and a(n) an assertion about the program output.

To prove that the program statements between points P(i) and P(i+1) are correct, it must be demonstrated that the application of the program statements separating these points causes a(i) to be transformed to a(i+1). If this verification is carried out for all adjacent points in the program, this will demonstrate that the input assertion plus the program leads directly to the output assertion. If the input and output assertions are correctly formulated and the program terminates (does not contain an endless loop), this process demonstrates the correctness of the program. A description of program verification techniques is given in McGettrick (1983).

A discussion of program-proving techniques requires a book to itself, so general techniques will not be covered here. Rather, two examples of program proofs are presented to demonstrate program verification. The first program is a trivial program which determines the maximum value in a sequence, and the second example is the well known binary search algorithm.

The notation used in these examples is not the familiar notation used in predicate logic. The existential quantifier is replaced by a function MEMB so that MEMB (X) can be read as 'there exists a member of X'. If X is ordered, this ordering is denoted by ORD(X). The logical operators are written as 'and', 'or' and 'not', with 'not' having the highest precedence followed by 'and' then 'or'.

Rather than use the universal quantifier, the notation X, where X is a set, sequence or array, is taken to mean all members of X. Part of a sequence or array may be written as $X(p..q)$ which means all members between X(p) and X(q). This notation may be extended to specify multiple parts. X(p..q,r..s) means all members of X between X(p) and X(q) and all members between X(r) and X(s).

A program to determine the maximum value in a sequence and its associated assertions is shown below. This program determines the largest value in a sequence with the model of sequences being that of Chapter 4. The sequence is made up of two lists, I.past and I.FUTURE. Notice that assertions are written as special comments introduced by the symbol $--|$.

```
    -- accepts sequence values and sets max to
    -- the value of the largest member of that sequence
      I : SEQUENCE OF INTEGER;
      MAX, A : INTEGER;
      --| max = UNDEFINED and length(I) > 0
   1. MAX := next(I);
      --| max >= I.past and max = MEMB (I.past)
   2. while LENGTH (I.FUTURE) > 0 loop
   2.1      A := next(I);
            --| max >= I.past and max = MEMB (I.past)
            --| or max < a and a = MEMB (I.past)
   2.2      if MAX < A then
            --| a > I.past and a = MEMB (I.past)
   2.2.1        MAX := A;
            --| max > I.past and max = MEMB (I.past)
            end if;
      end loop;
      --| max >= I and max = MEMB (I)
```

Proof of termination

The **next** operation is defined as reducing the length of I.FUTURE by 1 each time it is applied. Thus the length of I.FUTURE must eventually become 0 and the while loop at 2 terminates. This is always true because there are no reset statements in the program to affect the length of I.FUTURE.

Initial assertion

The program is valid if and only if the length of the sequence I is greater than 0.

Final assertion

The output assertion states that the value of MAX is greater than or equal to the values of all members of the sequence I. It also states that the value of MAX is equal to the value of a member of the sequence. This is obviously essential, as some large value which is not in the sequence might satisfy the first assertion.

Proof

To prove that this design is correct, it must be shown that the output assertion follows from the input assertion and the program. Consider each statement in turn.

1. The assertion that can be made before statement 1 is that max is undefined. This statement sets MAX to the first member of the sequence, thus defining it to be equal to a member of I.

2. At statement 2, MAX is greater than or equal to all members of the sequence considered so far. This is true on first execution as I.PAST consists of the first member of I and statement 1 sets MAX to this value.

3. The loop has no side effects, so assertion 2 holds before execution of statement 2.1. After execution either this assertion still holds or A > MAX.

4. Statement 2.2 selects case where A > MAX. When this statement is selected, A > I.PAST and A = MEMB (I.PAST).

5. Statement 2.2.1 assigns value of A to MAX. After this, statement 2 is executed. The invariant specified there subsumes this assertion (>= includes >), so the invariant at 2 is true if this statement is executed. On loop termination, therefore, the assertion MAX >= I.PAST and MAX = MEMB (I.PAST) always holds. But the definition of the empty condition specifies that I.FUTURE is empty when I.PART = I.

6. Therefore, the final condition MAX >= I and MAX = MEMB (I) is true and the program is correct.

A proof of this simple program has been covered in detail to demonstrate that even the verification of a simple program is lengthy.

As a further illustration of verification, consider a more complex program, namely a binary search routine. Assertions have been included as commentary in the program.

```
procedure BINARY_SEARCH (KEY : INTEGER;T : INTARRAY;
        FOUND : out BOOLEAN; L:out INTEGER) is
    M : INTEGER := T'FIRST;
    N : INTEGER := T'LAST;
    BOTT : INTEGER := M;
    TOP : INTEGER := N;
    MID : INTEGER;
begin
    --| 1. m <= n and m > 0 and ORD(T)
    L := (M+N) MOD 2;
    FOUND := T(L) = KEY;
    --| 2. found and T(L) = key or
        --| not found and key <> T(m..bott-1,top+1..n)
    while BOTT <= TOP AND NOT FOUND loop
        MID := (TOP + BOTT) MOD 2;
        IF T(MID) = KEY then
            FOUND := TRUE; L := MID;
            --| 3. key = T(mid) and found
        elsif T(MID) < KEY then
            --| 4. key /= T(m..mid)
            BOTT := MID + 1;
            --| 5. key /= T(m..bott-1)
```

```
        else
              --| 6. key /= T(mid..n)
              TOP := MID − 1;
              --| 7. key /= T(top+1..n)
        end if;
     end loop;
  --| 8. found and T(L) = key or
     --| not found and key /= T
  end BINARY_SEARCH;
```

Proof of termination

The program terminates when FOUND becomes TRUE or when BOTT becomes greater than TOP. If the search succeeds, that is if an element equal to KEY exists, FOUND is explicitly set TRUE thus causing termination. Initially BOTT < TOP. If FOUND is not set TRUE, either the statement BOTT := MID +1 or the statement TOP := MID − 1 must be executed. The effect of these statements is to reduce (TOP − BOTT) until eventually it is negative in which case bott exceeds top and the program terminates.

Initial assertion

The initial assertion specifies that T is in ascending order, that array bounds are non-negative and that the upper bound exceeds or is equal to the lower bound.

Final assertion

The final assertion specifies that either an element in the table is equal to the key and L is the index of that element, or the table does not contain an element equal to the key.

Proof

Again, proving this design correct involves demonstrating that the final assertion follows from the initial assertion. This may be accomplished as follows:

1. Assertion 2 specifies either that the required value does not lie in the portion of the table already examined or it is the value at the mid point of the table. This is true on the first entry to the loop because none of the table has been examined, so the required value does not lie in the portion of the table already examined.

2. Assertion 3 follows because of successful test, KEY = MID. If assertions 3, 5, and 7 are true then assertion 2 follows directly for subsequent entries to the loop.

3. Assertion 4 follows from the fact that T is ordered and T(MID) < KEY. All values between M and MID are less than KEY.

4. Assertion 5 follows by substituting BOTT−1 for MID.

5. Assertion 6 follows using a similar argument to 4 for values greater than key.

6. Assertion 7 follows from 6 by substituting TOP−1 for MID.

7. On termination, it follows from the loop invariant that T(L) = KEY and FOUND is TRUE or, alternatively, FOUND is FALSE and there is no value in the part of the table searched so far that equals KEY. However, on termination, BOTT is greater than TOP so the expression T(M..BOTT−1, TOP+1..N) includes the entire table so there is no value in T = KEY. Therefore, the binary search program is correct.

From the foregoing it is clear that a correctness proof is at least as long if not longer than the program whose correctness is being verified. The effort required to develop the proof normally exceeds the programming effort. Thus, developing a proof is a difficult and costly exercise requiring specially trained and motivated staff. Although some progress has been made in implementing software tools to assist verification, the development of such tools is still a research problem.

For these reasons, authors such as Jensen and Tonies (1979) do not consider program proving to be a cost-effective software engineering technique. On the other hand, reports of work at IBM's Federal Systems division (IBM, 1980) suggest that they make successful use of verification techniques in the development of large programming systems.

7.3 Code inspections

Whether or not a program verification has been carried out at some stage during the software development process, a validation technique which has proved to be cost-effective is code inspection. Code inspection is a formalization of egoless programming, described in Chapter 10, and involves a programmer conducting an inspection team through his code. The code inspection process involves distributing the design specifications in advance to the inspection team, who study these and attempt to understand the design. This may be supplemented by a preliminary overview presented by the designer. During the inspection itself, the programmer explains to the rest of the team how he has implemented the design. They follow his explanation closely and attempt to detect errors and anomalies in it.

When an error is detected, it is noted by the moderator and the inspection continues. No attempt is made to correct the error, even if the correction seems obvious. The task of the inspection team is detection, not correction.

Fagan (1976) suggests that the best size for an inspection team is four members. These are:

1. a moderator who is a competent programmer but not personally involved in the project,

2. the designer of the program,

3. the programmer involved in the implementation,

4. the individual responsible for testing the code.

If the same individual is responsible for the design and coding or the coding and testing, another outsider should be brought in to take over one of those roles.

The advantage of code inspections over testing is that the inspection finds many errors in a single session. When errors are discovered by testing, they often require correction before further testing can continue. This has the consequence that errors are discovered and corrected one by one. The time required to correct many errors all at once is much less than that required to detect and correct them one by one, so that the inspection process results in a decrease in the overall system validation effort.

7.4 Validation tools

The process of system validation is laborious and is often the most expensive stage of software development. For real-time systems, validation may consume up to half of the costs of software development, and for other classes of system, validation costs are about one third of development costs. It is thus usually cost-effective to make as much use as possible of automated software tools to assist the validation process.

After implementation tools, testing and debugging tools are probably the most widely used and best developed software tools. In this section, therefore, descriptions of several testing tools such as flow summarizers, file comparators and simulators are provided. Where appropriate, the actions of these tools are illustrated by example.

7.4.1 Test data generators

Test data generators are programs which automatically generate a large number of test inputs for some system. Unfortunately, it is not possible for test data generators to produce the corresponding outputs — otherwise they would be equivalent to the program under test.

Test data generators are most useful in situations where the performance of a system in a practical environment must be tested. For example, testing of a database management system may start by using very small databases and the testing is initially designed to detect program errors resulting in incorrect output being produced. This small-scale testing does not actually reflect the actual environment where the program is to be used — it would normally operate using very large databases. Given the specification of a database, a test-case generator can generate large amounts of data so that the performance of the system may be tested in a realistic environment.

Another instance where test data generators can be useful is that situation where the syntax of the output from a system can be specified in a formal way. A program can be written which checks that syntax. Given an input specification, the test data generator can produce a large volume of input data which is presented to the system under test. The output is presented to the syntax checker and, if discrepancies are found, this may be due to errors in the program under test.

An example of such a situation might be the testing of the syntax analysis phase of a compiler. The output from such a phase for a correct program may be simply whatever program was input whereas, if an incorrect program is presented, the output also includes error indicators. A test-data generator might accept a specification of the syntax of the language being compiled and from that generate correct and incorrect programs. The output from the compiler can be checked automatically to ensure that error messages are not generated for correct programs and, conversely, error messages are generated for incorrect programs.

7.4.2 Execution flow summarizers

Execution flow summarizers, such as that for ALGOLW described by Satterthwaite (1972), are programs used to analyse how many times each statement in some other program has been executed. They are sometimes called dynamic analysers and have two fundamental parts:

1. An instrumentation part which adds instrumentation statements to a program either whilst it is being compiled or before compilation. When the program is executed, these statements gather and collate information on how many times each program statement is executed.

2. A display part which collects the information provided by the instrumentation statements and prints it in a form which can be understood by the reader. Typically, this produces a program listing where each line is annotated with the number of times that line has been executed.

In order to instrument a program, all decision statements and loops must be identified and instrumentation code placed at the beginning of each loop and decision. A sequence of statements without loops or decisions need only have a single instrumentation section at the beginning of the sequence. Because the instrumentation phase needs knowledge of the language syntax, the easiest way to provide this facility is to build it into the compiler. The user may switch it on with a compiler directive. Alternatively this phase of the system may be implemented as a preprocessor which adds high-level language statements to collect information about the program execution. These are compiled by the standard compiler and flow information is output to a 'history' file.

This history file is then input to the flow display program which associates the history information with the statements in the original program. An example of the output produced by such a system is shown below. This was generated using the Pascal execution flow summarizer available under the Berkeley Unix system.

Berkeley Pascal PXP −− Version 2.12 (5/11/83)

Mon Apr 9 15:17 1984 pascflow.p

Profiled Mon Apr 9 15:20 1984

```
  1        1.−−|program primes(input, output);
```

{Prints all prime numbers between 3 and MAXPRIME.
Uses Sieve of Eratosthenes method}

```
  6              |const
  6              |   MAXPRIME = 700;

  8              |type
  8              |   boolvec = array [1..MAXPRIME] of boolean;

 10              |var
 10              |   primes : boolvec;
 11              |   i, j, k : 1..MAXPRIME;

 13              |begin
 14              |   for i := 1 to MAXPRIME do
 15      700.−−|   if odd(i) then
 16        350.−−|   primes[i] := false
 16        350.−−|   else
 18        350.−−|   primes[i] := true;
 19              |   i := 3;
 20              |   k := trunc(sqrt(MAXPRIME));
 21              |   while i <= k do begin
 23       8.−−|   j := i + i;
 24              |      while j <= MAXPRIME do begin
 26        688.−−|   primes[j] := true;
 27              |         j := j + i
 27              |      end;
 29              |      i := i + 2;
 30              |      while primes[i] and (i <= k) do
 31        4.−−|   i := i + 2
 31              |   end;
 33              |   i := 3;
 34              |   while i <= MAXPRIME do begin
 36      349.−−|   if not primes[i] then
 37        124.−−|   writeln(i, 'is prime');
 38              |      i := i + 2
 38              |   end
 38              |end.
```

Flow summarizers are useful for program testing as they allow those
program statements which have not been executed during a test run to be
detected. Subsequent tests can therefore be designed to exercise these
statements.

7.4.3 File comparators

A file comparator is a general-purpose software tool which reports differences between files and has an important role in system testing. As the activity of testing frequently involves the examination of large volumes of test output, it is not unusual for the reader to miss erroneous output. To avoid this, as much of the checking and comparison process as possible should be automated.

Automation involves preparing a file containing the output expected from a program if no errors are detected. The tests are then executed and the actual output directed to some other file. Both files may then be compared using a file comparator, and differences in the files highlighted. If the expected output from the program and the actual output are the same, the tests failed to detect any errors.

Another situation where file comparators may be used is in checking that procedures and functions do not have unwanted side effects which affect global program variables. A global dump is taken before and after exercising a function, and these dumps are then automatically compared. Notice that global dumping cannot be automated using an external tool but must be implemented using a specially written procedure. Those globals which have been changed are then highlighted by the file comparison program. This is illustrated in the example below, which shows the output produced by the Unix file comparator 'diff' after comparing dumps of globals used in a Pascal program. The first part of the example shows the input files which are the same except for the changed values shown in brackets. The second part illustrates how diff marks these changes.

```
X : integer = 20
Y : integer = 17 (18)
Z : integer = 34
name : chararray = 'J Smith' (F Jones)

diff df1 df2

2c2
< Y : integer = 17
— — —
> Y : integer = 18
4c4
< name : chararray = 'J Smith'
— — —
> name : chararray = 'F Jones'
```

Notice that it is not possible to assess, using this technique, whether global pointer-type variables have been modified, as their values have no meaning outside the program. The use of file comparators is particularly helpful when many tests are submitted to a program at once. Generally, only some of these tests will succeed and a file comparison program can detect these successful tests and bring them to the attention of the tester.

File comparators may be completely general purpose, comparing any two files character by character for equality. Alternatively, such programs can be constructed for a specific application and information about the structure of the test output built into the program. General purpose comparators are most useful when the expected output from a program is itself generated by a program. For example, when a program is to be extended, a set of tests might be run before the program is altered and the test output saved. After the program enhancement is made, the same tests can be re-run and the output file produced should be the same as that produced before modification.

General-purpose comparison programs are less useful when the expected output file is manually input. A trivial input error such as the input of an extra blank which does not affect the meaning will cause a character by character file comparison to fail. However, special-purpose programs can be useful in this situation as they can identify and abstract the important items of information from each file and compare these items.

7.4.4 Simulators

A simulator is a program which imitates the actions of some other program, hardware device, or class of devices. Simulators are often used in testing to replace hardware which is expected but not immediately available. They are particularly important in the testing of real-time programs because they allow a sequence of events to be repeated, thus allowing timing-dependent errors to be detected.

In some cases, it may be essential to use simulation to mimic the events a real-time system must process. For example, if a program is used for controlling a nuclear reactor, that program must obviously be able to deal with failure of the reactor cooling system. This failure will normally be signalled by sensor inputs indicating a rise in temperature, drop in pressure, etc. Obviously, this cannot be tested operationally so it is necessary to simulate these sensor inputs using some other program. The reactions of the reactor control program to these inputs may then be observed.

The ability of simulators to reproduce sequences of events exactly is of vital importance. Consider a situation where a system is accepting input from many user terminals and a system failure occurs. Each terminal will normally be presenting different commands, and the failure may be due to particular terminal commands being processed simultaneously or to some historical event sequence which has caused corruption of information. If the system is tested using real terminals with human operators it is impossible to reproduce the command sequences input at each terminal. However, if a terminal simulator is used, this accepts command sequences from a prepared script and the exact sequence and its timing can be repeated.

As well as providing repeatable inputs, terminal simulators also allow the system to be tested under load. If a system is required to support a number of terminals with an average response time of m seconds, a terminal simulator can be set up to imitate these terminals. The simulator can then measure the system response using different combinations of input to ensure that the average response is that required.

The Unix/PWB system discussed in Chapter 5 provides a general purpose terminal simulator called LEAP (Dolotta *et al.*, 1978). This simulator is designed to run on the Unix/PWB machine and to test programs running on some other mainframe connected to the PWB machine. This has the advantage that uncontrolled interactions between the program under test and the simulator are eliminated. Furthermore, high-level languages have been developed for use with LEAP, which allow the actions of terminal-operator pairs to be simulated.

7.4.5 Program verifiers

Whilst the notion of verifying the correctness of a program is an attractive one, the amount of work involved in this task means that formal verification is not a cost-effective validation technique for large software systems. However, some efforts have been made to develop automatic program verifiers to reduce this effort. This work is summarized by London and Robinson (1979).

Verification systems take a program, its specification and other verification information asserted by the user and attempt to prove that the program, as stated, meets its specification. They rely on a formal specification of language semantics, formal and complete program specifications and sufficient user information to carry out the verification task. Obviously, the development of such systems is hindered by the fact that formal specification techniques for both languages and programs are in need of much refinement.

Whilst program verifiers help with some of the mundane and error-prone tasks involved in verification, the really difficult and time-consuming tasks of specification and assertion development are still left to the user. Hence, program verifiers are an important first step towards automatic verification systems, but much work remains to be done in developing supporting tools and applying these to practical software systems.

Recent developments in this area, such as Anna (Kreig-Brucker and Luckham, 1980) have introduced the interesting idea of self-checking code where verification tool activation and program execution are integrated. The programmer includes verification information with his program and, during execution, this is automatically checked. If the verification tool signals a potential inconsistency, program execution may be suspended or some other exception-handling mechanism activated.

7.5 Program debugging

Program debugging is related to program testing in that it relies on test output to show the presence of errors. Debugging is the process of identifying those areas of the program which cause the errors and modifying them to correct the error. General principles of debugging are discussed below and the role of software tools in the debugging process is described.

The process of debugging involves two stages. Firstly, those parts of the program code which are incorrect must be located, and, secondly, the program must be modified so that it meets its requirements. After modification, program testing must be repeated to ensure that the change has been carried out correctly. In general, the first stage — error location — is the most difficult stage, and most debugging aids are intended to assist this activity.

The second stage of the process in many instances is straightforward. If the error is a simple coding error, it is usually fairly easy to correct without affecting other parts of the program. On the other hand, if the error is a design error or involves a misunderstanding of the program requirements, correcting this may involve much work.

In such cases, it may be necessary to redesign parts of the program and consequently retest the whole system. It is vitally important, therefore, that such errors be avoided wherever possible by making use of design reviews and validation before coding commences. Apart from avoiding such errors, all the programmer can do to minimize their effect is to program in such a way that the program is made up of independent functional units. If a design error is discovered, the chances are that it will affect a single unit and only that unit need be redesigned and recoded. The remainder of the programming system can remain unchanged.

If, on the other hand, the program units are logically dependent and make use of many shared variables, this is a recipe for disaster if a major redesign is required. In such a program, it is very difficult to determine the effects on the overall system caused by redesigning one module. An apparently straightforward modification can result in errors in functionally unrelated modules. This process may snowball as these errors are corrected, causing other errors whose correction then causes more errors and so on.

The most important aid for the debugger is the listing of the test results which display the error to be corrected. If the programmer is familiar with the code, the nature and location of the error can often be determined by examination of these results. Code examination can then determine which statement or statements are incorrect.

Many programmers approach code inspection thinking that they know what the program does and, subconsciously, they read the code as if its operation is what the programmer thinks it is. The most useful debugging aid is the ability to approach code in an open-minded, sceptical manner and to perform a 'thought execution' of that code. This ability, combined with good programming practice, significantly reduces the chore of debugging.

In some circumstances, however, code inspection alone is inadequate. Those circumstances arise where programming errors do not cause immediate failure or obvious corruption to test output. Rather, these errors may cause incorrect although not necessarily invalid output to be generated. In these cases, the execution of the program must be traced to determine where the corruption causing the error is taking place.

The most commonly used technique for this is to include program statements which print important data values at appropriate places in the program. Examination of the output involves comparing subsequent values of the same object and, when an anomaly is detected, the coding error must lie between the output statement which printed the correct values and the output statement which printed the incorrect values.

The process of adding output statements can be continued, if necessary, until individual statements are bracketed. At this stage, the statement where the error manifests itself can be determined. This need not necessarily mean that an individual statement is incorrect — the error may be a design error or may involve the failure of some program component, previously thought to be correct.

This technique is certain to detect the program statement where the error is manifested, although this need not be the statement in error, irrespective of how 'correct' the program appears to be. It is, however, a laborious and time-consuming process to include output statements and recompile the program after it has been written. It is much better to anticipate that there will be program errors and include some of these output statements when the program is first constructed.

Clearly, when the program is finally delivered, it should not produce debugging output so it is necessary to somehow switch off the statements used to produce diagnostic information. This can be accomplished in three ways:

1. Each statement can be identified by some string such as ***DEBUG*** and, using this string as an identifier, can be edited or commented out of the final program.

2. The output statements can be conditionally compiled into the program. When the program is being tested, a compiler directive can cause the output statements to be included, when the production version of the program is delivered the compiler directive is switched off so that no debugging code is included.

3. The output statements can be conditionally executed depending on some global debugging switch which may be set by the program user. The switch is set whilst the program is being debugged and unset in the production version of the program.

Each of these techniques has disadvantages. Editing out diagnostic statements is a final process — it requires time and effort to put them back. Conditional compilation, although potentially the best technique, is not offered by many existing compilers, and the permanent inclusion of diagnostic information increases the size of the program.

The inclusion of anticipatory diagnostic statements shares a disadvantage with a number of other error-location techniques provided by software tools. Unless carefully controlled, voluminous amounts of information can be generated. Examining all this information is a time-consuming process. Excessive output is most easily controlled by controlling diagnostic output via a multi-way, rather than a two-way switch. Levels of output detail can be controlled by switch settings — setting 1, say, may cause global information to be printed only at important checkpoints, whereas setting 5 might cause diagnostics to be output more frequently and in greater detail.

7.6 Debugging tools

Because of the problems involved in including output statements in programs, a number of debugging tools have been developed which perform the same function. They provide information which helps the programmer to locate errors. The debugging tools which have been developed are all concerned with the first stage in that they help the user locate the source of the error. At present there is no way to automate the second stage and provide automatic error correction.

The most crude and primitive debugging aid is the core dump. The name is historical, as core store is not now widely used, but essentially a core dump is a printout of the machine store content when the program error manifested itself. Manual analysis of core dumps is boring, detailed work and is frequently a waste of time. In order to be useful, debugging tools must present information in terms of the source program being executed. As core dumps present object information rather than information relating to the source program, they are of little use for debugging programs written in a high-level language.

7.6.1 Symbolic dump programs

Debugging tools which rely on the user manipulating store addresses are of little use to the high-level language programmer. When using high-level language the programmer needs a debugging tool which relates the names of the objects used in his program to their values. A symbolic dump program is such a tool.

Symbolic dumps can take two forms — an interactive form or a batch form. In the batch form the system lists the names of all program variables along with their values either when the program terminates or at the specific inclusion of a program directive. Such a system saves the programmer including explicit output statements to trace the values of his variables.

A properly designed symbolic dump will not only generate information about global variables but will also present information about local variable values in all activated procedures. It should associate the name of the appropriate procedure with the variable name in order to avoid confusion where variables of the same name are used in different procedures.

Symbolic dumps of this kind are much more useful than core dumps but they produce a voluminous amount of information, much of which is irrelevant to the current debugging task. One way round this is to adopt the approach described by Malone and McGregor (1980). This program compares store images before and after program execution and only displays information taken from those parts of the store image which have been changed by the program execution.

A more powerful tool is an interactive program for analysing the symbolic information. This allows the user to request the value of individual variables by name so that only relevant values need be examined. Again, local variables should be accessible by specifying the procedure name followed by the variable name.

An example of an interactive symbolic dump system is included in the Pascal debugging package pdx, available under Berkeley Unix. In combination with a Pascal interpreter, this system allows the user to request the values of variables, to set breakpoints in his or her code, to find out the types of variables, to find out where variables are used, etc.

Potentially, interactive tools of this kind are extremely useful if they allow the user to scan the dump information in a number of ways. He or she should be allowed to specify conditions relating to object values and all name/value pairs satisfying these conditions should be printed. It should also be possible to display structures involving pointers in some readable way. Many program errors are the result of misdirected pointers, and a facility to detect these is invaluable. This graphical display facility is difficult to implement and very few systems which include pointer display have been built. One such experimental system for Pascal is described by Getz *et al.* (1983).

7.6.2 Program trace packages

Symbolic dump systems allow the user to examine values once the program has terminated, but they do not provide information about the dynamic execution of the program. Program trace packages provide such information, printing information about procedure entry and exit, transfers of control, branch selection in if statements, etc.

An example of the output produced by the trace package built into the Pascal programming debugging system available under Berkeley Unix is shown below. The program traced is a modified version of the prime numbers program given in Section 7.4.2. The modification made is to print only the prime numbers to 36. Otherwise, excessive output would be produced.

The Pascal debugging system allows high-precision tracing to be specified so that the volume of output can be controlled. Trace options in this system include tracing the value of variables — in the example below *i* and *j* are traced. The user may also set up a line number trace, trace expression values, procedures, etc.

```
> initially (at line 14): i = 0
initially (at line 14): j = 0
trace:     14        for i := 1 to MAXPRIME do
after line 14:   i = 36
trace:     19        i := 3;
after line 19:   i = 3
trace:     20        k := 6;
```

```
trace:     21         while i <= k do
after line 21:  i = 7
after line 21:  j = 40
trace:     33           i := 3;
after line 33:  i = 3
trace:     34         while i <= MAXPRIME do
after line 34:  i = 37
```

execution completed

Trace packages involve instrumenting the program automatically so that the relevant information can be collected. This instrumentation obviously involves overhead both in terms of space and speed.

7.6.3 Static program analysers

Static program analysers do not require the program to be executed. Rather, when presented with the text of a program, a static analyser scans that text and searches for anomalies likely to result in errors in the program.

Static analysers are perhaps most useful when programming languages such as FORTRAN, which do not allow much compile time checking, are used. The analyser takes over much of the checking which would be carried out by the compiler in a more strict language such as Pascal. For example, an installation may have a rule that all variable names used in a FORTRAN program must be declared — the default conventions of the language are not to be used. A static analyser can scan a program and mark undeclared variables in the same way as a Pascal compiler can detect undeclared names.

As well as syntax checking, a static analyser can also check that no parts of the program are unreachable because goto statements always branch around the code, and it can check variable initializations by flagging instances where a variable name is used on the left side of an assignment statement before it is used on the right side of an assignment.

A number of static analysers such as DAVE (Osterweil and Fosdick, 1976), AUDIT (Culpepper, 1975) and FACES (Ramamoorthy and Ho, 1975) have been developed for use with FORTRAN programs. These analysers all detect anomalies and inconsistencies which normally cause errors. These tools check subroutine interfaces to ensure that the number and types of subroutine parameters are consistent with the routine declaration; they locate COMMON block errors and flag error-prone practices such as branching into a DO-loop.

Static analysers are not just useful with FORTRAN — a program called LINT (Ritchie et al., 1978) has been developed for use with C programs and its authors claim that use of LINT provides static checking equivalent to that provided by the compiler in a language such as ALGOL 68. Thus the reliability advantages of a strictly typed language are combined with the ability to generate very efficient code using a systems implementation language.

An example of the output product by LINT is shown below:

```
      include <stdio.h>
main ()
{
     int array[5]; int i; char c;
     printarray(array,i,c);
}
printarray(array)
int array;
{
     printf("%d",array);
}
```

lintit.c:
lintit.c(5): warning: c may be used before set
lintit.c(5): warning: i may be used before set
printarray: variable of args.lintit.c(9) :: lintit.c(5)
printarray, arg. 1 used inconsistentlylintit.c(9) :: lintit.c(5)

The program itself is, obviously, nonsense. However, the C compiler accepts it without complaint whereas the static analyser picks up and indicates the errors in the code.

7.6.4 Dynamic program analysers
As well as being a useful program testing tool, dynamic program analysers can also be used in debugging a program. Examination of the output from a flow summarizer can identify loops which do not terminate properly and help the user to find sections of code which are being executed when they ought not to be executed.

7.6.5 Interactive debugging environments
The most sophisticated debugging tools are systems such as EXDAMS (Balzer, 1969). These systems give the programmer the impression that he can interact with his program while it is executing and can display variable values, reverse execution sequences and so on.

In fact, such systems operate by executing the program and constructing a 'history' file recording all program state changes. They provide facilities for interrogating this history file in program terms. The user can watch control flow and/or data flow in his program as each statement executes and the statement causing the error can then be detected. Such systems are potentially very useful but require considerable resources and are not widely available.

More recently, the Cornell Program Synthesizer (Teitelbaum and Reps, 1981) which integrates the preparation, translation and execution of programs written in a subset of PL/1 has provided an interactive execution/ debugging environment for programs. In the Cornell Program Synthesizer, the execution of the user's program is controlled by an interpreter and, as particular statements in the program are executed, they are picked out by the cursor on the user's terminal.

Because of the interpretive nature of the system, the user can 'single-step' his program executing statements one by one until a previously observed error manifests itself. Should the user overshoot, the Cornell Program Synthesizer also provides a 'reverse gear' facility which allows backwards execution of the program. The user can thus quickly converge on the statement in error.

Further reading

The Art of Software Testing, G. J. Myers (1979), New York: Wiley.

A comprehensive and thorough review of practical software testing techniques.

'The Cornell Program Synthesizer: A syntax-directed programming environment', T. Teitelbaum and T. Reps (1981), *Comm. ACM*, **24 (9)**.

This paper discusses, amongst other things, the program testing and debugging tools which can be provided in a syntax-directed environment. Also useful background reading for the material covered in Chapter 5.

Chapter 8 DOCUMENTATION AND MAINTENANCE

Software documentation and maintenance are unexciting but essential parts of system production and use. There is little point in producing a software system if it cannot be understood, if it cannot be used except by its implementors, and if modifications to that system are difficult or impossible to make. For organizational reasons, documentation and maintenance are considered separately below. The reader should bear in mind, however, that this separation is somewhat artificial — without documentation the maintenance of large systems is impossible.

This chapter is composed of two parts — the first covers aspects of documentation, the second maintenance considerations. The documentation may describe how to use the program, why it was written and the techniques used in its construction, and should clarify any obscurities in the program. As maintenance — the process of making modifications after the program has been delivered — requires an understanding of the program, this is achieved by study of the program code and associated documentation. This chapter will only cover that documentation which is separate from the program itself. Associated with each program is intra-program documentation in the form of comments. These should be used in such a way that the function of the program code is made clear to the program reader.

Documentation is a topic which is often neglected in programming texts. This is in spite of the fact that, for large projects, as much effort may be involved in documentation as is required for software development. In this part of the book, the different types of documentation are described, a style of technical writing is proposed and software tools which aid the production and maintenance of documentation discussed.

As maintainability is considered to be one of the most important characteristics of a software system and is emphasized throughout the book, the section on program maintenance concentrates on maintenance costs and program understandability rather than how an easily maintained program can be constructed. Understanding a program is the key to effective maintenance and techniques of program reading to achieve this understanding are described. This is followed by a brief summary of research aimed at establishing metrics for gauging the understandability of a program.

8.1 Software documentation

All large software systems, irrespective of application, have a prodigious amount of documentation associated with them. This documentation may be classed as either user documentation or system documentation. User documentation is made up of those documents which relate to the functions of the system, without reference to how these functions are implemented. System documentation, on the other hand, describes all aspects of the system design, implementation and testing.

The documentation provided along with the system should satisfy a number of requirements. It must describe:

1. how to use the system — without this even the simplest system is useless;
2. how to install and operate the system;
3. the overall system requirements and design;
4. the system implementation and test procedures so that it may be maintained.

The documentation provided along with a system can be useful at any stage in the lifetime of the system. It need not necessarily be produced in the same order as the system itself. In fact, it is often useful during system specification to have user documentation available so that the specifier is aware of the constraints within which he or she must operate.

All kinds of documentation need effective indexing. A good index which allows the user to find the information he or she needs is probably the most useful feature that can be provided but, sadly, is often the most neglected part of document production. A comprehensive index can make a badly written document usable but, without an index, even the best written prose is unlikely to convince the reader that the document is effective.

8.1.1   User documentation

The documentation provided for system users is usually the first contact which they have with the system. It should provide an accurate initial impression of the system. It is not sales literature so it should not over-emphasize system features which are novel or very powerful, nor should it be unrealistic about the system's capabilities. It should not be necessary for the user to read most of the documentation to find out how to make simple use of the system. Thus the documentation should be structured in such a way that the user may read it to the level of detail appropriate to his or her needs.

There are at least five documents which might be considered under the heading of user documentation. These documents are:

1. a functional description, which explains what the system can do,
2. an installation document, which explains how to install the system and tailor it for particular hardware configurations,
3. an introductory manual, which explains, in simple terms, how to get started with the system,

4. a reference manual, which describes in detail all of the system facilities available to the user and how these facilities can be used,

5. an operator's guide (if a system operator is required), explaining how the operator should react to situations which arise whilst the system is in use.

The functional description of the system outlines the system requirements and briefly describes the aims of the system implementors. It should describe what the system can and cannot do, introducing small, self-evident examples wherever possible. For example, the functional description of an operating system which has a hierarchical file system might illustrate the structure of the file system as a tree, and instructions on how to move up and down the tree may be shown as examples.

The functional description of the system should not attempt to go into detail nor need it cover every system facility. Rather, it should provide an overview of the system and, when read in conjunction with an introductory manual, should enable the user to decide if the system is appropriate for his or her needs.

The introductory manual should present an informal introduction to the system, describing its 'normal' usage. It should describe how to get started on the system and how the user might make use of the common system facilities. It should be liberally illustrated with examples. The introductory manual should also tell the system user how to get out of trouble when things go wrong. Inevitably beginners, whatever their background and experience, will make mistakes. It is vital that easily available information on how to recover from these mistakes and restart useful work is provided.

The system reference manual is the definitive document on system usage. The most important characteristic of a reference manual is that it should be complete. Wherever possible, formal descriptive techniques should be used to ensure that completeness is achieved and, although the style of the reference manual should not be unnecessarily arcane or turgid, it is acceptable to sacrifice readability for completeness. This manual may assume that the reader is familiar with both the system description and introductory manual. It may also assume that the reader has made some use of the system and understands its concepts and terminology. As well as describing, in detail, the system facilities and their usage, the system reference manual should also describe the error reports generated by the system, the situations where these errors arise and, if appropriate, refer the user to a description of the facility which was in error.

The system installation document should provide full details of how to install the system in a particular environment. First and foremost, it must contain a description of the machine-readable media on which the system is supplied — its format, the character codes used, how the information was written and the files making up the system. It should then go on to describe the minimal hardware configuration required to run the system, the permanent files which must be established, how to start the system, and the configuration dependent files which must be changed in order to tailor the system to a particular application.

For systems which require an operator, an operator's manual must be provided. This should describe the messages generated at the operator's console and how to react to these messages. If system hardware is involved, it might also explain the operator's task in maintaining that hardware. For example, it might describe how to clear faults in the operator's console, how to change printer ribbons, etc.

Depending on the size of the system, these may be provided as separate manuals or bound together as one or more volumes. If the latter method of presentation is chosen, each document should be clearly distinguished so that readers may easily find and use the document that they require. This distinction might be made by separating the sections and providing thumb indexes, or might be accomplished by printing the different parts of the manual on different colours of paper.

As well as manuals, it may be appropriate to provide users with other easy-to-use documentation. For example, a quick reference card listing available system facilities and how to use them is particularly convenient for experienced system users. On-line help systems, which contain brief information about the system, are another facility which saves the user spending time in consultation of manuals.

Some organizations consider that the production of user documentation should not be the task of the software engineer. Rather, professional technical authors are employed to produce such finished documentation using information provided by the engineers responsible for constructing the system. There is some merit in this approach inasmuch as it frees software staff to do their principal job — construct software. However, it does have the disadvantage that communications between authors and software engineers can be almost as time consuming as writing the documentation so, in practice, the use of technical authors may not be cost effective.

8.1.2 System documentation

In this text, the term 'system documentation' is taken to mean all the documents pertaining to the implementation of the system from the requirements specification to the final acceptance test plan. Documents describing the design, implementation and testing of a system are essential if the program is to be understood and maintained. Like user documentation, it is important that system documentation is structured, with overviews leading the reader into more formal and detailed descriptions of each aspect of the system.

The documents making up the system documentation should include:

1. The requirements definition and, perhaps, an associated rationale.

2. An overall systems specification showing how the requirements are decomposed into a set of interacting programs. This document is not

required when the system is implemented using only a single program.

3. For each program in the system, a description of how that program is decomposed into components and a statement of the specification of each component.

4. For each unit, a description of its operation. This need not extend to describing program actions as these should be documented using intra-program comments.

5. A comprehensive test plan describing how each program unit is tested.

6. A test plan showing how integration testing, that is, the testing of all units/programs together, is carried out.

7. An acceptance test plan, devised in conjunction with the system user. This should describe the tests which must be satisfied before the system is accepted.

Each of these documents is a different representation of the same software system and one of the most common problems which arises during system maintenance is ensuring that all of these representations are kept in step when changes to the systems are made. To help with this, the relationships and dependencies between documents and parts of documents should be recorded along with the documents and, preferably, managed and checked with the aid of a software tool designed for this purpose.

It may also be appropriate to make use of configuration management tools such as MAKE and SCCS, described in Chapter 5, to maintain different versions of the documentation and to record when and by whom document changes were made.

8.1.3 Data dictionaries
A data dictionary is a document which provides details of each and every entity relevant to the system being described. The document is normally referenced using the name of the object of interest — hence the term data dictionary. Data dictionaries are an important part of the documentation in some application areas, particularly those involving database management systems. However, their use is not restricted to database applications. They are an extremely useful form of documentation which can be used with any kind of computing system.

The entities entered in the dictionary include objects which are named in the system being documented, such as procedures, records, files, modules, etc., and also entities in the real-world system modelled by the program. For example, consider a program which records and processes sales of goods made by some organization. Each sale might be represented by a record made up of the date of sale, the salesman, the quantity of goods sold, the product reference number and the customer. Under 'sale' in the data dictionary, this information would be recorded along with cross-references to other relevant dictionary entries. These cross-references would include reference to the program objects used to represent the sale.

Data dictionaries are of value to both system users and to those involved in maintaining the system. Users who intend to use the system to obtain information about some entity can look up the dictionary and, by tracing cross-references, work out how to retrieve the required information.

The value of data dictionaries to system maintenance staff is obvious. Much of the information conventionally gathered by cross-reference programs can be entered but, more importantly, information about the entity modelled by a program object is also available. When a program object is to be changed, reference to the dictionary can be made to ensure that the change is compatible with the modelled entity and that the change does not affect other system entities.

Because of the need for cross-referencing in a data dictionary, and also because the dictionary may be subject to change, the data dictionary for a system should always be maintained on-line. Except in exceptional circumstances, there is little point in providing users with a hard copy of the dictionary, which is liable to date rapidly and which is slow to use.

8.2 Document quality

It is a sad reflection on the current state of software engineering that the majority of computer system documentation is badly written, difficult to understand, out-of-date or incomplete. With some honourable exceptions, little attention has been paid to producing system documents which stand on their own as well written pieces of technical prose. Documentation is usually seen as something to be finished off quickly after the more interesting work of software development.

In fact, document quality is as important as program quality. Without information on how to use a system or how to understand it, the utility of that system is degraded. Producing good documents is neither easy nor cheap, and the process is at least as difficult as producing good programs. In this section, therefore, some hints on producing good quality software system documents are provided.

A standard procedure for producing, checking and laying out documentation is an important aid to document quality control. The importance of quality control mechanisms in document production cannot be over-emphasized. Poor quality documentation is likely to confuse rather than help the reader, with the consequence that minimal use is likely to be made of that documentation.

Documentation standards should describe exactly what the documentation should include and should describe the notations to be used in the documentation. Within an organization, it is useful to establish a standard 'house format' for documents and require that all documents conform to that. This standard might include a description of a front-cover format to be adopted by all documents, page numbering and page annotation conventions, methods of reference to other documents and the numbering of headings and sub-headings.

The numbering of headings and sub-headings may appear a trivial point. However, when a large number of separate documents are produced which reference each other, a consistent numbering scheme is vital. Documents should be subdivided using exactly the same system so that corresponding sections in each document each refer to the same entity. Explicit cross-referencing should be avoided wherever possible and, when unavoidable, should reference by section heading and section number.

8.2.1 Writing style

Although standards and quality assessment are essential if good documentation is to be produced, the most fundamental factor affecting documentation quality is the ability of the writer to construct clear and concise technical prose. In short, good documentation requires good writing. In a book of this nature, devoted to a technical subject, it may appear presumptuous to include notes on writing style. However, it is unfortunately the case that some people involved in software production have great difficulty constructing well written, clear and concise documentation. It is thus the intention of this section to provide some guidelines on technical writing style.

Writing documents well is neither easy nor is it a single-stage process. Written work must be written, read, criticized and then rewritten, and this process should continue until a satisfactory document is produced. As in many other aspects of software engineering, it is impossible to present a set of rules which govern exactly how to set about this particular task. Technical writing is a craft rather than a science and only broad guidelines about how to write well may be given. These guidelines, set out in a style that might be used in software instruction manuals, are:

1. *Use active rather than passive tenses.* For example, it is better to say 'You should see a flashing cursor at the top left of the screen' than 'A flashing cursor should appear at the top left of the screen'.

2. *Do not use long sentences which present several different facts.* It is much better to use a number of shorter sentences. Each sentence can then be assimilated on its own. The reader does not need to maintain several pieces of information at one time in order to understand the complete sentence.

3. *Do not refer to information by reference number alone.* Instead, give the reference number and remind the reader what that reference covered. For example, rather than say 'In section 1.1.1 ...' you should say 'In section 1.1.1, which described the process of software evolution, ...'.

4. *Itemize facts wherever possible.* It is usually clearer to present facts

in a list rather than in a sentence. You may have found this set of guidelines harder to read if they hadn't been itemized.

5. *If a description is complex, repeat yourself.* It is often a good idea to present two or more differently phrased descriptions of the same thing. If the reader fails to completely understand one description, he may benefit from having the same thing said in a different way.

6. *Don't be verbose.* If you can say something in five words do so, rather than use ten words so that the description might seen more profound. There is no merit in quantity of documentation — quality is much more important.

7. *Be precise and define the terms you use.* Computing terminology is very fluid and many terms have more than one meaning. Therefore, if such terms (e.g. module or process) are used, make sure that your definition is clear. If you need to define a number of words, or if you are writing for readers with little or no knowledge of computing terminology, you should provide a glossary with your document. This should contain definitions of all terms which might not be completely understood by the reader.

8. *Keep paragraphs short.* As a general rule, no paragraph should be made up of more than seven sentences. This is because of short-term memory limitations, described in Chapter 10. Our capacity for holding immediate information is limited, so by keeping paragraphs short all of the concepts in the paragraph can be maintained in short-term memory.

9. *Make use of headings and sub-headings.* Always ensure that a consistent numbering convention is used for these.

10. *Use grammatically correct constructs and spell words correctly.* To boldly go on splitting infinitives (like this) and to mis-spell words (like mispell) irritates many readers and reduces the credibility of the writer in their eyes.

One mechanism which can be used for checking and improving documents is to establish document inspections. These are to be used in the way that code inspections can be used for the detection of program errors. During a document inspection, the text is criticized, omissions pointed out and suggestions made on how to improve the document. In this latter respect it differs from a code inspection, which is simply an error-finding rather than an error-correction mechanism.

As well as personal criticism, it is also possible to make use of software tools whose function is to read text and find ungrammatical or clumsy uses of words. These tools might also point out where sentences and paragraphs are too long and where passive rather than active tenses are used. A set of such tools has been packaged together under Unix to form a so-called 'writer's workbench'. This is discussed in Section 8.3.

8.3 Documentation tools

This section discusses software tools which can be used to develop and maintain project documentation on a computer system. Although not essential, this should preferably be the same system as is used to develop the software system, so that programs and documentation can be developed together. There are a number of advantages which accrue from developing documentation in this way rather than manually or on some separate word processor system. These are:

1. *The documentation is always on hand.* The programmer need not search for a manual if he has access to the computer. In the case of user documentation, copies of this should be maintained on the same system as the application so that, again, reference to manuals may be unnecessary.

   The need for effective indexing of documents is particularly important when the documentation is maintained on-line. There is no point in having the information available if the reader cannot easily and quickly find the information that he or she requires.

2. *Documents are easy to modify and maintain.* This has the consequence that the project documentation is more likely to be kept up-to-date.

3. *Documentation may be formatted.* The documentation text can be automatically formatted and neatly laid out — in some circumstances, printing costs can be reduced by using a computer-driven phototypesetter.

4. *Documents may be analysed.* The documentation text can be automatically analysed in various ways to produce different types of index, and to check for spelling and typing errors.

5. *Documents may be shared.* Several individuals may work on the production of a document at the same time.

6. *Documentation management is simplified.* All the documents can be gathered together under a common heading and the state of development of these documents may be ascertained. It may be possible to make use of configuration management tools to maintain different versions of documents and to control changes to documents.

7. *Automatic information retrieval is feasible.* Information retrieval systems may operate on documents retrieving all documents which contain particular keywords, for example.

Clearly, the most important documentation tool is a powerful editing system which allows documents to be generated and modified. A general-purpose editor, as described in Chapter 5, may be used for this task, or a special word processing system specifically designed for producing text may be preferred. There are advantages and disadvantages to each approach.

Word processing systems are screen based and are organized so that the operations of text editing and formatting are combined. This means that the image of the document on the user's terminal is more or less the same as the final form of the printed document. Thus, finished layout is immediately obvious. Errors can be corrected and layout improved before printing the document. On the other hand, programmers who already use an editor for program preparation do not normally wish to learn how to use another type of editor and, for them, use of a separate editor and text formatting system may be more appropriate.

Using an editor, a computer terminal can simply be treated as a type-writer and the document formatted directly by the typist. Unfortunately, the screen size of most terminals is such that it does not conform to standard paper sizes. The typist must adapt to the smaller terminal screen and, when typing, mentally translate screen layout to layout on paper. Although each line is formatted as it will be printed, visualizing how changes affect lines which are not currently on the screen is a difficult task.

This problem can be avoided by processing input text using a text formatting program such as the NROFF/TROFF system (Kernighan *et al.*, 1978) provided under Unix. Such systems are very powerful. However, they are not particularly easy to use. Errors are invariably introduced into the book which have resulted from mistakes made by the author when using the text formatting system. A text formatter allows the typist to input text in free format. It then automatically rearranges that text and lays it out neatly on standard paper. The final layout of the document is specified by the author by interspersing formatting commands with the text of the document.

When the text is processed, these formatting commands are identified and interpreted. The text is laid out as specified by these commands. Such a system is more flexible than simpler screen-based systems, as it allows the user to vary the output format in different parts of the document. Further-more, some systems also allow the user to define his or her own macros — sequences of formatting commands — and they provide elementary text storage and decision-making capability. Using these facilities, powerful formatting features can be provided such as automatic subsection number-ing, automatic contents creation and footnote placement. It is also possible to redefine the document layout simply by rewriting some of the macros — it is unnecessary to make changes to the document text itself.

Preparing and storing documents on a computer system means that changes can be made to a document without the chore of retyping the complete document. Not only does this reduce the cost of producing documentation, it also means that higher-quality documentation is pro-duced. If documents are produced manually, there is a disinclination to make changes and improve the clarity of an explanation, say, because of the retyping effort involved. Without this retyping effort, authors can be encouraged to rewrite and reword documents to improve their quality. This rewriting, however, must be carefully controlled. If computerized document-editing facilities are readily available, authors may strive for perfection and expend much effort in relatively minor improvements. It is the responsibility of documentation management to ensure that this does not happen.

Although an editor and a text formatter are the most important documentation tools, there are a number of other programs which are useful in document production. These include programs to assist with proofreading, programs to help lay out complicated tables and mathematical expressions, graphics systems to assist diagram production, pattern matching systems for document retrieval, and programs to identify and control changes in documents.

Proofreading is one of the most onerous chores associated with authorship. Although the process cannot be completely automated, some help can be given if a machine-readable copy of the document is available. For example, a spelling checker program might be available which points out words which appear in the document but not in the system dictionary. Similarly, a punctuation checker can detect common errors such as unbalanced parentheses, spaces before punctuation marks, etc.

A spelling checker should be designed so that the dictionary may be passed as a parameter to the program. This means that, after a document has been checked using the standard system dictionary, the spelling checker can be re-run, checking those words not found in the standard dictionary against the user's private dictionary. This dictionary might contain specialized terms or proper names which are particular to a user or an application.

In addition to these very simple proofreading tools, which are widely available, a very comprehensive set of proofreading and document checking tools has been developed to run under the Unix system. This toolkit, called the 'writer's workbench', contains programs which detect common typographical errors such as repeated words, badly used spacing, etc. There are also programs which detect clumsy phraseology and suggest alternatives, programs to measure the clarity of the text, and programs which comment on the user's style. This writer's workbench system is described by Cherry and MacDonald (1983).

Programs which assist the user with complicated layout problems normally operate in conjunction with a formatting system. Rather than the user being forced to devise a complex set of formatting commands, he or she provides a table specification, say, along with the data to be included in that table. A table formatter reads the specification and the data and generates the appropriate sequence of formatting commands for inclusion in the user's document.

Most document production hardware, be it phototypesetter or high-quality printer, has some graphics capability. This can be utilized to produce diagrams, and software to make use of this graphics capability is of great value. Because the syntax of diagrams is complex, the most useful diagram production systems are those where the user draws or at least outlines his or her diagram on a terminal. The diagram generator program then translates this picture into the appropriate formatter commands to generate the diagrams on the printer.

Document retrieval software is, of course, generally useful but it has a specialized application in a document-production environment. If the document retrieval system includes a sufficiently powerful pattern matching system, a database of existing documents can be scanned to find any text which is associated with that being produced. This text may then, if appropriate, be re-used. As in program production, re-use of existing work can increase productivity and reduce the amount of proofreading (testing) and modification (debugging) required.

Information retrieval systems are also useful in bibliography production. When a document is produced, its bibliography may be added to a bibliography database and this database made publicly accessible. Not only does this help the user find source material, it also ensures that making references to other documents is simplified. The appropriate reference can be copied directly from the bibliography database, thus ensuring the correctness of the reference.

As documents are modified and new versions of the document produced, it is important that control is kept over these modifications. Furthermore, important new information should be clearly signalled to readers. Mashey and Smith (1977) report that the code control system SCCS (Rochkind, 1975), available under Unix, has been used to keep control over the different versions of documents and modifications to these documents.

The use of a file comparison program can identify changes made to documents by pinpointing lines in each copy of the document which differ. By combining the output from such a program with an editor preprocessor, those lines can be edited and marked with revision bars, indicating the changes to the user.

8.4 The maintenance of documentation

As a programming system is modified, the documentation associated with that system must also be modified to reflect the changes to the system. Unfortunately, documentation maintenance is often neglected, with the result that the documentation becomes out of step with its associated software. This introduces problems for both users and maintainers of the system.

It is important that all associated documents are modified when a change is made to a program. Assuming that the change is transparent to the user, only those documents describing the system implementation need be modified. If the system change is more than the correction of a coding error, this will mean revision of design and test documents and, perhaps, the higher-level documents describing the system specification and requirements.

As discussed earlier, one of the major problems in maintaining documentation is keeping different representations of the system in step with each other. The natural tendency is to meet a deadline by modifying code with the intention of modifying other documents later. Often, pressure of work means that this modification is continually set aside until finding what is to be changed becomes very difficult indeed. The best solution to this problem is to support document maintenance with software tools which record document relationships, remind software engineers when changes to one document affect another and record possible inconsistencies in the documentation.

If the system modification affects the user interface directly, either by adding new facilities or extending existing facilities, this should be intimated to the user immediately. In an on-line system, this might be accomplished by providing a system noticeboard which each user may access. When a new item is added to the noticeboard, users can be informed of this when they log in to the system. System changes can also be indicated on a real noticeboard and in a regular newsletter distributed to all system users. At periodic intervals, user documentation should be updated by supplying new pages which describe the changes made to the user interface.

This updating process is simplified if manual pages are not consecutively numbered but are numbered according to their chapter or section. For example, pages in chapter 3 would be numbered 3-1, 3-2, 3-3.... If this numbering scheme is adopted, parts of the manual may be replaced without disrupting page numbering in the unchanged parts of the document.

Paragraphs which have been added or changed should be indicated to the reader. New versions of documents should be immediately identifiable — the fact that a document has been updated should not be concealed on an inner page. Rather, the version number and date should be clearly indicated on the cover of the document and, if possible, different versions of each document should be issued with a different colour of cover.

The updating and maintenance of user and system documentation is simplified if the documentation is available in machine-readable form. Tools for producing documentation have already been described and these tools are equally, if not more, useful for implementing and controlling document modification. In addition, if a document retrieval system is available, the user may immediately obtain copies of modified documents — delays due to distribution are minimized.

8.5 The portability of documentation

When a computing system is moved from one machine to another, the documentation associated with that system must be modified to reflect the new system. In some circumstances, the work involved in this is comparable to the work involved in moving the programs themselves. If portability is a system design objective, the documentation must also be designed and written with the same aim.

Just as the property of self-containedness is the key to program portability, portable documentation should also be self-contained. This means that the information provided in the documentation should be as complete as possible. Reference should not be made to any other documents, such as an operating system manual, which are not directly associated with the system being documented.

For example, say a programming language allows the user access to mathematical functions such as sin, cos, tan, log, etc. In some installations, these functions may be provided in a library of similar functions shared by all of the programming languages implemented at that installation. When discussing available functions, the programming language documentation should not simply refer to the documentation describing the mathematical library. Should that language be implemented on another machine without a mathematical library, the language documentation would be incomplete. The language manual itself should describe fully the functions available.

Those parts of the system which generally cause portability problems are obviously the sections describing non-portable parts of the programming system. These include file organization, file naming conventions, job control, input-output, and so on. When the system is moved from one computer to another, those parts of the documentation must be rewritten.

In order to facilitate this rewriting, descriptions of system-dependent functions should be confined to separate sections. These sections should be clearly headed with information about their system dependence and replaced when the system is moved to another installation. If possible, other references to system dependent features should be avoided. If this is impossible, an index of such references should be maintained so that they may be located and changed when the program is moved.

As transporting a program and its documentation is really a specialized form of system maintenance, the availability of machine-readable documentation and appropriate software tools reduces the work involved in producing documentation for a new system. System-dependent parts of the document may be located, rewritten and a new version of the document produced automatically.

8.6 Software maintenance

Historically, the term 'maintenance' has been applied to the process of modifying a program after it has been delivered and is in use. These modifications may involve simple changes to correct coding errors, more extensive changes to correct design errors, or drastic rewrites to correct specification errors or accommodate new requirements.

As Turski (1981) has pointed out, this is a gross abuse of the term 'maintenance'. The addition of a new wing to a building would never be described as maintaining that building, yet adding new facilities to a program is considered as maintenance activity. However, as the term maintenance is widely and generally used, it will be used here to mean changing a program in order to correct errors and provide new facilities.

Software maintenance falls into three categories. These are:

1. perfective maintenance,
2. adaptive maintenance,
3. corrective maintenance.

Perfective maintenance encompasses changes demanded by the user or the system programmer; adaptive maintenance is maintenance due to changes in the environment of the program; and corrective maintenance is the correction of undiscovered system errors. A survey by Lientz and Swanson (1980) discovered that about 65% of maintenance was perfective, 18% adaptive and 17% corrective.

As described in Chapter 1, in the discussion of software evolution, it is impossible to produce systems of any size which do not need to be maintained. Over the lifetime of a system, its original requirements will be modified to reflect changing needs, the system's environment will change, and obscure errors, undiscovered during system validation, will emerge. Because maintenance is unavoidable systems should be designed and implemented so that maintenance problems are minimized.

The costs of maintenance are extremely difficult to estimate in advance. Evidence from existing systems suggests that maintenance costs are by far the greatest cost incurred in developing and using a system. In general, these costs were dramatically underestimated when the systems were designed and implemented. As an illustration of the relative cost of program maintenance, it was estimated that one US Air Force System cost $30 per instruction to develop and $4000 per instruction to maintain over its lifetime (Boehm, 1975).

These figures are perhaps exceptional as the system in question was a highly optimized, tightly coded control system. Almost certainly, performance was its principal requirement and this can sometimes be achieved by sacrificing the understandability and hence the maintainability of a program. Maintenance costs certainly vary widely from application to application but, on average, maintenance costs appear to be about four times development costs for large software systems.

Furthermore, Lientz and Swanson found that large organizations devoted about 50% of their total programming effort to maintaining existing systems and, as systems age, relatively more effort must be expended in maintaining those systems. One of the major problems which arises is that these systems may be written in obsolete programming languages which are no longer used for new systems development. Often, special provision has to be made to train staff members to maintain these programs. This problem is likely to become particularly apparent as Ada supplants languages such as FORTRAN and Pascal as the major systems development language.

It is certainly worthwhile to invest time and effort when designing and implementing a system to reduce maintenance and hence overall system costs. The guidelines and techniques discussed in previous chapters recognize this. They have been formulated with the explicit intention of explaining how an understandable and maintainable program can be designed, developed and tested. As the previous chapters are based on the assumption that the software engineer should produce easily maintained programs as a matter of course, no further discussion on how to construct such systems will be presented here.

8.6.1 Factors affecting maintenance costs

The cost of maintenance can be minimized if the requirements of the program maintainer are taken into account when the program is designed and implemented. Estimating maintenance costs for any particular program is very difficult. The difficulties arise because these costs are related to a number of relatively unpredictable factors which are unrelated to any technical characteristics of the software system. These include:

1. *The application being supported.* If the application of the program is clearly defined and well understood, the system requirements may be definitive, and perfective maintenance due to changing requirements minimized. If, on the other hand, the application is completely new, it is likely that the initial requirements will be modified as users gain experience with the system.

2. *Staff stability.* It is normally easier for the original writer of a program to understand and change a program rather than some other individual who must understand the program by study of its documentation and code listing. Therefore, if the programmer of a system also maintains that system, maintenance costs will be reduced. In practice, the nature of the programming profession is such that individuals change jobs regularly and it is fairly unusual for one person to develop and maintain a program throughout its useful life.

3. *The lifetime of the program.* The useful life of a program obviously depends on its application. The program will become obsolete if the application becomes obsolete or if its original hardware is replaced and conversion costs exceed rewriting costs. Historical evidence suggests that program lifetimes are much longer than originally anticipated — some systems running today were coded in the early 1960s.

   As a program is continually maintained throughout its life, maintenance costs tend to rise. This is a result of the inevitable deterioration of program structure which occurs as multiple modifications are made.

4. *The dependence of the program on its external environment.* If a program is highly dependent on its external environment it must be modified as that environment changes. For example, changes in a taxation system might require payroll, accounting and stock control programs to be modified. Taxation changes are relatively common

and maintenance costs for these programs will be related to the frequency of these changes.

On the other hand, a program used in a mathematical application does not normally depend on human decisions changing the assumptions on which the program is based. Maintenance costs for such programs are not usually affected by changes in human and political systems.

5. *Hardware stability.*   If a program is designed to operate on a particular hardware configuration and that configuration does not change during the program's lifetime, no maintenance costs due to hardware changes will be incurred. However, hardware developments are so rapid that this situation is relatively rare and computing hardware becomes obsolete very quickly. The program must be modified to use new hardware which replaces obsolete equipment.

This process is distinct from moving the program to another computer system as the required modifications normally involve enhancing the program to make use of improved hardware or modifying assumptions built into the program about the hardware.

Apart from these non-technical considerations, maintenance costs are also governed by less unpredictable, technical factors. Some technical factors affecting program maintenance are:

1. *Module independence.*   It should be possible to modify one program unit of a system without affecting any other unit.

2. *Programming language.*   Programs written in a high-level programming language are usually easier to understand (and hence maintain) than programs written in a low-level language.

3. *Programming style.*   The way in which a program is written clearly contributes to its understandability and hence the ease with which it can be modified.

4. *Program validation and testing.*   Generally, the more time and effort spent on design validation and program testing, the fewer errors in the program, and consequently decreased maintenance costs result from error correction. Maintenance costs due to error correction are governed by the type of error to be repaired. Coding errors are usually relatively cheap to correct, whereas design errors are much more expensive as they may involve the rewriting of one or more program units. Errors in the requirements specification are normally the most expensive to correct because of the drastic redesign which is usually involved.

5. *The quality and quantity of program documentation.*   If a program is supported by clear, complete yet concise documentation, the task of understanding the program can be relatively straightforward. Consequently, program maintenance costs tend to be less for well docu-

mented systems than for systems supplied with poor or incomplete documentation.

Because of this multiplicity of factors, it is impossible to present any technique of maintenance cost estimation which has general applicability. Such cost estimates can only be made using cost data from past projects and even then are only likely to be accurate when previous cost information was collected for the same type of system. However, if this information is available, the maintenance cost estimation algorithm described below may be useful.

8.6.2 Maintenance cost estimation

Using data gathered from 63 projects in a number of application areas, Boehm (1981) has established a formula for estimating maintenance costs. This is part of a general software cost estimation model which is discussed in Chapter 11 of this book. It is recommended that you read the material on this topic in Chapter 11 before reading this section on maintenance costs.

Boehm's maintenance cost estimation is calculated in terms of a quantity called the Annual Change Traffic (ACT) which he defines as follows:

> The fraction of a software product's source instructions which undergo change during a (typical) year either through addition or modification.

Boehm's estimation method for maintenance costs uses the ACT and the estimated or actual development effort in person-months to derive the annual effort required for software maintenance. This is computed as follows:

AME := 1.0 * ACT * SDT

AME and SDT are the annual maintenance effort and the software development time and the units of each are person-months (p.m.).

Therefore, if a software project required 236 person-months of development effort and it was estimated that 15% of the code would be modified in a typical year, the basic maintenance effort should be:

AME := 1.0 * 0.15 * 236 = 35.4 p.m.

Boehm does not claim that this formula gives any more than a rough approximation to maintenance costs. However, it serves as a basis for computing a more accurate figure. This is based on the notion that software costs and maintenance costs depend on the size of the software and a number of other factors including the reliability required, the type of software, hardware constraints and the skill of the software development personnel. Details of these factors and their effect on software costs are covered in Chapter 11.

The maintenance cost estimate may be refined by judging the importance of each factor which affects the cost and selecting the appropriate cost multiplier. The basic maintenance cost is then multiplied by each multiplier to give the revised cost estimate.

For example, say in the above system the factors having most effect on maintenance costs were reliability (RELY) which had to be very high, the availability of support staff with language and applications experience (AEXP and LEXP) which was also high, and the use of modern programming practices for system development (very high). From Boehm's table, reproduced in Chapter 11, these have multipliers as follows:

RELY   1.10
AEXP   0.91
LEXP   0.95
MODP   0.72

By applying these multipliers to the initial cost estimate, a revised figure may be computed as follows:

AME := 35.4 * 1.10 * 0.91 * 0.95 * 0.72 = 24.2 p.m.

The reduction in estimated costs has come about partly because experienced staff are available for maintenance work but mostly because modern programming practices had been used during software development. As an illustration of their importance, the maintenance cost estimate if modern programming practices are not used at all and other factors are unchanged is as follows:

AME := 35.4 * 1.10 * 0.91 * 0.95 * 1.40 = 47.1 p.m.

As Boehm also estimates that the use of modern programming practices reduces development costs, the figure of 47.13 p.m. is, in fact, an underestimate as initial development costs would have been greater if modern practices were not used.

This maintenance estimate is a gross effort for the entire software system. In fact, different parts of the system will have different ACTs so a more accurate figure can be derived by estimating initial development effort and annual change traffic for each software component. The total maintenance effort is then the sum of these individual component efforts. It is outside the scope of this book to look at cost estimation at this level of detail and interested readers are referred to the original source by Boehm.

One of the problems encountered when using an algorithmic cost estimation model for maintenance cost estimation is that it takes no account of the fact that the software structure degrades as the software ages. This means that using the original development time as the key factor in maintenance cost estimation is liable to be misleading as the software loses its resemblance to the original system. It is therefore not clear whether the cost estimation model is valid for ageing software systems.

The maintenance cost estimation model used by Boehm estimated maintenance costs which fitted reasonably well with measured actual costs. Boehm does not claim that his organization is necessarily typical and the estimation model may not work quite so well in other organizations or for other types of work.

However, the existence of a cost estimation model which takes into account factors such as programmer experience, hardware constraints, software complexity, etc., allows decisions about maintenance to be made on a quantitative rather than a qualitative basis. For example, say in the above example system that management decided that money might be saved by using less experienced staff for software maintenance. Assume that inexperienced staff cost $5000 per month compared to $6500 for experienced software engineers.

Using experienced staff, the total annual maintenance costs are:

$$AMC := 24.23 * 6500 = \$157\,495$$

Using inexperienced staff, the effort required for software maintenance is increased because the staff experience multipliers change:

$$AME := 35.24 * 1.10 * 1.07 * 1.13 * 0.72 = 33.89 \text{ p.m.}$$

Thus, total costs using inexperienced staff are:

$$AMC := 33.89 * 5000 = \$169\,450$$

Therefore, it is actually more expensive to use inexperienced staff rather than experienced engineers. Even if the actual costs are inaccurate, the model demonstrates how management decisions affect costs and, in this respect, is a very valuable tool for software maintenance management.

8.6.3 Program understanding

The key to effective program maintenance is program understanding. Unless a program is properly understood by the maintenance programmer, changing the program is likely to result in the introduction of errors. As one of the major themes of this book is the production of understandable programs, the writing of such programs is not discussed further here. Rather, this section concentrates on providing hints on how to read and understand a program written by some other software engineer.

The fundamental assumption which must be made at this stage is that the program reader has a thorough knowledge and understanding of the programming language used. Without this knowledge, it is unlikely that he will ever understand the program in sufficient detail to modify it successfully.

In this section, techniques of program reading are described. However, the usefulness of these techniques to any particular program depends on the application of that program, the style in which it was written and the program reader. If the reader has some experience of working with or implementing the type of program he is studying he or she will almost certainly read that program differently from a reader who has no experience of that application.

For example, a program reader who has experience of compiler writing knows that compilers all have a lexical analysis part, a syntactic and semantic analysis part and a code generation part. These parts normally communicate using a symbol table. When attempting to understand a compiler, that individual will naturally look for those parts as the first stage of the program comprehension process. The reader without experience must start at a different level and by studying program components, determine the functions of different parts of the program. Program documentation presenting a system overview can be exceptionally useful in such cases.

There appear to be no general program reading techniques which ensure that the different units in a program can be identified simply by code examination. The use of meaningful names and descriptive header comments, however, can be enormously helpful, and it is essential that their use is adopted in any large system. Although not an infallible guide to the function of an object, meaningful names provide semantic clues to the reader which help him or her deduce the actual function of that object.

Given that program units can be identified, the program reader must then discern how these units are activated and used. There are two ways of tackling this problem. The reader may study the functions of each program unit and, by understanding these functions, can work out how the units should be used. Reference to the program code can then confirm this usage. Alternatively, the reader may choose to examine the program code and trace how and where units in the system are called. By examining various parts of the program, the functions and usage of each of the units can be determined.

The first approach roughly corresponds to a bottom-up approach where the overall functions of a system are understood in terms of their sub-functions. The latter approach is a top-down approach where details of sub-functions are ignored so that a manageable overall picture may be obtained. There is no evidence to suggest that one technique is superior to the other and both would normally be used in practical situations.

Having identified the program units and how they are used, the program maintainer is generally faced with the problem of understanding one or more units in detail, so that they might be modified.

Given that the programming language is understood, there are various strategies which might be adopted to determine how a program unit operates. For example, the reader might first study the input and output statements to determine the unit's interaction with its environment, then the unit's data declarations, then procedure declarations and finally, with this background, the control statements to understand the unit's operation. On the other hand, the control statements might be studied first, then procedure declarations, then data definitions and so on. The particular approach adopted is at the discretion of the individual and there is no published evidence to suggest that one technique is better than another.

As an illustration of how program reading might be tackled, the approach adopted by the author in studying program units is described here as one possible way of tackling the problem of program understanding. A number of steps are involved:

1. The program is scanned to determine its structure and to see if program objects are ascribed meaningful names.

2. If not, an attempt is made to determine the function of each object in the program — constants, types, variables and procedures. A table of names and their probable functions is constructed.

3. Linear code sequences, loops and conditionals are then studied to find out their functions and the program listing annotated accordingly. This is a process of adding low-level comments in a form which is particular to the reader. Existing low-level comments in the program are deliberately ignored as experience has shown that they are often misleading.

4. The program logic is then traced step by step. Depending on the modifications to be made to the unit, this may mean tracing each statement or may involve only a few statements in one procedure.

Wherever possible, the latter stage in program reading is best carried out with another person who has also studied the program. Logic tracing is easier if one person explains to the other what the program is supposed to be doing. This verbalization clarifies individual thinking and has the additional advantage that oversights or misunderstandings by one reader may be detected by the other.

8.6.4 Measuring the maintainability of programs

Attempts have been made to devise techniques which quantify the maintainability of programs and to measure that maintainability automatically. These techniques equate maintainability with complexity — the more complex the program, the more difficult it is to understand and hence maintain.

Halstead (1977) suggests that the complexity of a program can be measured by considering the number of unique operators, the number of unique operands, the total frequency of operators and the total frequency of operands in a program. Using these parameters, Halstead has devised metrics allowing program size, programming effort and program 'intelligence count' to be computed.

McCabe (1976) has devised a measure of program complexity using graph theoretic techniques. His theory maintains that program complexity is not dependent on size but on the decision structure of the program. Measurement of the complexity of a program depends on transforming the program so that it may be represented as a graph and counting the number of nodes, edges and connected components in that graph.

Both of these techniques have some applicability, but both suffer from the same disadvantage that they do not take into account the data structures used in the program, the program comments or the use of meaningful variable names. Shepherd *et al.* (1979) have conducted experiments using both techniques. Their results were inconclusive.

Boehm *et al.* (1978) have devised a number of software metrics including a measure of the maintainability of a program. They consider that program maintainability is dependent on testability, understandability and modifiability. These factors are themselves dependent on program structuredness, program self-descriptiveness, program conciseness, etc., and empirical techniques have been devised to measure these characteristics.

Techniques for measuring program maintainability are rarely used in production programming environments, and existing evidence suggests that existing techniques are still in need of considerable refinement. The refinement of existing techniques and the development of new maintainability metrics is an important research area. With reliable metrics, improved programming techniques which reduce maintenance costs can be identified and adopted.

Further reading

Software Maintenance Management, B. P. Leintz and E. B. Swanson (1980), Reading, Mass: Addison-Wesley.

This is a thorough survey of software maintenance in data processing environments and, from their work, the authors provide useful hints for maintenance management. However, its concentration on data processing systems is perhaps a weakness as many systems which have extreme maintenance problems are real-time embedded systems.

Software Maintenance Guidebook, R. L. Glass (1981), Englewood Cliffs, NJ: Prentice-Hall.

Very pragmatic, practical advice on software maintenance.

'Documentation', G. Goos. In *Advanced Course on Software Engineering* (1970), Berlin: Springer-Verlag.

Very little indeed seems to have been published on this topic. This early paper summarizes a situation which has changed little.

ACM Sigdoc Newsletter.

An informal publication of the ACM Special Interest Group on Documentation. The articles in it are sometimes amusing and sometimes interesting but most of the material is, unfortunately, trivial.

Chapter 9 THE USER INTERFACE

This chapter deals with a topic which is not normally covered in texts on software engineering, namely the interface of the user with the software system. It may be thought that the user interface is the responsibility of the systems analyst rather than the software engineer but, as was made clear in the chapters covering software requirements specification, these roles should not be considered distinct.

The user interface is the yardstick by which the user judges system quality. If a system has a poorly designed interface, it is liable to be rejected, irrespective of the facilities which it offers. A badly designed interface can cause the user to make potentially catastrophic errors. If information is presented in a confusing or misleading way, the user may accidentally misunderstand the meaning of an item of information and, on that basis, initiate a sequence of dangerous actions.

This situation is most likely to arise when the user is dealing with information not normally presented by the system. Such a situation arises when a system malfunction occurs, so the consequences of a user error may be to compound that malfunction. The seriousness of a nuclear accident at a power station in the USA in 1979 may have been compounded by the complexity of the user interface to the reactor control system.

User interfaces can be classified as on-line interactive interfaces and off-line interfaces. In an on-line interface, the user directly interacts with the computer system through his or her terminal. An off-line interface, on the other hand, relies on the user preparing machine-readable input separately then presenting that to the computer system. The results of processing that input are returned to the user, often on specially designed forms.

Although off-line interfaces are common in business data processing systems, in future the majority of direct user interfaces will be interactive. Indirect interfaces such as that of a consumer to the billing computer of an electricity supply utility will still be oriented around a specialized form. This class of interface will not be discussed here.

Interactive user interfaces show a remarkable range of variation — a simple mnemonic interface may simply report system status and accept commands from the user; a business system interface may be the forms input to and generated by the system; and an engineering design interface may involve the user manipulating graphic representations of structures. To design an appropriate interface requires knowledge of both user procedures and what is practicable to provide using the computer system.

There are a number of styles of user/computer dialogue which may be implemented — mnemonic-based, quasi-natural language, forms-driven, menu-type and question-answer dialogue. The first three of these may be classified as user-initiated dialogues and the latter two as computer-initiated dialogues. Computer-initiated dialogues are most useful for untrained users, whereas user-initiated dialogues are best where the user is trained and interacts with the computer on a regular basis.

Serious consequences can result if a poorly designed or inappropriate interface is used. At best, an inappropriate interface will result in increased training costs and a higher proportion of user errors; at worst, it will result in the system being completely abandoned. Eason *et al.* (1975) have identified three characteristic responses which result from poor interface design.

1. The user refuses to make use of the computer system. After initial 'testing', he or she deems it inadequate for his or her needs.

2. The user learns a few commands 'parrot fashion' and restricts usage of the system to these commands. Because the user has no real understanding of the system, he or she cannot make use of all the system facilities.

3. The user interacts with the computer system by using an intermediary who becomes the local system expert.

An individual's particular reaction to an inappropriate interface depends on the organization using the system, the status of the individual and the nature of the system itself. Whereas a manager may decide not to use a management information system or may delegate an intermediary to use the system, a secretary using a word processor system does not, generally, have such options. In this case, minimal system facilities are learned and used. The full capability of the system is ignored.

As computer systems become more pervasive because of reduced hardware costs, more and more individuals will use computers as everyday tools. Interface design should reflect this and should ensure that the computer is seen as a useful and powerful tool. The interface should not have human characteristics, otherwise the user may ascribe human abilities to the machine. Human abilities and computer power are complementary and it is the task of the interface designer to ensure that they work well together.

Section 9.1 briefly discusses psychological issues which should be taken into account in designing a user interface. This is followed by a general discussion of user interface design where a distinction is made between user-initiated interfaces and computer-initiated interfaces. Natural-language interfaces are also discussed. The final sections of the chapter discuss interfaces which are not based on a standard alphanumeric terminal. The need to use graphics to improve the immediacy and readability of output displays is discussed, and Section 9.4 examines situations where a specially designed terminal might be used.

9.1 User psychology

In order to design an acceptable user interface, the psychology of the system user should be carefully considered. There are some interface design issues which are directly related to user psychology and are independent of the background of experience of the individual user. Shneiderman (1980) discusses some of these issues. These include information overloading, task complexity, system response time and the degree of control over the system which the user is allowed.

Information overloading is a situation where the interface presents the user with too many distinct items of information. Miller (1957) suggests that human memory is hierarchical with a short-term memory made up of about seven locations. This is supplemented by other more permanent memory to which information is transferred. If a user interface presents more than seven distinct items of information to the user at the same time, they may not all be retained in short-term memory and some are likely to be forgotten.

In designing an interface, therefore, information should be presented in units rather than in groups so that the user has time to assimilate that information and, perhaps, transfer it to more permanent memory. This allows short-term memory locations to be kept free for use in problem-solving operations.

Because of short-term memory limitations, an individual feels relief when an operation has been completed and the short-term memory may be cleared. As a result, there is an inherent desire for closure — the completion of a task and the subsequent relief. Each time a user types a command or completes a session of editing, closure is achieved and relief gained.

Because of this desire for closure, user interfaces are best organized as a sequence of short operations rather than a single large, complex task. Even although this may involve more typing, informal studies reported by Shneiderman suggest that users prefer short operations in sequence rather than a single, more complicated, operation. This fact may account for some of the success of the Unix system interface which is based on simple operations but which includes mechanisms (pipes and macros) to combine these simple operations, to create more powerful commands.

The response time of an interactive system is possibly the most important factor influencing the user's opinion of that system. If the user considers the response time to be excessive, he or she may think that the system is a poor system irrespective of the facilities provided. If the response is prompt, he or she may be quite prepared to overlook some system inadequacies.

It is not possible to provide a standard acceptable response time because user expectations vary depending on the complexity of the operation being executed by the system. Users expect instant echoing of characters which they have typed and very fast response to editing or login requests. On the other hand, if a user knows that a task is complex or involves a large amount of information processing, he or she is prepared to wait much longer. Examples of such operations might be compiling a program or retrieving information from a database.

If it is necessary to include facilities which may involve long response times, the user should be given the option of finding out how the task is progressing. For example, if the task is processing a number of items, periodic status reports might be produced setting out the number of items processed so far. This is particularly important when response times are variable and depend on the loading on the system. Without some indication of how long the task will take, the user cannot readily make use of the time spent waiting for the system to respond.

Strangely, there are situations where too rapid a response can cause the user anxiety. This is particularly likely if the users are inexperienced and a computer-initiated interface (described below) is in use. If the response is fast, the user may be surprised and his or her thinking may be disrupted. She may feel that she is being driven by the machine to work at an excessive speed. In such situations, it may be desirable to delay responses and minimize the variance in response time.

As users become more experienced in computer usage, their desire to control the computer increases. They are not content simply to be passive and accept the computer as the dominant partner in their interaction. As a result, they feel resentful if system messages suggest that they are not in charge or if they are forced to follow a prescribed verbose routine with which they are familiar.

Because of this need for control, interactions whose progress is controlled by the machine are only suitable for casual, irregular computer users. Regular system users should be provided with an interface which makes them feel that the computer is a tool which they can control.

9.2 User interface design

The design of a user interface should not be undertaken by the software engineer alone. It is essential to consult with system users and discuss their background and their needs. In some situations, it may be impossible to develop a single interface which is suitable for all system users. In such cases, multiple interfaces should be provided, each tailored for a particular class of user.

User interface systems can be broadly classified as:

1. user-initiated interfaces,
2. computer-initiated interfaces.

In the former case, the user is in charge, controlling the progress of the user/computer dialogue. In the latter case the computer system originates the dialogue, the user replies and, on the basis of that reply, the computer selects the next stage in the interaction. As a general rule, user-initiated interfaces are most suitable for experienced or regular computer users, whereas computer-initiated interfaces are best for inexperienced or casual users. Of course, situations exist where the most appropriate interface is made up of combinations of each interface class.

The most fundamental principle in user interface design is that the interface must be designed to suit the needs and abilities of the individual user. Users should not be forced to adapt to an interface which is convenient to implement or which is suited to the systems designer. Tailoring the interface to the user means that the interface must be couched in terms familiar to the user and that the objects manipulated by the system should have direct analogues in the environment with which the user is familiar.

For example, if a system is designed for use by secretarial staff, the objects manipulated should be letters, documents, diaries, folders, etc., at least as far as the secretary is concerned. In practice, these objects will be implemented using different files but the secretary should not be forced to cope with such computing concepts as workfiles, directories, file identifiers and so on. The allowed operations might be 'file', 'retrieve', 'index', 'discard', etc.

Examples of systems based on an office metaphor are now commercially available. In these systems, the user is presented with pictures (called icons) of familiar office objects such as calculators, wastebins, pencils, erasers, etc. To select an operation, the user points at the appropriate picture and that operation is initiated. For example, to perform calculations he or she points at the calculator icon, to draw diagrams he points at the pencil icon, to discard items the wastebin icon is indicated and so on.

This type of interface is very suitable for users with no previous experience of computers as they are not intimidated by the terminology associated with the machine. It is, however, very expensive in both hardware and software terms. It also has the further disadvantage that completely new operations which have no non-automated analogue cannot be represented with a familiar icon. Indeed, it may be very difficult to devise any kind of icon for automated operations. For example, how might multi-file comparisons be pictorialized?

The second principle of interface design is that the user interface must be consistent. Consistency should be maintained within a system and across sub-systems running on the same machine. Interface consistency means that system commands should have the same format, parameters should be passed to all commands in the same way, and command punctuation should be similar.

A consistent interface means that when a user takes time to learn about one command of the interface that knowledge is applicable to all other commands in the system. For example, say system commands accept parameters which may be filenames or which may be flags controlling command operation. If it is necessary to distinguish flags from filenames by some means — such as preceding flags with a '-' character — this should be the convention for every system command whether or not there is any ambiguity in a particular command between filenames and flags.

If a particular flag name is used to signify a particular operation in one system command, exactly the same name should be used in all compatible commands. For example, if a command to print a file takes a flag '-d' specifying that the file is to be deleted after printing, the same flag name should be used in every other command which can delete a file such as archive commands, copy commands, etc.

Interface consistency across sub-systems is equally important. Many large systems are made up of sub-systems which can be independently activated and these sub-systems should be designed so that commands with similar meanings in different sub-systems are expressed in the same way. It is very dangerous for a command, say 'k', to mean 'keep this file' in a system editor and 'kill this transaction' in an information retrieval system. Users of both systems will inevitably confuse the commands with dire consequences.

The third principle of interface design is that the interface should have built-in 'help' facilities. These should be accessible from the user's terminal and should provide different levels of help and advice — from very basic information on how to get started with the system up to a full description of system facilities and how to use them. These help facilities should be structured so that the user is not overwhelmed with information when he or she asks for help.

> help [command input by user]

First-level output from this help command might be as follows:

> The help command is designed to give you information about system facilities. In short, you should type help followed by the name of the facility you are interested in. For example, if you want to know how to send files to be printed on the line printer type:

> > help lpr

> If you want to find out about the Pascal system, type:

> > help pascal

> If you are just starting with the system you might like to type:

> > help system

> This will tell you what facilities are available. If you want more information about help, type:

> > help -m

> Any command may take a -m(ore) flag which results in more detailed information being provided.

Notice that this help output does not overwhelm the reader with information but provides enough detail for him to explore further using the help command.

User-initiated interfaces fall into two approximate classes:

1. *Command-driven interfaces.*   In this type of interface the user inputs commands or queries which are interpreted by the computer.

2. *Forms-oriented interfaces.* In these interfaces the user calls up an image of a form to his or her screen and fills in that form by overtyping appropriate parts of the screen.

Under some circumstances, forms-oriented interfaces might be considered as computer-initiated, particularly where the user has little or no control over what forms are actually filled in. In other cases, he or she has virtually complete control of everything from form layout to the contents of the form. This simply illustrates that there is no clear dividing line between interface classes.

9.2.1 Command-driven interfaces

Command-driven interfaces involve the user inputting a command to the computer system which takes some action depending on the command. The command may be a query or the initiation of some sub-system, or it may call up a sequence of other commands.

At the time of writing, this class of user interface is, by far, the most common. The user interacts with the system via a terminal made up of a typewriter keyboard and a display screen which can display discrete alphanumeric characters or very limited graphics characters. The size of the screen is such that normally 24 lines of 80 characters can be displayed.

This class of interface is a direct derivation from off-line interfaces where data was punched onto cards and input to the system. It is a relatively straightforward task to convert from an off-line interface to a simple on-line text interface. Because of this, because terminals to support this class of interface are cheap, and because the software techniques of text handling are well understood, the majority of general-purpose computer systems support this class of interface.

For many applications, this form of user interface is eminently suitable. Much of the information which is processed by computer systems is best gathered, input and displayed as text and there is no need for capabilities apart from those required to input and output text. They are suitable for environments where the majority of work carried out is program development, documentation and maintenance.

Unfortunately, because this type of interface is derived from punched card systems, some user interfaces of this type are based entirely on upper-case letters. This is completely artificial as text-based information is normally presented using both upper-case and lower-case letters. Upper-case letters are only used in distinguished positions. Upper-case only interfaces are obsolete and text-based user interfaces should always support both upper and lower-case letters.

Command systems may involve the user actually providing a command such as 'print' or 'edit'. Alternatively, the command may be implicit with the user simply providing details of the entity to which his command relates. An example of this latter type of command might be an information retrieval system which does not allow users to modify information in a database — a library catalogue, for example. The retrieval and display operation is implicit and the user inputs key details about the information he or she wishes to retrieve.

The design of such interfaces, where the command is implicit, is usually straightforward and readily derived from the application. Situations where the user must actually input commands tend to be more complex and the design of those systems depends on the application being developed and on the experience, background and ability of the system users. When designing such an interface, the software engineer must decide if the commands input by the user are to be functional mnemonics (such as ed to initiate the editor) or if they are to be expressed in full.

If a decision is made to implement a system using mnemonic commands, the system designer is faced with the problem of choosing appropriate mnemonics to represent the possible system operations. Mnemonic choice should be governed by the following criteria:

1. Mnemonics should be easily remembered and semantically related to the operation they represent. For example, an edit operation might be represented as 'ed', a print operation by 'pr' and a copy operation by 'cp'.

2. Mnemonics should be unambiguous — if there are more commands than can be accommodated using initial letter mnemonics, two- or three-letter mnemonics should be used. Single and multiple letter mnemonics should not be used in the same system as this may cause confusion. For example, a system may have a command to print files and a command to purge files. It is poor practice to use a mnemonic 'pr' for print and 'p' for purge as a mix-up, with serious consequences, is liable to occur. In such a situation, mnemonics such as 'pr' for print and 'pu' for purge would be better choices.

3. If mnemonics are chosen by abbreviating the name of the operation, a consistent abbreviation convention should be adopted. For example, the mnemonic may consist of the first two or three letters of the operation name. Therefore, users who are not completely familiar with available mnemonics but who know which operation is required can make a guess at the appropriate mnemonic.

The decision on whether to use mnemonics or full commands must be taken by considering the system users. When users become familiar with a system, it is irritating for them to have to type lengthy system commands or to be presented with wordy, well known system messages. Such users generally prefer a mnemonic system involving the minimum amount of typing and are content with terse system messages.

On the other hand, inexperienced and casual system users are less likely to be intimidated by an interface if it accepts meaningful commands and generates friendly responses. The inexperienced user is far less likely to make mistakes if commands must be given in full. For example, if the user wishes to compile a Pascal program, the command:

    compile myprogram with Pascal

is more meaningful than the terse:

    pc myprogram

Unless a system is intended for a single class of user, such as programmers (who normally want a concise interface), system commands should be expressible in both a concise and a verbose form.This can easily be accomplished by providing a command processing system which includes a macro processor. The basic command may be the concise version but, by defining a full version of the command as a macro, both terse and verbose forms can be made available.

The provision of a macro processor system as part of the interface interpreter allows the user to combine commands into a named sequence which may be initiated simply by typing the macro name. The interface translator expands that name into the command sequence and executes each command in turn. In such systems, it is usually possible to parameterize commands, allowing them to be generalized.

Some interfaces provide constructs which may be used to control which interface commands are executed. The user interface is a special-purpose programming language manipulating entities associated with the system application. For example, if the interface is an operating system interface, the objects manipulated may be data files and program files. Control constructs such as if-then-else conditionals and while loops allow interface commands to be skipped or to be executed a number of times.

The example below illustrates how commands provided by the Unix c-shell (the Unix system interface is called the shell) may be combined. This shell program defines a print command which initiates the Unix text formatting system and, depending on an input flag, directs the output to either the user's terminal, a fast printer or a typewriter-quality daisy-wheel printer.

```
/* set up short names for files */
setenv T /usr/rsch/is/consts/tform
setenv P /usr/rsch/is/consts/prelude
/* if prelude exists, override default */
if (-e prelude) setenv P prelude
switch ( $1 )
      case "-t": /* user terminal */
```

```
    nroff -mis -Tlpr $3 $4 $5 $6 $P $2.h $2 | more;
    breaksw
    case "-tr": /* terminal but with shorter lines */
    nroff -mis -Tlpr $3 $4 $5 $6 $P $T $2.h $2 | more;
    breaksw
    case "-p": /* line printer */
    nroff -mis $3 $4 $5 $6 $P $2.h $2 | lpr;
    breaksw
    case "-d": /* next three are daisy wheel printers */
    nroff -mis -e -Txerox12 $3 $4 $5 $6 $P $2.h $2 | lpr -Pdaisy -h;
    breaksw
    case "-d10":
    nroff -mis -e -Txerox $3 $4 $5 $6 $P $2.h $2 | lpr -Pdaisy -h;
    breaksw
    case "-q":
    nroff -mis -e -Tqume-12 $3 $4 $5 $6 $P $2.h $2 | lpr-Pdaisy -h;
    breaksw
endsw
```

The use of interfaces such as the Unix shell is most appropriate when the system users have some programming experience (Mashey and Smith, 1977) although non-programmers may be able to make use of some of their facilities.

The notion of translating one form of a command to an equivalent form has not been extended to system replies, except on an experimental basis (Sommerville, 1981). The advantage of this extension is that system replies can be tailored to user's background — casual users can have full explanatory replies regular users concise replies. In the absence of such a mechanism, the best approach is to provide concise system messages expressed in a form suitable for regular users. These should be supplemented by an easy-to-use 'help' facility such as the typing of a single question mark. If the user does not understand a reply, he or she can ask for help and a fuller, more explanatory version of the reply can be provided by the system.

9.2.2 Natural language interfaces

One class of imperative user interface is those interfaces based on natural language. It is argued that computer systems will not become truly accessible to casual users until natural or quasi-natural language exchanges with the computer system become possible. A number of such interfaces to large database systems such as LADDER (Hendrix et al., 1978) and PLANES (Waltz, 1978) have been implemented and are reportedly successful. The particular systems are information retrieval systems geared to queries concerning a particular type of subject — ships in the case of LADDER, aircraft in the case of PLANES.

Both of these systems are interfaces to database systems and it is intended that they should be usable by people with no computing experience. Examples of the type of query, taken from the paper by Hendrix et al., which may be posed in the LADDER system are:

What is the next port of call of the Santa Inez?
How many ships carrying oil are within 300 miles of the Enterprise?
Where are they?
Where are they headed?

Notice that the system is sophisticated enough to recognize context so that queries such as 'Where are they?' are processed in the context established by the previous query.

The language-processing techniques used in these systems are of a general-purpose nature and have been modified to provide interfaces to other database systems holding information on other topics.

The software problems involved in implementing quasi natural-language interfaces are immense — natural languages are inherently ambiguous and resolving ambiguities is generally difficult and sometimes impossible. Systems such as PLANES and LADDER only operate successfully because knowledge about the entities in the database is built into the user interface. Using this knowledge, many ambiguities can be resolved. All natural-language systems presently implemented confine themselves to very specialized applications and techniques for developing a general-purpose natural-language understanding system have not been devised. An excellent survey of this area is given in Barr *et al.* (1981).

Even if the implementation of a quasi natural-language system such as LADDER is feasible, it is not necessarily the case that a natural-language interface is the most acceptable to users. The fundamental problems with such an interface are:

1. It is verbose — users have to type long commands.

2. The resolution of ambiguities may involve much time-wasting system/user dialogue. Thus even more typing is involved.

Whilst the principal means of communicating with a computer system is via a keyboard, quasi natural-language interfaces are less convenient than other types of user interface because of the unnecessary typing involved. If general-purpose speech recognition and understanding systems can be developed, this situation may change. The verbosity of the language will no longer be a problem as users will be able to talk directly with the computer. However, there is no evidence from current research that speech understanding systems are likely to be available in the near future.

A further problem which may result from the use of a natural-language interface is that inexperienced users might overestimate the capabilities of the computer system. If the computer appears to communicate like a human, it is natural for those unfamiliar with computers to ascribe other human abilities to the machine, such as the ability to make deductions on the basis of incomplete information. The consequent disappointment may discourage users from investigating the real potential of the system and may even cause them to abandon usage of the system altogether. However, there is no doubt that the flexibility and ease-of-use of natural language means that it has an important role to play in user interfaces. Perhaps it may be used in conjunction with graphical interfaces and pointing devices to provide a flexible interface without excessive verbosity.

9.2.3 Forms-oriented interfaces

User interfaces which are forms-oriented involve the user calling up an image of a form to the terminal. He or she then fills in the form by typing in the appropriate screen locations. Such systems rely on terminals with a cursor which may be moved anywhere on the screen.

Forms-oriented interfaces are considered to be user-initiated because it is assumed that a library of different forms is available. Exactly which form is filled in is under the control of the user. In general, forms-oriented interfaces are more limited in scope than command-driven interfaces and are most suitable for use in situations where the users have little experience or understanding of computing.

This type of interface is often the best choice when an existing manual paperwork system, based on standard forms, is to be automated. The interface design may be based on forms already in use. If that automated system resembles the existing manual system, users are unlikely to be intimidated by the system and will accept the new automated system. Furthermore, both manual and automated systems may easily run in parallel without confusion and without the overhead of high user-training costs.

One of the most sophisticated forms-oriented interfaces is the Office-Talk (Ellis and Nutt, 1980) system. This experimental system is the basis of a number of office systems which are now commercially available. Office-Talk was built as a research vehicle to investigate how to automate the activities in any office and provides powerful facilities for creating and manipulating forms. Individual forms may be examined in more or less detail. The OfficeTalk terminal is designed to mimic a desk, with several forms on it as shown in Fig. 9.1. OfficeTalk avoids one of the limitations of conventional forms-oriented systems, namely that forms can only be viewed singly. By using a graphics display, several forms may be viewed simultaneously by the user on different parts of the screen.

Forms-oriented interfaces must be combined with a simple version of some other interface type which allows forms to be called up, saved and printed. This may be a command-driven interface where the user requests the form by its number or a menu-type interface where the user is presented with a list of possible forms and operations. He selects from this list by indicating the appropriate entry using a pointing device such as a light pen. In OfficeTalk, a menu is provided and a 'mouse' is used to point at commands which the user wishes to initiate.

9.3 Computer-initiated interfaces

Computer-initiated user interfaces are those user interfaces where the computer system guides the progress of the user/computer dialogue.

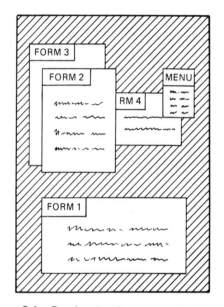

Figure 9.1   Overlapping forms on a 'desk' image.

Information is displayed, the user responds in some simple fashion, and, on the basis of that user response, the computer takes action or displays further information. The computer leads the user through his or her interaction with the computer by presenting alternatives and acting according to the user's reaction.

Computer-initiated interfaces are most suitable for situations where the users have little or no experience in using computers and who do not make regular use of a computer system. This type of interface has the advantage that the user need remember little or nothing about how to interact with the system — all necessary information is presented to him as the terminal session proceeds.

Computer-initiated interfaces fall into two rough classes:

1. menu systems where the user is presented with a list of alternatives and chooses one of these alternatives,
2. question-answer systems where the computer asks the user a question and takes action on the basis of his or her reply.

The general problem with computer-initiated interfaces is that as they become familiar to the user, he or she may feel frustration caused by the lack of control over the computer system. She knows the system questions and replies and is angered by unnecessarily verbose communications with the machine. It is therefore important that the user should be allowed to abbreviate replies and shorten system messages once he or she becomes used to the interface.

9.3.1 Menu systems

In a menu-type interface, the user must select one of a number of possibilities and indicate his or her choice to the machine. There are several ways in which the choice may be indicated. The user may type the name or the identifier of the selection; he or she may point at it with a mouse or some other pointing device; he or she may use cursor-moving keys to position the cursor over it or, on some types of touch-sensitive terminals, he or she may even be able to point at the selection with her finger.

An example of a menu system is an information retrieval system where the user is presented with a number of document names and a summary of each. Associated with each document is a number and to display a document, the user simply types that document number. This is illustrated in Fig. 9.2.

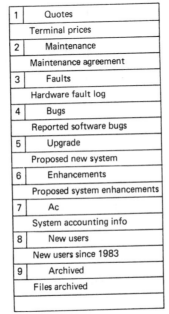

Figure 9.2 An information retrieval system menu.

Menu systems suffer from the restriction that there must be sufficiently few choices that all possibilities can be displayed on the terminal screen at the same time. In some cases, this is no problem but, in others, there may be tens, hundreds or thousands of possibilities. Techniques must be devised to classify these possibilities and to allow the user to identify his or her requirements with the minimum number of interactions.

An example of a menu-driven system with thousands of possibilities is the UK's Prestel system. This is an on-line information retrieval system containing pages of information. It is publicly accessible via the telephone network and the pages may be displayed on a domestic television set. Prestel offers about 250 000 separate pages and, to allow a menu-type

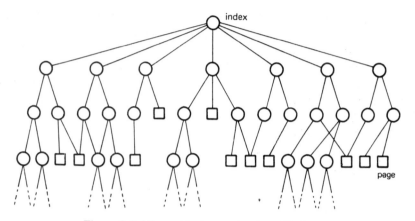

Figure 9.3 Hierarchical organization of indexes.

interface to be used, classifies these pages as information pages and index pages. A tree structure of indexes exists and, by starting at the root of this tree, the user works his or her way through the indexes, keying in an abbreviated version of the page number of the next page required. This hierarchical organization is illustrated in Fig. 9.3. All pages in the system have a unique number rather than a number relative to some index, so the system does not suffer from the most common drawback of hierarchically indexed systems. On many such systems, the user must progress through every level in the hierarchy from 1 to $(n-1)$, in order to reach level n. This is necessary because items at some level m are only identified to the higher level $(m-1)$. Using Prestel, the user may access any page by keying in the number of that page.

On the other hand, when there is no such relationship between an index and its entries, it is not normally possible for the user to work his or her way up the index hierarchy from level n to level 1. There is no physically recorded relationship between an index and its entries. The user must always start at the top and work his or her way down the indexes.

An alternative to providing an index hierarchy is to present the user with a screenful of information with the added choice of 'go on to next page'. If the user selects this the following page is displayed and the process may continue until the required item is finally displayed. This method is suitable for situations where there are tens rather than hundreds or thousands of possibilities. With such a system, it is important to include a skip forwards and backwards capability so that the user can flip through the pages looking for the one which is required. Otherwise, should the user accidentally miss the required page, he or she must start all over again at page 1.

Menu systems are likely to become increasingly widespread as more and more computers equipped with graphics and pointing devices become available. Whilst using a menu system on a conventional terminal is rarely quicker than typing commands, picking menu commands with a mouse (say) is a much faster operation than typing these commands. However, if commands have a number of optional parameters, menu systems are not necessarily faster as a menu is required for each parameter set.

For example, say an information retrieval system was built into a programming environment. This is intended to provide information about which software components are available, who designed what component, etc. Examples of possible queries are:

LIST components, project=viewdata_system,
    owner=J.Smith, status = untested

LIST projects, members = J.Smith, A.Jones
    manager=A.J.Black

Although it is possible to devise menu systems to express such complex queries, they are not particularly convenient to use. Experienced computer workers would probably prefer a command-driven interface. An interface for less experienced users might be a forms-oriented interface such as Query-by-Example (Zloof and de Jong, 1977). In this system, the user provides examples of the information he or she wishes to retrieve and the system deduces his or her query from these examples.

9.3.2 Question-answer interfaces

Question-answer interfaces are user interfaces where the progress of the person/computer dialogue is governed by the user's answers to questions posed by the computer. The most widespread use of this type of interface is in computer learning systems, but medical interviewing systems using this class of interface have also been developed. This type of interface would be used in preference to menu-type interface in situations where some overall picture of the user's requirements has to be built up by considering responses to a number of queries.

The design of question-answer interfaces is very dependent on the application being implemented. They appear to be most successful in situations where the number of possible user responses to a question are limited. For example, consider a medical interviewing system intended to find out how many cigarettes a patient smokes in a day. If the system poses the question:

How many cigarettes do you smoke in a day?

There are a variety of possible responses such as:

NONE	Twenty five	2 packs
0	20	about 15

A very sophisticated pattern-matching system must be used to recognize the user response as it may be couched in a number of equivalent ways. If the response cannot be recognized, the question must be reformulated and asked again. This may alienate the user, particularly as he or she is liable to have little experience or understanding of computer systems.

In such a dialogue, it is much better to formulate a series of questions which the user can answer simply with 'yes', 'no', or 'don't know'. For example:

> Do you smoke cigarettes?
> Do you smoke more than 10 cigarettes a day?
> more than 20?
> more than 30?
>   . . .

This particular dialogue terminates when the user answers 'no' to a question. In particular areas of medicine such as gastro-intestinal medicine, these interviewing systems are remarkably successful. They are as good as senior doctors in diagnosing particular complaints and have been well received by patients.

Question-answer systems of this type have been implemented using a special terminal with a restricted number of keys. Typically, these are numeric keys plus keys marked 'yes', 'no' and 'don't know'. An interesting result that has emerged from the use of the interviewing system is that patients not only enjoy using the system but are actually more honest with it than with medical staff (Lucas, 1977). They appear to feel less inhibited about answering personal questions posed by a machine probably because they feel that whatever they say the computer will not disapprove.

9.4 Error message design

The design of error messages is an important part of user interface design. As user errors are inevitable, the system's response should be helpful and should provide information on the nature of the error and, perhaps, its possible cause. Brown (1983) suggests that this is a critical but neglected area of the person-machine interface.

The error messages provided by the system should be polite, concise, consistent and constructive. Under no circumstances should they be abusive and, if the user's terminal might be in a public place, the error-handling system should not cause audible tones to be emitted which might embarrass the user. Error messages should include a reference to the appropriate user manual which describes the error in more detail and which might explain how the error can be corrected.

The background and experience of the user should be anticipated when designing error messages. Lengthy, detailed messages are irritating if the user is experienced, but essential if the user is a novice. For example, assume a system user is a nurse in a intensive-care ward in a hospital. Patient monitoring is carried out by a computer system. One command in such a system might be a command to display a patient's status. This command is initiated by typing the word 'display' followed by the patient's name:

display J.Jones

This would display the monitor readings for patient J.Jones. However, say the nurse was new to the system and rather than type 'display', he or she typed 'print'. A badly designed system might respond with an error message as follows:

*** ERROR *** Unrecognizable command

A much better error message would be:

Your instruction (print) is not a command which I understand. For a list of commands and their functions type the command 'help'.

Alternatively, the nurse might make an error in typing the patient's name. The nurse might type:

display J.Janes

A badly designed error message would be:

*** ERROR *** Invalid patient-id

This may be compared with the much friendlier response:

There is no patient J.Janes registered on the system. Perhaps you have made a typing mistake?

Notice that the friendlier system responses are couched in human terms rather than in computer terminology. Whilst anthropomorphization of computers is not without dangers (human abilities may be attributed to computers) it is sometimes a sensible way to approach error-message design. This is particularly true when building systems for inexperienced or infrequent computer users.

In situations where users are experienced and interact regularly with the computer system wordy human-like responses from the computer tend to become annoying after a few repetitions. Such users prefer more concise messages although these messages should still be expressed in plain language rather than jargon.

Much work remains to be done in this area, particularly in the tailoring of error messages to different classes of user. Many systems have both experienced and inexperienced users and, if they make regular use of the system, inexperienced users soon become experienced. Current thinking in such situations is for the system to hold a model of each user and to modify its error output depending on the type of user. However, exactly how this can be done in an economical way remains a research problem.

9.5 The use of graphics

Although interactive computer graphics systems have been available for several years their use until recently has been relatively limited. Because of the cost of terminal hardware and the processor power needed to drive the graphics display, user interfaces based on interactive graphics have only been used in systems where there is no possible alternative. Examples of applications which have made use of graphical interfaces include computer-aided design, computer animation and computer-aided mapping. It is not the intention to describe the technicalities of computer graphics here. These are outside the scope of this book and are covered in detail by Newman and Sproull (1979) and Foley and VanDam (1982). This section simply concentrates on the advantages and the potential of graphical user interfaces.

Decreasing processor and memory costs now mean that the cost of graphics display terminals has been significantly reduced. Low-cost graphics systems using domestic television technology and based on a microprocessor are now available on almost every personal computer. These systems can either act as stand-alone systems or be used as a graphics terminal connected to some larger system. As a result, it is now realistic to consider using a graphical interface for many types of application system.

Graphical systems have the advantage that the information stored and processed by the computer can be displayed in such a way that the user can gain an overall impression of the entities described by that information. For example, consider a system which records and summarizes the sales figures for a company on a monthly basis. These figures may be presented exactly, using alphanumeric text.

Jan	Feb	Mar	April	May	June
2842	2851	3164	2789	1273	2835

By reading those figures, it can be seen that higher sales were recorded in March and much lower sales in May. To abstract this information requires each monthly figure to be studied.

Graphical presentation of this information as a histogram makes the anomalous figures in March and May immediately obvious as shown in Fig. 9.4. Once an overall impression is gained, further, more precise details can be obtained from these figures.

This type of overall impression is what many computer users require. A manager, using an information system, is often more interested in trends and patterns in her data than in exact figures. These trends can be difficult to discern if the data is presented alphanumerically, particularly when correlations are sought. Graphic display of the data, on the other hand, makes trends immediately obvious.

The ability of graphics systems to present approximate information in an easily assimilated way can also be used in designing the user interface to built-in computer control systems. Consider, for example, the sensor information available to the pilot of an aircraft. Traditionally, this information is displayed on electromechanical dials. Glancing at a dial provides enough information to tell the pilot whether action is needed or not. He does not necessarily need to see the exact value registered on the dial — the

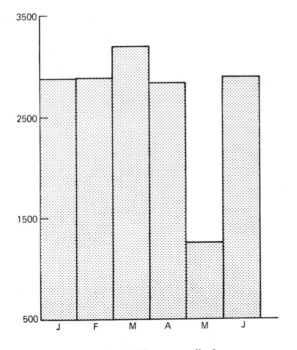

Figure 9.4 Histogram display.

needle position is enough to tell him that all is well or that some corrective action is required.

The introduction of computer-controlled sensor and display systems has meant that it is easier, cheaper and more reliable to display information electronically rather than using an electromechanical dial. The most common electronic display is a digital display based on liquid crystal technology which shows exact values. The operator must examine and mentally check the information rather than acquire this information from a needle position.

Where a large number of sensor displays are provided, digital displays are confusing and time consuming to check. Rather than use digital displays in such situations, it is better to convert the display output to an analogue form and display this graphically. A dial can be simulated on a display screen by blocking in segments of a circle or, alternatively, an expanding/contracting line whose length is proportional to the value displayed may be used. When such at-a-glance displays are provided, they may be supplemented by more exact digital displays activated at the request of the user or displayed alongside the graphical output. This is illustrated in Fig. 9.5.

Colour is another parameter which can be used to improve the readability and immediacy of graphic displays. Again, the use of domestic television technology means that colour graphics systems are relatively cheap and they

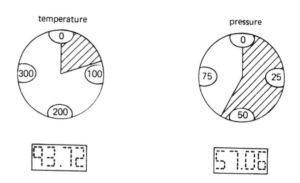

Figure 9.5   Graphical and digital information display.

offer an opportunity to the software engineer to improve the ergonomics of his output displays.

Consider the previous example where sensor data is displayed using a graphical interface. If colour graphics are available, data from a number of sensors can be displayed on the same screen and distinguished by their colour. Displays may be programmed to change colour if the sensor values fall below or rise above the acceptable range, with the usual conventions of red for danger, green for safety adopted.

Another reason for making use of colour graphics displays is the increasing audiovisual sophistication of the population in general. This is a result of exposure to high-quality television technology. If a user interface whose technical quality is less than that broadcast is used, some potential users will consider the associated system to be of low quality and decline to make use of it.

As well as presenting information in a form which is more acceptable than text to many classes of user, graphical interfaces may also have associated input devices which are easier and more convenient to use than a conventional keyboard. Because some computer users, such as managerial staff, are unable to type and are unwilling to learn this skill, they have an inbuilt resistance to keyboard-controlled terminals. If such users can be provided with an alternative, easier to use input device and a user interface built around that device, they are more likely to make personal use of the computer system.

Examples of such input devices include graphics tablets, light pens and cursor 'mice'. Using a graphics tablet, the user draws on a metal board with a stylus. His or her movements are sensed and the lines drawn on the tablet are displayed on the screen of the terminal. A light pen is a device used to touch the display screen. Its position can be detected by the graphics system and appropriate action taken. Light pens are fairly low-resolution devices so they are not suitable for drawing on the screen. They are best used for marking the position of an object of interest on the screen.

Cursor 'mice' are also devices for screen marking. They consist simply of a ball which can be moved in the $x-y$ directions. As this ball (mouse) is moved, the screen cursor follows its movement. This type of device is cheap and simple and a more convenient way of cursor movement than the usual terminal function keys. At the time of writing, several commercial micro-computer systems have recently come on the market which include a mouse and a high-resolution, bit-mapped graphics display as standard peripherals.

These systems not only allow the presentation of high-resolution graphics, they also allow text and graphics to be mixed on the same screen. This is not possible with many present microcomputer systems which only permit the mixing of text and low-resolution graphics. Furthermore, bit-mapped graphics display allows different type fonts and sizes to be displayed. As such systems become more common, user interfaces which incorporate some graphics will become the norm rather than the exception.

9.6 Special terminal hardware

For some types of application, it is not practical to base a user interface design on standard alphanumeric or graphics terminals. The needs of some classes of user are such that they are best accommodated by providing a special-purpose terminal specifically designed to support the application. General-purpose terminals may either be too generalized and difficult to use or may not provide the facilities required by the computer system.

For example, the interface of an air traffic control system with the traffic controller consists of a display screen presenting information derived from radar inputs and the aircraft themselves. The traffic controller has special function keys pertinent to traffic control such as a key which allows him to lock on to a particular aircraft and follow its flight path.

Some banking systems use special terminals which read information from a special plastic card presented by the customer making the transaction. These terminals perform some of the functions of a bank teller such as cash dispensing. Similarly, retail organizations might use cash register terminals which can read product codes and act as a cash dispenser and collector.

Banking and retail terminal systems present very little information to the user. They are designed for a very particular function and there is no need for any complex interactions. Other special-purpose terminals, such as those used in some word processing systems, have more extensive interactive capabilities and are tailored to a specific application by dedicating special functions to certain keys.

As well as a normal qwerty keyboard, a word processing system may also have a set of function keys. These keys might initiate actions such as the loading of a document into the machine, the printing of a document or document editing. Because the operations allowed to the user are restricted, the problem of designing user commands can be avoided if a function key is provided for each command.

There are two sets of circumstances where it may be appropriate to use special-purpose terminals:

1. when the terminal and computer costs represent a relatively small part of the overall system costs,
2. when the system is intended for use by people who are completely unfamiliar with computing equipment.

When the computer system acts as a controller for some larger system, such as a power station or telecommunications network, the computer is intended for use by technicians familiar with the application but not, necessarily, with the computer system itself. In this case, the cost of the terminal system is only a small part of overall system costs. The extra costs incurred by using a special terminal rather than an off-the-shelf device are justified by the increased usability of the system.

In banking and retail systems, where special-purpose terminals may also be required, the terminal costs make up the major part of system expenditure. Such systems where the terminal users are untrained in and uninterested in the computer system need a specially designed terminal to facilitate speedy and safe transactions. The cost of a such a terminal, tailored towards the specific needs of an organization is such that it can only be justified in those cases where very large numbers of terminals are to be purchased.

Most requirements for this type of terminal are satisfied by purchasing off-the-shelf banking or retail terminal systems and designing the application to use these terminals. The user interface design is completely dependent on the hardware characteristics. The market for such systems is sufficiently large, when all possible users are taken into account, that economies of scale allow terminals to be built and sold at a realistic price.

It is the responsibility of the system designer and software engineer to decide when it is cost-effective to use special-purpose terminals. In the situations described above, the decision is straightforward — special terminals are essential. In other situations, the decision is not so clear cut. The advantages offered by special hardware must be offset against the increased cost of such hardware. Furthermore, building the user interface into the hardware is liable to be expensive in situations where the system requirements and facilities change with time. As the system evolves, the interface built into the terminal may become inadequate. Updating that interface may require complete replacement of the terminal.

An alternative to designing a special-purpose terminal for some applications is to use an off-the-shelf intelligent terminal with an extended or restricted keyboard. Special functions can be provided by programming the terminal so that each key represents a particular function — there is no need for the same key to mean the same thing on every terminal. Removable key overlays may be used to label each key with the function it represents.

Programmable terminals avoid the problems of interface obsolescence described above — as the system requirements evolve, the terminal can be reprogrammed and the keys relabelled. As hardware costs fall, intelligent terminals will become widely used and their potential for individually tailored user interfaces exploited.

Further reading

Design of Man-Computer Dialogues, J. Martin (1973), Englewood Cliffs, NJ: Prentice-Hall.

Although over ten years old, the material in this book is not really out-of-date. Martin presents a very thorough discussion of the different types of user interface and when each might be used.

'The humanisation of computer interfaces', Special Issue (1983) *Comm. ACM*, **26 (4)**.

This special issue contains a number of papers in this area covering topics such as error-message design, the ease of use of various text editors, etc.

Chapter 10 SOFTWARE MANAGEMENT PSYCHOLOGY

Effective software management is important if large programming projects are to be completed on time, to specification and within budget. To be effective, the software manager must understand the technical aspects of programming management. Furthermore, he or she must also understand staff as individuals and how these individuals interact with each other. This chapter concentrates on these psychological fundamentals — how programmers behave as individuals and in groups. Chapter 11 is concerned with more practical aspects of software management — software cost estimation and control, project team organizations and management tools.

Because software engineering is a cognitive activity, psychology — understanding thought processes — is of vital importance. A better understanding of the psychology of programming helps us to understand the human limits involved and to tailor software projects so that programming staff are not set unrealizable objectives. With such an understanding, the software manager is less likely to form project groups whose members' personalities clash, and can gain insights into aspects of individual behaviour.

The material covered in this chapter is separated into three sections — the programmer as an individual, the programmer as a group member and the effects of the working environment on programmer performance.

Section 10.1 considers aspects of the individual activity of programming. It presents a cognitive model of the programming process and describes some implications of that model. For example, the model explains why gotoless programming is better than programming with gotos and why programming ability is language independent. This section also discusses programmer aptitude tests and concludes that aptitude test performance is unlikely to be a useful guide to programming ability.

Section 10.2 discusses programming group behaviour. It describes different personality types and how they interact and discusses some of the problems managers can have in keeping control of groups. Group communications, the implications of group loyalty, the relationship between group structure and system structure, and the role of the group leader are covered here.

Section 10.3 concerns the effect of the physical work environment on performance. It concludes that there is a need to design that environment to facilitate both individual working and group interactions.

10.1 The programmer as an individual

Software development is an individual, creative task. It is comparable with composing music, designing buildings and writing books. Although a programmer may work as part of a team, the team is only necessary because the required software system is so large that it cannot be produced by one person in a reasonable amount of time. Within the team, the work is partitioned and each individual programmer works on his own, creating his or her part of the project. An understanding of individual programmer performance is therefore of importance to the programming manager.

In this section, aspects of the psychology of the programmer as an individual are described. A model of the cognitive processes used in problem solving is presented and the implications of that model discussed. This is followed by an examination of the influence of personality on programming performance and the section concludes with a discussion of the reliability of programmer selection techniques.

10.1.1 A cognitive model of programmer behaviour

This section describes a model of the human cognitive process and the implications of that model to programmer behaviour. The model was suggested by Greeno (1972) and is described in some detail by Shneiderman (1980).

The model suggests that human memory structure is hierarchical. Input from the outside world first enters a relatively small short-term memory and, from there, it is either transferred to a 'permanent' long-term memory or forgotten. The long-term memory seems to have an unlimited capacity. There may also exist a 'working' memory which is more permanent than short-term memory but considerably less permanent than long-term memory.

When problems are posed, new information from short-term memory is integrated with existing, relevant information from long-term memory in a working memory. The result of this integration forms the basis for the problem solution and may be stored in long-term memory for future use. A diagram of this hierarchy is shown in Fig. 10.1.

The knowledge acquired by a programmer and stored in long-term memory appears to fall into one of two distinct classes:

1. *Semantic knowledge.*   This is the knowledge of concepts such as the operation of an assignment statement, the notion of a linked list and how a hash search technique operates. This knowledge is acquired through experience and learning and is retained in a representation-independent fashion. The manner in which the concept was presented to the programmer does not appear to affect the way in which this knowledge is stored.

2. *Syntactic knowledge.*   This is the knowledge of details of a representation such as how to write a procedure declaration in Pascal, what

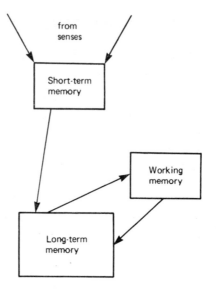

Figure 10.1 Memory organization.

standard functions are available in a programming language, whether an assignment is written using an = or := sign, etc. Because this knowledge is detailed and arbitrary, it is more likely to be forgotten than semantic knowledge.

Semantic knowledge is acquired by experience and through active learning where new information is consciously integrated with existing semantic structures. Syntactic knowledge, on the other hand, seems to be acquired mechanically, and new syntactic knowledge is not necessarily integrated with existing knowledge. In fact, new syntactic knowledge may interfere with existing knowledge, as it can only be arbitrarily added to that knowledge rather than integrated with it.

The different acquisition modes for syntactic and semantic knowledge explains the typical situation which arises when an experienced programmer learns a new programming language. Normally, the experienced programmer has no difficulty with the language concepts — these are embodied as semantic knowledge. The language syntax, however, tends to get mixed up with the syntax of familiar languages. For example, the FORTRAN programmer learning Pascal might write the assignment operator as = rather than :=; the Pascal programmer might write 'type x = . . .' rather than 'type x is . . .' when learning Ada, etc.

On the other hand, the novice programmer has two problems when learning to program. Not only must he or she master the semantic concepts implied in the computational model, he or she must also master an arbitrary and sometimes obscure syntax. This has the implication for programming language designers that non-obvious syntax rules should be avoided. For example, in Pascal semicolons usually follow statements except before an 'end'. Either semicolons should be unnecessary or they should be required everywhere.

Cognitive processes are constrained by the size of the short-term memory. In a classic paper, Miller (1957) found that the short-term memory can store about seven quanta of information. A quantum of information is not a fixed number of bits — it may be a telephone number, the function of a procedure or a street name. Miller also describes the process of 'chunking', where information quanta are collected together into chunks. These chunks can themselves be collected into larger chunks, etc. This chunking process appears to be the basis of our ability to form abstractions.

Shneiderman conjectures that this chunking process is used in understanding programs. The program reader abstracts the information in the program into chunks and these chunks are built into an internal semantic structure representing the program. Programs are not understood on a statement-by-statement basis. Once the internal semantic structure representing the program has been established, this knowledge is not readily forgotten. Furthermore, the structure can readily be represented in different notations. Hence, it is usually straightforward to translate an understood program from one programming language to another.

10.1.2 Practical implications of the model

This model of how we understand programs may be used to explain a number of aspects of programming practice. For example, it explains why a structured program should be easier to understand; why programmer ability is language independent; and what is the best way to learn a new programming language.

Structured programming should make a program easier to understand because it allows the chunking process to be more effective. If a program can be read top-to-bottom, the abstractions involved in forming chunks can be made sequentially, without reference to other parts of the program. The short-term memory can be devoted to a single section of code. It is not necessary to maintain information about several sections connected by arbitrary goto statements.

For the same reasons, if a programmer actively endeavours to program without the use of goto statements, he or she is less likely to make programming errors. His short-term memory can be devoted to information relevant to the program section being coded. There is no need to retrieve information from working memory about other parts of the program which interfere with that section.

The process of devising and writing a program is, basically, a problem-solving situation. The problem must first be understood, a general solution strategy must be worked out and, finally, this strategy must be translated into specific actions. The first stage involves the problem statement entering working memory from short-term memory. It is integrated with existing knowledge from long-term memory and analysed. The second stage uses this analysis to work out an overall solution. Finally, some method, such as the top-down development process described in Chapter 4, is used to develop the general solution and construct a program.

The development of the solution (the program) involves building an internal semantic model of the problem and a corresponding model of the solution. Once this model is built, it may be represented in any appropriate syntactic notation. An experienced programmer who understands a number of programming languages will have approximately the same degree of difficulty in representing that solution, irrespective of which language is actually used. Programming ability is the ability to formulate correct solutions and is language independent.

However, the representation is more likely to be free of errors if the syntactic facilities of the notation match the lowest-level semantic structures which are formulated. Programs written in languages such as Pascal should contain fewer errors than those written in FORTRAN or assembly code. Languages such as Pascal are more expressive than FORTRAN and offer higher-level constructs. Consequently, if the final representation is to be in Pascal, the internal semantics need not be developed to such a level of detail as would be required if the program is represented in FORTRAN. Because such a detailed model is not required, more of that model can be retained in short-term memory. Programmer errors caused by unexpected interaction of parts of the model are less likely to occur.

Because programming ability is language independent and programming language knowledge is held in a representation independent way, it is relatively easy for programmers who are familiar with one programming language to learn a new language of the same type. All that must be learnt is a new syntax — the concepts are already understood.

This is only true, however, if the computational model underlying both of these languages is the same. For example, a FORTRAN programmer should have little difficulty learning Pascal as both languages are based on the model of a sequential Von Neumann computer. On the other hand, the same programmer could have great difficulty learning PROLOG (Clocksin and Mellish, 1983) as its underlying model is completely different. In fact, beginners may find learning such a language easier than experienced programmers, as they would not attempt to fit the language into an existing, understood model.

The managerial implications of this are twofold. Firstly, the common practice of hiring programmers on the basis of programming language knowledge is not justified. Programming ability and programming language knowledge are quite different and knowledge of or even virtuosity with a programming language is no measure of programming ability.

Secondly, when organizing programmer education, experienced programmers and inexperienced programmers have quite different requirements. Experienced programmers require to know the syntax of a language whereas inexperienced programmers need to be taught the concepts — how an assignment statement works, the notion of a procedure and so on. It is unlikely that a training course can provide these differing requirements at the same time. Consequently, it is probably cost-effective to provide training courses tailored for inexperienced programmers and to allow experienced programmers to learn a new language by self-teaching.

10.1.3 Programming and personality

Intuitively, it seems likely that programmer performance is influenced by personality factors. An individual's personality is made up of a number of traits and the presence of one or more particular traits may make that person more or less suited to programming work.

There has been little psychological research carried out to identify those personality traits which might influence programming ability. Using a personality test devised for job aptitude, Perry and Cannon (1966) produced a programmer profile by testing existing programmers. If new recruits are tested and their profiles matched with this profile, it may be possible to gauge their suitability for programming.

However, as Weinberg (1971) points out, this is not necessarily the case. Different personalities may be suited to different aspects of programming such as systems design, testing, etc. Should the tests attempt to identify a 'programming personality' or should they be more precise and identify program design personalities, program testing personalities, and so on?

The ideal personality profile was obtained by testing programmers already in the profession but without reference to their ability. There is no guarantee that the sample of the programming profession chosen is representative of the most competent programmers. Finally, an intelligent programmer filling in personality tests might cheat. Instead of presenting their true personality to the tester, they might present the personality which they think the tester wants. This is a natural human reaction to any kind of assessment and no more culpable than an individual trying to present a favourable picture of himself at a job interview.

Because of the lack of concrete evidence, any attempt to assess the influence of distinct personality traits on programmer performance is conjectural. However, it seems likely that some personality traits play a more important role than others.

One example of such a trait is the ability to withstand a certain amount of stress. The nature of software projects is such that the schedule for the project is imposed on the programmer. Work must be completed by a particular date. As that date approaches, the stress imposed on the programmer becomes greater and his or her performance may suffer unless he or she is able to cope with that stress.

Another personality trait which seems likely to be important is adaptive ability. The rate of change of both hardware and software technology is extremely rapid and programmers must be able to adapt to these changes. Without adaptive ability, individuals tend to continue with obsolete practices to the detriment of overall performance.

Although individual personality traits may be important, there is no evidence to suggest that any one type of personality, as a whole, makes an individual suited or unsuited to programming. Personality factors cannot be ignored, however, as they are probably most important at the programming team level, when individuals interact. This is discussed later in this chapter.

10.1.4 Programmer selection techniques

Although a personality profile has been devised for programmers it is not widely used to assess the suitability of individuals for programming. Rather, a programming aptitude test is used by many organizations in their selection of programming staff. This section examines aptitude tests and considers their suitability for assessing programming ability.

There have been a variety of different aptitude tests devised. Most of these have derived from a test developed by IBM and made up of a number of components. These include:

1. arithmetic reasoning — the examinee must do sums;
2. geometric relationships — the examinee must choose the next related figure in a series or identify the relationship between figures;
3. number series — the examinee must derive the next number in a series;
4. letter series — the examinee must derive the next letter in a series.

These tests are normally completed in a relatively short time — typically 20 to 30 minutes. Promoters of the tests suggest that high test scores correlate with programming ability.

It has already been suggested that the cognitive process of developing a program involves building an internal semantic model of the problem and its solution. Given that this conjecture is correct, programming ability is directly related to the ability to construct such a model. Building this model may involve utilizing existing knowledge and, except for trivial problems, is an iterative process. A solution is formulated, evaluated and, on the basis of that evaluation, refined so that the final solution is actually approached in a step-wise fashion.

In order to be successful, programmer aptitude tests ought to measure the ability of an individual to build internal semantic models. Although definitive evidence does not exist on this point, it is intuitively unlikely that they do so. The reasons for this are:

1. The time available for aptitude tests is in no way related to the time available for even the simplest programming task. Aptitude test participants are placed under stress by this time limit and only those able to withstand high levels of stress are likely to succeed in these tests. Although the ability to withstand stress is important for programmers, aptitude tests impose a completely unrealistic stress level.
2. The arithmetic reasoning component of aptitude tests simply measures an individual's facility for fast mental arithmetic. Problem

solving only occasionally involves arithmetic and then only in a minor role. This part of the aptitude test therefore measures an ability which is quite irrelevant.

3. Aptitude tests offer no facilities for refining a solution or presenting reasons explaining how a particular answer was derived. It is often the case that the pattern matching parts of the test are ambiguous with several possible answers to a question. Only one answer is considered 'correct', however, that first thought of by the devisers of the test. This militates against the creative individual who can identify patterns which are not obvious.

In short, the only aptitude which aptitude tests reliably measure is the aptitude of an individual for aptitude tests. Furthermore, the more often an individual attempts aptitude tests, the better his or her scores. An individual who is first assessed by aptitude tests as having little programming ability can become an ideal candidate simply by practicing aptitude tests!

In view of the model of the programming process described above and our lack of knowledge concerning the personality factors affecting programming ability, it is presently impossible to devise a simple test of programming ability which does not actually involve program writing. The psychology of computer programming is not sufficiently understood to allow important factors to be identified and assessed.

10.2 Programmers in groups

The popular image of a programmer is of a lone individual working far into the night peering into a terminal or poring over reams of paper covered with arcane symbols. This image of programming as a profession for lone workers is also held by programmers themselves. In a survey by Cougar and Zawacki (1978), it was discovered that data processing professional staff feel that they have a negligible need to work with other individuals.

Whilst there are many programming staff working on their own, the majority of staff working on large projects work in teams which vary in size from two to several hundred people. In a study undertaken by IBM (McCue, 1978), it was discovered that 50% of a typical programmer's time was spent interacting with other team members, 30% working alone and 20% of his or her time was spent in activities, such as travel and training, which were not directly productive. Clearly, the interaction between team members plays an important role in overall performance so, in this section, aspects of group psychology which are relevant to programming groups are discussed. The topics covered here include the interaction of personalities within a group, the role of the group leader, the notion of egoless programming and how the structure of a system is influenced by the structure of the group building that system. Particular programming group organizations such as chief programmer teams are covered in Chapter 11.

10.2.1 Personalities in groups

The formation of a software engineering group brings together individuals, each with their own distinct personality. These personalities sometimes work extremely well together and sometimes clash so dramatically that little or no productive work is possible. This section attempts to describe why personality clashes sometimes occur and why some groups work together very successfully.

Very roughly, individuals in a work situation can be classified into three types:

1. *Task-oriented.* This type of individual is motivated by the work itself.

2. *Interaction-oriented.* This type of individual is motivated by the presence and actions of co-workers.

3. *Self-oriented.* This type of individual is motivated by a desire for personal success.

Obviously these classes are not rigid and each individual's motivation is made up of elements of each class. Normally, however, one type of motivation is dominant.

In an experiment by Bass and Dunteman (1963), task-oriented persons described themselves as being self-sufficient, resourceful, aloof, introverted, aggressive, competitive and independent. Interaction-oriented individuals considered themselves to be unaggressive, with low needs for autonomy and achievement, considerate and helpful. They preferred to work in a group rather than alone. Self-oriented individuals described themselves as disagreeable, dogmatic, aggressive, competitive, introvert and jealous. They preferred to work alone. In the same experiment, it was found that males tended to be task-oriented whereas females were more likely to be interaction-oriented. Whether this latter observation is a result of natural tendencies or of role stereotyping is not clear.

When individuals worked in groups which were composed entirely of members belonging to the same personality class, only that group made up of interaction-oriented persons was successful. Task-oriented and self-oriented group members felt negatively about their groups — there was, perhaps, an oversupply of leaders. The difficulties encountered when individuals of the same personality class worked together suggest that the most successful groups are made up of individuals from each class with the group leader task-oriented.

With reference to programming groups, Weinberg (1971) suggests that, in practice, two group members often emerge to take different and complementary roles. These are the roles of task specialist and interaction specialist. The task specialist sets, allocates and co-ordinates the work of the group, whereas the interaction specialist sorts out conflicts among group members and between group goals and individual goals.

Observation suggests that the majority of those involved in computer programming work are task-oriented individuals, motivated primarily by their work. This implies that programming groups are likely to be made up of individuals each of whom will have his or her own idea on how the same project should be undertaken. This is borne out by frequently reported problems of interface standards not being adhered to, systems being re-designed as they are coded, unnecessary system embellishments, etc.

The implication of this for software management is that careful atten-tion must be paid to group composition. Selecting individuals who comple-ment each other in terms of personality may produce a better working group than a group selected simply on the basis of programming ability. If a selection on the basis of complementary personalities is impossible, a like-ly situation bearing in mind most programmers are task-oriented, the tendency of each group member to go his or her own way implies that strict managerial control may be necessary to ensure that individual goals do not transcend the overall goal of the group.

This control may be more readily achieved if all the members of a project group are given the opportunity to take an active part in each stage of the project. Individual initiative is most likely when one group member is instructed to carry out a task without being aware of the part that task plays in the project as a whole. Say a program design is presented to an individual for coding. That individual may see how that design can be improved but, without understanding how that design was arrived at, these improvements could have serious implications. If the programmer is involved in the design right from the start, the individual is more likely to identify with that design and to strive to maintain rather than to modify it.

Clearly, the involvement of all group members at each stage of the project is impossible if the group is large. This implies that, for psycho-logical reasons alone, large groups are less likely to be successful than small groups. This is borne out by a number of experiences of project failure and cost overrun where large programming groups were used and the failure was attributed to the lack of effective group communications. When a large system requires a large amount of effort, the organization which is most psychologically sound is to partition that system into independent sub-systems which are each designed and developed by separate small program-ming groups.

10.2.2 The role of the group leader

The group leader plays a vital role in group functioning and his or her performance may govern the success or otherwise of a software project. While most programming groups have a titular leader appointed by higher management, that individual may not be the real leader of the group as far as the technical work of the project is concerned. Some other more techni-cally capable individual may adopt this role with the official leader being responsible for administrative tasks. This is not necessarily a bad organiza-tion. Technical competence and administrative competence are not necessarily synonymous and the roles of technical leader and administrative leader may be complementary.

The actual leader in a programming group is that group member who has most influence on other group members. The leadership may change at different stages of a project. Because of expertise or experience at a particular stage, the best qualified group member may command respect and take over leadership for that stage of the project.

For this reason, and because of the similar motivations of each member of the programming group, the traditional role of a leader responsible for directing, disciplining and rewarding in an autocratic fashion is not one which is likely to be successful with programming groups. In fact, a classic experiment by Lewin *et al.* (1939) suggests that the traditional leader's role as an autocrat is only suited to situations, such as arise in military engagements, where very rapid decision making is essential.

Their study showed that when a democratic style of leadership is adopted, group productivity is higher, individual members work better without supervision and are more satisfied with their work. This confirms the intuitive notion that participation of group members at all stages of a project is likely to result in members adopting group goals and co-operating rather than competing.

The leader of a programming group will, in most cases, emerge as the individual who is most technically competent at each stage of the project. If this is not recognized by higher management and an unwanted leader is imposed on the group, this is likely to introduce tensions into the group. The members will certainly not respect the leader and may reject group loyalty in favour of individual goals. This is a particular problem in a fast-changing field such as software engineering where new members may be more up-to-date and better educated than experienced group leaders.

The implication of this for management is that competent individuals should not be promoted out of programming. It is necessary to provide an alternative career structure for technically able individuals so that they may be properly rewarded yet remain involved in programming. Such a structure has been created by IBM and other organizations in chief programmer teams, described in Chapter 11.

10.2.3 Group loyalties

Being a member of a well led group tends to induce individual loyalty to that group. Each group member identifies with group goals and with other group members. He or she attempts to protect the group, as an entity, from outside interference. Group loyalty implies that there is a coherence in decision making and universal acceptance of decisions once they have been made.

In general, this is a good thing. Group loyalty means that individuals think of the group as more important than the individual members. If a strong group feeling exists, membership changes can be accommodated. The group can adapt to changed circumstances, such as a drastic change in software requirements, by providing mutual support and help.

There are, nevertheless, two important disadvantages of group loyalty which are particularly obvious when the group is cohesive and tightly knit. The disadvantages are the resistance of group members to a change in leadership if there is a need to introduce a new group leader and a loss of overall critical faculties because group loyalty overrides all other considerations.

If the leader of a tightly knit group has to be replaced and the new leader is not already a group member, the group members tend to band together against the new leader irrespective of whether he or she is competent or not. The new leader will not have the same feelings of group loyalty as the rest of the group and may attempt to change the overall goals of the group. These changes are likely to be met with resistance from existing group members with a consequent decrease in overall productivity. The only practical way of avoiding this situation is, whenever possible, to appoint a new leader from within the group itself.

Another consequence of group loyalty has been termed 'groupthink' by Janis (1972). Groupthink is the state where the critical faculties of the group members are eroded by group loyalties. Consideration of alternatives is replaced by loyalty to group norms and decisions. The consequence of this is that any proposal favoured by the majority of the group tends to be adopted without proper consideration of alternative proposals. Janis suggests that groupthink is most prevalent under conditions of stress. For a programming group, this may be as deadlines and delivery dates approach when it is particularly important to make reasoned decisions.

Software management should make active efforts to avoid groupthink. This may involve formal sessions where group members are encouraged to criticize decisions and the introduction of outside experts who can offer comments on the group's decisions. Personnel policies can also be used to avoid groupthink. Some individuals are naturally argumentative, questioning, and disrespectful of the status quo. Such people are positive assets in spite of the fact that they may appear to be troublesome. They act as a devil's advocate, constantly questioning group decisions, thus forcing other group members to think about and evaluate their activities.

10.2.4 Group communications

The time a group member spends on communications is non-productive time. When an individual is communicating, he or she is not programming. In terms of time alone, therefore, it is desirable to minimize intra-group communications.

A further incentive for minimizing communications is that the greater the number of separate communications a group member is involved in, the more difficult these communications are to manage. Consequently, when large numbers of interpersonal communications become the norm, errors are more likely to occur.

Effective communication amongst the members of a programming group is essential if that group is to work efficiently. There appear to be a number of factors which affect the effectiveness of intra-group communications. These are:

1. the size of the group,
2. the structure of the group,
3. the status and personalities of group members,
4. the physical work environment of the group.

This latter factor will be covered later in this chapter. This section concentrates on the first three factors governing communication effectiveness.

As the size of a programming group increases linearly, the number of potential communication links between individual members increases as the square of the group size. For example, if there are two members, A and B, there are two links, AB and BA. If there are three members A, B and C, there are six links and, in general, for n-member groups the number of links is proportional to the square of n. Therefore, even in relatively small groups there are a large number of potential communication channels.

There are two ways of minimizing the number of necessary intra-group communications:

1. The group can be structured in such a way that all communications pass through some central coordinator.
2. The group size can be kept to a minimum and all communication channels used.

Research by Leavitt (1951) and Shaw (1964, 1971) suggests that the second alternative is the more effective. In their experiments, the group members preferred to work in loosely — rather than rigidly — structured groups and they also implied that the problem-solving performance of loosely structured groups is superior to that of groups which have a centralized structure. On the other hand, groups where the communication passed through a centralized co-ordinator seem to be superior for relatively simple tasks such as the collection and dissemination of information.

Further evidence of the superiority of small, loosely structured groups has been provided by Porter and Lawler (1965). They found that the size of an organization correlates negatively with job satisfaction and productivity. It correlates positively with absenteeism and staff turnover. Although their work related to fairly large organizations, their results probably apply to programming groups.

As well as size and structure, the effectiveness of group communications is also influenced by the status, personalities and sexes of group members. Communications between group members of higher and lower status tend to be dominated by higher to lower communications. The lower status member is inhibited in opening communications because of his or her status. The effect of status on communications can be minimized by active efforts of the higher-status individual to encourage uninhibited communication by lower-status members.

The effectiveness of group communication and hence group efficiency can be influenced by personality clashes between group members. These personality clashes may be due to all members being task-oriented (too many leaders) as discussed previously, or may be the result of personal likes, dislikes and prejudices. Such clashes are difficult for management to resolve — people cannot be coerced into liking each other. If group effectiveness is hampered by personality clashes, the best solution is to reorganize the programming group, transferring some members elsewhere.

The sexual composition of groups also affects intra-group communication. The importance of interaction-oriented individuals has already been discussed and, as women tend to be more interaction-oriented than men, it seems likely that mixed-sex groups will communicate more effectively than single-sex groups. Furthermore, a study by Marshall and Heslin (1976) has shown that both men and women prefer to work in mixed-sex groups.

10.2.5 Group structure and system structure

It is an observable fact that the structure of a programming system tends to reflect the structure of the group producing that system. For example, if a three-person group is working on a compiler, the result is likely to be a three-pass system, with each pass written by one member of the group. On the other hand, if the group structure is hierarchical, with a dominant leader and subordinates, the resulting system is likely to be hierarchical with the leader coding the main program which calls components coded by his or her subordinates.

This tendency for systems to reflect the structure of their programming groups should be recognized by software management and taken into account when the system structure is designed. Ideally, the system is designed using the most appropriate structure and a project group assembled whose structure matches the project structure.

In practice, this is rarely possible. The software manager must use existing staff who are available when the project is to start and only occasionally has the luxury of putting together a new team specifically for each project. Furthermore, the ideal system structure may not be suitable for any type of team structure. If this is the case, the team tends to modify the ideal structure into a suitable form for team implementation, thus negating some of the efforts of the system designer.

This phenomenon appears to be inevitable and attempts to coerce a group into adopting an unnatural working technique are unlikely to succeed. To minimize these clashes between system structure and group structure, the entire programming group should be involved at the system design stage. An appropriate system structure can then be agreed by group members. This structure can take the group structure into account and also the strengths and weaknesses of individual group members. Naturally this is only possible if small programming groups are used.

10.2.6 Egoless programming

The notion of egoless programming was introducing by Weinberg (1971) in his book *The Psychology of Computer Programming*. Egoless programming is a style of project group working which considers programs to be the common property and responsibility of the entire programming group irrespective of which individual group member was responsible for their production.

Weinberg suggests that this is a good way of working because it makes program production a group rather than an individual effort. His argument is based on the notion that an individual identifies a program as 'his' or 'hers' so is loath to accept that the program may contain errors. This idea is based on the theory of cognitive dissonance, put forward by Festinger (1957).

This theory argues that individuals who hold a set of beliefs or have made a particular decision avoid anything which contradicts those beliefs or that decision. For example, supporters of a political party will normally only attend political speeches made by a member of the same party, in spite of the fact that the material presented in the speech is probably familiar.

On the same basis, the programmer who considers himself personally responsible for a program tends to defend that program against criticism, even if it has obvious shortcomings. The programmer's ego is tied up with the program itself. If, however, the programmer does not consider his or her work to be a personal possession but instead common group property, he or she is more likely to offer that program for inspection by other group members, to accept their criticisms of it, and to work with them to improve it.

The most important distinguishing feature of egoless programming is that it considers programming errors to be normal and expected. No individual blame is ever associated with these errors. It is not a method of programmer assessment or program quality control. Rather, it is a collective programming effort where the individual who actually coded the program has the same responsibility as all others in the group and is usually undertaken on an informal basis.

The technique of code inspection described in Chapter 7 is a formalization of the idea of egoless programming. However, it differs from egoless programming in that some of the code inspectors are taken from outside the programming group itself. Although individual criticism is avoided in the inspection process, program inspection as such does not encourage the group development of software.

As well as improving the quality of programs submitted for inspection, the practice of egoless programming also improves intra-group communications. It effectively draws the members of a programming group together and encourages uninhibited communications without regard to status, experience or sex. Individual members cannot go off and 'do their own thing' but must actively co-operate with other group members throughout the course of the project.

10.3 Programmer performance and physical environment

The physical work environment has unquantifiable but extremely important effects on the performance of those working in that environment. Psychological experiments have shown that individual behaviour is affected by room size, furniture, temperature, humidity, brightness and quality of light, noise and the degree of privacy available. Group behaviour is affected by factors such as architectural organization and telecommunication facilities.

There has been relatively little attention paid to tailoring the design of buildings specifically for programming. Most programming work takes place in environments designed for other functions, principally business offices. An exception to this is an IBM programming laboratory described by McCue (1978).

The design of this laboratory was carried out in conjunction with the programmers who would use the facilities. The most important environmental factors identified in that design study were:

1. Privacy — each programmer requires an area where he or she can concentrate and work without interruption.

2. Outside awareness — people prefer to work in natural light and with a view of the outside environment.

3. Personalization — individuals adopt different working practices and have different opinions on decor. The ability to rearrange the workplace to suit working practices and to personalize that environment is important.

Obviously, it is not always possible to custom design buildings specifically for programming. Nevertheless, software management should recognize the importance of the working environment to the individual and provide a pleasant and congenial workplace.

One important implication of McCue's study is that the common practice of grouping programmers together in open-plan offices is not likely to be the most productive organization. Not only are individuals denied privacy and a quiet working environment, they are also limited in the degree to which they can personalize their own workspace.

It is also important to provide each programmer with individual access to a computer terminal. In the present situation, where software costs far exceed hardware costs, it is not cost-effective to delay or hinder software production by limiting terminal availability. Furthermore, when each team member is equipped with a terminal, effective electronic mail systems become possible which can lead to significant improvements in productivity.

Although individual privacy and terminal facilities make for better productivity, they have the disadvantage that it is more difficult for informal communications between members of the same or different programming groups to take place. Weinberg suggests that this type of communication is extremely important as it allows problems to be solved and information to be disseminated in an informal but effective way. He cites an anecdotal example of how the removal of a coffee machine to stop programmers 'wasting time' chatting to each other resulted in a dramatic increase in the demand for formal programming assistance.

This implies that management should recognize the value of this informal communication and make implicit provision for it by providing coffee rooms and other informal meeting places as well as formal conference rooms and individual offices.

As well as individual effectiveness, group effectiveness and communications are also affected by the physical environment. Programming groups require areas where all members of the group can get together as a group and discuss their project, both formally and informally. Individual privacy requirements and group communication requirements seem to be exclusive objectives but the resolution of this problem, described by McCue, is to group individual offices round larger central rooms which can be used for group meetings and discussions.

Intra-group communication is inherently complex and it is very important that provision for face-to-face group meetings be available. These meeting rooms must be able to accommodate the whole group in privacy — it is unreasonable to expect group meetings to take place in the corner of some open-plan office.

As well as provision for face-to-face meetings, adequate telephone communications are necessary and an electronic mail system should be made available. Indeed, if powerful telecommunication facilities such as teleconferencing and electronic mail are available, they may substitute for a good deal of face-to-face communication. An example of a successful project carried out, almost entirely, using telecommunications was the design of the programming language Euclid (Lampson *et al.*, 1977). In future, as telecommunication facilities improve, it is likely that much more use will be made of electronic mail and teleconferencing, and major projects will be completed by disparate groups who only meet face-to-face one or two times per year.

Further reading

The Psychology of Computer Programming, G. M . Weinberg (1971), New York: Van Nostrand.

> This is a very readable book which uses mainly anecdotal evidence to suggest how programming groups and individual programmers should be managed. It ought to be compulsory reading for every software manager.

Software Psychology, B. Shneiderman (1980), Cambridge, Mass: Winthrop Publishers.

This is a more academic approach to software psychology which describes various experiments undertaken in this research area. The topics covered are wide ranging from the modelling of conception to how indentation affects program understanding.

'Computer programming and the human thought process', W. J. Tracz (1979), *Software — Practice and Experience*, **9 (2)**.

Using a model of thought processes, the author discusses topics such as software tools, top-down design and structured programming. His brain/computer analogy is interesting.

Chapter 11 PRACTICAL SOFTWARE MANAGEMENT

The failure of several large software projects, such as operating system development projects, brought the peculiar problems involved in software management to light. These projects did not fail because the project managers or programmers working on the project were incompetent. Indeed, the nature of these large projects was such that they attracted people of above average ability. The fault lay in the management techniques used. As these were the first really large programming projects, management techniques derived from small-scale development projects were used and these proved to be inadequate. The delivered software was late, unreliable, cost several times the original estimates and often exhibited poor performance characteristics (Brooks, 1975).

As discussed in the introduction, the experience gained from these project failures was directly responsible for the emergence of software engineering as a discipline. Improved methodologies for specification, design, implementation and validation of software have been developed and some progress has been made in understanding the difficulties of software management. However, much less progress has been made in this area than in design and implementation methodologies. It is still not possible to produce a set of general guidelines describing how to manage software production.

The software manager is responsible for planning project development and overseeing the work, ensuring that it is carried out to the required standards, on time and within budget. Whilst good management cannot guarantee project success, bad management or inadequate management techniques will almost certainly result in software which is delivered late, exceeds cost estimates and which may be expensive to maintain.

Traditional management structure is hierarchical with individuals at each level in the hierarchy reporting to the level above. Typically, a manager might be responsible for 12–25 subordinates. This hierarchical structure is retained to some extent in software management except that each software manager should only handle about six direct subordinates because of the complexity of the software projects under his control.

In a large organization undertaking a number of simultaneous software development projects, the software management structure might be as shown in Fig. 11.1.

The software department manager is responsible for the running of that part of the organization devoted to software production. He has little direct

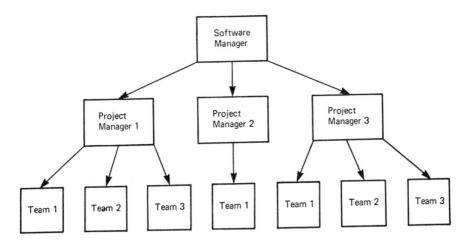

Figure 11.1   Software management structure.

contact with the process of software development except, perhaps, when problems arise. The project manager is involved with a particular project and is responsible for one to six programming teams each working on a particular part of the project. These teams may themselves be organized in the classical hierarchical fashion with a team leader making decisions which are carried out by his subordinates. However, later in this chapter, alternative team organizations will be described which have proved to be more successful than teams organized in a classical fashion.

The material covered in this chapter is relevant to both the project manager and programming team leader who must plan, estimate and control a particular project. The chapter includes sections on programmer productivity, project planning, software quality assurance, and software tools. In addition, a major part of the chapter is devoted to software cost estimation using an algorithmic costing model.

11.1 Programmer productivity

The productivity of a programmer is a measure of the amount of programming or associated work which can be completed in a given time. In this section, factors which affect programmer productivity are described and the problems of establishing a unit of productivity discussed.

The measurement of programmer productivity is important for two reasons. Firstly, without some estimate of productivity, project scheduling is impossible — productivity measurement provides data which allows estimates to be made. Secondly, some of the advantages accrued from the use of new programming methodologies and management techniques can only be demonstrated by showing that their use results in improved productivity over the whole of the software life cycle.

A number of different units have been devised to measure programmer productivity. These include:

1. lines of code written per programmer-month,
2. object instructions produced per programmer-month,
3. pages of documentation written per programmer-month,
4. test cases written and executed per programmer-month.

The most commonly used measure is lines of source code per programmer-month. This is computed by taking the total number of lines of source code delivered and dividing that number by the total time in programmer-months required to complete the project. This time includes analysis and design time, coding time, testing time and documentation time.

As Jones (1978) points out, this measure of productivity is subject to a number of problems. The most fundamental of these problems is determining exactly what is meant by a line of code. Programs are made up of declarations, executable statements and commentary, and may also include macro instructions which expand to several lines of code. Different counting techniques adopt different definitions of a line of code. Some consider executable statements only, some executable statements and data declarations, and some each distinct non-blank line in the program, irrespective of what is on that line. Because of these different conventions, published measures of programmer productivity cannot readily be compared.

Another problem which arises when languages such as Pascal are used is how source lines containing more than a single statement should be treated. If such lines are treated as a single line, this implies that higher productivity can apparently be achieved by the judicious use of newlines!

There is no evidence that any one line-counting technique is superior and, as long as the same technique is used consistently, comparisons can be drawn. However, a more serious problem which results from using lines of code/month as a measure of productivity is the apparent productivity advantages which it indicates when assembly code is used. The problem also occurs, to a lesser extent, when programs in different high-level languages are compared.

This paradox results from the fact that all tasks associated with the programming process (design, documentation, testing, etc.) are subsumed under the coding task in spite of the fact that the coding time normally represents much less than half the time needed to complete a project. The measure places undue emphasis on coding and considers other stages of the life cycle less important.

For example, consider a system which might be coded in 5000 lines of assembly code or 1500 lines of high-level language code. Analysis, design and documentation time are language independent and might take a total of 10 weeks. Coding time for machine code might be 8 weeks with an associated testing time of 10 weeks. For the high-level language, coding time might be 4 weeks and testing time 6 weeks. In total therefore, 7 months (28 weeks) are required to produce 5000 lines of assembler and 5 months (20 weeks) to complete 1500 lines of high-level language code. The assembler programmer has a productivity of 714 lines/month and the high-level language programmer less than half of this — 300 lines/month. Because of this paradox, it is necessary to establish productivity standards for each programming language used and to avoid productivity comparisons between projects coded in different languages.

To avoid some of the problems associated with using lines of code per month as a productivity measure, an alternative method uses the number of object instructions generated per programmer-month. Although this unit is more objective than lines of code — there is no difficulty in defining what is meant by an object instruction — there are also disadvantages in using this measure of productivity.

Firstly, it is difficult to estimate the source code/object code expansion ratio with most compilers. This means that object code/month is not useful for productivity estimation before code is actually produced. Secondly, the amount of object code generated by a compiler is very dependent on high-level language programming style. A programmer who takes more care over coding and produces tight code is apparently less productive than a programmer who codes in such a way that large object programs are generated.

Other measurements which have been used, such as pages of documentation/programmer-month, also suffer from disadvantages. If productivity is measured simply by volume of documentation produced, this militates against the documenter who takes time to express himself clearly and concisely.

The problem with all productivity units expressed in volume/time is that they take no account of the quality of the finished system. They imply that more always means better and take no account of the fact that apparently higher raw code productivity may ultimately involve increased system maintenance costs. It is very difficult to measure productivity over the whole of the system life cycle, so productivity over the software development stage is measured. If poor-quality software is produced quickly, the programmers may appear to be more productive than those programmers who produce reliable and easy-to-maintain systems. There is a need for a productivity measure which considers software quality as well as the size of the finished system.

11.1.1 Factors affecting programmer productivity

Although the present units for measuring programmer productivity are imperfect, let us assume that productivity can be roughly measured and examine what factors influence productivity.

A study by Sackman et al. (1968) showed that individual productivity differences can be very large — the best programmers may be 10 times more productive than the worst. This aptitude factor is likely to be dominant in individual productivity comparisons. Accordingly, the factors discussed below are only relevant to programming teams which are made up of programmers who have a range of abilities.

Walston and Felix (1977) carried out a productivity survey to identify productivity improvements which resulted from using methodologies such as top-down development, structured programming, etc. They collected data from over 60 projects ranging from small commercial DP programs to large complex process control systems. They selected 68 variables for analysis and identified 29 of these as correlating significantly with productivity. These variables included characteristics of the system being developed, the experience of the developers, hardware constraints, the use of new system development technology, program design constraints and the quantity of documentation required.

The most important single factor affecting productivity was the complexity of the customer interface. Projects with a low complexity interface showed a productivity of 500 lines/programmer-month whereas high complexity interfaces were produced at 124 lines/programmer-month.

The other most significant factors were found to be the extent of user participation in requirements definition and the overall experience of the programming team. Where the user did not participate in requirements definition, productivity was measured at 491 lines/programmer-month, but where there was significant user participation this dropped to 205 lines/month. Teams with a good deal of experience produced at a rate of 410 lines/programmer-month, whereas inexperienced teams produced at 132 lines/month.

The effects on productivity of customer interface complexity and team experience are what might be intuitively expected although the study by Walston and Felix is useful for quantifying the effects. It might also be expected that if the user had little to do with requirements definition, productivity would be higher although, in such cases, there must be some dubiety that the finished product is exactly what is required by the user.

Design and programming methodologies such as structured programming, design and code reviews and top-down development had a positive influence on productivity although this was not as great as the factors previously discussed. However, productivity improvements resulting from the use of these techniques must be seen as a bonus as their principal function is to improve the reliability and maintainability of software.

Another factor which obviously affects productivity is the amount of time that a software engineer actually spends working on software development. Ignoring holidays and leave, each member of a software development team spends time training, attending meetings and dealing with administrative tasks. If a project involves new techniques, training will be required; if the project involves more than one geographical location, travel time between locations is involved; and the larger the programming group, the more time must be spent communicating.

Because of the difficulties in establishing a unit of productivity measurement and because of the variety of factors which influence productivity, it is very difficult to give a figure which can be taken as the average productivity of a programmer. For large, complex real-time systems, productivity may be as low as 30 lines/programmer-month, whereas for straightforward business application systems which are well understood, it may be as high as 600 lines/month. Effective estimation, within an organization, can only be carried out using historical data derived from previous projects using the same programming language and carried out to the same quality standards. Without such data, productivity estimation is simply guesswork.

11.2 Programming team organizations

It is now generally accepted that software projects should not be tackled by large homogeneous teams of software engineers. Large teams mean that the time spent in communication amongst team members is greater than the time spent programming. Furthermore, it is usually impossible to partition a software system into a large number of independent units. This has the result that, if a large programming team is used, each member is responsible for a program unit whose interface with the rest of the system is complex. Consequently, the probability of interface error is high and software testing is difficult and time consuming.

Programming team sizes should be relatively small — between two and eight members. When small teams are used, communication problems are minimized — the whole team can get round a table for a meeting. However, if the magnitude of a project is such that it cannot be tackled by a single team in the time allowed, multiple teams must be used. They should work independently, with each team tackling a large part of the project in an autonomous way. The overall system design should be such that the interface between the parts of the project produced by the independent teams is well defined and as simple as possible.

As well as minimizing communication problems, small programming teams have a number of other benefits. These include:

1. A team quality standard can be developed. Because this is arrived at by consensus, it is more likely to be observed than arbitrary standards imposed on the team by software management.

2. Team members work closely together and can learn from each other. Inhibitions caused by ignorance are minimized as mutual learning is encouraged.

3. Egoless programming can be practised. Programs are regarded as team property rather than personal property.

4. Team members can get to know each other's work so that continuity can be maintained should a team member leave.

It is usual for small programming teams to be organized in an informal way. Although a titular team leader exists, he or she carries out the same tasks as other team members. Indeed, as discussed in the previous chapter, a technical team leader may emerge who effectively controls software production without having the title of team leader

In an informal team, the work to be carried out is discussed by the team as a whole and the tasks allocated to each member according to ability and experience. High-level system design is carried out by senior team members, but low-level design is the responsibility of the member allocated a particular task.

Informal teams can be very successful, particularly where the majority of team members are experienced and competent. The team functions as a democratic team, making decisions by consensus. Psychologically, this improves team spirit with a resultant increase in cohesiveness and performance. On the other hand, if a team is composed mostly of inexperienced or incompetent members, the informality can be a hindrance. No definite authority exists to direct the work, causing a lack of co-ordination between team members and, possibly, eventual project failure.

A very serious problem which can arise in some organizations is the lack of experienced team members. Teams tend to be composed of relatively inexperienced members because the career and reward structure of the organization is such that able and experienced team members are promoted to management positions. They are not directly involved in software development. This situation is exacerbated by distinctions made between so-called systems analysts and programmers, where design and programming work are separated. Programmers are reduced to simple coders with the result that talented people strive to get out of programming as soon as possible.

In order to utilize the skills of experienced and competent programmers, these individuals should be given responsibility and rewards commensurate with what they would receive in a management position. A parallel technical career path should be established to achieve this without any implication that it is inferior to a management-oriented career path. The team organization discussed below is one way of achieving this.

11.2.1 Chief programmer teams

An alternative programming team organization to the informal democratic team was suggested by Baker (1972) and also described, in a slightly different form, by Brooks (1975) and Aron (1974). The development of this approach was motivated by a number of considerations:

1. Projects tend to be staffed by relatively inexperienced people, as discussed above.

2. Much programming work is clerical in nature, involving the storage and maintenance of a large amount of information.

3. Multi-way communications are time consuming and hence reduce programmer productivity.

The chief programmer team is based on utilizing experienced and talented staff as chief programmers, providing clerical support for these programmers using both human and computer-based procedures, and funnelling all communications through one or two individuals.

The chief programmer team has been compared to a surgical team undertaking an operation. The ultimate responsibility in such a team rests with the surgeon but he or she is helped by skilled, specialized staff members such as an anaesthetist, chief nurse, etc., who carry out particular roles.

The nucleus of a chief programmer team consists of the following members:

1. A chief programmer who is experienced and highly qualified. He or she takes full responsibility for designing, programming, testing and installing the system under development.

2. A backup programmer who is also skilled and experienced. He or she works with the chief programmer and should be able to adopt the role if necessary. His or her main function is to provide support by developing test cases and analyses to verify the work of the chief programmer.

3. A librarian whose role is to assume all the clerical functions associated with a project. The librarian is assisted by an automated library system.

Depending on the size and type of the application, other experts might be added temporarily or permanently to a team. These might include:

1. A project administrator who relieves the chief programmer of administrative tasks.

2. A toolsmith who is responsible for producing software tools to support the project.

3. A documentation editor who takes the project documentation written by the chief programmer and backup programmer and prepares it for publication.

4. A language/system expert who is familiar with the idiosyncrasies of the programming language and system being used and whose role is to advise the chief programmer on how to make use of these facilities.

5. A tester whose task is to develop objective test cases to validate the work of the chief programmer.

6. One or more support programmers who undertake coding from a design specified by the chief programmer. These support programmers are necessary when the scale of the project is such that detailed programming work cannot be carried out by the chief programmer and backup programmer alone.

The principal objective of using a chief programmer team is to improve productivity, and measurements by Baker (1972) and Walston and Felix

(1977) suggest that a chief programmer team is approximately twice as productive as teams which are not organized in this way. However, it is not clear whether this improvement is a result of the team organization or whether it results simply from using better programmers who would be more productive in any case.

Shneiderman (1980) points out that there may be psychological problems in introducing chief programmer teams. These derive from the position of the chief programmer who is the kingpin of the project and, if the project is successful, takes the credit for this success. Other team members may feel that they have no definite function and be resentful of the status of the chief programmer.

Other political problems in using chief programmer teams are described by Yourdon (1979). In large organizations it may be impossible to fit the chief programmer team into the existing organizational structure and adequately reward the chief programmer. Tne introduction of chief programmer teams may entail the complete reorganization of existing staff and this might be resisted. It may be impossible to attract suitably qualified chief programmers to work in certain application areas.

In spite of these disadvantages, the basic premise underlying chief programmer teams — the need to utilize the talent of experienced programmers — is sound. The practice of programming is too difficult and important to be left entirely in the hands of novices.

11.3 Project planning

Effective management of a software project depends on thoroughly planning the progress of the project, anticipating problems which might arise and preparing tentative solutions to those problems in advance. It will be assumed that the project manager is responsible for planning from requirements definition to the delivery of the completed system. The planning involved in assessing the need for a software system, the feasibility of producing that system, and the assignment of priority to the system production process will not be discussed. For a discussion of these topics, the reader is referred to Fried (1979) and also to Pressman (1982).

The planning discussed here is that required for a large programming system which requires multiple teams to tackle the project so that it may be completed in a given time. However, much of the discussion is relevant to the production of smaller systems tackled by a single programming team, although, for such systems, planning can be less formal.

Metzger (1973) defines a project plan to be made up of 11 distinct sections. These are:

1. *Overview*. This describes the project in general, describes the plan organization and summarizes the remainder of the document.
2. *Phase plan*. This discusses the project development cycle — requirements analysis, high-level design phase, low-level design

phase, etc. Associated with each phase should be a date specifying when that phase should be complete and an indication of how different phases of the project might overlap.

3. *Organization plan.* This defines the specific responsibilities of each group involved in the project.

4. *Test plan.* This outlines the testing required and the tools, procedures and responsibilities for carrying out the system test. It does not include specific test cases.

5. *Change control plan.* This sets out a mechanism for implementing changes which are requested as the system is being developed.

6. *Documentation plan.* This is intended to define and control the documentation associated with a project.

7. *Training plan.* This describes training of the programmers involved in the project and training of the users to make use of the delivered system.

8. *Review and reporting plan.* This discusses how the project status is reported. The formal reviews associated with the progress of the project are defined here.

9. *Installation and operation plan.* This describes the procedure for installing the system at the user's site.

10. *Resources and deliverables plan.* This summarizes the critical plan details — schedules, milestones and all items to be delivered under contract.

11. *Index.* This shows where to find things in the plan.

Some of the sections in this plan have already been covered in other parts of the book. Here, attention will be concentrated on project scheduling, reporting and change control.

11.3.1 Project reporting

It is extremely important that information about the progress of a project is fed back to management at regular intervals. Without this information, control of the project is lost and cost estimates and schedules cannot be updated.

When planning a project, a series of milestones should be established. At each milestone, a formal progress report should be presented to management. As Metzger points out, it is important that these milestones each represent the culmination of a distinct stage in the project. There is little point in planning indefinite milestones where it is impossible to decide unequivocally if a milestone has been reached. A good milestone is characterized by finished documentation, for example, 'High-level design complete' or 'Test plan formulated'. On the other hand, a poor milestone is something like 'Coding 80% complete' — what exactly does this mean and how can it be determined if coding is 80% complete or not?

A useful starting point for identifying milestones is a detailed view of the software life cycle. The macro life cycle view where the life cycle is broken into five stages is too coarse for this purpose and each stage must be broken into sub-stages for reporting.

There is no single definitive detailed view of the software life cycle. The particular organization of each phase must depend on a number of factors such as the application being developed, the programming team organization, the project documentation required by the contractor, etc. One possible micro life cycle view with reporting milestones associated with each sub-stage is shown in Fig. 11.2.

Milestones should not necessarily be established for each and every project activity, otherwise the project team will spend more time on management reporting than on system development. If bar charts are drawn up for scheduling, these can be annotated with the project milestones which should

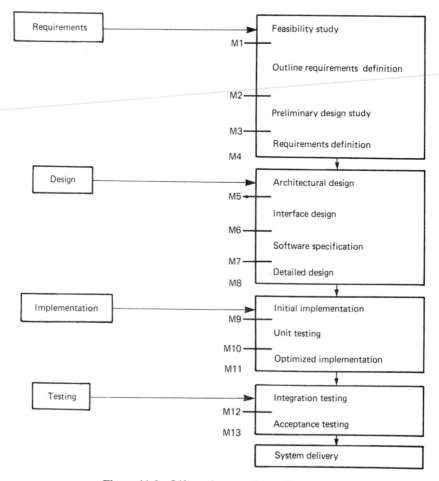

Figure 11.2   Life cycle reporting milestones.

occur, roughly, once every two or three weeks until the system is delivered for integration testing. After this stage, there may have to be a longer gap between milestones as integration and acceptance testing may take several weeks. Milestones part way through these stages are probably not particularly useful.

11.3.2 Bar charts and activity networks

Bar charts and activity networks are graphical notations which can be used in project scheduling. Bar charts illustrate who is responsible for each part of the project and when that part is scheduled to start and finish.

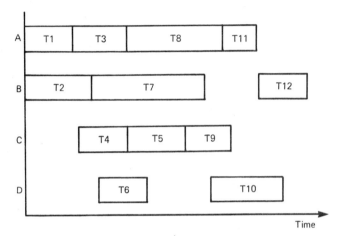

Figure 11.3 Bar chart for project scheduling.

The chart, illustrated in Fig. 11.3, shows a project undertaken by four programmers and made up of 11 distinct tasks. Notice that this chart does not show all team members to be occupied all the time. In the slack periods they may be doing other work, have scheduled leave, attend training courses, etc.

It is not generally useful to subdivide tasks into units which take less than a week or two to execute. Finer subdivisions mean that a disproportionate amount of time must be spent on estimating. It is also useful to set a maximum amount of time for any task on the chart — about 10–12 weeks is reasonable.

One of the problems with bar charts is that they do not show task dependencies. In the above chart, T10 might be dependent on T7 and T5 being complete. Should T7 be delayed, it may be impossible to start T10. A graphical method which can be used to show these interdependencies is the activity network or PERT chart.

An example of an activity network for showing the interdependencies of the tasks in the bar chart shown in Fig. 11.3 is shown in Fig. 11.4.

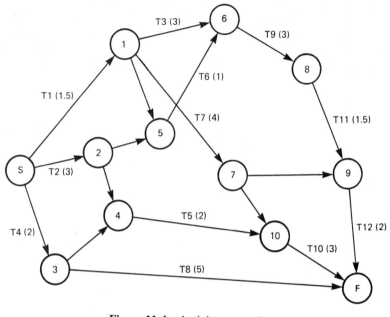

Figure 11.4 Activity network

Each node on the activity graph is called an event and represents the culmination of one or more activities. If an arc is labelled, the label is the name of the activity followed by the estimated time it will take to complete that activity. It is sometimes necessary to create dummy events to cater for the situation where mutually independent tasks are each dependent on the same activity. Arcs from dummy events are unlabelled and take zero time to execute.

Before progress can be made from one event to another, all activity paths leading to that event must be complete. For example, activity T9, shown in Fig. 11.4, cannot be started until both T3 and T6 are complete. The diagram shows the interdependence of activities, illustrating what activities can be carried out in parallel and what must be done in sequence.

The duration of the project can be estimated by considering the longest path in the activity graph. This is called the critical path. In the above diagram, the critical path is S-1-6-8-9-F which takes 11 time units. Delays in any of the activities in the critical path will necessarily result in delays in the final project, whereas a delay in T8, say, assuming it was not excessive, would have no effect on the project completion date.

PERT charts are a more sophisticated form of activity chart where, instead of making a single estimate for each task, pessimistic, likely and optimistic estimates are made. Considering each of these and combinations of them makes critical path analysis very complex and it is best carried out automatically.

As well as using activity graphs for estimating, it is useful for management to construct these charts when allocating project work. They can provide insights into the interdependence of tasks which are not intuitively obvious. In some cases, it may be possible to modify the system design so that the critical path is shortened. The duration of the project may be reduced because the time spent waiting for activities to complete might be reduced.

Inevitably, initial project schedules will be incorrect and, as the project develops, it is important to compare estimates with actual elapsed time. This comparison can be used as a basis for revising the schedule for later parts of the project. When actual figures are known, it is also important to review the activity chart and perhaps repartition the later project tasks in order to reduce the critical path.

11.3.3 Change control

All software development is an iterative process. As software is designed, flaws in the requirements definition are revealed; as it is implemented, flaws in the design are shown up, and so on. Changes are both essential and inevitable. However, the changes can easily get out of hand and it is important for management to plan for changes and establish a procedure for documenting and evaluating the effect of these changes.

Changes fall into two categories — those required to correct minor mistakes and those which either add or remove functions or change the way a function is implemented. The first type of change must be carried out and there is not, generally, any need for managerial approval of the change. However, if a mistake is discovered at a later stage in the project from that in which the mistake was made (say a design error during implementation), it is important that the change be formally documented using a standard change control procedure. If this is carried out, it is possible to check that all documents affected by the change have actually been modified to record the change.

The second type of change should always be subject to managerial approval. Some formal change evaluation procedure should exist and all changes of this type must be subjected to this procedure in order to assess the cost of the change and its ramifications on the rest of the software system. If the cost of the change is relatively low and the change does not affect the rest of the system it should normally be approved.

If, on the other hand, the cost of the change is high or its impact significant, a decision must be made whether to accept the change or not and, if accepted, who is to be responsible for paying for the change. Clearly, if the change is requested by the software customer, they must take the responsibility for paying for that change. Otherwise, some kind of cost-benefit analysis must be carried out to determine if the overall benefits resulting from the change are worthwhile. Again, the change should be formally documented and promulgated to all other relevant documents such as the requirements definition, high-level design, etc.

The activity of change control is part of the general process of software configuration management. Configuration management involves ensuring that change control practices are established, that software releases and versions can be built and rebuilt, that documents associated with software are updated, etc. Without automation, configuration management is a very difficult and error-prone process. Thus, one of the most important tools for software management is a configuration control system.

11.4 Software scheduling and cost estimation

Software scheduling and cost estimation are closely related. The majority of costs in a major software project are simply the costs of paying people to write software. The project cost is directly proportional to the number of person-months required to complete the work. There are, of course, other costs such as hardware costs, travel costs, training costs, etc., but these are less difficult to compute. They are not based on imponderables such as programmer productivity and source program size estimation.

The most commonly used technique for estimating software costs is to estimate the size of the programming system to be delivered and hence compute the number of programmer-months required to construct the system using either historic productivity data or intuition. The overall system cost is based on the figure plus overheads. If the software is being developed for an external agency, a profit figure is added to this cost estimate.

The system size is estimated by carrying out a preliminary design study to establish the units making up the system. An estimate is made of the size of each unit. This estimate is normally based on experience and intuition. These estimates are then summed to give the estimated size of the total system. This method is based on the assumption that programmer productivity for a given part of the system can be predicted in advance. It also assumes that the preliminary design is not oversimplified and accurately reflects the system which is to be produced.

We have already seen that programmer productivity is affected by a multiplicity of factors and cannot be accurately estimated by considering the size of each unit to be developed. Other factors, such as the programmer's experience, the newness and complexity of the application and the implementation constraints must also be taken into account. Ideally, these factors should be considered for each distinct unit rather than the system as a whole. As a large system may have several hundred units, cost estimation is a time consuming and costly business.

Rather than estimate costs using historical productivity data expressed in production of code/programmer-month, Jones (1978) suggests that cost units based on cost per thousand lines of code are more useful and versatile in cost estimation. Cost units are computed by taking the overall cost of a project and dividing this by the size of the delivered program.

An advantage of using cost units is that all costs associated with a project may be expressed in the same way. This contrasts with estimates based on productivity measures which must compute the production cost as described above then add overheads such as computer costs, support staff costs, documentation costs and travel costs. When cost units are used, all these extra costs can be subsumed under the same heading.

For cost estimation, Jones introduces the notion of a probability rectangle. This technique still relies on an estimate of program size but, rather than a specific estimate, best case and worst case estimates are made. Historical data can be used to derive the previous unit costs of programs similar to that being estimated. Typically, these will also lie in a range. To display the minimum and maximum software costs, these can then be plotted as a productivity rectangle as shown in Fig. 11.5. Assume that the minimum program size estimate is 8000 lines and the maximum 11 000 lines. If the minimum cost unit is $20 000/thousand lines and the maximum is $26 000 per thousand lines, the probability rectangle shown in Fig. 11.5 results.

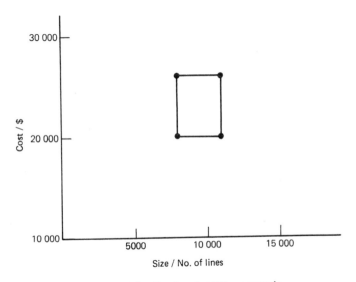

Figure 11.5 Cost/probability rectangle.

The minimum development cost of the program is 8000 lines at $20 000 per thousand, that is, $160 000, whereas the maximum cost is 11 000 lines at $26 000 per thousand, a total of $286 000. As the project develops and more accurate size estimates are produced, new cost estimates can be produced from the probability rectangle.

So far, cost estimating for complete projects has been discussed but it is also important to estimate costs in more detail and establish estimates for each phase of the project. Figures quoted by Boehm (1975) and Wolverton (1975) suggest that major costs of software development are incurred in requirements analysis, software design and software testing. The figures vary for the type of system under development. For example, about 50% of the costs were incurred in system testing and 35% in system design in the development of command/control systems, whereas for business systems 44% of the costs were expended in analysis and design and only 28% were spent on testing.

In order to estimate the costs of each phase these figures can be used to calculate the proportion of costs incurred at each stage of system development. If costs are monitored as the project progresses, overall estimates can be improved by comparing actual costs and estimated costs of the early stages of the project. The overall estimate is updated according to the goodness-of-fit of the estimated and actual costs.

A survey of various techniques of software cost estimation is given by Boehm (1981). He identifies seven different techniques. These are based on algorithmic modelling, expert judgement, estimation by analogy, Parkinson's Law (a project will cost what you have to spend on it), pricing to win (a project will cost what the customer has to spend on it), top-down estimation and bottom-up estimation. Each technique has advantages and disadvantages, but the important point made by Boehm is that no single technique is adequate in isolation.

He suggests that for large projects several cost estimation techniques should be used in parallel. If these predict radically different costs this implies that not enough costing information is available. However, it is important to avoid investing unnecessary effort in detailed software costing if only order-of-magnitude cost figures are required. The costing model described below may be very useful in this respect as a relatively fast way of computing approximate costs.

11.4.1 Project scheduling

Project scheduling is one of the most difficult tasks of software management. For many projects, previous experience is of limited relevance unless the project being scheduled is similar to a previous project. Typically, projects break new ground with the consequence that previous estimates cannot be directly modified. Different projects use different programming languages and methodologies which further complicates the task of estimating the project schedule. Because of these uncertainties, scheduling is an iterative process. An initial schedule must be estimated but this should not be considered inviolate. As the project progresses, information is fed back to the scheduler and the initial estimate modified.

The preparation of the initial schedule must be based on the experience and intuition of the manager. If the project is technically advanced, the initial estimate will almost certainly be optimistic in spite of endeavours to consider all eventualities. In this respect, software scheduling is no different from scheduling any other type of large advanced project. New aircraft, bridges and even motor cars are frequently late because of unanticipated problems and it is unrealistic to expect software projects to be different from other complex engineering projects.

Project scheduling involves separating the total work involved in a project into distinct tasks and assessing when these tasks will be completed. When a number of individuals or teams are working on a project, some of these tasks are carried out in parallel. The project scheduler must co-ordinate these parallel tasks and organize the work so that his workforce is used optimally. The scheduler must strive to avoid a situation arising where the whole project is delayed because a critical task is unfinished.

In estimating schedules, it should not be assumed that every stage of the project will be problem free. Individuals working on a project may fall ill or leave, hardware may break down and essential support software or hardware may be late in delivery. If the project is new and technically advanced, certain parts of it may turn out to be more difficult and hence take longer than originally anticipated. A rule of thumb in estimating is to estimate as if nothing will go wrong, increase that estimate to cover anticipated problems and then add a 'fudge factor' to cover unanticipated problems. This extra factor must be determined by the manager's experience and knowledge of his staff.

As a rough guide for the scheduler, requirements analysis and design normally takes twice as long as coding. So too does validation. To estimate the total time required for the project, the system size must be estimated and divided by the expected programmer productivity to give the number of programmer-months required to complete the project. The resulting figure is very approximate because of the difficulties involved in estimating system size and the variations in programmer productivity.

Estimating the actual duration of a project cannot simply be carried out by dividing the number of programmer-months by the number of available programmers. There are two reasons for this. Firstly, as the number of programmers increases, communication problems arise and productivity falls. Indeed, Fried suggests that once the number of programmers working on a project exceeds a certain maximum, productivity is actually negative. This is also suggested by Lehman's Laws, discussed in Chapter 1. Secondly, some tasks are indivisible and, no matter how many programmers work on them, the time required cannot be reduced. Again, experience is required to identify these indivisible tasks and to estimate the duration of a project.

11.4.2 A model for software costing
The most scientific approach to software costing and scheduling and, potentially, the most accurate cost-estimation technique is to use an algorithmic costing model. Such a model can be built by analysis of the costs of completed projects and a mathematical formula established linking costs with project size, number of programmers, etc.

There have been a number of such models built and used in software costing and these are compared by Mohanty (1981) and Boehm (1981). Mohanty exercised a number of these models with the same hypothetical project data. He received cost estimates ranging from $362 000 to $2 766 667 for the same input data.

This vast discrepancy in these figures does not, in itself, discredit algorithmic cost modelling but it does illustrate that the parameters associated with each model are highly organization-dependent. Because of different measurement techniques for quantities such as lines of code, the number of days in a person-month, etc., it is not possible to establish a single costing model which is applicable across a wide range of organizations and projects. Rather, any model must first be configured, using historical data, to match the requirements and methods of the model's users.

The best documented software costing model whose parameters can be tailored to particular modes of working is the COCOMO model described by Boehm (1981). The COCOMO model exists in basic (simple), intermediate and detailed forms but a full description of all of these is outside the scope of this book. Rather, an overview of the basic and intermediate COCOMO models is presented with the intention of introducing algorithmic cost modelling and to illustrate the advantages to management of using this technique.

The basic COCOMO model is intended to give an order of magnitude estimation of software costs. It uses only the estimated size of the software project and the type of software being developed. Versions of the estimation formula exist for three classes of software project:

1. *Organic mode projects.*   These are projects where relatively small teams are working in a familiar environment developing applications with which they are familiar. In short, communications overhead is low, team members know what they are doing and can quickly get on with the job.

2. *Semi-detached mode projects.*   This mode of project represents an intermediate stage between organic mode projects and embedded mode projects described below. In semi-detached mode projects, the project team may be made up of experienced and inexperienced staff. Team members have limited experience of related systems and may be completely unfamiliar with some (but not all) aspects of the system being developed.

3. *Embedded mode projects.*   The principal characteristic of embedded mode projects is that they must operate within tight constraints. The software system is part of a strongly coupled complex of hardware, software, regulations and operational procedures. Therefore, requirements modifications to get round software problems are usually impractical and software validation costs are high. Because of the diverse nature of embedded mode projects, it is unusual for project team members to have a great deal of experience in the particular application which is being developed.

The formulae to compute costs or, more precisely, the effort required for software development are as follows:

Organic mode $PM = 2.4 \, (KDSI)^{1.05}$

Semi-detached mode $PM = 3\,(KDSI)^{1.12}$
Embedded mode $PM = 3.6\,(KDSI)^{1.20}$

The quantities involved in these equations are PM, the number of person-months required to complete the project, and KDSI which is the number of thousands of delivered source instructions. In the version of the COCOMO model described by Boehm a person-month is defined as consisting of 152 hours of working time. This figure takes into account the average monthly time off for holidays, training and sick leave.

More contentiously, the definition of a delivered source instruction normally excludes undelivered support software even although the effort involved in this may be significant. A delivered source instruction is taken to be a line of code where a line of code is any code on a line terminated by a line feed character. Comments are excluded. Therefore, if there are two or more statements on a line this counts as a single delivered source instruction and if a statement is spread over five lines this counts as five DSIs.

The basic COCOMO model assumes that the software requirements will not be significantly changed after software development. There is also an implicit assumption that the project will be well managed by both the customer and the software developer.

As well as providing effort equations, the basic COCOMO model also provides equations to estimate the development schedule of a project. The development schedule is the time required to complete the project given that sufficient personnel resources are available. The development schedule equations for the different modes of the project are:

Organic mode $TDEV = 2.5\,(PM)^{0.38}$

Semi-detached mode $TDEV = 2.5\,(PM)^{0.35}$

Embedded mode $TDEV = 2.5\,(PM)^{0.32}$

To illustrate the basic COCOMO model, assume that an organic mode software project has an estimated size of 32 000 delivered source instructions. From the effort equation, the number of person-months required for this project is:

$PM = 2.4\,(32)^{1.05} = 91$ p.m.

From the schedule equation, the time required to complete the project is:

$TDEV = 2.5\,(91)^{0.38} = 14$ months

The number of personnel required to complete the project in the timescale is:

$N = PM\,/\,TDEV = 91\,/\,14 = 6.5$ people

Consider now a large embedded mode software project consisting of about 128 000 delivered source instructions. The basic COCOMO equations give results as follows:

$$PM = 3.6 \,(128)^{1.20} = 1216 \text{ p.m.}$$

$$TDEV = 2.5 \,(1216)^{0.32} = 24 \text{ months}$$

$$N = 1216 \,/\, 24 = 51 \text{ people}$$

The basic COCOMO model is intended to give an order of magnitude estimate of the effort required to complete a software project. Before going on to look at the intermediate COCOMO model which takes factors apart from system size and type into account, let us look at some of the assumptions which underlie the basic COCOMO model.

First of all, the model has an implicit productivity estimate built into it which was presumably derived from existing project data. In the case of the organic mode system above, the productivity is 352 DSI/p.m., which is about 16 instructions per person day. The effort required for the embedded system implies a productivity of 105 DSI/p.m., which is about 4 instructions per person day.

A more interesting implication of the COCOMO model is that the time required to complete the project is a function of the total effort required for the project and not a function of the number of software engineers working on the project. This confirms the notion that adding more people to a project which is behind schedule is unlikely to help that schedule to be regained.

Unfortunately, the COCOMO model is not particularly helpful in estimating schedules when personnel resources are limited but delivery schedules are flexible. It is not clear whether a project schedule of 14 months for 6.5 people can be simply upped to 30 months if only 3 people are available.

The basic COCOMO model is a useful starting point for project estimation but it is clear that there are many factors apart from project size and type which affect the effort involved in a project. The intermediate COCOMO takes some of these factors into account.

The intermediate COCOMO model for software estimation takes the basic COCOMO effort and schedule computations as its starting point. It then applies a series of multipliers to the basic COCOMO figures which take into account factors such as required product reliability, database size, execution and storage constraints, personnel attributes and the use of software tools. In all, fifteen factors are taken into consideration. These are divided into four classes — product attributes, computer attributes, personnel attributes and project attributes.

Product attributes are:

1. *Required software reliability (RELY).* This is rated on a scale from very low where a software failure would only result in slight inconvenience, through nominal where a failure would result in moderate recoverable losses, to very high where failure involves risk to human life.

2. *Database size (DATA).* This is rated from low where the size of the database (in bytes) is less than 10 times the number of DSIs, through nominal where the database size is between 10 and 100 times the system size, to very high where the database is more than 1000 times larger than the program.

3. *Product complexity (CPLX).* This is rated on a scale from very low to extra-high. Low complexity code uses simple I/O operations, simple data structures and 'straight line' code. Nominal complexity implies some I/O processing, multi-file input/output, the use of library routines and some inter-module communication. Very high and extra-high complexity means possibly re-entrant or recursive code, complex file handling, parallel processing, complex data management, etc.

Computer attributes are those hardware constraints such as speed and space constraints which affect software productivity. There are four attributes which are classed as computer attributes. These are:

1. *Execution time constraints (TIME).* This is rated from nominal to extra-high. A nominal rating means that less than 50% of available execution time is used and an extra-high rating means that 95% of available time must be used.

2. *Storage constraint (STOR).* This is rated in the same way as TIME, with a nominal value meaning that less than half the available store is used and an extra-high rating meaning that 95% of available store is used.

3. *Virtual machine volatility (VIRT).* The virtual machine is the combination of hardware and software on which the software product is built. A low rating for this factor means that it is only changed occasionally (once a year), a nominal rating implies major changes every six months, and a very high rating suggests that the virtual machine will change once every two weeks.

4. *Computer turnround time (TURN).* This is rated from low which implies interactive systems development to very high which means that turnround time is more than 12 hours.

There are five personnel attributes taken into consideration which reflect the experience and capabilities of development staff working on the project. These attributes are analyst capability (ACAP), application experience (AEXP), virtual machine experience (VEXP), programmer capability (PCAP) and programming language experience (LEXP). These are all rated from very low which means little or no experience, through nominal which means at least one year's experience, to very high which means more than three years experience.

The project attributes are concerned with the use of software tools, the project development schedule and the use of modern programming practices. Boehm defines modern programming practices as practices such as top-down design, design and code reviews, structured programming, program support libraries, etc. It was decided to classify these under a single heading rather than attempt to assess the effect of each factor in isolation.

The project attributes are as follows:

1. *Modern programming practices (MODP).* This attribute is rated on a scale from very low which implies no use of such practices, through nominal which implies some use, to very high which means that the use of modern practices is routine and that staff are experienced in their use.

2. *Software tools (TOOL).* The availability of software tools can have a significant effect on the effort required to develop a software system. A very low value assessment of this attribute means that only very basic tools such as an assembler are available. A nominal value means that a more complete set of implementation, testing and debugging tools are available, and a high value suggests that tools to support all life-cycle phases are available.

3. *Required development schedule (SCED).* This attribute is a measure of how well the required development schedule fits the nominal development schedule estimated using the basic COCOMO model. A very low value for this attribute means an accelerated schedule whereas a high value implies an extended schedule. Both low and high attribute values actually increase the effort required for product development.

The multipliers associated with each of these 15 attributes are shown in Table 11.1 reproduced from Boehm (1981). Note that VL means very low, L means low, N means nominal, H means high, VH means very high and EH means extra high. In the estimation of maintenance costs, discussed in Chapter 8, these ratings are the same for all attributes except RELY, MODP and SCED. In maintenance cost estimation, the original development schedule is irrelevant so this attribute always has a nominal value. The use of modern programming practices has a more significant effect on maintenance costs and this effect increases with product size. A low value for the reliability attribute reduces development effort but this is liable to mean increased maintenance effort will be required. Furthermore, a high development reliability means that achieving high reliability in the maintained product is easier than with a product which exhibits lower development reliability.

The modified values for RELY and MODP, also taken from Boehm (1981), are as follows:

	Maintenance effort multipliers				
	VL	L	N	H	VH
RELY	1.35	1.15	1	0.98	1.10

Table 11.1 Project attribute multipliers

Cost driver	Ratings					
	VL	L	N	H	VH	EH
RELY	0.75	0.88	1.00	1.15	1.40	—
DATA	—	0.94	1.00	1.08	1.16	—
CPLX	0.70	0.85	1.00	1.15	1.30	1.65
TIME	—	—	1.00	1.11	1.30	1.66
STOR	—	—	1.00	1.06	1.21	1.56
VIRT	—	0.87	1.00	1.15	1.30	—
TURN	—	0.87	1.00	1.07	1.15	—
ACAP	1.46	1.19	1.00	0.86	0.71	—
AEXP	1.29	1.13	1.00	0.91	0.82	—
PCAP	1.42	1.17	1.00	0.86	0.70	—
VEXP	1.21	1.10	1.00	0.90	—	—
LEXP	1.14	1.07	1.00	0.95	—	—
MODP	1.24	1.10	1.00	0.91	0.82	—
TOOL	1.24	1.10	1.00	0.91	0.83	—
SCED	1.23	1.08	1.00	1.04	1.10	—

Tables 11.1 and 11.2 are reproduced from *Software Engineering Economics*, B.W. Boehm (1981), by permission of Prentice-Hall Inc.

The MODP attribute depends on the size of the delivered product in KDSI:

Table 11.2 MODP attribute values

Product size	MODP rating				
	VL	L	N	H	VH
2	1.25	1.12	1.00	0.90	0.81
8	1.30	1.14	1.00	0.88	0.77
32	1.35	1.16	1.00	0.86	0.74
128	1.40	1.18	1.00	0.85	0.72
512	1.45	1.20	1.00	0.84	0.70

The basic and intermediate COCOMO models may be criticized because they are based on variables which are extremely difficult to estimate (product size) and use attributes whose assessment is inevitably subjective and approximate. Furthermore, the intermediate COCOMO model does not take into account attributes such as the type of application being developed, the amount of documentation required, personnel continuity, interface quality, etc. It also assumes little change in product requirements and high-quality project management.

Deficiencies such as these are characteristic of all cost-estimation models. However, the consistent use of the COCOMO model or any other cost-estimation model within an organization is likely to lead to improved software cost estimation. It is not, however, possible to compare costs in different organizations using algorithmic modelling because of the subjective nature of assumptions about product attributes which may be made.

In fact, after some experience of using an estimation model such as COCOMO it may be discovered that the constants built into the model should be changed to reflect local circumstances. Boehm discusses how the model may be recalibrated by comparing actual costs to predicted costs and by using a least squares approximation to fit estimated to measured costs. This allows the constant factor and the scale factor in the basic COCOMO model to be recomputed.

Furthermore, depending on particular modes of working within an organization, it may be possible to eliminate or combine intermediate COCOMO attributes or to add new attributes which are of particular importance. For example, the personnel attributes might be combined into a single attribute, interactive working may be the only development mode and the use of a standard development system such as Unix may mean that a standard toolset is always available. New attributes which might be added include the effect of working with classified data and its associated security and privacy considerations and an attribute reflecting the type of application being developed.

One of the most important benefits of using an algorithmic cost estimation technique is that it provides some quantitative basis for management decision making. This is very valuable even if the actual cost estimates produced by the model are approximate. This benefit has already been illustrated in Chapter 8 where the use of an estimation model showed that it was not cost-effective to use inexperienced staff for software maintenance. It is demonstrated further in the following examples.

Consider a situation where the basic COCOMO model predicts an effort of 45 p.m. to develop an embedded software system on micro-computer hardware. The hardware consists of a 16-bit processor running at 4 MHz and 64K bytes of store. The effort multipliers for the intermediate COCOMO model all have nominal values apart from the following:

RELY   1.15
STOR   1.21
TIME   1.10
TOOL   1.10

Thus, using the intermediate COCOMO model to estimate development effort gives the following figure:

$$PM = 45 * 1.15 * 1.21 * 1.10 * 1.10 = 76 \text{ p.m.}$$

Given that the costs per software engineer amount to $6000 per person per month, the total cost of developing this project is:

$$C = 76 * 6000 = \$456\,000$$

From the effort multipliers, it is clear that hardware constraints have a significant effect on the total software costs. Say a proposal was made to use a compatible 8 MHz processor with 128K of store. However, this requires special interfaces to be developed so the total additional hardware cost is $30000. Furthermore, it would mean that the TOOL attribute would be very low rather than low but, because the hardware is compatible, personnel attributes are not affected.

With this new processor, both TIME and STOR attributes are reduced to nominal values so the predicted software cost is:

$$C = 45 * 1.24 * 1.15 * 6000 = \$384\,000$$

Thus, a saving of $42000 can be achieved by investing in upgraded hardware.

Say a further proposal was made to invest in a Unix development system at a cost of $150000. The effect of this on the cost attributes would be to reduce the turnround attribute because of interactive working, increase the virtual machine experience attribute because the project team are not familiar with Unix and decrease the TOOL attribute because of the wide range of tools available under Unix. The revised project cost if such a development system were used is:

$$C = 45 * 0.91 * 0.87 * 1.10 * 1.15 * 6000 = \$270\,000$$

Thus the cost of the development system would almost be recovered in the savings for this project alone. Given that Unix is a general-purpose development environment which would be available for future projects, investment in such a system is almost certainly cost effective.

These examples illustrate how even a simple costing model can assist management decision making. Boehm shows how costs may be estimated for different life cycle phases and how component level rather than product level estimating can result in more accurate cost estimates. Space does not permit a discussion of these refinements here and the interested reader must turn to the original source text for more information.

11.5 Software quality assurance

The activity of software quality assurance is closely related to verification and validation activities carried out at each stage of the software life cycle. Indeed, in many organizations there is no distinction made between these activities. However, quality assurance and other verification and validation activities are actually quite separate, with quality assurance being a management function and verification and validation being part of the process of software development.

An appropriate definition of software quality assurance is provided by Bersoff (1984):

Quality assurance consists of those procedures, techniques and tools applied by professionals to ensure that a product meets or exceeds prespecified standards during a product's development cycle; and without specific prescribed standards, quality assurance entails ensuring that a product meets or exceeds a minimal industrial and/or commercially acceptable level of excellence.

This definition is, of course, a fairly general one and it suggests that, firstly, software standards can be established and, secondly, the level of excellence of a software product can be estimated.

The development of software engineering project standards is an extremely difficult process. A standard is some abstract representation of a product which defines the minimal level of performance, robustness, organization, etc., which the developed product must attain. At the time of writing, some software standards have been developed by the IEEE, ANSI and military organizations.

These standards describe configuration management plans, documentation, specification practices, software comparisons, etc. Other standards which are currently under development include standards for reliability, measurement, the use of Ada as a PDL, software testing and others. Branstad and Powell (1984) describe both existing and planned software standards as well as discussing standardization in more general terms.

The problem with national software standards is that they tend to be very general in nature. This is inevitable as, unlike hardware, we are not yet capable of quantifying most software characteristics. Effective quality assurance within an organization thus requires the development of more specific organizational standards.

Of course, the problem which arises in developing software standards for quality assurance and which makes the assessment of the level of excellence of a software product difficult to assess is the elusive nature of software quality. Boehm *et al.* (1978) suggest that quality criteria include but are not limited to:

Economy	Correctness	Resilience
Integrity	Reliability	Usability
Documentation	Modifiability	Clarity
Understandability	Validity	Maintainability
Flexibility	Generality	Portability
Inter-operability	Testability	Efficiency
Modularity	Re-usability	

Exactly how some of these criteria may be quantified is not clear. Furthermore, as Buckley and Poston (1984) point out, parts of this definition may have no value for a particular product. It may be possible to transfer a system from a microcomputer to a large mainframe but this is often a nonsensical thing to do. Assessment of software quality thus still relies on the judgement of skilled individuals, although this does not mean that it is necessarily inferior to quantitative assessment. After all, we cannot assess a painting or a play quantitatively yet this does not preclude a judgement of its quality.

Within an organization, quality assurance should be carried out by an independent software quality assurance team who report directly to management above the project manager level. The quality assurance team should not be associated with any particular development group but should be responsible for quality assurance across all project groups in an organization.

The activity of quality assurance involves sitting in on design reviews, program walkthroughs, etc., and reporting on the overall quality of the product as it is developed. It also involves checking that the finished product and its associated documentation conform to those standards which exist. The quality assurance team may also assess if the different representations of a product (requirements, design, code) are consistent and complete.

Notice that quality assurance is not the same as system testing. It is the development or testing team's responsibility to validate the system, with the quality assurance team reporting on both the validation and the adequacy of the validation effort. This naturally involves quality assurance being closely associated with the final integration testing of the system.

Software quality assurance is now an emerging sub-discipline of software engineering. As Buckley and Poston point out, effective software quality assurance is likely to lead to an ultimate reduction in software costs. However, the major hurdle in the path of software management in this area is the lack of usable software standards. The development of accepted and generally applicable standards should be one of the principal goals of research in software engineering.

11.6 Software tools for management

The activity of software management is probably no more complex that any other large project management task. However, software managers do have the peculiar problem that the product under development is not visible. It is possible to see how well the building of a bridge is progressing, but there is no visual evidence of progress in software system development. Furthermore, software costs are virtually all 'people costs', with little or no material or manufacturing costs associated with a software project.

Some general-purpose management tools may be used by software management. Accounting and budgeting systems can be used to keep track of day-to-day running costs, and simple graphics systems may be used to maintain and update bar charts, cost distributions and other graphical representations of project attributes. PERT packages are widely used general management tools and their use may be adopted by software management for critical path analysis and project scheduling.

Configuration management tools for version control have already been described in Chapter 5. The tools described there are principally aids for software developers, but enhanced versions of such systems incorporate change control and management reporting facilities. With the incorporation of these features these version control systems may be considered to be project librarians (PSLs).

The role of a PSL is set out by Bersoff (1984). In short, it is to collect system components in a database and ensure that they are documented according to standards laid down by project management. If change control is to be automated, this requires information about component owners, permitted modifiers, etc., to be incorporated in component documentation. Generally, therefore, entering a component into a library requires a standard 'soft' form describing the component to be filled in by the component developer. This is then held in the library along with the component and used by the configuration management system.

The PSL may be responsible for ensuring that all users of a component are notified when a change is proposed, may automatically check that documentation has been provided and may produce management reports about the state of components which it controls. Indeed, if sufficient information is collected when the component is entered in the library, the PSL may incorporate a general-purpose management information system which can be used to give information on component developers, usage, costs, etc. Such a system is seen as an essential part of the Ada programming support environment.

The simple version of the COCOMO cost-estimation model discussed earlier in this chapter does not require automated support. A calculator is all that is necessary for effort and cost computation. However, more detailed versions of the model must be implemented on a computer, which not only simplifies initial computations but also makes experimentation with the effort multipliers a much easier task.

The prime requirement of management tools is that they provide the project information required for effective management. Unfortunately, most management tools have been developed on an ad hoc basis and integrated management toolkits are not yet in use. The development of such systems integrated with other software tools is likely to lead to significant improvements in the practice of software management.

Further reading

Software Engineering Economics, B. W. Boehm (1981), Englewood Cliffs, NJ: Prentice-Hall.

> This is the definitive text on algorithmic cost modelling which covers the use of the COCOMO model in great detail. However, its scope is much wider than this as it discusses many other wider aspects of software management. This is an excellent book, although not for the faint-hearted.

The Mythical Man-Month, F. P. Brooks (1975), Reading, Mass: Addison-Wesley.

> One of the first and one of the best books on software management. Brooks was the manager of one of the largest software development

projects which exhibited most of the problems associated with large software systems. This book is a distillation of his experience with that system and, because it is very well written, has now become a minor classic.

Software Engineering — A Practitioner's Approach, R. S. Pressman (1982), New York: McGraw-Hill.

This is a general text on software engineering which is somewhat patchy in its coverage of the subject as a whole but which has excellent chapters on software planning and management.

IEEE Trans. Software Engineering (1984), **SE-10 (1).**

This special issue has a number of up-to-date papers on the practice of software management.

Appendix A SOFTWARE ENGINEERING EDUCATION

The term 'software engineering' was first brought to prominence around the end of the 1960s when it was realized that the development of large software systems was a problem more akin to engineering problems than to problems in mathematics or natural science. Since then, there has been a great deal of discussion about the implementation of large computer systems and a number of important techniques of large-scale software development have been developed. Some of these have been described in this book. These include formal or semi-formal languages for specifying software requirements, software design representations, top-down development and software cost estimation.

In spite of these advances, the task of building large software systems remains immensely difficult. It is still common for large systems to be delivered late, to cost more than was originally estimated, to be unreliable, and to be inadequately documented. We do not yet completely understand many aspects of implementing these large software systems but some of the failures of today's software projects are due to the fact that existing techniques are not used in developing these systems. Those responsible for the implementation of these systems are inadequately trained in software engineering. Indeed, the Alvey committee in the UK, set up to review developments in information technology, identified software engineering to be of particular importance to the future prosperity of the nation and suggested that expenditure in software engineering education should be significantly increased.

Software engineering education has been the subject of some discussion by authors such as Freeman and Wasserman (1976), Fairley (1978) and Mills (1980). Although the views of different authors differ in detail, the concensus seems to be that software engineering education should be based on a firm theoretical foundation but should also include practical topics such as management science, problem solving and communication skills.

In the remainder of this appendix, the problems of integrating undergraduate courses in software engineering with computer science courses are discussed and this is followed by a description of the structure of software engineering courses given to computer science undergraduates at the University of Strathclyde. These courses are practically oriented and particular attention is paid to coursework completed by groups of students.

The final sections of this appendix are made up of a list of tutorial questions and a description of the project specifications used in our final-year practical work. These specifications are deliberately vague. The tutorial questions are intended to assist with self-study and the answers to many of the questions may be found in the text of the book.

A.1 Software engineering and computer science

Computer science and software engineering have an uneasy relationship with each other. Although they accept that a knowledge of some aspects of computer science is essential, many working software engineers are dubious of the value of computer science courses as the topics covered there often seem to be divorced from the 'real world' of software development. Many teachers of computer science are wary of software engineering because it lacks a coherent core of theoretical principles. They prefer to teach topics such as lambda calculus because its academic rigour is clearly discernable. This attitude comes out clearly in the ACM's Curriculum 78 proposals where there is no explicit mention of software engineering as a distinct subject area.

Part of the problem arises because there is no generally agreed definition of either software engineering or computer science. In some institutions, computer science is treated as a very theoretical subject, in some its bias is towards computer hardware and in yet others the computer science course concentrates on the development of systems software. Software engineering, similarly, has a diversity of interpretations. In some cases, it is concerned with the hardware/software interface, in others it is the theory (such as there is) of software development, and sometimes software engineering is concerned with the practical problems of developing large software systems.

We favour the latter interpretation of software engineering and, as such, there are three problems which the developer of courses in this subject must tackle. These are:

1. Computer science students in the early years of their course lack the maturity or experience to realize that large software systems are not simply scaled-up versions of the small, fairly trivial programs which they write as educational exercises. It is only towards the end of their course, after they have experience in writing non-trivial programs and after using practical software systems, that they understand that software engineering is not simply the same as computer programming.

2. Many present-day computer science faculty members have a background in mathematics or natural science and do not appreciate the need for an engineering type of course. Opposition is particularly apparent when the introduction of software engineering courses means the reduction in courses in some other more conventionally accepted computer science topic.

3. Because the development of large software systems takes a long

time, it is quite impossible to simulate the process realistically in the time available to undergraduate students. This fact alone has meant that many courses have concentrated on particular aspects of software development without considering the topic as a whole.

Given that the need for courses in software engineering is accepted, the problem then remains of integrating these courses with the remainder of the computer science curriculum. The immaturity of students necessarily restricts these courses to the latter years of a computer science course although we believe that emphasis should be placed from the start on the production of reliable and maintainable programs. Furthermore, we do not believe that software engineering courses should themselves have a significant theoretical element but that the theory should be covered elsewhere in the computer science course. The job of the teacher of software engineering should be to show how theory can be applied and is a useful tool for the software engineer.

A.2 Software engineering at Strathclyde

The computer science course at Strathclyde University is a four-year course in which students study computer science in all four years and mathematics in the first three years. The introductory programming language is Pascal and, as well as a first year course in that language, students must also take an 'advanced programming' course in their second year. This course covers fundamentals of programming and introduces the importance of programming style and software validation.

These courses are prerequisites for students who wish to take the third-year and the fourth-year courses in software engineering. Students who specialize in computer science must take both the third- and fourth-year courses as part of their degree. Other students may choose only the third-year course.

Both the third-year and the fourth-year courses are based on this book. In the third year, the emphasis is on software design and programming so the work is concentrated around Chapters 4 to 7. However, the notion of a software life cycle is also introduced in this course. After introducing the life cycle model, we discuss software design and then go on to describe programming practice. Programming language features and their influence on reliability and maintainability are described and the course concludes with a comprehensive discussion of testing and validation.

Our final-year course tends to concentrate on the non-programming aspects of software development; namely, requirements specification, software design, documentation, software economics and software management. By this stage, most students have an adequate understanding of programming and are usually fairly disciplined in their programming style, so we consider it unnecessary to discuss programming techniques here. Thus, we make use of Chapters 1–3, Chapter 8 and Chapters 10 and 11 in the fourth-year work.

We start by looking at requirements definition and then go on to formal software specification. This is followed by further work on software design, and the notion of object-oriented design is introduced. We then spend quite a lot of time discussing software management, including maintenance and documentation management. Previously, user-interface design was part of this course but it is now offered as a separate option. In parallel with software engineering, fourth-year students must also take a course in formal methods. This covers topics such as program verification and software specification in more detail and with greater rigour.

The students are expected to work at their own pace through the software engineering course material. To assist them, a number of tutorial problems have been provided ranging from very simple tasks to fairly complex design exercises. The material in the notes is not reiterated in lectures — there are no formal lectures associated with the course — but tutorial periods are available where the student may seek advice and guidance on the topics covered in the course notes. A selection of problems is listed in a later section of this appendix.

All of the formal class contact associated with this course is devoted to discussion of practical work, the development of communication skills (both oral and written) and general discussion of topics in software engineering. In this respect, the course differs from most classes offered at UK universities where a major part of the time is spent in formal presentation of the coursework in lectures.

Our experience with this method of presentation is that students prefer it because they have good, comprehensive notes which can be read in advance and they can spend class periods in understanding rather than assimilating material. Teachers prefer it because it is much more stimulating (although harder work) than standing up and talking for an hour to an often unreceptive audience.

A.2.1 Practical work

As our approach to software engineering is a practical one, our software engineering courses place great emphasis on project work. This project work has a number of objectives. Its primary objective is to show students some of the problems involved in developing large software systems, particularly those which arise in specifying and costing the system. Its secondary objectives are to develop students' communication skills, to reinforce material in the course notes, and to show them what it is like to work as a member of a group rather than as an individual programmer.

However, designing suitable practical exercises is very difficult indeed because of the limited time which the students can devote to the coursework. In essence, there are two alternative possibilities:

1. The project chosen can be relatively small and well defined so that a group of students can complete the specification, design and implementation in the time allocated for the course.

2. The project can be larger and more comprehensive, with only parts of the system completed by the students.

Neither of these alternatives is entirely satisfactory. If a small well defined system is chosen, the tasks of specification and high-level design are trivial and appear to be unimportant. However, in real software systems it is these aspects of the development process which are often the most difficult and costly and we wish to demonstrate this to students.

In our third-year course, we adopt the first option, where the software engineering coursework is integrated with coursework in a computer architecture class. Students must build a simulator for a virtual memory system. This is assessed as a software 'product' rather than simply according to its usefulness as a tool for the computer architect.

Our approach in the final year of the course is to use a larger, more realistic example system, but this has the disadvantage that the students cannot complete the whole process of development because of time limitations. In fact, we expect them to concentrate on the specification, design and costing of the project. In parallel with this work, each student is also involved in a major programming project as part of his or her general assessment.

However, before students start on their final-year project work we set them a small piece of practical work at the very beginning of the course. We ask them to modify the memory simulation program which they worked on in the previous year. The idea underlying this work is to demonstrate the problems of program maintenance — for most students it is the first time that they have ever had to change an existing program which they had not seen for some time. Their reactions have indicated that this is a very useful exercise, demonstrating the value of disciplined programming and sensible program commenting. It emphasizes that maintenance can be a time-consuming and difficult activity.

The main project work centres round an example of a fairly large but comprehensible system. Examples which have been used include an electronic mail/teleconferencing system and a real-time patient monitoring system such as might be used in a hospital intensive care unit. These are described in Section A.4.

The initial information given to the students is intentionally vague as it is intended that each project group must question the instructor to ascertain the detailed requirements of the system. The instructor attempts to act like a typical user during this questioning phase deliberately suggesting impossible objectives and contradictory requirements. The students must identify these in their report as well as providing a full specification of what the system is actually required to do.

The work is carried out in project groups of three or four students and each group must submit three reports:

1. The detailed requirements of the system must be defined using some requirements definition language.

2. The high-level design of the system must be specified. This document sets out the distinct parts of the system and their inter-relationships, but does not describe detailed algorithms which might be used.

3. Finally, each group must complete a report setting out the system costs, and the time which would be required to complete the system. As part of this report, they must prepare a PERT chart showing the dependencies of the different parts of the system and the time required to complete each part.

As one of the objectives of the course is to develop students' communication skills, particular emphasis is placed on the quality of the technical description in all of these reports. The instructor takes care to provide detailed comments on technical writing style and report layout. We have noticed that there is a marked improvement in the quality of technical writing as students assimilate these comments in initial reports and bear them in mind when preparing later reports. In order to develop oral communication skills, all students are required at some time in the course to make a presentation in front of the class describing some of the work which they have done.

We believe this practical work has two fairly original features:

1. Problems of software maintenance are demonstrated by requiring that students should modify a program which they have written in a previous year of the computer science course.

2. The instructor acts as a 'typical' software customer and makes conflicting and self-contradictory demands on the students. It is up to the students to recognize and reconcile these contradictions.

There are, of course, a number of disadvantages associated with this approach to practical work:

1. It requires a great deal of work on the part of the instructor to mark and to comment in detail on project reports. This marking must be completed quickly so that the comments are useful for the student in subsequent reports.

2. There can be problems with the assessment of group projects where one member of a group does not play a full part in the work. Other members feel resentful if that individual is assessed on the same level as they are. Although this is obviously a potential problem, our experience is that it is relatively rare.

3. This type of project organization is probably only viable with a relatively small class size. For large classes, it is unrealistic to expect all students to make presentations about their work simply because of the time required for such talks.

In spite of these disadvantages, we believe that the approach we have adopted to software engineering practical work meets our primary objective, namely to demonstrate the difficulties of software specification, design and costing. It also meets our secondary objectives of reinforcing the course material, developing communication skills, and showing students some of the difficulties of group working. This supposition is based on comments by students about the course, their performance in the practical work, where a marked improvement is shown from the first project to the last, and their performance in formal examinations where a fairly high class average mark has been attained.

As far as the students are concerned, informal surveys have shown that they find the project work challenging and an interesting change from programming. Their performance in the practical work is significantly better than in examinations and, as practical work makes up a third of the overall course assessment, they improve their final mark by their practical performance. They also find that potential employers are very interested in this work and it seems to enhance their chances of finding a job on leaving the university.

A.3 Tutorial examples

The tutorial examples below are representative of the examples given to our students to help them read and understand the course material. The first section here introduces a number of simple problems which are referred to in a number of questions below. This is followed by a list of fairly short questions, organized into different subject areas.

A.3.1 Program examples

Example 1
A program is required which will search a text file and print all the lines which contain a given textual pattern. The pattern is to be identified using the following metasymbols:

%	Beginning of line
$	End of line
*	Zero or more repetitions of the preceding character
?	Matches any single character

Any other character appearing in the pattern represents itself. For example:

%The	Matches line beginning with The
end$	Matches line ending with end
d?g	Matches 'dig', 'dog', etc.
ab*	Matches ab, abb, abbb, etc.
?*	Matches everything

A pattern may not exceed 20 characters.

Example 2
A program for processing examination marks expects lines of data containing the following fields:

Student number	7 digits
Student name	Terminated by comma
Student initials	Separated by spaces, terminated by a colon
Five marks	Integers, range 0. .100, separated by commas

Input is free format and spaces between fields are not significant. A valid student number must start with two digits in the range 72. .84. For each student, the program should print all marks and compute the average mark. It should also print the average mark for each distinct examination.

Example 3
A text justification program accepts a continuous stream of characters as input, and outputs these characters as lines of some specified length. These lines are left and right aligned at the left and right margins. The character input is made up of words which are separated from each other by one or more blanks. The following conditions hold for this program:

1. Newline characters in both input and output act as blanks in that they are treated as word separators.

2. An input sequence made up of more than one blank or an input sequence consisting of only blanks and newline characters is output as a single blank or, if appropriate, a newline character.

3. Words are never hyphenated and each output line ends with a complete word.

4. A line of input never begins with a blank.

5. The last output line should not be justified.

A.3.2 Requirements definition

1. What do you understand by the terms functional and non-functional requirements?

2. What are the advantages and disadvantages of using formal notations to define software requirements?

3. Discuss problems which might arise if the following natural language statements were presented as a requirements definition.

   The routine tabulate should accept input consisting of strings, one per line, and should output these strings in four columns across the terminal screen. For example:
   one
   two
   three
   four
   five
   should be output:
   one two three four
   five

4. Formulate a more formal requirements definition of the above routine using an Ada-like definition language.

5. Under what circumstances is software prototyping likely to be a cost-effective technique?

6. Comment on the suitability of the Unix shell as a tool for prototype development.

7. Compare and contrast the life cycle model of software development to an evolutionary model based on software prototyping. Illustrate the advantages and disadvantages of each approach.

8. Discuss the usefulness of simulation and prototyping in requirements validation.

9. Describe the uses of the requirements/properties matrix.

10. Suggest software tools which might be useful for analysing requirements specifications.

11. If you are familiar with a language such as Prolog or APL, comment on its suitability as a tool for developing software prototypes. Explain how the language might be extended to enhance its usefulness in this area.

A.3.3 Software design

1. Using top-down structured design, derive designs for the three examples presented in Section A.3.1. Express these using an Ada/ PDL or some other PDL with which you are familiar.

2. Repeat the design process but use an object-oriented approach to the software design.

3. Construct formal specifications for what you think are the programs defined in Section A.3.1. Notice you can't be exactly sure as they are not formally specified.

4. Construct algebraic specifications for the following abstract data types:

> Circular queues
> Mailboxes in an electronic mail system
> Linked lists

5. Write specifications for and express the following algorithms in some program description language:

> Bubblesort
> Shellsort
> An algorithm to create a linked list in sorted order
> An algorithm which splits a document into words
> An algorithm which compares strings and returns how many characters in each string match.

6. Justify the correctness of these algorithms using some non-formal correctness argument.

A.3.4 Programming

1. Develop your designs for the example programs from Section A.3.1 into programs in Pascal or some other language. Experiment with both top-down and bottom-up development.

2. Under what circumstances is a static program analyser most useful?

3. What do you understand by the term 'programming environment'?

4. What are the major factors which must be taken into account in the design of a programming environment?

5. Discuss the suitability of the Unix system as a programming environment and suggest facilities which might be added to that system to enable all stages of the life cycle to be supported.

6. Explain why software should be made portable. Give general guidelines on how to make software portable. Under what circumstances is non-portability of software unavoidable?

7. Pascal is a language designed to teach beginners how to write well structed programs. Criticize the language from this point of view giving examples and suggesting possible improvements to Pascal.

8. Explain why standard Pascal is not a suitable language for the implementation of large software systems and outline enhancements which would be necessary for such an environment.

9. Identify two features of Pascal which should be modified in order to make it a better language for writing safe programs. Justify your answer and give examples.

10. Describe the considerations which must be taken into account when choosing a programming language for a major project.

11. Under what circumstances might you recommend the use of FORTRAN as the development language for a large software project?

12. Explain why 'modules' are a useful aid for system structuring.

13. Discuss problems that might arise with Ada's exception-handling facilities.

14. Discuss the adequacy of Ada's case statement design.

15. Using examples, show how the use of meaningful names can improve program readability.

16. Discuss the advantages and disadvantages of syntax directed program editors.

17. What are the factors which most affect program portability?

18. Discuss the notion that a universal job control language would significantly reduce software costs.

19. Given that a structured design for a large system has been created, compare the possible strategies of top-down and bottom-up implementation. In each case, explain how the program is built up and how each stage might be tested.

20. A programmer takes great pride in producing 'clever programs' which few people can understand. Explain why he is not the best person to employ on a large programming project.

21. You are responsible for the teaching of a group of trainee programmers. Assuming that they have successfully compiled a program, write a set of guidelines to assist them in finding bugs in the program. Any diagnostic aids which you suggest should be described with examples of their use.

22. You have been appointed to the post of software manager in an organization which is about to undertake a number of large software projects. Write a short report, aimed at senior management, explaining the importance of producing software which is both easy to maintain and portable. Your report should include a brief review of problems in these areas. Include a checklist of policy decisions which will aid the production of portable software. Outline a set of guidelines for programmers to assist them in writing programs which can be easily maintained.

23. When choosing a programming language for a major software project, what considerations must be taken into account?

24. Under what circumstances might you recommend the use of assembly code for developing a major software system?

A.3.5 Testing and validation

1. Devise sets of test cases to test the programs described in the examples in Section A.3.1.

2. What is the purpose of testing a program? Explain why the programmer is not the best person to test a program.

3. Describe the difference between program testing and debugging.

4. What do you understand by the terms 'equivalence partitioning' and 'boundary value analysis' used when referring to program testing techniques?

5. Show how testing can never establish that a program is free from errors. Explain why the same is true for program verification.

6. Discuss the notion that software tools for debugging are unnecessary if a strongly typed programming language with array bound checking is used for software development.

7. Describe how static and dynamic program analysers might be used during software validation.

8. Discuss the peculiar problems which arise in testing real-time systems.

A.3.6 Documentation and maintenance

1. Write a document describing how to use the programs described in Section A.3.1.

2. Make the following changes to these programs:

   Example 1. The program should be changed so that the user may define the special pattern matching symbols for himself or herself.

   Example 2. The examination mark processing program should be changed so that it can handle any number of examination marks associated with each student. The marks are input as <examination number>.<mark>, e.g. 52101.57, 52202.75. The program should print the average mark for all examinations whose marks have been entered.

   Example 3. The program should be changed so that the user may embed formatting commands with his or her text. Formatting commands always start with '.' and appear on a line by themselves. The formatting commands which should be handled by the system are:

br	Break — start a new line
sp	Leave a blank line
na	Switch off justification

3. What do you understand by the term 'software maintenance'? Describe three distinct classes of software maintenance which can be identified.

4. Discuss the notion that the formal verification of programs will significantly reduce the costs of software maintenance. Hint: It won't.

5. Describe the major non-technical factors affecting the maintenance costs associated with a software system.

6. What documentation should be supplied with a large software system? Discuss the notion of a self-documenting program.

7. Find parts of this book which you think are badly written. Rewrite them to make them more clear. Send your suggestions to the author.

8. Suggest documentation tools which you would find useful in producing software system documentation.

A.3.7 User interface design

1. It is intended to use the pattern matching system described in Example 1 above interactively. Design a user interface for this system.

2. Suggest how the user interface to the nroff text processing system might be improved.

3. Discuss the use of graphics in user-interface design.

4. Describe how short-term memory considerations should influence the design of user interfaces.

5. Under what circumstances are menu-type systems most useful? Comment on their advantages and disadvantages.

6. Design a 'help' facility for the Unix system.

7. Design an interface to a student information system which is to be used by administrative staff with no knowledge of computers.

8. Under what circumstances would you recommend the use of special terminal hardware?

9. Explain how programmable terminals might be used to make user interfaces more friendly.

10. There are now a number of implementations of Unix on bit-mapped terminals equipped with pointing devices. Suggest how the Unix shell might be modified to take advantage of the capabilities of these systems.

A.3.8 Software management

1. Describe the use of bar charts and activity charts for project scheduling.

2. Describe the most common technique used to measure programmer productivity and discuss the limitations of that technique.

3. List the major factors which affect programmer productivity.

4. Discuss software cost estimation based on cost units. Explain why this cost-estimation technique is superior to software cost-estimation techniques based on programmer productivity estimates.

5. Discuss the limitations of using the formula below to estimate the time required to complete a large programming project.

$$T = S / (N * P)$$

Note that T = estimated time, S = system size in lines of source code, N = number of programmers and P = programmer productivity.

6. A programming project may be split into a number of related tasks and a separate time estimate prepared for each task. Tasks are not necessarily independent and some may not be started until other tasks are complete. Table A.1 shows the time estimate for each task and its dependencies.

Construct an activity chart for this project and identify the critical path.

7. Explain why different software cost-estimation models give different results when presented with identical project estimates.

Table A.1 Time estimates

T1	3 weeks	—
T2	2 weeks	—
T3	4 weeks	T1
T4	1 week	T2, T3
T5	6 weeks	T2
T6	3 weeks	T4
T7	2 weeks	T2
T8	2 weeks	T6, T7
T9	5 weeks	—
T10	6 weeks	T5, T8
T11	1 week	T9
T12	3 weeks	T10, T11

8. A major software project consisting of approximately 1 000 000 lines of source code is to be tackled by a project team consisting of 40 software engineers. Given that at least 10 of these have some experience in the application being implemented, describe how the project might be organized and estimate the total project cost.

    Assume that a programmer can produce 25 lines of code per day and costs $60 000 per year.

    What assumptions must be made in constructing the cost estimates? Assuming that this is an 'organic-mode' project, use the basic COCOMO model to estimate the effort required to complete the system. Are the results different from your other estimates? Why?

9. Suggest two software tools which might be used to assist the activity of software management.

10. Compare the chief programmer and specialist team organizations for a programming team, emphasizing the similarities and differences between these two approaches.

11. Using the cost-modelling technique described in Chapter 11, experiment with project estimates to see how the various modifiers affect project costs.

12. A programming project is running several months behind schedule. Explain why increasing the manpower allocated to the project will probably lengthen the overall duration of the project.

13. Describe a model of human cognitive structure and explain how learning a new programming language fits with this model.

14. Why do psychological considerations predict that structured programs are easier to understand that unstructured programs?

15. Describe why a programming team consisting entirely of task-oriented individuals with an autocratic leader is unlikely to be successful.

16. What are the most important environmental considerations which affect programmer productivity? Suggest how your own physical environment might be improved to make it more conducive for software development.

17. Discuss the advantages and disadvantages of every software engineer being equipped with a personal computer terminal.

18. Describe three ways of measuring programmer productivity.

19. There is a wide variation in the published estimates of the number of lines of fully tested code that a programmer is capable of producing per day. Explain the factors which affect these estimates of programmer productivity.

20. Do you foresee significant improvements in programmer productivity in the near future? If not, why not?

21. Will the widespread use of Ada increase programmer productivity?

22. What are the individual plans which should be prepared as part of the overall plan for a large software project?

23. Prepare activity charts for the following activities:

    Organizing a holiday in the tropics in a country which requires a separate visa.
    Organizing an examination for several hundred students.

A.4 Project specifications

The system description set out below is that issued to students taking our final-year undergraduate course in software engineering.

A real-time patient monitoring system

When a patient in hospital is seriously ill and taken to an intensive care unit, that patient's condition must be constantly monitored to check for deterioration and to alert staff if such deterioration occurs. Part of this monitoring can be done by machine with a display at the patient's bedside and, in some cases, this display is also fed to a central console where it can be watched over by a nurse.

It is common to monitor a patient's heartbeat automatically, but other factors such as blood pressure, temperature and breathing are more often monitored by frequent manual checks. There is no technical reason, however, why these cannot be automatically monitored.

The aim of this project is to design a computerized monitoring system to collect the output from an array of instruments checking heart rate, temperature, blood pressure and breathing rate, to record this information for future analysis, to display it in a convenient form both at the patient's bedside and at a central console, and to alert staff if potentially dangerous changes in the patient's condition are detected.

The following conditions apply to the system:

1. It should be able to handle the monitoring of at least eight patients and to display information about all of these patients at the same time.

2. Although initially it should be designed to support the monitoring of the parameters specified above, it should be capable of expansion so that further patient parameters may be added at a later date.

3. The system should provide different levels of warning ranging from 'take immediate action' for a cardiac arrest, say, to 'look when you have time' when a change in blood pressure, say, is detected.

4. The system should provide facilities to summarize the collected data about patients and to display and print these summaries in a convenient form for study by medical staff or inclusion in the patient's medical record.

It is an obvious requirement of such a system that reliability is of the utmost importance. The system therefore should include extensive self-checking facilities and should also be able to assess the feasibility of the information which is being presented to medical staff.

Requirements specification

The first practical work in this course is to develop a comprehensive requirements specification for the patient-monitoring system described, in not very much detail, below. This requirements specification is the document which is used by the system designer to formulate the initial design of the system and it should be expressed in a semi-formal notation such as that used in the book associated with this course.

In order to mimic real conditions, the initial statement of needs has been deliberately generalized. It is the task of project groups to find out more detailed needs by asking questions of the lecturer as to what is required of the system. The replies to these questions may also mimic real life — they may ask for contradictory or impossible features to be included in the system. It is your task to assess the replies and to provide a consistent and complete requirements specification.

System design

The object of this practical exercise is to use the requirements specification which you have prepared to complete a preliminary high-level design of the patient monitoring system. Your design should be expressed using data-flow diagrams, structure charts if appropriate and PDL. The level of detail provided should be sufficient that a technically qualified reader should understand the system design, but it is not necessary to express the design for programming.

Note that you will be expected to estimate the system size at some later stage. You may find this a useful guide for deciding on the level of detail in your design.

System estimation

The object of this project is to use the system requirements and design documents to estimate the time required to complete the project by *your* project group. Your report should contain the following sections:

1. An estimate of the individual programming productivity of the group members based on the assumption that the system is to be pro-grammed in a high-level language which has facilities to directly address peripherals; that is, all programming, including hardware control, can be done without dropping into machine code. This estimate should be in terms of raw code, i.e. given a program design, how many lines of commented code can be produced per day?

2. A description of the different project tasks which your group considers to be indivisible and a statement of who is responsible for what task.

3. An individual estimate for each of these tasks of the time required to complete that task.

4. An activity chart showing the interdependence or otherwise of the individual parts of the system.

5. A bar chart, showing the overlapping of activities.

6. A statement of your overall assumptions regarding the proportion of the total project completion time allocated to design, implementation, validation and documentation.

7. An estimate of the overall time required to complete the project from the present stage of high-level design to handing over a properly documented and validated software system.

As well as this practical exercise, the exercise described below has also been used in our software engineering course. Essentially, the same was expected of students, so only a brief description of the work is given here.

An electronic mail/teleconferencing system

As part of its office automation strategy, a large organization has decided that it has a need for an electronic mail and teleconferencing system for use by management. The system should support the following facilities:

1. A message exchange facility whereby users may send mail to one or more other users who may or may not be logged on to the system. Some of the messages exchanged may be confidential.

2. A conferencing facility where one or more logged on users may converse with each other using their terminals. The system must implement a protocol to ensure that conversations are not mixed up.

It is your responsibility to take this broad statement of needs and derive a requirements definition for this system.

REFERENCES

Abbot, R. (1983), 'Program design by informal English descriptions', *Comm. ACM*, **26 (11)**, 882–94.

Alford, M. W. (1977), 'A requirements engineering methodology for real time processing requirements', *IEEE Trans. Software Engineering*, **SE-3 (1)**, 60–9.

Aron, J. D. (1974), *The Program Development Process*, Reading, Mass: Addison-Wesley.

Backus, J. (1978), 'Can programming be liberated from the Von Neumann style? A functional style and its algebra of programs', *Comm. ACM*, **21 (8)**, 613–49.

Baker, F. T. (1972), 'Chief Programmer Team management of production programming', *IBM Systems J.*, **11 (1)**.

Balzer, R. W. (1969), 'EXDAMS — extendable debugging and monitoring system', *AFIPS*, **34.**

Balzer, R. M., Goldman, N. M. and Wile, D. S. (1982), 'Operational specification as the basis for rapid prototyping', *ACM Software Engineering Notes*, **7 (5)**, 3–16.

Barr, A., Cohen, P. and Feigenbaum, E. A. (1981), *The Handbook of Artificial Intelligence*, London: Pitman.

Bass, B. M. and Dunteman, G. (1963), 'Behaviour in groups as a function of self, interaction and task orientation', *J. Abnorm. Soc. Psychol.*, **66**, 419–28.

Bell, T. E., Bixler, D. C. and Dyer, M. E. (1977), 'An extendable approach to computer aided software requirements engineering', *IEEE Trans. Software Engineering*, **SE-3 (1)**, 49–60.

Berg, H. K., Boebert, W. E., Franta, W. R. and Moher, T. G. (1982), *Formal Methods of Program Verification and Specification*, Englewood Cliffs, NJ: Prentice-Hall.

Bersoff, E. H. (1984), 'Elements of software configuration management', *IEEE Trans. Software Engineering*, **SE-10 (1)**, 79–87.

Blank, J. and Krijger, M. J., eds. (1983), *Software Engineering: Methods and Techniques*, New York: Wiley-Interscience.

Bochmann, G. V. (1973), 'Multiple exits from a loop without the goto', *Comm. ACM*, **16 (7)**, 443–5.

Boehm, B. W. (1974), 'Some steps towards formal and automated aids to software requirements analysis and design', *IFIP 74*, 192–7, Amsterdam: North-Holland.

Boehm, B. W. (1975), 'The high cost of software'. In *Practical Strategies for Developing Large Software Systems*, ed. E. Horowitz, Reading, Mass: Addison-Wesley.

Boehm, B. W., Brown, J. R., Kaspar, H., Lipow, M., Macleod, G. and Merrit, M. (1978), *Characteristics of Software Quality*, TRW Series of Software Technology, Amsterdam: North-Holland.

Boehm, B. W. (1981), *Software Engineering Economics*, Englewood Cliffs, NJ: Prentice-Hall.

Boehm, B. W. (1984), 'Prototyping vs. Specifying: Some experimental results and software life cycle implications', *Proc. 1st Software Process Workshop*, Egham, UK.

Bohm, C. and Jacopini, G. (1966), 'Flow diagrams, turing machines and languages with only two formation rules', *Comm. ACM*, **9 (5)**, 366–71.

Booch, G. (1983), *Software Engineering with Ada*, Reading, Mass: Addison-Wesley.

Bourne, S. R. (1978), 'The UNIX shell', *Bell Systems Tech.J.*, **57 (6)**, 1971–90.

Branstad, M. and Powell, P. B. (1984), 'Software engineering project standards', *IEEE Trans. Software Engineering*, **SE-10 (1)**, 73–8.

Brooks, F. P. (1975), *The Mythical Man-Month*, Reading, Mass: Addison-Wesley.

Brown, P. J., ed. (1977), *Software Portability*, Cambridge: Cambridge University Press.

Brown, P. J. (1983), 'Error messages: The neglected area of the man/machine interface', *Comm. ACM*, **26 (4)**, 246–50.

Buckley, F. J. and Poston, R. (1984), 'Software quality assurance', *IEEE Trans. Software Engineering*, **SE-10 (1)**, 36–41.

Chen, P. (1976), 'The entity relationship model — Towards a unified view of data', *ACM Trans. Database Systems*, **1 (1)**, 9–36.

Cherry, L. and MacDonald, N. H. (1983), 'The Unix writer's workbench software', *BYTE*, **8 (10)**, 241–52.

Clocksin, W. and Mellish, C. (1982), *Programming in Prolog*, Heidleberg: Springer-Verlag.

Chu, Y. (1978), 'Introducing a software design language'. In *Structured Analysis and Design*, Infotech State of the Art Report, Maidenhead, UK.

Codd, E. F. (1970), 'A relational model of data for large shared data banks', *Comm. ACM*, **13**, 377–387.

Cole, A. J. and Morrison, R. (1982), *An Introduction to Programming with S-ALGOL*, Cambridge: Cambridge University Press.

Constantine, L. L. and Yourdon, E. (1979), *Structured Design*, Englewood Cliffs, NJ: Prentice-Hall.

Cougar, J. D. and Zawacki, R. A. (1978), 'What motivates DP professionals', *Datamation*, **24 (9)**.

Culpepper, L. M. (1975), 'A system for reliable engineering software', *IEEE Trans. Software Engineering*, **SE-1 (2)**, 174–8.

Dahl, O. J., Dijkstra, E. W. and Hoare, C. A. R. (1972), *Structured Programming*, New York: Academic Press.

Davis, W. S. (1983), *Systems Analysis and Design*, Reading, Mass: Addison-Wesley.

Davis, C. G. and Vick, C. R. (1977), 'The software development system', *IEEE Trans. Software Engineering*, **SE-3 (1)**, 69–84.

DeRemer, F. and Kron, H. H. (1976), 'Programming in the large versus programming in the small', *IEEE Trans. Software Engineering*, **SE-2 (2)**, 80–6.

Dijkstra, E. W. (1968a), 'A constructive approach to the problem of program correctness', *BIT*, **8**, 174–86.

Dijkstra, E. W. (1968b), 'Goto statement considered harmful', *Comm. ACM*, **11 (3)**, 147–8.

Dijkstra, E. W. (1975), 'Guarded commands, nondeterminacy, and formal derivation of programs', *Comm. ACM*, **18 (8)**, 453–7.

Dijkstra, E. W. (1976), *A Discipline of Programming*. Englewood Cliffs, NJ: Prentice-Hall.

DoD (1980), *Requirements for Ada Programming Support Environments: Stoneman*, US Department of Defense.

Dolotta, T. A., Haight, R. C. and Mashey, J. R. (1978), 'The programmer's workbench', *Bell Systems Tech. J.*, **57 (6)**, 2177–200.

Eason, K. D., Damodaran, L. and Stewart, T. F. M. (1975), 'Interface problems in man-computer interaction'. In: *Human Choice and Computers*, Amsterdam: North-Holland.

Ellis, C. A. and Nutt, G. J. (1980), 'Office information systems and computer science', *ACM Computing Surveys*, **12 (1)**, 27–60.

Fagan, M. E. (1976), 'Design and code inspections to reduce errors in program development', *'IBM Systems J.*, **15 (3)**, 182–211.

Fairley, R. E. (1978), 'Towards model curricula in software engineering', *Proc. 9th SIGCSE Symposium on Computer Science Education*, Pittsburgh.

Feldman, S. I. (1979), 'MAKE — A program for maintaining computer programs', *Software — Practice and Experience*, **9**, 255–65.

Festinger, L. A. (1957), *A Theory of Cognitive Dissonance*, Evanston, Ill: Row Peterson.

Floyd, R. W. (1967), 'Assigning meanings to programs', *Proc. Symposium Applied Maths.*, 19–32.

Foley, J. D. and VanDam, A. (1982), *Interactive Computer Graphics*, Reading, Mass: Addison-Wesley.

Freeman, P. and Wasserman, A. I. (1976), *Software Engineering Education: Needs and Objectives*, Berlin: Springer-Verlag.

Fried, L. (1979), *Practical Data Processing Management*, Virginia: Reston.

Frost, R. A. (1981), 'ASDAS — A simple database management system', *Proc. 6th ACM European Conf. Systems Architecture*, London.

Getz, S. L., Kalliyiannis, G. and Schach, S. R. (1983), 'A very high level interactive graphical trace for the Pascal heap', *IEEE Trans. Software Engineering*, **SE-9 (2)**.

Gladden, G. R. (1982), 'Stop the Life Cycle, I Want to Get Off', *ACM Software Engineering Notes*, **7 (2)**, 35–9.

Goguen, J. A., Thatcher, J. and Wagner, E. G. (1977), 'Initial algebra semantics and continuous algebras', *JACM*, **24 (1)**, 68–95.

Greeno, J. G. (1972), *The Structure of Memory and the Process of Problem Solving*, Univ. of Michigan: Human Performance Center, Tech. Rep. 37.

Gomaa, H. (1983), 'The impact of rapid prototyping on specifying user requirements', *ACM Software Engineering Notes*, **8 (2)**, 17−28.

Guttag, J. (1977), 'Abstract data types and the development of data structures', *Comm. ACM*, **20 (6)**, 396−405.

Guttag, J. V., Horowitz, E., and Musser, D. R. (1978), 'The design of data type specifications'. In *Current Trends in Programming Methodology, Vol IV*, ed. R. T. Yeh, Englewood Cliffs, NJ: Prentice-Hall.

Halstead, M. H. (1977), *Elements of Software Science*, Amsterdam: North-Holland.

Hendrix, G. G., Sacerdoti, E. D., Sagalowicz, D. and Slocum, J. (1978), 'Developing a natural language interface to complex data', *ACM Trans. Database Systems*, **3 (2)**, 105−47.

Heninger, K. L. (1980), 'Specifying software requirements for complex systems. New techniques and their applications', *IEEE Trans. Software Engineering*, **SE-6 (1)**, 2−13.

Hill, A. (1983), 'Towards an Ada-based specification and design language', *Ada UK News*, **4 (4)**, 16−34.

Hoare, C. A. R. (1969), 'An axiomatic basis for computer programming', *Comm. ACM*, **12 (10)**, 576−83.

Hoare, C. A. R. and Wirth, N. (1973), 'An axiomatic definition of Pascal', *Acta Informatica*, **2 (3)**, 335−55.

Howden, W. E. (1982), 'Contemporary software development environments', *Comm. ACM*, **25 (5)**, 318−29.

IBM (1980), 'Software development', *IBM Systems J.*, **19 (4)**.

Iverson, K. E. (1962), *A Programming Language*, New York: Wiley.

Ivie, E. L. (1977), 'The programmers' workbench — A machine for software development', *Comm. ACM*, **20 (10)**, 746−53.

Jackson, K. (1977), 'Language design for modular software construction', *IFIP 77*, 577−82, Amsterdam: North-Holland.

Jackson, M. A. (1975), *Principles of Program Design*, London: Academic Press.

Jackson, M. A. (1982), *System Development*, London: Prentice-Hall.

Jamsa, K. (1984), 'Object-oriented design vs. structured design', *ACM Software Engineering Notes*, **9 (1)**, 43−8.

Janis, I. L. (1972), *Victims of Groupthink. A Psychological Study of Foreign Policy Decisions and Fiascos*, Boston: Houghton Mifflin.

Jensen, R. W. and Tonies, C. C. (1979), *Software Engineering*, Englewood Cliffs, NJ: Prentice-Hall.

Jones, C. B. (1980), *Software Development — A Rigorous Approach*, London: Prentice-Hall.

Jones, C. B. and Bjorner, D. (1982), *Formal Specifications and Software Development*, London: Prentice-Hall.

Jones, T. C. (1978), 'Measuring programming quality and productivity', *IBM Systems J.*, **17 (1)**, 39−63.

Kernighan, B. W., Lesk, M. E. and Ossanna, Jr., J. F. (1978), 'Document preparation', *Bell Systems Tech. J.*, **57 (6)**, 2115–35.

Kernighan, B. W. and Plauger, P. (1976), *Software Tools*, Reading, Mass: Addison-Wesley.

Knuth, D. E. (1974), 'Structured programming with go to statements', *Computing Surveys*, **6 (4)**, 261–301.

Kreig-Bruckner, B. and Luckham, D. C. (1980), 'ANNA: Towards a language for annotating Ada programs', *ACM Sigplan Notices*, **15 (11)**, 128–38.

Lampson, B. W., Horning, J. J., London, R. L., Mitchell, J. G. and Popek, G. L. (1977), 'Report on the programming language Euclid', *ACM Sigplan Notices*, **12 (2)**, 1–79.

Leavitt, H. J. (1951), 'Some effects of certain communication patterns on group performance', *J. Abnorm. Soc. Psychol.*, **8 (1)**, 38–50.

Lehman, M. M. and Belady, L. A. (1976), 'A model of large program development', *IBM Systems J.*, **15 (3)**, 225–52.

Lehman, M. M. (1980), 'Programs, Life Cycles and the Laws of Software Evolution', *Proc. IEEE*, **68 (9)**, 1060–76.

Lehman, M. M. (1984), 'A further model of coherent programming processes', *Proc. 1st Software Process Workshop*, Egham, UK.

Lewin, K., Lippit, R. and White, R. K. (1939), 'Patterns of aggressive behaviour in experimentally created "social climates"', *J. Social Psychology*, **10**, 271–99.

Lientz, B. P. and Swanson, E. B. (1980), *Software Maintenance Management*, Reading, Mass: Addison-Wesley.

Linger, R. C., Mills, H. D. and Witt, B. I. (1979), *Structured Programming — Theory and Practice*, Reading, Mass: Addison-Wesley.

Liskov, B. and Zilles, S. (1974), 'Programming with abstract data types', *ACM Sigplan Notices*, **9 (4)**, 50–9.

Liskov, B. and Berzins, V. (1979), 'An appraisal of program specifications. In *Research Directions in Software Technology*, ed. P. Wegner, Cambridge, Mass: MIT Press.

London, R. L. and Robinson, L. (1979), 'The role of verification tools and techniques'. In: *Software Development Tools*, ed. W. E. Riddle and R. E. Fairley, New York: Springer-Verlag.

Lucas, R. W. (1977), 'A study of patients' attitudes to computer interrogation', *Int. J. Man-Machine Studies*, **9**, 69–86.

Malone, J. R. and McGregor, D. R. (1980), 'STABDUMP — A dump interpreter program to assist debugging', *Software — Practice and Experience*, **10**, 329–32.

Mander, K. C. (1981), 'An Ada view of specification and design', *Tech. Rep.* **44**, Department of Computer Science, University of York, York, UK.

Manna, Z. (1969), 'The correctness of programs', *J. Computer System Sci.* **3**, 119–27.

Marshall, J. E. and Heslin, R. (1976), 'Boys and girls together. Sexual composition and the effect of density on group size and cohesiveness', *J. Personality and Social Psychology*, **36**.

Mashey, J. R. and Smith, D. W. (1977), 'Documentation tools and techniques', *Proc. 2nd Int. Conf. Software Engineering*, 177–81.

McCabe, T. J. (1976), 'A complexity measure', *IEEE Trans. Software Engineering*, **SE-2**, 308–20.

McCarthy, J. (1962), 'Towards a mathematical science of computation', *IFIP*, **62**, 21–8, Amsterdam: North-Holland.

McCracken, D. D. and Jackson, M. A. (1982), 'Life cycle concept considered harmful', *ACM Software Engineering Notes*, **7 (2)**, 29–32.

McCue, G. M. (1978), 'IBM's Santa Teresa Laboratory — Architectural design for program development', *IBM Systems J.*, **17 (1)**, 4–25.

McDermid, J. and Ripkin, K. (1984), *Life Cycle Support in the Ada Environment*, Cambridge: Cambridge University Press.

McGettrick, A. D. (1983), *Program Verification using Ada*, Cambridge: Cambridge University Press.

McGregor, D. R. and Malone, J. R. (1980), 'The FACT database: A system based on inferential methods', *Proc. Cambridge Symposium Research and Development in Information Retrieval*, Butterworth.

McGuffin, R. W., Elliston, A. E., Tranter, B. R. and Westmacott, P. N. (1979), 'CADES — Software engineering in practice', *Proc. 4th Int. Conf. Software Engineering*, Munich.

McKeeman, W. M., Horning, J. J. and Wortman, D. (1970), *A Compiler Generator*, Englewood Cliffs, NJ: Prentice-Hall.

Metzger, P. W. (1973), *Managing a Programming Project*, Englewood Cliffs, NJ: Prentice-Hall.

Miara, R. J., Mussleman, J. A., Navarro, J. A. and Shneiderman, B. (1983), 'Program indentation and comprehensibility', *Comm. ACM*, **26 (11)**, 861–67.

Miller, G. A. (1957), 'The magical number 7 plus or minus two: Some limits on our capacity for processing information', *Psychological Review*, **63**, 81–97.

Millington, D. (1981), *Systems Analysis and Design for Computer Applications*, London: Ellis Horwood.

Mills, H. D. (1980), 'Software engineering education', *Proc. IEEE*, **68 (9)**.

Mohanty, S. N. (1981), 'Software cost estimation: Present and future', *Software — Practice and Experience*, **11 (2)**, 103–21.

Myers, G. J. (1975), *Reliable Software through Composite Design*, New York: Van Nostrand.

Myers, G. J. (1979), *The Art of Software Testing*, New York: Wiley.

Naur, P. (1972), 'An experiment on program development', *BIT*, **12**, 347–65.

Newman, W. M. and Sproull, R. F. (1979), *Principles of Interactive Computer Graphics*, New York: McGraw-Hill.

Osterweil, L. J. and Fosdick, L. D. (1976), 'DAVE — A validation, error detection and documentation system for FORTRAN programs', *Software — Practice and Experience*, **6**, 473–86.

Pagan, F. G. (1981), *Formal Specification of Programming Languages — A Panoramic Primer*, Englewood Cliffs, NJ: Prentice-Hall.

Parnas, D. (1972), 'On the criteria to be used in decomposing systems into modules', *Comm. ACM*, **15 (2)**, 1053–58.

Parnas, D. (1979), 'The role of program specification'. In *Research Directions in Software Technology*, ed. P. Wegner Cambridge, Mass: MIT Press.

Perry, D. K. and Cannon, W. M. (1966), 'A vocational interest scale for programmers', *Proc. 4th Annual Computer Personnel Conf.*, ACM, New York.

Peters, L. J. (1980), 'Software representation and composition techniques', *Proc. IEEE*, **68 (9)**, 1085–93.

Porter, L. W. and Lawler, E. E. (1965), 'Properties of organisation structure in relation to job attitudes and job behaviour', *Psychol. Bull.*, **64**, 23–51.

Pressman, R. S. (1982), *Software Engineering — A Practitioner's Approach*, New York: McGraw-Hill.

Ramamoorthy, C. V. and Ho, S. F. (1975), 'Testing large software with automated software evaluation systems', *IEEE Trans. Software Engineering*, **SE-1 (1)**, 46–58.

Randell, B. (1975), 'System Structure for Software Fault Tolerance', *IEEE Trans. Software Engineering*, **SE-1 (2)**, 220–32.

Ritchie, D. M., Johnson, S. C., Lesk, M. E. and Kernighan, B. W. (1978), 'The C programming language', *Bell Systems Tech. J.*, **57 (6)**, 1991–2020.

Ritchie, D. M. and Thompson, K. (1978), 'The UNIX time sharing system', *Bell Systems Tech. J.*, **57 (6)**, 1905–29.

Robson, D. (1981), 'Object-oriented software systems', *BYTE*, **6 (8)**, 74–9.

Rochkind, M. J. (1975), 'The Source Code Control System', *IEEE Trans. Software Engineering*, **SE-1 (4)**, 255–65.

Ross, D. T. (1977), 'Structured analysis (SA). A language for communicating ideas', *IEEE Trans. Software Engineering*, **SE-3 (1)**, 16–34.

Royce, W. W. (1970), 'Managing the Development of Large Software Systems: Concepts and Techniques', *Proc. WESCON*.

Sackman, H., Erikson, W. J. and Grant, E. E. (1968), 'Exploratory experimentation studies comparing on-line and off-line programming performance', *Comm. ACM*, **11 (1)**, 3–11.

Salter, K. G. (1976), 'A methodology for decomposing system requirements into data processing requirements', *Proc. 2nd Int. Conf. Software Engineering*, San Francisco.

Satterthwaite, E. (1972), 'Debugging tools for high level languages', *Software — Practice and Experience*, **2**, 197–217.

Schoman, K. and Ross, D. T. (1977), 'Structured analysis for requirements definition', *IEEE Trans. Software Engineering*, **SE-3 (1)**, 6–15.

Scowen, R. S. (1979), 'A new technique for improving the quality of computer programs', *Proc. 4th Int. Conf. Software Engineering*, Munich.

Sharman, G. O. H. and Winterbottom, N. (1979), 'NDB: Non programmer Database Facility', *IBM Technical Report* TR 12.179', IBM Hursley, UK.

Shaw, M. E. (1964), 'Communication Networks'. In: *Advances in Experimental Social Psychology*, New York: Academic Press.

Shaw, M. E. (1971), *Group Dynamics. The Psychology of Small Group Behaviour*, New York: McGraw-Hill.

Shepherd, S. B., Curtis, B., Milliman, P., Borst, M. and Love, T. (1979), 'First year results from a research program in human factors in software engineering', *AFIPS*, 1021–7.

Shneiderman, B. (1980), *Software Psychology*, Cambridge, Mass: Winthrop Publishers Inc.

Sommerville, I. (1981), 'Providing the user with a tailor made interface', *Proc. 6th European ACM Conf. Systems Architecture*, London.

Standish, T. A. (1981), 'ARCTURUS — An advanced highly integrated programming environment'. In: *Software Engineering Environments*, ed. H. Hunke, Amsterdam: North-Holland.

Stoy, J. E. (1977), *Denotational Semantics: The Scott Strachey Approach to Programming Languages*. Cambridge, Mass: MIT Press.

Strachey, C. and Milne, R. (1976), *A Theory of Programming Language Semantics*. London: Chapman and Hall.

Stucki, L. G. and Walker, H. D. (1981), 'Concepts and prototypes of ARGUS'. In: *Software Engineering Environments*, ed. H. Hunke, Amsterdam: North-Holland.

Tanenbaum, A. S., Klint, P. and Bohm, W. (1978), 'Guidelines for software portability', *Software — Practice and Experience*, **8**, 681–98.

Teichrow, D. and Hershey, E. A. (1977), PSL/PSA: 'A computer aided technique for structured documentation and analysis of information processing systems', *IEEE Trans. Software Engineering*, **SE-3 (1)**, 41–8.

Teitelbaum, T. and Reps, T. (1981), 'The Cornell program synthesizer: A syntax-directed programming environment', *Comm. ACM*, **24 (9)**, 563–73.

Turski, W. (1981), 'Software stability', *Proc. 6th ACM European Conf. Systems Architecture*, London.

Van Leer, P. (1976), 'Top down development using a program design language', *IBM Systems J.*, **15 (2)**, 155–70.

Wallis, P. J. L. (1982), *Portable Programming*, London: Macmillan.

Walston, C. E. and Felix, C. P. (1977), 'A method of programming measurement and estimation', *IBM Systems J.*, **16 (1)**, 54–73.

Waltz, D. (1978), 'An English language question answering system for a large relational database', *Comm. ACM*, **21 (7)**, 526–39.

Warnier, J. D. (1977), *Logical Construction of Programs*, New York: Van Nostrand.

Wasserman, A. I. and Shewmake, D. T. (1982), 'Rapid prototyping of interactive information systems', *ACM Software Engineering Notes*, **7 (5)**, 171–80.

Weinberg, G. M. (1971), *The Psychology of Computer Programming*, New York: Van Nostrand.

Wichman, B. A. (1978), 'Performance of system implementation languages'. In: *Constructing Quality Software*, Amsterdam: North-Holland.

Willis, R. R. (1981), 'AIDES: Computer aided design of software systems'. In: *Software Engineering Environments*, ed. H. Hunke, Amsterdam: North-Holland.

Wirth, N. (1971), 'Program development by stepwise refinement', *Comm. ACM*, **14 (4)**, 221–7.

Wirth, N. (1976), *Systematic Programming, An Introduction*, Englewood Cliffs, NJ: Prentice-Hall.

Wolverton, R. W. (1975), 'The cost of developing large scale software'. In: *Practical Strategies for Developing Large Software Systems*, ed. E. Horowitz, Reading, Mass: Addison-Wesley.

Yeh, R. T. and Zave, P. (1980), 'Specifying Software Requirements', *Proc. IEEE*, **68 (9),** 1077–85.

Yourdon, E. (1975), *Techniques of Program Structure and Design*, Englewood Cliffs, NJ: Prentice-Hall.

Yourdon, E. (1979), *Managing the Structured Techniques*, Englewood Cliffs, NJ: Prentice-Hall.

Zahn, C. T. (1974), 'A control statement for natural top down structured programming', *Symposium on Programming Languages*, Paris.

Zilles, S. (1974), *Algebraic Specification of Data Types*. Project MAC, Progress Report 11, Cambridge, Mass: MIT.

Zloof, M. M. and de Jong, S. P. (1977), 'The system for business automation (SBA): Programming language', *Comm. ACM*, **20 (6),** 385–96.

INDEX